W9-BXO-778

Collaborative Intervention
in Early Childhood

Collaborative Intervention in Early Childhood

Consulting With Parents and Teachers of 3- to 7-Year-Olds

Deborah Hirschland

TOURO COLLEGE LIBRARY
Kings Hwy
WITHDRAWN

OXFORD

UNIVERSITY PRESS

2008

KH

OXFORD
UNIVERSITY PRESS

Oxford University Press, Inc., publishes works that further
Oxford University's objective of excellence
in research, scholarship, and education.

Oxford New York
Auckland Cape Town Dar es Salaam Hong Kong Karachi
Kuala Lumpur Madrid Melbourne Mexico City Nairobi
New Delhi Shanghai Taipei Toronto

With offices in
Argentina Austria Brazil Chile Czech Republic France Greece
Guatemala Hungary Italy Japan Poland Portugal Singapore
South Korea Switzerland Thailand Turkey Ukraine Vietnam

Copyright © 2008 by Deborah Hirschland

Published by Oxford University Press, Inc.
198 Madison Avenue, New York, New York 10016

www.oup.com

Oxford is a registered trademark of Oxford University Press

All rights reserved. No part of this publication may be reproduced,
stored in a retrieval system, or transmitted, in any form or by any means,
electronic, mechanical, photocopying, recording, or otherwise,
without the prior permission of Oxford University Press.

Library of Congress Cataloging-in-Publication Data
Hirschland, Deborah.
Collaborative intervention in early childhood: consulting with parents and teachers of
3- to 7-year-olds/Deborah Hirschland.
p. ; cm.
Includes bibliographical references and index.
ISBN 978-0-19-533120-2
1. Behavior disorders in children. 2. Emotional problems of children.
3. Problem children—Mental health services. 4. Developmentally disabled children—
Mental health services.
I. Title. [DNLM: 1. Early Intervention (Education) 2. Child Behavior.
3. Child Development. 4. Child, Preschool. 5. Child.
6. Developmental Disabilities—rehabilitation. WA 320 H669c 2008]
RJ506.B44H57 2008
618.92'89—dc22   2007048237

9 8 7 6 5 4 3 2 1

Printed in the United States of America
on acid-free paper

9/3/09

To
My parents, Evelyn Polk and Henry Hirschland
and
My fine three

Preface

I first began working on this book in a small cabin in Northern Maine, a place that offered a respite from my varied responsibilities as a clinician who specializes in early childhood. Settling into the wicker chair at my makeshift desk, I'd look through the window at the birches down by the lakeshore and hope to catch sight of a loon or two. Then I'd get started.

It was a wonderful place to think and write. Something about the uncomplicated quality of time spent in the Maine woods mirrored my desire to find simple ways to frame the complex process of understanding and helping worrisome three- to seven-year-olds. I'd spent countless hours over twenty-five years talking with parents, playing with children, asking questions of teachers and childcare providers, and observing kids in their classrooms and with their families. After a while, I began teaching and supervising others who found this work as compelling as I did.

As my experience grew, the field's knowledge base did too; information on the intricate workings of young brains, the impact of trauma, and the power of culture and gender was added to what we already understood about the importance of early relationships, about family functioning, and about cognitive and psychological development. The challenge of integrating new information with old was ever-present, as was the task of using both to come up with practical approaches "on the ground." Because clinicians in early childhood practice need to be well versed in the world of theory without getting lost in it, using their expertise to empower parents and teachers to develop their own.

The job of figuring out how to capture such aspects of early childhood work lay at the heart of those early writing sessions in Maine. How could I convey central elements of the knowledge base on which clinicians rely, and explore the kinds of down-to-earth approaches to intervention that parents and teachers yearn for? How might I highlight the importance of valuing the wisdom these adults bring to conversations about the children everyone wants to help, and the necessity for flexibility in response to the richly varied, sometimes highly stressful worlds of three- to seven-year-olds? The content, structure, and goals of this book grew out of the answers to these questions—its intent to provide practitioners with the perspectives they need to do this work with skill, compassion, and creativity.

It is work that relies on the power of collaboration and, in particular, on the ideas that emerge out of discussions with concerned parents and teachers. As such discussions unfold, those of us involved get increasingly focused on puzzling out the reasons for a child's troubling behavior. Whatever the issue at hand, we put our heads together and ask questions—questions about the child's temperament and history and about life at home and in school. We assume that if things aren't progressing as smoothly as we'd hope, some combination of constitutional, emotional, and familial issues is probably at play, and the way people are reacting to the problem may be making it worse rather than better. We laugh together about the mistakes we all make, and the ways in which we can get as stuck as the children we're trying to help. Then we start to develop a reasonable hypothesis for why the challenges in question are unfolding in just the way they are. Finally, we brainstorm about how to begin turning things around.

When these discussions go well, parents and teachers leave with fresh perspectives about the kids they've been worried about, rekindled energy for the work ahead, and an assortment of creative approaches to try at home or in school. It's this mix of optimism and pragmatism that I want to capture in these pages. By offering an easily shared language with which to understand early childhood difficulties, as well as step-by-step strategies that support growth, I hope to reach the practitioners whom parents and teachers approach for help, thus supporting the partnerships in care that are so crucial to young children who aren't thriving.

I'd like to think that these explorations will leave readers with some new ideas for practice, a commitment to home-school collaboration, and an appreciation for the challenge of remaining accessible in our approach without being simplistic in our thinking. If they do, there are countless others besides myself who deserve credit; many of this book's conceptual frameworks and most of its strategies are extrapolated from gifted practitioners and thinkers in the field of child development, or have been designed in partnership with the parents and teachers with whom I've had the privilege to work. I am grateful to them all.

Acknowledgments

This book is about people joining together in an effort to change children's lives. Without those who joined me throughout the process of thinking and writing, it could never have been completed. That process required significant amounts of time, and I am very fortunate to have had the backing of the Health Foundation of Central Massachusetts, which provided the opportunity to pilot this material over the two years of an early childhood mental health seminar, then supplied funding so that I could complete the manuscript. Its commitment to forward-thinking early childhood initiatives makes a truly important contribution to the lives of young children in Massachusetts and beyond.

I am grateful, too, to the members of the Somerville Community Partnerships' Early Childhood Study Group, who have given me the chance to be in extended conversation about young children's well-being with an extraordinary group of professionals, to Libby Zimmerman of the Connected Beginnings Training Institute and Lynn Hennigan of the Together for Kids Project for offering needed encouragement and intellectual company, and to my colleagues at the Newton Community Partnerships for Children, the Newton Early Childhood Association, WarmLines Parent Resources, and the Guild of Accessible Practitioners, whose friendly support throughout this endeavor has been matched only by their tolerance for my limited presence during its end stages.

Any clinician would count herself lucky to have the company and input of colleagues like mine. Thanks to Judith Kneen and Candace Saunders, my partners in teaching, thinking, and playing, and to Betsy Abrams, Joan Abramson, Amy Bamforth, Roxy Leeson, Nellie Loring, Laura O'Meara, Fran Roznowski, Susan Stone, and Loretta Wieczner, whose warmth and creativity in supporting kids have taught me so much. Gratitude also, in memoriam, to Ellen Sondheimer and Barbie Greenspan, whose wisdom about children I still appreciate and whose companionship I still miss.

I have been incredibly fortunate to have had a group of gifted practitioners, writers, and theoreticians who generously agreed to read and critique sections of this manuscript in their areas of expertise. This book is far better because of their feedback, though its limits are solely my own. Thanks to Joan Abramson, Marilyn Augustyn, Holly Bishop, Cassandra Clay, Ann Flynn, Eliana Gil, Betsy Groves, Jerome Kagan, Judy Medalia, Maryann O'Brien,

Ellen Perrin, Judith Sampson, George Scarlett, Susan Stone, Kathleen Trainor, Edward Tronick, Loretta Wieczner, Andy Wizer, and Libby Zimmerman. Their help was invaluable.

A few individuals offered much-needed mentorship along the way. Many thanks to Nancy Boyd Webb who offered wise counsel and encouragement near the project's beginning; to Eliana Gil, Patricia Albjerg Graham, David Hirschland, and Zick Rubin who provided friendly advice about the publishing process; and to Jan Surrey and Steve Bergman, whose interest, suggestions, and support helped me stay the course.

Special thanks to a few friends, without whose dedicated company during this journey I might never have begun and could not have persevered. To David Feingold, treasured friend and consummate intellectual, I owe more gratitude than can be conveyed in words. His love of clear thinking and good writing is with me always, and it is a great sorrow that he isn't here for this book's completion. Thanks many times over, also, to Sage Sohier, whose ability to picture the world in her way encouraged me to write about it in mine, and to Susan Goodman, writer and editor extraordinaire, without whose expertise, guidance, and friendship this book would never have made it to publication.

I am lucky to have had such good companionship throughout this process. Thanks to dear friends Adrienne Asch, Marilyn and Martin Feinberg, Donna Fromberg and Michael Owings, Gill Garb and Colin Sieff, Cyndi Mason, Lucy and Will Ogburn, Joyce Rosen Friedman, Dana Schaul-Yoder, Rick Schaul-Yoder, and Andy Wizer and Rob Vecchi, whose support—and uncomplaining acceptance of my dazed presence throughout the writing process—made a huge difference.

Those of us involved in social services feel especially fortunate to be surrounded by the support and love of family. Thanks to my mother Evelyn Polk, whose loving and wise advice helped me hear the music of prose, to my father Henry Hirschland and his wife Janet, with appreciation for their wonderful support and upbeat "How's the book?," to my sister Madi Hirschland, whose generous editorial help and belief in the project buoyed me up all the way through, and to my brothers David and Richard, for always being there. Gratitude also to my grandparents Eric and Joan Polk, whose postretirement pleasure in working with preschoolers started me down this path, and to my mother-in-law Esther Fine, whose belief in the power of teaching to transform the lives of young people has been an inspiration.

Any clinician who works with children and caregivers owes much of her wisdom to their willingness to be open about their struggles and their lives. Thanks, always, to the many teachers and directors who so graciously invite me into their classrooms, gently correct me when I get too full of myself, and constantly add to my understanding of young children's development. Gratitude also to "Jeremy" and his parents, for their warmth, humor, and honesty, and to all the royal racers and their families, so many of whom have generously agreed to share their stories.

I am fortunate indeed to have had the support and assistance of my editors at Oxford University Press, without whom this book would have been a rambling and confusing epic: Mariclaire Cloutier, who believed in the project from its earliest incarnation and then—with clarity and wisdom—helped refine its vision, and Julia TerMaat, whose cheerful, painstaking, and skillful work was a godsend all along the way. Thanks also to my capable research assistant Anneke Schaul-Yoder, whose upbeat presence near the end of this project was such a help and such a pleasure.

Finally, and with all my love...deep appreciation to my wonderful daughters Sarah and Shoshanna, the first who served as an affectionate and insightful editor-in-waiting, the second who offered hugs, encouragement, and ample doses of good humor whenever needed. And to my husband Jeffrey—partner, friend, and favorite colleague—thanks doesn't even come close. Your unwavering commitment to meeting those who seek your help accessibly and humanly lights the way for us all.

Contents

Part IV   Questions and Conclusions

*Collaborative Intervention
in Early Childhood*

Introduction

Nothing matches the energy and enthusiasm of three- to seven-year-old children who are thriving. Full of curiosity about themselves and the world, eager to play and quick to laugh, kids this age can bring indescribable pleasure to the adults who spend time with them. When things aren't going so well, however, young children may leave parents and teachers feeling concerned and discouraged, even incompetent. The behaviors that cause such distress cross class and culture. An easily frustrated youngster can't keep her emotional thermostat regulated, while a nonstop wiggler zooms impulsively from kitchen to bedroom and back again. An intensely shy child holds back from talking to his friendly teacher or beloved uncle, while one with a particularly strong will refuses to bend even an inch with her peers. A dreamy scientist-in-the-making recites detailed information about dinosaur species, yet can't focus on the simplest requests for attention.

As such difficulties take up more and more space in a family or classroom, concerned adults may seek guidance from a mental health professional. Those of us approached for such help practice in a range of situations. Some of us are embedded in early care settings, Head Start programs, and elementary schools. Some go from one childcare program to another, offering consultation funded by state and local initiatives. Still others provide help to families and educators through clinics or in private practice.[1] Whatever its context, our job of supporting and mentoring the important adults in a young child's life has significant implications for development; research suggests that early childhood consultation helps foster success in school, skill in friendship, and well-being at home (Brennan et al., 2005; Gilliam, 2005; Bean, Biss, and Hepburn, 2007; Perry, Woodbridge, and Rosman, 2007).

This work takes many forms, even in a single day. A clinician may start his or her morning sitting on a child-sized chair in a classroom, drawing out teacher concerns about a youngster's worrisome behavior, offering some thoughts that shed light on the issues at hand, then suggesting step-by-step strategies to help jumpstart a process of change. Later, that same practitioner might be found in an office talking with a set of nervous parents about whether to have their child go through a neuropsychological evaluation, or with a single mother about how to help her four-year-old settle down at bedtime. Then it might be on to a parent training on limit setting, a staff discussion about social skill development, or a home visit. In fact, variability is this work's hallmark, and is what makes it both so satisfying and so challenging. It requires a combination of clinical sophistication, flexibility, and practicality—a mix that allows clinicians to draw from a wide-ranging knowledge base, yet offer information in a way that feels easily accessible and quickly useable to the parents and teachers asking for their help.*

This book aims to deepen practitioners' understanding of this mix, providing both the conceptual frameworks that anchor early childhood work and the step-by-step strategies that drive its thrust toward mastery. It offers an approach to collaborative intervention in which clinicians are therapeutic agents (though not necessarily therapists) offering parents and teachers the support, knowledge, and skill set they need to help children overcome a range of emotional, behavioral, and developmental challenges. This approach rests on what we now know about the science of brain development and the way constitutional factors play a role in a child's style of connecting and learning. It draws on both clinical and research-based explorations of how behavioral principles shape a youngster's way of functioning, and how early history can have a profound effect on later well-being. But most importantly, it nests development squarely within the relationship-filled worlds in which it unfolds. For at the heart of any approach must be the recognition that children rely on warm connections with caregivers in order to change and grow.

Guiding parents and teachers successfully relies on an ability to communicate simply yet cogently, to work with—not against—the nuances of family and classroom life. Language has great power, and the language clinicians use in talking with parents and teachers can either convey a respectful and collaborative stance, or leave them feeling both alienated and intimidated. Thus this book will not just explore the knowledge base and strategies on which we rely, but also look at how we offer our expertise in user-friendly ways. For this reason, there are points when a term or concept from the clinical world is explained, and then a more accessible variation offered as an entry point for conversations with concerned adults.

The book's content is anchored by the explorations of Part 1, *Foundations for Intervention*. Chapter 1 introduces the process of consultation, a progression that is framed with three questions: *What do we see? What do we think? What do we do?* These questions capture the idea that our first job as clinicians—together with the parents and teachers who are our "partners in care"—is to collect as much information as possible about a child, to observe him closely in an effort to learn about his life both past and present.†

* "Teacher" is used throughout this book to denote professionals working in a variety of settings, including family childcare providers, agency-based early care and education staff, and both preschool and elementary school teachers. Similarly, "school" refers to the range of environments in which these adults teach and care for young children, while "parent" designates parents, foster parents, and other primary caretakers.
† From this point on, in order to combine gender-neutral writing with ease of readability, children will be referred to as "he" or "she" in alternate chapters or chapter sections.

To help us gather enough data to come up with reasonable guesses about why he isn't thriving, we need to understand a few elements thoroughly. One is the nature of the developmental tasks that all kids work on in their early years; these "building blocks" are explored in Chapter 2.

Practitioners also need to be familiar with the many variations in temperament and learning styles that kids are born with. (Research has substantiated what parents have always known—children come into this world "built" very differently [Chess and Thomas, 1996; Kagan and Snidman, 2004]). Chapter 3 outlines some of these variations in what is often called "hard-wiring," so that clinicians can help caregivers look underneath behavior to the inborn factors that may contribute to it. Then, since the nature of family history and interplay has such a powerful effect on children's development, Chapter 4 explores what we might call family dances, the never-ending interchanges that we all engage in with the people we live with and love.

Part II, *Foundations for Intervention*, lays the groundwork for the day-to-day approaches that clinicians offer parents and teachers. It begins with an exploration of frameworks and principles for observation and intervention in Chapter 5, then continues with a look at how to coach parents in setting and enforcing sensible expectations in Chapter 6. Chapter 7 outlines the ways in which clinicians mentor teachers in the multifaceted process of providing classroom-based support to challenging children and challenging groups.

Part III, *Specific Approaches for Specific Difficulties*, explores the nuts and bolts of collaborative intervention for six areas of difficulty commonly seen in early childhood. Its chapters—one for each area—open with a summary of contributing issues, follow with a "points to remember" list, then outline concrete strategies for fostering mastery at home and in school. Finally, in-depth case material teases out the specifics of how these strategies are used "on the ground."

Part IV, *Questions and Conclusions*, touches on adaptations needed in work with traumatized youngsters, the challenges of helping families navigate life in our media-driven age, approaches to supporting children and parents through loss and illness, and other issues that regularly confront clinicians. Then, the book's final chapter looks at the predictable ups and downs all children go through as they progress toward adolescence, and highlights how the understanding gained through work on a youngster's earlier difficulties can inform approaches to challenges he faces later on.

No one volume can cover all that a clinician needs to understand in the field of early childhood practice. What this book offers is a comprehensive, practical approach to collaborative intervention. It does not attempt to explore the nature of intensive child or family therapy, although each can be tremendously useful. Nor does it delve into the advocacy efforts—and systems of care—that can be essential to families experiencing stressors connected to poverty, immigration, substance abuse, domestic violence, or serious mental health issues. Furthermore, although important (and sometimes hotly debated) questions about medication and diagnosis arise with great frequency in this work, neither area is given center stage here.[2]

In this book, development takes that place. And because development proceeds in contexts full of people and places, of things to do and hardships to endure—and because to do his or her job well, a clinician must understand complex narratives of experience—these explorations will be illustrated with stories of children's lives, stories culled mostly from this author's practice as an early childhood consultant. One of those children is Jeremy, whose struggles at home and in school will introduce the next chapter's look at the process of consultation.

Part I

Foundations for Understanding

1

When Young Children Need Help

What Do We See? What Do We Think?
What Do We Do?

Jeremy sat on my office floor constructing a racetrack out of blocks. He grabbed a red car from the nearby toy bin and propelled it wildly around the track, all the while recounting the woes of its thrill-seeking driver. After finding a satisfying end to the tale, he asked me to write it down, carefully dictating every detail.

> Once there was a kingdom that had a royal racer. She raced so fast, she raced faster than all the others. Then the king set up a racetrack for her, but she didn't like it, because it only went round and round in the same place and she wanted to explore all over. One time the ninjas told her they wanted a ride but she raced so fast they fell off. They said, "Ouch, royal racer, would you go a little slower?" But she said, "No, I want to go as fast as I can!"
>
> One day, she heard that there was a secret treasure buried far away from the kingdom. So, she jumped from a very, very high royal race jump and speeded off into America to look for that treasure. She drove so fast, her car broke down! Then she took the car to a mechanic shop and the mechanic said, "You need to speed slower." But the royal racer yelled, "I AM THE ROYAL RACER AND I WANT TO GO FAST!!!" The mechanic said, "Whoa—I didn't know you were the royal racer. You can race as fast as you want. And I will work on your car so that you won't break down ever again . . ."

Jeremy's parents and teachers reached out for professional guidance during his last year of preschool. An initial visit to his classroom had revealed an articulate child with large dark eyes, a lumbering gait, and a propensity for making cheerful pronouncements about the workings of the universe in a loud, slightly monotone voice. Kids were very drawn to this boy. His ideas for play were compelling and, in addition, tended to push just to the limits of adult tolerance—something that has as much appeal to the preschool set as it does to adolescents. Jeremy could be scary though: If blocked in his intentions, he might just throw a punch.

Jeremy's teacher enjoyed his upbeat nature. But she was ready to tear her hair out over his difficulty getting along with his peers, following directions that required him to put aside an engrossing activity, or leaving space for others to speak when he had something to say (which he almost always did). His parents loved his warmth and playful intelligence, yet tiredly wished that his willfulness and energy were easier to contain in their family of five.

Like so many of the young children about whom clinicians are contacted, Jeremy desperately wanted approval from the often-frustrated adults and kids who spent time with him. But—as is also common—the distance between this boy's wanting that approval and his having the wherewithal to get it was large indeed. After all, Jeremy's world was full of treasures, scientific knowledge (of which he already had an impressive amount), new words to be learned and used, interesting places to see and explore: How could he stop to make room for the ideas and needs of others? Furthermore, there were far too many things in life that just went round and round—the routines of the classroom, the repetitive nature of circle time, bathing, brushing teeth, and putting away toys at home. Why should he have to pause and attend to those annoyingly boring activities in the face of all he had to think about and to do?

The Consultative Agenda: Understanding, Appreciation, and Compassionate Intervention

By the time Jeremy created the royal racer's story, his parents, teachers, and I had spoken together many times, and the changes resulting from those conversations were encouraging—Jeremy was becoming easier to live with at home, had made his first real friend, and was beginning to negotiate play ideas at school. But, magical as his growing mastery might sound, those changes grew out of a slow process of consultation and intervention. In the first stage of that process, Jeremy's parents, teachers, and I developed a shared understanding that his internal focus, intensity, and drive—inborn traits all—lay at the heart of his difficulties. Soon afterward, Jeremy's parents came to see that in the effort to nurture their son's gifts, they had allowed his inner focus too much free rein. Finally, we focused on the kind of friendly help he'd need at home and in the classroom in order to live in the world of others with more give-and-take.

In fact, far from being magical, Jeremy's successes in learning a different style of royal racing were hard won; as is so often true, in order to change, he had to fight against both his intense temperament and some deeply ingrained patterns of behavior. As a result, he sometimes got very frustrated with his team of dedicated mechanics—mainly his parents and teachers, with me seeing him occasionally and offering guidance from behind the scenes. But in the end, though he still wished to speed along unhindered, Jeremy seemed to realize that this group of adults understood his dilemmas, and was helping him move through his days in such a way that others could now hang on for the ride.

Jeremy's story will continue later, with an in-depth look at how his parents and teachers learned to give him the assistance he so badly needed. For now, it's worth noting that his experience is what we always shoot for in the consultative process: that struggling youngsters feel increasingly understood and appreciated for who they are, at the same time that they get ongoing help with the challenges they face. To accomplish this sometimes-difficult double agenda, caring adults need a hefty dose of patience, a sense of just what is keeping such kids from thriving in the way they might, and a set of easily useable strategies that can help them gain the mastery they need. They are our royal racers, and with this kind of knowledge and thoughtful intervention, we can help them become successful explorers of the treasures within themselves and in their worlds.

The Consultative Outlook: Embracing Collaboration, Problem-Solving, and Hope

When Jeremy's parents first contacted me, they alternated between wondering what interesting path he might eventually take as an inventor or writer and fearing that he would become a rigid, isolated young man. And like this loveable, quirky boy, many of the three- to seven-year-old children clinicians hear about evidence both great promise and the possibility of future hardship. On the one hand, parents and teachers imagine the wonderful grown-ups they may be at twenty-five or forty: inspired artists, competent builders, nurturing parents and friends. On the other, those same adults fret that a youngster's current difficulties will lead to less favorable outcomes and worriedly envision school troubles, conflicted friendships, scuffles with the law. Daily, struggling children face challenges both internal and external, and parents and teachers look on with apprehension, noting the strengths and vulnerabilities they bring to their playing, loving, and learning.

Luckily for all concerned, young children are strikingly adaptable. Though their basic natures seem quite clear by three or four, the difficulties they have in coping with their lives haven't yet become hardened into parts of their characters, and the unfolding stages of early development provide countless opportunities for overcoming the challenges that have given them trouble. But, all too often, even the most optimistic parents and teachers see where a youngster's difficulties lie without understanding how to offer ongoing assistance in a useful way. Furthermore, young children who are getting stuck in some aspect of their lives can't explain (at least not accurately) what is tripping them up. The adults who care for them have to puzzle out what's going on in order to help them get on track.

Concerned adults can find it hard to gauge what "on track" means for this age group, however. What is normal for three- to seven-year-old children ranges so widely that the behavioral signs that suggest difficulty can also be quite unremarkable. Parents end up wondering whether their child's actions are just an intense version of normal behavior or whether there is cause for concern. Pediatricians and teachers wonder the same.[1] It's when the people who care daily for a child can't figure out whether to be concerned—or how to help if they are—that a mental health professional may get contacted for assistance. It is at this point that the power of the consultative process to spur growth may make itself felt: In partnering up with a child's caregivers, clinicians can often contribute to an understanding of what is getting in the way of her doing well. Then, as this collaborative undertaking continues with the design and implementation of step-by-step approaches to intervention, things frequently change for the better.

One of the factors propelling this shift is that the adults who take care of young kids usually haven't given up hope. When clinicians work with an adolescent who has been testy and explosive for a long time, the grown-ups around her—parents, teachers, principals—have often begun to lose faith in her ability to do better. Things have gotten entrenched in her and in her world. Much can happen to make the situation improve, but there's a kind of hopelessness, both in the teenager and in the people who deal with her each day, which must first be fought long and hard. It can be quite a battle. But the parents and teachers of a young child who isn't thriving usually still sense, with a kind of desperate immediacy, the potential just beneath the surface of her problematic behavior. They see it shine through on occasion (or perhaps even more often), and they imagine that she could function differently and much better. Add this hope to the pliability of the kids themselves, and the wonder and spark early childhood specialists experience in their work isn't hard to understand. Everyone is plugging for change, and change is often not so hard to reach.

A Common Problem: Unsuccessful Patterns of Response to Children's Difficulties

All this said, parents and teachers don't usually convey hope in their first conversations with clinicians, but a painful triangle of worry, frustration, and helplessness. Because when a child remains stuck despite the ongoing efforts of the adults who care for her, those adults may become as tangled up as she is. Parents sometimes broadcast a kind of tense self-reproach in these initial meetings—they sense the way their child's behavior is embedded in family life and are distressingly aware of how they have contributed to her difficulties. A father ruefully admits that his temper is as hard to control as his daughter's; a mother shamefacedly relates that when her shy son whines and clings to her side at family gatherings, while his cousins greet their relatives with cheerful hugs, she responds with irritated lectures that she knows only make things worse. Teachers, too, sometimes acknowledge that they've reached the end of their rope, conceding that they spend far too much time correcting a child and not enough supporting her. One recounts that Sammy's desperate need to slam his way into being first in line on the way to the gym—*every single time*—leaves her feeling disquietingly judgmental, not just of him but of his parents too. Another describes that, glancing over to the loft and seeing Julia once again curled up in a sad bubble of isolation, she is alarmed to notice herself thinking, "Go ahead, if that's what you really want. *I just can't try to draw you out any more.*"

Worry, frustration, and helplessness: By the time adults seek professional consultation, they're often feeling this demoralizing triple jeopardy, and are usually desperate for a plan of action. However, they need to figure out why a youngster's difficulties are occurring before deciding on what to do. This sounds obvious at first hearing, but the truth is that parents and teachers often intervene with kids in the same unsuccessful fashion over and over again, without really understanding what is causing their difficulties. In the heat of the moment, it can be hard for them to slow down and think, "What is bothering me here? Why is it happening? What can I do to get things moving in a different direction? If I do the first thing that comes to mind, is it going to have the effect I want?" In fact, the helplessness these adults experience in the face of a young child's difficulties, perhaps the most problematic leg of the triangle, often suggests that they are using strategies in just this way, repetitively and unproductively. They know it, but don't know what else to do. They need to stop and think before they act, but they must first learn what to think about.

Three Core Questions: What Do We See? What Do We Think? What Do We Do?

The job of a consulting clinician is to join parents and teachers in answering an expanded version of the questions just listed: What do we see that's worrying us? How can we observe carefully to discover what factors might be contributing to a youngster's struggles? How can we best understand the behaviors that are of concern? Using the provisional understanding we develop as our guide, what strategies can we design to support the growth we hope for? After we start using these strategies, how can we figure out which ones work and which ones don't?

I've deliberately used the words "we" and "us" because it has been my experience that the more the adults who care about a young child team up in answering these questions, the more potent the thrust toward growth becomes. Using the word "we" to stand in for this idea of partnerships in care, this series of questions can be boiled down to three: *What do we see? What do we think? What do we do?* Once we begin trying out the strategies that answer the last question, we figure out which ones are useful by asking the first once again. The process of helping a struggling youngster to thrive is an ongoing one, with lots of successes and failures along the way, and we do best when we track both. Thus a better way to illustrate our set of three questions would be:

The Work's Intention: Striving for Mastery, Not Management

The heart of this looping progression lies in the question, *What do we think?* We gather information so that we may answer it well, and the strategies we devise follow directly from the content of that answer. There's nothing surprising about the importance of this question; looking at it is the stuff of parent-teacher conferences, and of conversations that parents have with friends and that teachers have with colleagues. How it is answered is often deeply influenced by the culture in which it is asked. In the United States, for example, there is currently a tendency to look to biological explanations for behavior, and to encapsulate our understanding with diagnoses of mental and learning disorders. Children whose energy seems relentless and who have trouble harnessing attention may be understood to have attention-deficit/hyperactivity disorder (ADHD). Youngsters whose emotions get intense quickly and who have difficulty staying calm for extended periods may be given a diagnosis of bipolar disorder. Kids who worry endlessly and can't be easily soothed by their caretakers may be thought to have a generalized anxiety disorder. And so on.

In the midst of this trend toward medical diagnosis, it makes sense that the adults trying to understand a child's troubles find themselves wondering about the possibility of biologically based disorders to account for what they see. Surely, having specific research and theory-based knowledge about the constitutional issues that contribute to such difficulties can be useful (Shonkoff and Phillips, 2000). But, placing kids in large and amorphous diagnostic categories—grouping them by the most striking aspects of their worrisome behaviors—creates problems of its own (Levine, 1995). Children who share behavioral characteristics can function in that manner for very different reasons and in quite different ways (Greenspan and Wieder, 1998). By labeling kids in this way, we are in danger of not understanding what drives their behavior and of coming up with strategies to help them that fail to address the underlying reasons for their actions. Such strategies frequently backfire.

Other drawbacks, too, accompany this tendency to diagnose young children. For one, it often leaves families feeling deeply insecure about their ability to help their kids overcome the challenges they face. For another, it can lead to a precipitous use of medication (Willis, 2003). Through the lens of a label, parents, teachers, and specialists may be inclined to see rigid problems rather than fluid possibilities, and to work toward the management of disorders rather than the mastery of developmental challenges.[2] Furthermore, labels can be dangerous; these days, we hear parents saying things like "She is ADHD," as if the diagnosis we use to describe a child's challenges suddenly becomes a boxed-in truth about who she is—a worrisome possibility to be sure.

It can be far more effective to consult with the adults who care most about a child and then, using all the knowledge we have at our disposal, to come up with an individualized profile for her.[3] Developing this kind of pro-file requires a careful look at the intersection between a child's inborn nature, the particulars of the family and community in which she lives, and the tasks of development that she has faced in her early years—the work of exploring how these three factors come together is a primary focus of this book.

Hence the approach offered here, while not disregarding contemporary understandings of childhood difficulties, rarely uses the language of medi-cine and disability. It emphasizes that some things can be *hard for* rather than *wrong with* children, targets *mastery of* developmental tasks rather than *man-agement of* disorders, and leans toward looking at *constitutional vulnerabilities* rather than *biological givens*. I hope to take the best from current biophysi-ological understandings of behavior, yet remain grounded in the real world in which a child lives, plays, and learns—the world of the sandbox and circle time in school, of birthday parties, gatherings with grandparents who require hello kisses, and bedtimes with just one more glass of water and a nightlight. And, as highlighted earlier, I'll do this in words that can be easily shared with our parent and teacher partners—it's often true that if we can't describe what we know without using extensive professional jargon, we probably need to ask ourselves how clearly we understand the content in question.

Consultative Process in Action: Getting Specific and Then Getting to Work

The process we're about to explore in depth is one in which we observe widely, think carefully, and develop a provisional understanding of what is driving a child's behavior. Avoiding overly general categories to account for why she is having difficulty, we aim for specificity and clarity in our analysis. Then, and only then, do we partner with caregivers to design a set of strategies that target her challenges in a way that is tailored to her unique profile. We're finally able to answer the question, *What do we do?* This process could be described as one of "getting specific" and then "getting to work," phrases that we'll return to in future chapters. In order to do the first, clinicians need a solid understanding of the important elements of early childhood mastery. It is these "building blocks of development" that are explored in the next chapter.

2

Seven Building Blocks of Development

Understanding Core Emotional, Behavioral, and Social Competencies

A teacher stops her program's early childhood consultant in the hallway, eager to talk about a distractible four-year-old who has her concerned. A mother calls her kindergarten son's school social worker after reluctantly acknowledging that his provocative behaviors just aren't getting any better. A couple shows up for an appointment at a mental health clinic, full of worry about how disengaged their daughter seems compared to her siblings and classmates. Whatever the context, clinicians hear a set of familiar refrains when a young child isn't thriving at home or in school. "She doesn't seem to know how to play with other kids." "It's really hard to get his attention." "I can't get her to calm down when she's upset, and she's upset a lot." "It's so difficult to understand what he's trying to tell us." "She's always on the move." Each of these descriptions relates to what we sometimes call a developmental trajectory.

Developmental Trajectories and Early Childhood Mastery

The idea of developmental trajectories is embedded in child development literature, and suggests a process of growth across a range of important early childhood challenges (Shonkoff and Phillips, 2000; Aber et al., 2003). Theorists and researchers have explored these challenges in different ways through the years—looking at, among other areas, a child's ability to engage with others; to pay attention; to store, retrieve, and organize information; to regulate emotions; and to grasp the idea that not all minds think and feel alike. Furthermore, the organizing constructs that drive different theoretical paradigms range widely. Some, for example, put cognition at their core, while others stress connection as the foundation for all growth.[1]

Detailed information about these paradigms can be found elsewhere.[2] What is important to note here are three ideas that hold steady across many theoretical frameworks: the notion that the developmental pathways of children are individual in nature, that mastery in multiple areas of functioning is an important feature of successful growth, and that vulnerabilities in one area of development often impact competency in others. As clinicians, we base our thinking on these ideas, assuming that although every child is unique, a core group of developmental challenges carries great weight for them all. We also keep in mind that mastery across a range of such challenges often leads to a youngster being not only competent but also likeable. If a child is stumped by one or more of them, on the other hand, daily life can become difficult for everyone.

The seven "building blocks of development" outlined in this chapter are culled from a longer list of those articulated by developmental theorists. They are far from comprehensive. Instead, they're offered as a practical look at a set of developmental trajectories that have a large impact on how kids handle the ins and outs of life from ages three to seven.[3] They'll rest at the center of our investigation of how a child isn't thriving, and as the jumping off point for the strategies we'll use to help out.

Seven Building Blocks of Development

1. *Feeling Safely and Warmly Connected*—the building block that supports them all: experiencing trust, interest, and pleasure in relationships.
2. *Tuning In*—being able to harness and sustain attention, to focus on people, ideas, requests, and expectations.
3. *Communicating Effectively*—understanding others and making others understand, both verbally and nonverbally.
4. *Regulating Energy*—being able to shift from one energy level to another; having the capacity to slow down and stay calm for periods of time.
5. *Regulating Feelings*—managing small difficulties without large reactions; being able to regain composure after getting upset; maintaining self-control in the face of frustration.
6. *Changing Tracks and Being Flexible*—being able to adapt reasonably to change; knowing how to share space and ideas; having the ability to end one activity when it's time to begin another.
7. *Feeling Capable and Confident*—the building block that follows from the rest: having a sense of resourcefulness, competence, and optimism.

The First Building Block: Feeling Safely and Warmly Connected

Sophie sits cross-legged amidst a jumble of puzzle pieces, animatedly discussing which piece goes where with a classmate. Paula, the classroom's lead teacher, heads over to where the two are hard at work. She kneels down. "Hi Sophie, hi Emma, that puzzle is coming along! Sophie, can you look up for a minute?" She waits until the child's eyes meet hers. "I'm going to get snack and I'll be back soon. Can you say, 'Good-bye Paula, I'll see you soon'?" Sophie echoes thinly, "Good-bye Paula, see you soon." Her teacher smiles and says, "Good-bye Sophie, I'll be back soon."

About five minutes later, the teacher returns and goes over to the girl, who is now flipping through the pages of a book. She kneels down once again. "Hi Sophie." Sophie glances up. "I'm back Sophie," she says, looking into the child's dark brown eyes. "Okay Paula." The teacher stays for a few moments, commenting on the book's pictures as Sophie nestles up against her. Then she delivers a gentle farewell pat and leaves to supervise several other kids.

Why would a teacher go over to a happily involved four-year-old and engage in a rather stiff, scripted interchange about her upcoming and brief absence from the room? To answer this question, let's return to my first observation of Sophie, three months earlier. What I note then verifies Paula's worried description when she called my office: On the few occasions when Sophie isn't actually shadowing Paula around the room, her intense brown eyes vigilantly follow her teacher's movements. In addition, this girl appears terrified any time Paula leaves the classroom and, with increasing alarm, calls out her name over and over again until she returns. Throughout the observation, Sophie rarely spends relaxed time with other kids. On the way out to the playground, she insists on grabbing a favorite book, and won't let it go even as she clambers up the slide. She is frightened of anyone sneezing, and cries inconsolably if she gets even a tiny paper cut. All the staff who deal with this girl express tremendous concern about her. And for good reason: Sophie is experiencing more distress than any child should ever have to feel.

There are many reasons behind Sophie's profound uneasiness. Her twenty-two-year-old mother struggles with substance abuse, and has been an inconsistent and confusing presence in her life. Her grandmother Maria, with whom she lives, is kind but exhausted and has some bothersome, though not life-threatening, medical problems. When Maria isn't feeling well, she leaves Sophie in the care of a wide array of relatives, often without much warning. This lack of warning is problematic in and of itself; the additional question of abuse at the hands of one of these relatives remains unanswered. To further complicate matters, Sophie has some medical problems of her own. A year earlier, following a bad cold, her chronic asthma intensified so alarmingly that she was hospitalized for several days, an understandably unsettling experience. All in all, there is little about this child's life that has been predictable, and it isn't surprising that she doesn't trust the world, or the people in it, to be safe and secure. In fact, Sophie has experienced Paula as her most consistent connection over the previous year and a half, and it is with this teacher that she plays out her fears about relationships for all to see.

Fortunately, the adults who care for Sophie are slowly able to help her feel more trusting. Her loving but overwhelmed grandmother comes to see that she needs to be more thoughtful about whom she finds to care for her granddaughter and how she helps the child prepare for her stays away from home. In addition, she gives permission for Sophie to begin weekly meetings with a seasoned clinician. Then there is Paula's simple, repetitive goodbye-hello ritual, which we design in order to help this girl overcome her paralyzing terror about loss. Paula also works to spend less one-on-one time with Sophie, instead offering herself as a comforting anchor from which her student can safely connect with other adults and kids. It's a thrill to walk into the classroom three months after my initial consult and find Sophie off in a corner playing with Emma, no adult in close proximity. Paula beams as she tells me that the day before, Sophie forgot to bring her book out to the playground. The two of us guess that we can soon try shortening and then letting go of the goodbye script, but agree that we'll be careful not to move too quickly.

The Importance of Secure Connections: Lessons From the Study of Attachment

Shortly, we'll look at the reasoning behind the interventions just described, and the ways in which it reflects the importance of secure connections in children's lives. Clinicians' understanding of this importance stems in great part from the study of attachment, the well-known construct first articulated by Bowlby (1969) and Ainsworth (1973), and later elaborated upon by Main and Solomon (1986), Siegel (1999), Shore (2001a, 2001b), and others. In response to the work of such theorists and researchers, it is now seen as a given that kids need to feel safely embedded in their caretaking relationships, to have confidence that the adults who watch over them can be relied on for comfort, care, and assistance. Without this assurance, children often don't dare to explore their worlds, to learn and grow and make friends (National Scientific Council on the Developing Child, 2004).

Part of the experience of secure attachment involves the infant's or child's growing sense of being bonded to at least one or two people; such experiences of bonding allow children to learn what a warm back-and-forth with another human being feels like. This back-and-forth is not one of constant attunement between child and adult, however; the experience of losing and regaining connection—what Tronick and Weinberg refer to as "error and repairs, deviations and disruptions" (1997, p. 54)—is, by many, believed to be part of the process of relational strengthening and emotional growth.

Lessons learned from the study of attachment deepen our understanding of children's reactions to trauma and abilities to be resilient in the face of hardship. They have implications for learning as well.[4] At this juncture, however, we'll focus on two central ideas that have tremendous implications for work with parents and teachers. The first is that, within reason, it's normal for adults to sometimes be "out of synch" with the children they care for: Relational "misses"—and the reconnections that follow—are a part of healthy development. The second is that it's through the cumulative experience of connection that children come to feel secure within themselves, and in their families, schools, and communities.[5] It is these ideas that we hold in mind while looking to understand why a child's mastery of the first building block is at risk.

Getting Specific: Understanding Why Children Struggle With Connections

Although the specifics of Sophie's hardships are her own, her level of suffering is widely shared. Clinicians are all too familiar with the problematic circumstances that can play a role in children's and parents' difficulties feeling pleasure and ease in their mutual connections: the chaos of homelessness, overcrowded housing, or frequent relocation; the devastation of neglect, abuse, or a violent household; the bleak experience of a parent's addiction or a mother's postpartum depression. The list goes on and on.

There is no doubt that such situations may contribute to a lack of comfort in relationships, but it is important to remember that children in more fortunate circumstances can have trouble feeling trust and connectedness as well. Sometimes kids are born with an inner focus that leaves them naturally less interested in connections than most youngsters. Parents don't always know how to "find" such children, feeling, after a while, that it is just easier to leave them contentedly in their own worlds. Distance grows slowly but inexorably in these situations. Sometimes there is an awkward mismatch between the temperament of a parent and that of a child—each reaches out but finds it hard to connect to the other (Bates and MacFadyen-Ketchum, 2000). Sometimes early feeding or medical problems get in the way of a warm bond. Sometimes a superficially easy, undemanding child gets lost in a pack of siblings and becomes, quietly, more and more withdrawn. Now and again a child gets so easily overwhelmed by sound or touch or smell that he feels too uncomfortable to get close to anyone (Stock Kranovitz, 1998). Occasionally, the circumstances preceding a child's adoption gave him a less than optimal experience of nurturing connection and initially, post-adoption, he can't feel securely engaged with those who care for him (Rutter et al., 1998).

A child's difficulty feeling trust and pleasure in relationships can show up in a number of ways. Kids may be deeply unsettled, like Sophie. They may be interested in but anxious about getting close, or prickly, or just plain withdrawn.[6] When we have an intuition that a child isn't feeling comfortably connected, we look to see if he makes good eye contact, whether he responds to warm attention, if he seeks comfort from others when he is upset, and whether he shares pleasure in his accomplishments.[7] We note whether he shows interest in those around him, and empathy for them when they are distressed. If a number of these behaviors are lacking, it is likely that this developmental building block is at risk. We'll need to tailor our response to him in a way that encourages him to feel more connected to others. As always, the strategies we'll use will depend on our understanding of *why* he's experiencing difficulty. Often, a core element will involve supporting the development and deepening of "circles of connection."

Getting to Work: Encouraging Trust and Pleasure in Relationships

The idea of circles of connection flows directly from Greenspan's influential work on how connection and communication unfold between children and their caretakers. It is based on his practical yet elegant way of conceptualizing what he calls "circles of *communication* (italics mine)," a construct that informs parents', teachers', and specialists' work on fostering sustained and pleasurable exchanges between themselves and the children they care for. This construct is used in its original form in the upcoming exploration of building block three. Here it is tweaked slightly, with an altered focus on the element of connection in its own right, but the construct's core visual metaphor maintained: circles that are initiated (opened) by one member of a duo, responded to by the other, then completed (closed) by the first (Greenspan, 1992, Greenspan and Wieder, 1998).

Consider how these interchanges play out in everyday life by envisioning the energy that flows between two people in a relationship as a series of circles. Paula catches Sophie's eye and smiles. Sophie sidles up to her teacher, gazing at her face all the while. Paula offers her a welcoming pat on the arm. A circle of connection has been opened and then closed, from one person to the other and back again. Dad looks at three-year-old Carlos and makes a funny face. Carlos giggles and makes a silly face back. Dad imitates his son's expression as they smile together. Another circle of connection has been opened and closed. If Carlos then says a nonsense word, dad adds to it, and then both laugh, a second circle has looped around. Circles of connection happen with words and without. Babies and their caretakers start getting them going very early on, teenagers sometimes engage in them by fighting with their parents, and lovers know their feel on a profoundly intimate level.[8]

Young children who have comfortable relationships engage in easy circles of connection many, many times a day. And when relationships are reliable and warm, kids begin to carry within themselves a sense of security and wholeness, even when the adults who hold them dear are not immediately available. One way of understanding Sophie's terrified behavior in the classroom is that her ongoing experiences have gone beyond the normal relational disruptions and repairs discussed earlier. As a result, her ability to tolerate even minor separations is minimal—she's too afraid that the circles of connection she relies on to feel safe may be broken at any moment. In response, she fearfully shadows Paula to try to keep them intact. The purpose of our goodbye-hello ritual is to allow her first to feel a warm circle loop between herself and her beloved teacher, then to hear and say words that remind her that another circle will soon be available and, finally, to open and close a last circle that tells her that she's once again in Paula's comforting presence. Our hope is that over time, with a soothing and almost hypnotic repetition of this ritual, she'll be able to hold the certainty of her connection to Paula within herself, and that the temporary loss of Paula's presence won't leave her feeling so alone and vulnerable. To our relief, the ritual seems to fulfill just this purpose.

The approach to helping Sophie works because it is carefully thought out in response to our understanding of her situation. The strategies we use to encourage other kids to feel ease and openness in their relationships will be as varied as the reasons that their connections are at risk. A thorough look at these strategies will come later. But we should note here that without the ability to feel pleasure and safety in relationships, children often experience difficulty with many of the other building blocks. Feeling trust and enjoyment in connection is truly the building block that supports them all.

The Second Building Block: Tuning In

> Gabe shambles contentedly into his kindergarten classroom each morning, eager to get started on a puzzle or science corner activity. He reads at a high second grade level, can manipulate numbers in his head like a fourth grader, and has an ever-growing fund of knowledge about the way the world works. However, halfway through the school year, this boy still doesn't know the names of the other kids in his group. He's more generally out of synch with what is going on around him too. Gabe is usually thinking intently about something, and frequently talks in depth about his ideas to classmates who are clearly not listening. When it's his turn to speak at circle time, it can take three or four repetitions of his name for him to respond. Then, after he finally looks up, he's often unsure of the topic at hand.

Gabe is having trouble tuning in. He loves the world of ideas, but struggles in day-to-day life because it is hard for him to harness his attention, to emerge from his inner experience and thoughts and become aware of what is going on around him. He appears to be a happy dreamer, but his parents and teachers are increasingly concerned, not only that he doesn't have real friends, but also that he may eventually fall behind in school because he won't be able to pay attention to what is being taught. Not surprisingly, Gabe has started showing signs of frustration. The more he misses the social signals that are going on all around him, the further behind he falls in knowing how to negotiate sibling and friendship relationships, and learning to handle conflict when it arises. Recently, he's begun crying more at home, especially when his rather bossy older sister uses his foggy inattention to get the better of him.

Four-year-old Emily also has trouble with attention. Motoring her way through her days, flitting from activity to activity, Emily often can't rein in her relentless energy enough to focus on what people are saying to her.

Emily's single mother Dana finds her overwhelming, and feels frustrated that it so often takes a harsh yell to get the girl she thinks of as a "human whirlwind" to listen. Emily's preschool teachers have also noted how hard it is for her to slow down enough to tune in, mentioning to Dana that because her daughter's friendships and play have had to develop on the fly, both are beginning to suffer. They wonder whether Emily will be ready for kindergarten next year and fear that if she goes, it may be hard for her stay attentive to the varied demands of the long school day.

The Elements of Tuning In

Though there is more to learn about these two children, the different qualities of their temperaments and their inattention are already noticeable. Yet they are each having trouble tuning in, and the nature of this developmental task can be understood similarly for both. Harnessing attention is something we all do all the time. We do it while listening to the news, when trying not to get distracted during a child's rambling recitation of last night's dream, and when noting the sad expression in a friend's eyes. You are doing it now as you read this page—your eyes peruse these words, you register their meaning, make some connection that is all your own, and then emerge to read a bit more. It happens quickly, seamlessly, and mostly without notice. But if you are getting restless and hungry, you may suddenly realize that though your eyes are moving ahead on the page, you have no idea what you've just read. Instead, you are debating whether to go to the kitchen and grab a snack. Then, recognizing that your thoughts have meandered off, you direct yourself to focus again on these words.

There has been a great deal written on the nature of attention, and even more on that of inattention. Often, inattention is addressed in tandem with its frequent partner, hyperactivity. In this section of the book, the two remain separate. (They'll be paired in our later exploration of intervention.) Looking briefly at how theorists deconstruct the ability to pay attention, we see a number of elements: competence in discriminating between what is important versus unimportant; the ability to sustain focus in the face of distracting visual, auditory, and tactile stimuli; and skill in maintaining consistent mental alertness (Levine, 2001). Research informs us about how competently attentive individuals can grasp the nature and passage of time and are able to suppress responses to compelling stimuli and impulses in the present in order to attend to information and expectations with import for the future (Barkley, 1998). This last ability, which is a particular challenge for children who are both inattentive and highly active, is what Barkley describes as "behavioral inhibition" (1997a). Many of the elements listed here are tied together under the umbrella of "executive function," what we might think of as the ability of the mind to oversee its activities and monitor its performance (Zelazo, Qu, and Mueller, 2005).[9]

As clinicians, we easily tie such theoretical understandings of inattention to what we see in kids: a boy fidgeting with his shirtsleeves instead of listening to group instruction for an upcoming math project, a girl losing interest before finishing a simple block construction that was entrancing only moments earlier. To help parents and teachers make this leap from abstract ideas to the real world, we need a straightforward language that captures what we know. So let's go back to your experience of reading these paragraphs and, somewhere along the way, losing track of their words. What do you do if you want to regain focus? You tell yourself, in essence, to *pop up* out of your mental wanderings, and *tune in* to what you are reading. These phrases point us toward a parent- and teacher-friendly explanation of the process of attending, one that outlines a sequence of four actions:

The Process of Attending

In order to harness attention successfully, we

1. *Pop up*—emerge from whatever we've been thinking, feeling, or doing, and direct our consciousness to a specific piece of input.
2. *Tune in*—focus our attention on the information at hand. Tuning in often involves vision, frequently requires hearing, and sometimes includes taste, touch, and smell too. It also requires that we screen out unimportant stimuli: irrelevant thoughts, intriguing sights and sounds, and interesting but off-task impulses to act.
3. *Take in*—make sense of the information to which we have just attended.
4. *Pop down*—return to a more internal state, thinking or feeling in response to the information we've just absorbed, and forming our reaction to it.

We pop up, tune in, take in, and pop down over and over again throughout our waking hours. Success in school requires children to pop up and tune in countless times a day; success with friends requires the same. After all, to be able to get along with other kids, a child must notice their facial expressions and pay attention to their words and tones of voice, something that Gabe is particularly unskilled at doing.

Getting Specific: Understanding Why Children Struggle to Harness Attention

There are many reasons that children have problems harnessing attention. Challenges in understanding or using language; a constitutionally based inner focus or naturally high energy level; biologically driven vulnerabilities in the brain functions that support self-monitoring and impulse control; exposure to toxic substances in utero; the experience of being chronically overwhelmed by sound or touch or smell; distressing emotional issues—all these and more can leave a child struggling to tune into the information swirling around her (Shonkoff and Phillips, 2000). In fact, the wide-ranging reasons for attentional problems suggest that we must be careful about making premature assumptions. It's all too easy, for example, to decide that a child has a genetically based predisposition toward distractibility when, in fact, it may be emotional overload from a history of trauma that is at work (Cole et al., 2005).

No matter what the cause, when kids don't tune in easily, a secondary problem often emerges; they get so used to hearing annoyed voices telling them to "stop" or "look at me" that they start willfully shutting out requests for attention. Both Gabe and Emily have begun to do this, and it's now hard for their frustrated parents and teachers to figure out when they are intentionally unresponsive versus when popping up and tuning in is truly difficult. It's a dilemma for everyone involved with these two, and is often at the heart of the irritable interactions that other inattentive kids have with the adults who care for them.

Getting to Work—Helping Kids Learn to Harness Attention

Gabe is a quiet middle child, nested between a powerhouse of an older sister and a lively, assertive younger brother. As his siblings fill the house with their raucous games, Gabe unobtrusively assembles complex puzzles or flips through the science books his dad brings home from the library. But now, after seeking professional guidance, his parents are trying out some new strategies to help their son tune in more successfully. Joining Gabe when he is contentedly absorbed in an activity, they watch for a short while, and then ask him to stop what he is doing "just for a few moments." It often takes time for him to comply, but they remind themselves not to get annoyed or to nag. When he finally responds, they do their best to meet his eyes, and then express curiosity about what he's up to. By showing warm interest in his responses, and continuing to meet his gaze as they converse with him, they're bolstering his ability to harness attention. Their strategy has two parts. First, *they mostly ask for Gabe's attention at a time when what he'll be rewarded with when he gives it is wholly positive.* (We often tend to "reward" the eventual focus of inattentive kids with a request to do something they won't like or a criticism of what they are already doing. Understandably enough, this doesn't encourage them to tune in more often [Barkley, 1997b, 2000]). Second, *they work on supporting attention in this way at least twenty or thirty times a day,* offering him steady skill-building assistance in an area of vulnerability. What they are finding is that by doing the attentional equivalent of thirty sit-ups with Gabe each day, he is indeed strengthening his ability to pop up and tune in.

Shortly after wandering into his classroom on a recent Monday morning, Gabe walks over to his teacher, looks right into her eyes, and declares: "Ms. Alper, your hair looks different!" She knows that he's really saying, "Your new haircut looks funny." But even in the midst of her amused dismay at his honesty, she notes that Gabe is making progress. He's tuned in to what he sees and has stayed tuned in as he talks with her about it.

Feeling comfortably related to others is indeed the developmental building block that supports all others, but harnessing attention follows closely in its wake. When children find it hard to pop up and tune in, they miss much of what they need to learn easily and make friends happily. Not only that, but attending and communicating are intimately connected (Greenspan, 1992; Nelson, 2007). If kids don't tune in to the people around them, they often have trouble both understanding and being understood. At the same time, if they can't communicate with ease, they often end up struggling with attention. That leads us to our next building block.

The Third Building Block: Communicating Effectively

Peter is scowling again. His teacher Leanne is pretty sure that if she doesn't quickly reach the corner where he's been playing with his friend Nathan, there is going to be another explosion. She goes over to lend a hand, crouching down next to the tall, heavyset boy. "Peter, you look unhappy. Is something wrong?" "HE, HE WON'T LET ME, HE WANTS TO BE BLUE, I CAN'T BE, I WANT TO BE A RED ONE." "A red what, Peter?" Leanne puts her arm around his shoulders. "A RED ONE, A RED SPACE GUY." Nate chimes in, "I want to be a blue alien, a bad guy." "YEAH, I DON'T WANT THAT, I WANT TO, I DON'T WANT TO, I WANT TO BE RED." "Okay, so Nate, you want to be a blue alien, a bad guy, and Peter wants to be a red space guy . . . is that a problem for you Nate, if Peter is a red space guy?" Nathan looks puzzled, and replies that it isn't a problem at all. Peter can be what he wants, but *he* wants to be a bad blue alien.

"Peter, Nate wants to be a blue alien that's bad, and you want to be a red guy." "YEAH, A GOOD GUY. I DON'T WANT TO BE BAD." "Oh, you don't want to be a bad guy?" Peter begins to calm down. "No, I don't LIKE to be the bad guy." His eyes tear up. "Peter, were you worried that you had to be a bad guy too?" Peter's relieved assent makes it clear that he finally feels understood.

Peter is having trouble keeping up with the rapid-fire language used by other children in his preschool classroom of four- and five-year-olds. All the kids in the class will be going on to kindergarten next year, and most of them are busy playing and chatting with each other, using complex strings of sentences to share ideas and solve problems. But Peter takes much longer than the other youngsters to comprehend what he hears, and to respond with his own ideas. Often, he misunderstands what his classmates have in mind, and gets left behind as narrative play quickly unfolds among a group of children.

Peter's vulnerabilities in language processing are causing a ripple effect developmentally. He is having trouble learning the give-and-take involved in play with friends, not because he is by nature inflexible, but because he is uncertain about the meaning of what is going on around him. Furthermore, as he gets more and more confused in the midst of interactions with his peers, he isn't managing frustration well, losing his temper a number of times a day in the classroom. Last year, Peter had an easier time of it in preschool. Many of the other youngsters were also still developing basic language skills; the length of their statements was shorter and the pace of conversation slower. But recently, his mother heard him describe himself as stupid, and she frets that her son is beginning to lose confidence.

Across the hall from Peter's room is a class of three-year-olds. Within minutes of entering the "purple room," a visitor might note a steady stream of children tearfully running to their lead teacher to complain about Anjali. "Martha, Anjali took my doll!" "Martha, Anjali hit me." "Martha, I was first. Anjali pushed me!" Martha knows that this girl's family speaks mostly Hindi at home. She knows, too, that the range of language ability in the purple room is always wide; some kids this age converse in long sentences, while others only have phrases of a few words. But Anjali isn't using much language at all. Furthermore, in addition to the grabbing and pushing kids so dislike, she skitters from one activity to another, doesn't respond to simple instructions, and seems mystified by most of what goes on at circle time. Anjali's parents relate that she isn't doing much better either speaking Hindi or behaving at home, and everyone is beginning to worry. This child's trouble understanding and using language is impairing her ability to control herself, to slow down and tune in, and to relate to others. Like Peter, she is falling further and further behind as the rest of the class takes off.

Second grader Renee is also having social difficulties. This child's use of language is just fine. In fact, teachers are bowled over by her sophisticated vocabulary and long, precise descriptions of weekend events. Renee's face, though, remains impassive while she speaks, and her voice has a flat, unenthusiastic quality. Ask her to understand the meaning of a child's annoyed gesture or irritated grimace, and she often doesn't have a clue. Gifted in the use of language, she has trouble comprehending the nonverbal world. She too is struggling with some of the basics of communication.

Communication as a Three-Part Process

The study of communication has captivated theorists for many years, with attention being focused on questions both large and small. Is there a special "language acquisition device" in every child's brain that allows him to produce grammar from a universal template programmed into his genetic system (Chomsky, 1965)? How do children test out their hypotheses about the connections between things in the world and the words that describe them (Brown, 1958)? How do they proceed from sound recognition to word recognition, from word production to rule usage, and from there to strikingly nuanced expressions of meaning, all in the course of a few years (de Villiers and de Villiers, 1979)? How does the process of language acquisition help children join the "community of minds," the symbol-filled culture in which they live (Nelson, 2007)?

As the result of such detailed explorations, we've learned that the process of acquiring and using language is a subtle one involving many interacting factors. These factors include, to name only a few, the ability to engage in turn-taking, to grasp the rhythm and cadences of speech patterns, to understand and use syntactic rules, and to have—and be able to access on demand—an adequate repertoire of vocabulary words (Campbell, 2002; Landy, 2002; Shonkoff and Phillips, 2000). The more we know about this process as clinicians, the more acute are our abilities as diagnosticians, especially when we suspect that subtle language processing issues are responsible for distressing behavioral problems. However, it is usually too time consuming—and often unnecessary—for clinicians to fully explain the workings of communication to teachers and parents. As a result, we take some central constructs from our knowledge base in order to offer these adults a framework for understanding this building block.

Elements of this framework, outlined shortly, are evident in the vignette of Peter and Nathan. Peter's good buddy Nathan, of bad blue alien fame, communicates with ease. Notice how he responds to his teacher's question about whether it is a problem for him if Peter is a red space guy. No, it's not, he answers, Peter can be whatever he wants, but he, Nathan, has his own agenda. Nathan understands the question, figures out his answer, and then expresses that answer logically and simply. Peter, on the other hand, keeps backing up, as if to get a running start, then switches what he has to say several times before landing on a vague statement of his problem: "He, he won't let me, he wants to be blue, I can't be, I want to be a red one." "A red what," his teacher must ask. "A red one, a red space guy," he replies. With a few more prompts, he adds the information that he doesn't like being a bad guy, never actually stating that he believes Nathan wants him to be just that. With many more words than his friend, Peter has expressed himself with far less precision.

When talking with the concerned parents and teachers of children like Peter, clinicians emphasize that communication can be visualized as a three-part process that includes intake, reflection, and output (Buckley, 2003). The actions on the intake and output ends of this process are commonly called "receptive" and "expressive" communication. The reflection that goes on in between these ends might be described as internal processing. When a child communicates with the kind of facility Nathan demonstrates, these actions happen rapidly and sometimes even simultaneously (Bonniwell Haslett and Samter, 1997). Of course, before any child can use spoken language to communicate successfully, he must be able to hear sounds at various volumes and pitches. Because mild to severe hearing loss sometimes accounts for a youngster's difficulty communicating, we make sure to have hearing checked if using or understanding language is a problem. But assuming that a child hears well, he, like Nathan, must experience success in all three prongs of the following process in order to communicate with ease:[10]

The Process of Communication

Intake—Receptive Communication

As he works to take in information, a child must:

- Attend to sounds, faces, and gestures
- Decode the sounds he hears into words and sentences
- Make sense of these strings of language
- Maintain his memory of the sequencing and meaning of what he's heard early on, as he attends to more information
- Attend to cues he sees and hears in facial expressions and gestures, and in the tone and volume of voices
- Figure out the meaning of this nonverbal information, for example, understanding what communication is meant as humorous or sarcastic and what is intended as serious or important

Reflection—Internal Processing

Once he's made sense of what has been communicated, he has to:

- Think about what he's heard and seen
- Form a response that logically connects to what he's understood

Output—Expressive Communication

In order to convey ideas successfully, he needs to:

- Find the words he needs to communicate his thoughts accurately
- Organize those words into logically sequenced phrases and sentences
- Get the attention of those he is addressing
- Articulate his response in a way that is intelligible
- Use gesture, tone of voice, and facial expression to help get across his meaning

Understanding this series of steps allows us to form hunches about what elements of the communication process may be challenging for a child like Peter. However, that's only one part of what we need in order to help out. We must also be aware of how these skills develop over a child's first years.

Learning to Communicate: The Power of Naming and Narrating

The process of learning to communicate unfolds slowly. Parents notice that their six-month-old babbles in a way that suggests meaning, and wait expectantly for hints of real words nested in his unintelligible jabber. They rejoice in the first recognizable "ma" he uses while smiling at his mother, and laugh when he calls all creatures on four legs "doggy," including the elephant at the zoo.[11] Later, they sit back in awe when—now a toddler intoxicated by the magic of language acquisition—he careens around the house mumbling treasured words, or proclaims gleefully throughout the day, "See tha ball? Thasa ball!" "See tha cat? Thasa cat!"[12]

As a child develops, he begins using words, as well as gestures that reflect his desires and interests, to communicate with the people who matter most in his life. At first, for example, he may attach the word "mama" to the friendly face leaning over his crib. Then he learns to call that word out when he sees mama passing by. Soon, he is stringing together the mama word with others he's learned, adding nonverbal expressions of intent, and organizing a short sequence of language and action that gets him what he wants. Thus we might observe a fourteen-month-old toddling determinedly to the kitchen, pointing to the cookie jar, and saying, "Mama, mama, cookie, cookie, mama, mama, mama." Translation: "Mom, pay attention mom. I want a cookie from that thing over there. Come mom. Help me mom."

These two words, repeated in their particular configuration, convey not only a beginning mastery of language, but developing cognitive abilities as well. Such a child knows that cookies exist in a place where he can't see them. He knows that his mother has gotten such tasty morsels for him before, and that her actions can make that happy event happen once again. Kids this age aren't just learning about cause and effect, they are learning how language allows them to cause just the effect they want.[13]

As a youngster becomes more skilled at combining words and gestures, he moves toward increasingly complex versions of a phenomenon introduced in this chapter's exploration of the first building block, one best described by using Greenspan's construct of "circles of communication" (1992). Greenspan sees these circles as looping interactions between two people in which words and gestures support a feeling of connectedness and an exchange of content. As the child gets older, he can "open and close" increasing numbers of these circles.[14] At the same time, the unfolding of thought and language becomes ever more sophisticated in its construction and meaning. This last development happens gradually. At first, we see kids begin to think, play, and talk about the things they've seen and done in their young lives. A rectangular red block becomes a telephone as an eighteen-month-old places the block on his ear and chats happily. A two-year-old puts a small plastic man in the front seat of a toy truck, and drives it away with a "rrrmmm...rrrrrmmm." These little bits of play can be thought of as comprising simple units of meaning (Greenspan and Wieder, 1998).

Not long after these simple units emerge in a child's play and conversation, we begin to see him connect one to another, thus creating increasingly complex progressions of thought, representation, and language. With a two-year-old, this linking up of units may be rather simple: Now the figure in the truck stops to get gas. As children get older, a number of these smaller elements are joined together, allowing them to narrate the stories of their lives (Greenspan and Thorndike Greenspan, 1985). Four-year-old Susannah, for example, finds it hard to keep up with her eight-year-old brother and his friends. One day, as she sits eating lunch, she glances up. "Know what Mom? I have a friend named Jessica. And Mom, I can boss her all the time and she doesn't mind. And I never have to share and it's okay. And know what? She flies to wherever I am if I want her to, and she sleeps with me at night when it's dark." This girl uses language to create a poignant expression of imagination and yearning, one that allows her to feel safer and stronger in what must sometimes feel like an overpowering universe. It is when children have this kind of ability to manipulate words and ideas that they are able to tell us their concerns and play out their stories.

Getting Specific: Understanding Why Children Struggle With Communication

Language helps children connect to themselves, each other, and the adults who care for them. Language allows them to figure out how to solve problems. It is a means through which they share humor and explain frustration, the foundation for asking and getting answers to questions about the big world in which they live. No surprise, then, that three- to seven-year-olds who can't communicate with ease begin to feel lost and frustrated.

When we are wondering whether to be concerned about a child's ability to communicate, we keep in mind that children learn to express themselves comfortably at different rates. Some three-year-olds appear to speak in complete paragraphs. Others use just a few halting words at a time. Kids who speak one language at home and another at school sometimes learn both more slowly than their buddies who only hear a single language throughout each day (Genesee, Paradis, and Crago, 2004). None of these variations, in and of itself, need create cause for concern. On occasion, however, the adults involved sense that something is awry. When this happens, we encourage them to contact appropriate speech and language specialists, both for diagnostic help and possible intervention.

Before such help is successfully accessed, it's often wise for us to puzzle out what we can about a youngster's struggles. Services aren't always available quickly and, as first responders, we may need to suggest preliminary ideas for language-based intervention. Even after speech and language specialists arrive to offer their expertise, practitioners may still have a role to play. So many of the social issues about which we are consulted involve language. Understanding the nature of a youngster's struggle to communicate allows us to help teachers and parents support friendly conversations at the snack table, successful negotiations in the block corner, and engaging playtimes with cousins, neighbors, and the children of parents' friends.

Communication problems usually stem from difficulty with one or more elements of the intake–processing–output sequence.[15] Some children rarely tune in to the people and sounds around them, and don't get the practice they need to understand what they hear. Some have brains that don't easily translate raw sound into pieces of meaning; they're experiencing vulnerabilities in "auditory processing." Others process information very slowly. Some kids have trouble holding on to what they've heard while they take in what comes next, or remembering the second part of what they want to say while articulating the first part. (These children have difficulty with what we call "working memory.")

Some youngsters struggle with word retrieval. They know what they want to say, but can't locate the words they need. Often, if we supply a desired word for them, they smile with recognition and relief, as if to say, "Yes, that's it—that's exactly the word I wanted. Where was it when I wanted it?" Then there are children who have trouble sequencing information. They know what they want to tell us, but putting their ideas in order eludes them. They rarely tell a story logically, sometimes starting in the middle of a compelling narrative.

Some kids can do all these things, but getting their tongues and mouths to perform the precise actions needed to make sounds come out properly is a real challenge. They chatter away to their siblings or playmates, and then have the frustrating experience of seeing mystified looks on the faces around them. (These children have trouble with articulation, or with what we call "oral motor" actions.) Children like Renee, the verbally gifted 2nd-grader whom we met earlier in this chapter, have none of these issues. Instead, they can't easily decode nonverbal information. They don't instinctively grasp which tone of voice conveys silliness and which sarcasm, when a playmate's expression communicates affection and when annoyance. They can have trouble understanding how much physical distance to put between themselves and others as they speak too. Kids like Renee often seem, at first glance, like brilliant communicators. A second look tells us otherwise.

As we work on figuring out what aspect of the communication process is causing a child difficulty, we also pay attention to his level of language development. We note that kids like the purple room's three-year-old Anjali are stuck at an earlier stage of language acquisition than those like four-year-old

Peter across the hall. Whether in Hindi or in English, Anjali neither recognizes nor uses many words. Her behavior and play are not progressing well because she lacks the organizational thrust that developing language provides. Peter is fully capable of stringing together sequences of words. But he needs a lot of time to do it, and finding the words he wants isn't always easy. It's a given, then, that intervention with these two children will look very different. However, both will benefit from a focus on *lending an ally* to support communication skill.

Lending an Ally: A Core Approach to Supporting Developmental Mastery

"Lend-an-ally" work rests at the core of many of the strategies we suggest to bolster the development of all seven building blocks. *When we lend an ally, we figure out what aspects of a building block challenge a particular youngster. Then we offer help in those areas by joining with that child in doing things that are inherently interesting to him.* We join kids in their play, their conversations with friends, their storytelling. We sit with them as they eat lunch, or as they are working on a building project. We let them feel the safety and support of our presence for periods as short as one or two minutes to as long as half an hour. During these periods, we provide what the influential Russian psychologist Vygotsky first described as "scaffolding," support for the emergence of skills that they cannot yet demonstrate on their own (1978). *When we lend an ally successfully, we meet children right where they are in their development. Then we stay just a quarter step ahead of them as we offer the assistance they need to increase mastery in areas of vulnerability.*[16]

When the teacher of an abused child kneels down to offer an extra dose of warmth and interest, she can be understood to lend an ally—lend some safe connection. When parents initiate interactions that strengthen their child's ability to pop up and tune in, they lend an ally—lend some focus. Similarly, when the purple room's lead teacher Martha crouches down as she joins Anjali in the doll corner, tenderly rocks one of the dolls, and articulates clearly, "Baby is sleeping," she begins a session of lend an ally—lend some communication skill. If Anjali then reaches for her doll, mouths a quiet "Buba supin" and Martha slowly repeats, "Yes, baby is sleeping," adult-initiated scaffolding has resulted in an important moment of skill development.

Using a Child's Strengths to Help Us Work on Any Vulnerabilities

When we lend an ally, we don't just meet a child where she is in her development, *we rely on her strengths to help us work with any weaknesses.* Since Anjali is a highly visual child, her teachers make eye contact before speaking, and pair cues she can see with things she hears. This is why Martha rocks the doll, pairing language with an action whose meaning Anjali easily recognizes. Peter loves to please, so Leanne uses her genuine enjoyment of his company to reinforce his laborious efforts to share what he is thinking. What we find is that such carefully targeted work can have a powerful effect, not only on a child's skill level, but also on the way he feels about himself.

When children struggle to understand and use words, life can feel endlessly frustrating. When they use words easily, but don't comprehend the nonverbal cues that fill in meaning, problems arise as well. By working to understand their difficulties, then offering the skill-building assistance they need to communicate proficiently, we give them access to the underpinnings of social and academic success, and a boost that can have a lasting impact on their development.

The Fourth Building Block: Regulating Energy

"I grabbed her arm so tight, I'm surprised she doesn't have a bruise. And then I gave her a huge swat on the bottom." Dana's angular face looks even longer than usual, and her eyes well up. "I really can't say I was in control. And I swore I'd never do that to Emily. I was banged around a lot as a kid by my mom, and it's taken me all this time to forgive her."

Luis, one of the more vocal members attending the parenting group, nods his head as Dana goes on. "She really drives me crazy, and the things I finally explode over aren't any worse than anything else she does—something in me just pops and then I start screaming or . . ." Despite her efforts to stay in control, Dana begins to sob. The room echoes with the sound. Finally, Luis begins speaking. "Man, do I know how you feel. I had a really bad blowout with Juan last night when he wouldn't stop jumping around after his bath."

I've come to call the group of children who share Emily and Juan's restless, pulsing energy "the wiggly ones," as a parent- and teacher-friendly way of describing a set of qualities that can test the patience of even the calmest adult. A short, slight child, Emily behaves like a cross between a bull and a butterfly. Fluttering from her classroom's art table to its housekeeping corner, never remaining at one activity for more than a minute or two, she doesn't appear to be totally anchored on the floor. Yet Emily's will is powerful. Her teacher Linda reports "if Emily wants to she will, otherwise forget it." In addition, her preschool's director once mentioned having the odd feeling that "Emily needs to smack into the world in order to live in it." A twenty-three year veteran of early childhood education, she declares that she's never had a child who is as difficult to settle at naptime.

Unlike Emily, Juan lives firmly grounded on his feet. As coordinated dribbling a soccer ball as he is when leading classmates in a line dance, Juan zips through the morning at school. And wherever he is, he always appears to be on his way to somewhere else. Juan is as eager to please as any child in his classroom. Yet his teacher Maryann relates that she'd felt obliged to give him a long time out the previous morning because for three days running, he'd squirted water from the sink on one of the other boys in the class. She says that Juan had looked straight at her as he did the very thing he'd just been warned about. "I know he wants to be good…it's almost as if he is listening to me but can't use what he hears."

The Nature of Regulating Energy

Emily and Juan are children whose energy levels are not well regulated. Both have trouble settling into and staying focused on interesting activities. Both spend so much time on the move that they don't easily focus attention on requests from playmates and grown-ups. In addition, each finds sitting still during group time to be a formidable challenge. Kids who comfortably regulate energy shift naturally and easily from higher energy levels to lower ones and can remain in that slowed-down state for a while. If they are charging around outside and dad tells them it's time to come in for dinner, they can usually settle down as they approach the kitchen. If a teacher asks them to line up from recess, they can calm themselves enough that they aren't in danger of knocking a classmate down the stairs as they head to their basement classroom. In essence, they can send messages from their brains to their bodies that say it's time to slow down, and their bodies will usually respond (Routh, 1978; Shonkoff and Phillips, 2000; Landy, 2002).

One way of conceptualizing the process of regulating energy is by visualizing a graph.[17] Up its left side are notations for speed, numbered from zero at the bottom, to seventy-five at the top. Zero represents the body at rest. We're at zero when we are asleep or napping in a chair. Fifteen is what might register when we are eating or sitting doing a puzzle. Twenty-five reflects a leisurely walk. At fifty, we're moving along, taking a morning run or playing an easygoing game of basketball. At seventy-five, we're pushing our limit. When a young soccer player comes off the field, red-faced from a dramatic run down midfield, she's been up near the top of the scale.

Across the bottom of the graph are markings for times throughout day—at the left end, morning, at the far right, evening. If we graphed the experience of a child who regulates energy fairly well, we'd see a number of wave-like curves. There would be steady periods hovering around the middle of the scale, some spikes heading to the upper range, and then curves back down again. The representation of a wiggly one's day wouldn't look even remotely the same. These kids often start up around fifty or so. They have a hard time coasting down to a lower energy level and an even harder time staying there. Their graph would show the steadiest periods toward the top of the scale, with brief dips down to the middle.

There are exceptions, of course. Some children who struggle with energy regulation do just fine when they are engrossed in an interesting activity

(Sears and Thompson, 1998). Others have trouble during unstructured periods but can be read to for hours. Many of these children settle down quickly in front of a television or computer, though this fact may be problematic in its own right.[18] The importance of monitoring "screen time" will be explored in Chapter 14, but it bears noting here that the calm focus children show when they are settled in this way emanates from the outside not from the inside, and thus screen time can't be thought of as a useful tool when we're aiming to foster skill in body-state regulation. It's too bad it can't, because the parents of high-energy kids often crave the break screen time offers them—that's why we encourage them to allow it when it's really needed while seeking alternatives when it's not.

Getting Specific: Understanding Why Children Struggle to Regulate Their Energy Levels

In order to understand children's difficulties in modulating their activity levels, we look to a few areas of theory and research. One of those is the study of temperament, an area covered in more depth in the next chapter. Explored early on by Thomas, Chess, and Birch in their influential New York Longitudinal Study (1968)—and brought to the attention of parents and teachers in Turecki's widely read *The Difficult Child* (2000)—the construct of temperament points to a child's worrisomely high activity level as, in some cases, an inborn trait.

Other researchers have studied problems in energy regulation as part of a more general set of challenges nested in the category of self-regulation. Such researchers don't dispute the idea of temperamental predispositions, but look more deeply at how constitutionally based difficulties relate to the functioning of a child's autonomic nervous system (Landy, 2002). In doing so, they note challenges in motor control, and tendencies toward sensory overload, irritability, and distractibility, all of which may accompany—and perhaps even help account for—a child's difficulties in staying calm (DeGangi et al., 1991; DeGangi, Craft, and Castellan, 1991; see also, Shonkoff and Phillips, 2000, pp. 93–123).

The paradigms cited earlier bear a close connection to models that examine how a child's ability to process sensation (what we call sensory integration) relates to energy regulation (Ayres, 1979; Greenspan, 1992; Greenspan and Wieder, 1998). It is on such models that the work of sensory-focused occupational therapists is based, work that teaches us a great deal about the nuts and bolts of intervention with high-energy children (Williams and Shellenberger, 1996; Stock Kranovitz, 1998). Finally, there is the work of researchers who study this developmental trajectory in tandem with issues related to attention and self-control (See Barkley, 1997a for an overview), and the contribution of those who have tied children's high activity levels to emotional and physiological overload connected to highly stressful experiences (National Scientific Council on the Developing Child, 2005).

Each of these paradigms is useful as we examine the everyday functioning of high-energy children. They help us understand, for example, that although youngsters like Emily and Juan may look similar at first glance, they behave the way they do for quite different reasons. If kids can be thought of as having engines, Juan's runs continually on high.[19] A child whose high energy is connected to his temperament, Juan started crawling at five months, was walking three months later, and figured out how to throw himself out of his crib shortly after his first birthday. Long after his brothers or classmates yearn to take a break from physical activity, Juan is still raring to go. Luis has noticed that the more tired his son gets, the more "revved up" he becomes.

The influence of temperament on the behavior of children like Juan is apparent in their first year (Brazelton, 1983). Little motor babies, they move their bodies a lot even when they can't yet roll over. Long before they master crawling, they are intoxicated with being on the go, intently hauling themselves forward on their bellies or haphazardly propelling backwards to parts unknown. Parents often mention that such high-energy youngsters have trouble giving into sleep, or that they go from nonstop motion to sleep in one quick transition (Kaplan et al., 1987). Kids with this inborn nature don't just need many opportunities to move in order to be content. Their make-up doesn't allow them easy access to pathways from high-energy levels to calmer ones, even when a teacher or parent is utterly clear in communicating that slowing down is in order (Barkley, 2000). At their best, these children are a joy: They are vivid, alert, and wonderfully active participants in anything interesting. At their hardest, they are tremendously exhausting to parent and to teach.[20]

A close look at Emily's difficulties suggests that her behavior stems from another constitutional source: Her sensory system is off-kilter. As a result, she has a hard time processing and organizing the physical sensations we all experience all the time. Kids like Emily crave extra sensation in order to feel comfortable and grounded, and we notice them seeking out frequent opportunities for movement, body contact, even the taste of spicy or sour foods (Ayres, 1979). (Emily, in fact, "smacks into the world" so that she can feel at ease, though it might be hard for us to imagine that her frequent bangs into furniture and walls could be experienced as pleasurable.) On the other hand, although youngsters with Emily's sensory issues crave sensation, they easily get over-stimulated too. Sounds, sights, and smells may overwhelm them, and certain tactile experiences—the feel of grass on the soles of their feet or a shirt label against their skin—send them into a tizzy (Stock Kranovitz, 1998).

Over-stimulation can cause the behavior of another group of high-energy kids—this time, reactivity that connects to our understanding of self-regulation. Youngsters in this group process sensory information just fine, but other aspects of their lives quickly overwhelm them. Transitions or changes in schedule, shifts in caretakers or housing, unusual amounts of attention during family gatherings or play-dates, all these and more cause such children to lose their equilibrium. They then show their difficulties in handling stimulation by becoming active and cranky (Greenspan with Salmon, 1995).

Finally, there are the youngsters we encounter whose high activity levels stem from the neurobiological and emotional consequences of domestic violence or trauma. Children in the latter group aren't wiggly because they were born that way; things have gone on in their young lives that have made it hard for them to stay centered and calm (Shonkoff and Phillips, 2000; Groves, 2002). That's why any time a child is charging her way through her days, we first ask if there is something happening at home or elsewhere that she's telling us she can't handle.

The Relationship of Regulating Energy to Attention and Self-Control

Research reinforces what parents and teachers know already: Vulnerabilities in regulating energy are often paired with inattention and difficulty responding to behavioral expectations (Barkley, 2005). In response to a sharp, "Did you HEAR what I just said?" Juan may be able to repeat verbatim that Luis wants him to stop jumping on the couch this minute. But he hasn't slowed down enough to do what he's being asked, nor to take in that his dad's red face indicates an imminent explosion. Closely connected to this problem—and often driven by vulnerabilities in brain function—is that these children have trouble thinking before they act, in exerting the behavioral inhibition first noted in our earlier discussion of attention. When kids (and adults) show self-control, they put space between the impulse to do something and the behavior of doing it. In that space comes thought, thought that allows them to ask: "*Should I do this? What will happen if I do? Maybe I'd better not, even though I feel like it.*" The internalization of this kind of "self-talk" is in part what allows four-year-olds to behave far better than toddlers (Winsler et al., 2003). When Juan stares right at his teacher Maryann as he prepares to once again drench his friend, he isn't able to make use of the consequence she threatens. The misery on his face when he indeed has to sit out comes, in part, because it's only in retrospect that he can take in the reality of her words, and that despite the fact that Maryann is nothing if not patiently consistent.

High-energy kids sometimes struggle with other developmental tasks too. Speeding through their days, full of energy but lacking in focus and impulse control, they don't easily settle into periods of extended play. Such youngsters also get bored more quickly than others, making it even harder for them to stay put (Barkley, 2000). As a result, while other children are learning the give-and-take involved in getting along socially, or gaining language facility as they create increasingly complex imaginary stories, these youngsters often miss out (Shonkoff and Phillips, 2000). While their buddies develop skill in letter formation, or learn the engineering behind block building, these wiggly ones may still be restlessly cruising the room.

Perhaps most important of all, children like Emily and Juan, despite their better intentions, often irritate the people around them. Parents start scolding a lot. Teachers give endless commands to slow down. Other kids begin yelling in frustration. Over time, high-energy kids get used to screening out the negatives. It's this phenomenon, combined with their original vulnerability in attending to the cues they hear, that leads some of these children to appear not to care about the feelings and requests of their parents and friends. When Dana swears that today she won't lose her temper, then hates herself for screaming at Emily once again, she senses that she's stuck in a pattern of parental annoyance and child defiance. Though Dana has an especially hard task because she's parenting on her own, she is experiencing a pattern that is all too familiar to many parents of the wiggly ones.

Thinking in Advance So We're Ready in Response

This pattern, which Turecki has aptly described as a "vicious circle," is one we see happening both in families and in classrooms (2000). It doesn't just apply to high-energy kids. A child has a vulnerability that leads her to struggle with one of the developmental building blocks, and the way she struggles isn't much fun to be around. Parents and teachers see that she isn't behaving "the way she should" and, over time, get increasingly frustrated. They tell her to "*please* stop." They give her advice. They cajole and lecture, threaten, and offer bribes. Eventually, they lose their temper. Then they try to collect themselves once again, realizing that they are expending a lot of energy getting nowhere.

Though adults would love to believe that they do an excellent job of masking such intense frustration, they rarely do. Most children have good antennae for how people are feeling about them, and the child in question begins to think that she may be loved but is not much liked. She doesn't actually understand how to do better, and she begins to give up. She blocks out the annoyed voices, the lectures, and the threats. Sometimes, she stops trying to please entirely and becomes quite defiant. It's a vicious circle indeed, and getting out of it isn't easy. [21] That said, doing so is essential to the child's well-being, and parents and teachers may need our help in instigating the change.

In the six months since the start of the parenting group, Dana has learned to think both more calmly and more proactively. *Rather than being surprised and frustrated by Emily's difficult behavior, she assumes it is coming and is ready with skill-building help when it does.* [22] Emily's teacher Linda has been doing the same. The help they provide partly involves offering sensory calming activities when Emily needs to regain her equilibrium. Dana and Linda have also separated the slowing down process into manageable bits, so that Emily can develop skill regulating her energy in a step-by-step fashion. What they are doing is "chunking down" expectations for growth—*shooting for small, steady increments of mastery that, cumulatively, allow a child to thrive.* Now, both at home and at school, adults patiently take time to make sure that Emily settles into a state of calm focus before they make a request of her. She still needs numerous cues in order to do so, and it can take her a minute or two to get there. When she does, she's much more likely to comply. The pleasure her mother and teachers are taking in her more positive behavior is palpable.

Getting to Work: Helping Active Kids Slow Down

This combination of thinking in advance and chunking down expectations for growth lies at the heart of the work we do with all kinds of children. It's a crucial part of our efforts to help active children learn both to slow down, and to slow down and think. Knowing that they can't focus on what is being said to them when they are in "go mode," we start by helping them learn what it feels like to ramp down their "engine speed." At the same time, we begin basic work on strengthening attention, making sure that most of our requests for attention are followed by positive interactions. *Finally, we ask children to pair these two skills, to calm their bodies and focus their minds before we relay important information or requests.* It can take many months for a high-energy child to have consistent success in doing both, but once she does, wonderful growth often follows. Juan's teacher Maryann knows this firsthand, as she gives his father the kind of update that we hope to hear about any wiggly one: "You know, it hasn't been easy for him this week. It's been so cold and icy that we haven't been able to go out, and he's had even more energy than usual. But I'm so proud of him; he's handled himself really well."

The Fifth Building Block: Regulating Feelings

Five-year-old Sean appears to walk around with a personal weather system. Some mornings he wakes up or strides into school and his parents and teachers can almost see a storm brewing over his head. Sean can be a delight, but when the thunderclouds begin gathering, everyone—kids and adults alike—know to give him a wide berth. At these times, a loud "I hate you" often reverberates across kitchen or classroom, and a toy (or fist) may go flying. One day, after a particularly rocky transition to school, Sean hurriedly constructs a cardboard guitar, then sings and dances around his classroom with phenomenal rhythm. Later, he announces, "I want to be a rock and roll king. You know, they can get up on stage and smash their guitars, and everybody claps!"

Diane has requested some consultation. Her daughter Marianna is doing fine at home, she relates, but is crying for long stretches at school. And her teachers don't understand why things aren't improving. A subsequent visit to the classroom reveals four-year-old Marianna whimpering in a far corner.

When her teacher Nadine comes near, she begins crying in earnest. Nadine looks mildly exasperated as she sits down next to Marianna. "Marianna, could you stop crying so that you can tell me what's wrong?" "NOOO, I DON'T KNOW...I CAN'T STOP!" Nadine speaks softly. "You can stop, Marianna. Take a nice, deep breath and relax." Marianna lets out a cross between a sigh and a hiccup. "There, that's good. Now, why don't you tell me what is bothering you so I can help?" The tear-streaked girl begins wailing once again. Further observation makes it clear that what often sets off Marianna's long upsets at school are situations with friends in which she doesn't get her own way.

The Nature of Regulating Emotion: Managing Minor Difficulties Without Major Reactions

Most three to seven-year-olds have occasional trouble sorting through upsetting situations, and rightly so. But although they are still very young, many kids this age manage to stay calm a good portion of the time. When distressed about something, they may find an adult to comfort them or to help them problem-solve.[23] They may talk through a conflict with a friend, or just take a minute or two away from the fray to regain their composure (Bretherton et al., 1986; Calkins and Johnson, 1998). Sean rarely uses any of these strategies. Easily frustrated when denied a request, intensely annoyed when he can't manage an attempted task, Sean gives scant notice before his emotional state shifts from mild irritation to extreme anger.

Faced with situations where the people around her don't instantly adjust the environment to suit her, Marianna also shows little capacity to stay calm. Once thoroughly upset, she doesn't even seem to know what is bothering her. Other children experience a slightly different version of this dilemma. They manage frustration just fine but are easily swamped by anxiety. Then there are the youngsters who struggle with intense sadness. As the stresses and strains of their young lives pull them down, we feel deep concern about how often they are in the grip of unhappiness. These children need adults to investigate and help change whatever it is that is so overwhelming to them. They need support and help in expressing and working through their feelings safely too (Fitzgerald Rice and Groves, 2005). But they may also require support in learning to contain their distress so that they approach the positive aspects of their lives in a more hopeful, upbeat state of mind.

Learning to regulate emotion is one of the central developmental challenges of early childhood. Research on resilience tells us that children who thrive in the face of dramatically difficult situations often show great strength in this area (Masten and Coatsworth, 1998; Werner, 2000). Knowing that life can, sometimes very unexpectedly, bring real hardship, we pay special attention to helping all kids develop the abilities that contribute to the mastery of this challenge. Children who regulate emotion manage minor difficulties without major reactions. They find ways to soothe themselves or get comfort from others, and are able to regain composure fairly quickly after they get upset. They control their behavior even when frustrated. And they learn to solve problems rather than to be overwhelmed by them.

Getting Specific: Understanding Why Children Struggle to Regulate Their Feelings

Children who get overwhelmed frequently do so for a variety of reasons. Some are born with very intense natures—they react forcefully and quickly to whatever happens to them. (The mother of one such child described that her daughter got "happy right down to her bone marrow and angry in every cell.") Some have constitutions that don't allow them to adjust easily to new or uncomfortable situations. Even as infants, these youngsters are easy to upset and hard to soothe (Chess and Thomas, 1996). Some have headstrong, persistent natures; they don't give in comfortably, seeming almost intoxicated by battles of will (Forehand and Long, 1996).

Then there are the children whose difficulties stem from family or community life. Some of the youngsters in this group encounter poor or inconsistent limit setting at home. The way their behavior has been handled over time has led to worsening rather than improving self-control (Barkley, 1997b). Others face conflict-ridden situations involving parents or siblings, the emotional aftermath of which they carry into daily life (Webster-Stratton and Hammond, 1999). Still others are overwhelmed by experiences of abuse or neglect, or have witnessed terrible violence taking place around them (Van der Kolk and Streck-Fischer, 2000).

Whatever the cause, once a child has trouble regulating emotion, the way others respond to him often ends up amplifying the original problem (Barkley, 1997b). Children like Sean, who lash out rather than work things out, usually frustrate the people around them. The way those people react—often seesawing between compassion and anger—doesn't give these kids a chance to develop skill in soothing themselves or in solving problems. Children who are frequently sad or worried may end up with a slightly different dilemma, sometimes pulling the adults who care for them into a messy mixture of irritation-filled attention and concerned frustration. These youngsters get neither the warm support they need, nor the clarity required to help them learn to wrap up painful feelings and move on. Marianna is in just such a predicament.

Getting to Work: Managing Frustration

A postobservation conversation with Marianna's parents sheds some light on the reasons for her difficulties. Marianna is far happier at home than in school, that is true—as the youngest child in a family with much older half-siblings, life in the household revolves around her. Delighted by her radiant smile when they attend to her and having little need to cross her, Diane and Sonia have unwittingly given in to most of their daughter's requests. In consequence, as soon as something starts bothering Marianna, her world rearranges itself to make her unpleasant feelings go away. Thus at age four, she has not yet had the opportunity to learn to handle even minor frustrations, nor to let her own agenda go in order to ease the way with others. Faced with the complex social and emotional demands of school, Marianna is floundering. She needs help both at home and in the classroom.

It doesn't take long to begin turning things around. Marianna's parents first begin working on the task of waiting, judiciously choosing when to give Marianna clear directives that *this time* she'll have to postpone getting her needs met. When Marianna unravels in response to such requests for patience, they warmly but firmly tell her that she'll be fine. Mostly ignoring her responses, going about their business for a few minutes, they sometimes gently remind their whining, crying four-year-old that everyone has to wait for what they want from time to time. Once Marianna begins showing a developing ability to wait, Diane and Sonia start setting other limits too.

Marianna's teachers embark on a parallel process at school. Shifting the majority of their attention from the moments when Marianna is unhappy to the times when she's calm, they make sure to have as many positive interactions with her as they can manage. As they work to support these circles of pleasurable connection, they take advantage of Marianna's impish sense of humor to encourage her to bring her more playful side into the classroom. They initiate "lend an ally—lend some social skill" sessions too, sitting with Marianna and a group of friends and modeling the process of give-and-take. When Marianna becomes upset, which happens frequently at first, they briefly give her some support. They sympathetically remind her that it's okay to feel sad and that they know she'll figure out how to feel better soon. Reiterating that once she feels calmer, they'll be happy to help her find something fun to do, they then leave her on her own. If she is still struggling after five or ten minutes, they check in with her quickly and compassionately, reminding her of much the same.

Marianna starts brightening at school within days. The happy child her parents have described begins emerging in the classroom, though with the change in expectations, she has some intense tantrums too. But soon the number and intensity of tantrums diminishes, especially as Marianna's ability to solve social problems increases. This four-year-old girl is beginning to show signs not only of regulating feelings, but also of becoming more flexible.[24]

Tracking Behavioral Feedback Loops That Surround Problematic Behavior

Looking carefully at how Marianna's teachers and parents support this turnaround, we notice an important version of the "what do we see–think–do" progression. First of all, everybody carefully observes what they do when Marianna is unhappy. As a result, they realize that the attention she's been getting for her upsets has tended to encourage those upsets to continue though that, of course, has been no one's intent. As a result of their new understanding, Marianna's parents and teachers attempt to be far more attentive when she's doing well than when she becomes overwhelmed.

When concerned adults carefully observe the interactions surrounding a child's difficulties, they are *tracking behavioral feedback loops.* This construct, which comes from the worlds of family therapy and systems theory, points to the ways in which an individual's behavior unfolds in the context of interactional patterns. It opens up the option of seeing children's difficulties as stemming, at least in part, from their embedded place in a relational universe. As stated by Minuchin, Colapinto, and Minuchin (2007), "from a systems point of view, behavior is explained as a shared responsibility, arising from patterns that trigger and maintain the actions of each individual" (p. 22). The importance of this idea can't be underestimated: it allows us to note that, as in Marianna's case, the reactions a child elicits sometimes end up encouraging the very difficulties everyone is worrying about.[25] Becoming aware of these loops, and helping parents and teachers change them when necessary, is thus an important piece of clinical consultation. In order to clarify our explanations of how they operate, we can introduce these adults to the easily understood differentiation between "leaning in" and "leaning out."[26]

Leaning In and Leaning Out: The Importance of Clarity

When we *lean in*, we offer children extra support and skill-building assistance in areas that are hard for them. When we *lean out*, we choose to kindly but firmly set guidelines for behavior. Lending an ally, of course, is one of the basic strategies we use to lean in. For example, when Marianna's teachers join her and some block-building classmates in order to gently guide her as she learns to negotiate play ideas with friends, they are leaning in. Other strategies are included in the category as well. When a youngster has many worries and a special time is set aside for him to talk about what's on his mind, leaning in is at work too. Planning out what an easily frustrated child can do if he loses the Go-Fish game he's about to play is just one more example, especially if a goofy puppet plays out the sore loser role to make problem-solving more palatable.

Part of thinking in advance involves making quick decisions about when to offer the support of leaning in and when not. In leaning out, we lay out specific expectations for behavior that will foster the growth we feel a child is ready for. Sometimes, those expectations are backed up by a limit, sometimes not. When Diane and Sonia declare that Marianna will need to wait at least ten minutes before they play house with her, they are leaning out. When her teachers tell her kindly that they know that she can figure out how to stop feeling so sad and then walk away, they are leaning out too. Making clear decisions about when to set such behavioral expectations and when to offer extra support is not easy. *When a child is having trouble, a sloppy mix of the two is often contributing to her difficulties.* Nadine's exasperated attempt to console Marianna qualifies as just such a sloppy mix.

Helping Marianna learn to feel steadier in the midst of the everyday strains of life at home and at school isn't difficult. Once her parents and teachers figure out what is causing her upsets, they find strategies that allow things to turn around quickly. Helping Sean feel calmer and behave better is not nearly as easy. The narrative of his troubles, and of his slow but steady mastery of a challenging building block, is a lengthy one. As is sometimes true for kids who struggle to control their anger, a complex set of interacting variables rests at the heart of his difficulties, and sorting out those difficulties requires paying attention to all of them. (We'll come back to Sean's story in Chapter 11, when we look further at how we help kids regulate emotion.)

Sean and Marianna's struggles to maintain emotional composure are shared by many a young child, like one intense six-year-old boy who informed his mother that he hated being "marooned on the island of agitation." Learning to wrap up feelings allows kids to stay off that awful island, and gives them the strength to handle life's many frustrations. If children handle big feelings when things aren't going their way, they are usually flexible with others. Being a flexible son or daughter and a flexible friend often leads a child to be well liked and well respected as he grows older. To explore more about this quality, we'll move on to our next building block.

The Sixth Building Block: Changing Tracks and Being Flexible

> Jeremy and I sit on the floor as he builds a prison on the planet Callask. One of his many, vividly imagined pretend characters, young Callamina has just been whisked off to this planet along with her defenseless parents, and its residents have anointed her with a new and honored name: Boblambishwab. Callamina has often been chastised for not listening well at home. With a new name—and a new set of child-friendly planetary rules—she revels that her parents are to be incarcerated as soon as the prison is complete. Then she'll be free to do as she wishes.

Jeremy has great difficulty exiting his own agenda in order to leave room for anyone else's thoughts. This boy is smart, creative, and endlessly curious—about the stars and the names of plant species, about the exact location of Serbia and the meaning of the word "extravagant." But his curiosity doesn't extend to other people's ideas, unless those ideas dovetail precisely with what he's thinking about at a particular moment. Even then, he interrupts constantly.

Though Jeremy is only four, his parents and teachers worry that his vulnerabilities are already getting in the way of his connections with other kids, and may soon impact his ability to learn if a subject area doesn't immediately captivate him. Not only that, but his preschool director fears that if he can't get better at ending activities he enjoys when asked to participate in those he doesn't, he'll quickly get the reputation as a difficult, annoying kindergartener when he heads off to elementary school in the fall. A child with impressive intellectual gifts, his trouble being flexible with and responsive to others is causing a widening and alarming split between his cognitive and social development.

Flexibility as a Prime Life Skill: The Interplay Between Adaptability and Likeability

When a child knows how to be flexible, she can recognize other people's needs and balance them with her own. Using language we've already defined, children who have mastered this building block can stay emotionally regulated when faced with situations that aren't to their liking (Bradley, 2000; Eisenberg, 2002). Kids like this make good playmates: They don't lose their cool the minute one of their buddies suggests an idea that conflicts with theirs, and they remain in good spirits through the endless negotiating of play possibilities that drives young children's connections with each other (Fabes et al., 1999). These youngsters sometimes give up their own agenda in order to keep the peace, and other children look to them for help in solving thorny conflicts of interest. When we look to see which children in a first grade class are universally liked, we often find that a good-natured flexibility lies at the heart of their place in the social world. Flexibility is an asset in family life too. When mom must answer the phone right when she was about to set out snack, a flexible child waits without too much fuss. When dad has to do an unexpected errand after a long drive in the car, such a youngster can, at least sometimes, hang in there for a few more boring minutes. Youngsters who are flexible often tend to get along fairly well with their brothers and sisters too.

A child's ability to "change tracks" bears a close relationship to this capacity for flexibility. When a youngster changes tracks comfortably, she can, with a little warning, switch from one activity or situation to another—even if the second is less pleasing to her than the first. When it's time to end free play at school, she'll pitch in to clean up rather than continue her dress-up game, even if she doesn't much enjoy sitting at the group meeting that comes next. If she was absolutely counting on her favorite curly noodles for dinner but her nana has run out of pasta, she'll grumble for only a minute or so before settling for hotdogs instead.

One way of understanding the internal process required for this kind of switching gears is to visualize an actual train track. A child is traveling down this track, with a clear picture of where she's heading. Maybe she thinks she will get to have an ice cream cone after her trip to the dentist. Or perhaps she is dead set on an outing to the park with Uncle Joe once he finishes repairing the porch railing. But at some point, something—or someone—gets in the way of her travel plans. The dentist ran late, and the ice cream trip must now wait until after her sister's school pickup. Uncle Joe walloped his finger with a hammer and, grimacing as he nurses it with a cold pack, shows no interest in the park. It's as if a gate has descended over the track and the youngster sees that she must take a different route, one that bears off to the right. A flexible child stops her forward motion, quickly moves through her initial disappointment, readjusts her thoughts as to where she's headed, and makes the turn.

Kids who haven't yet developed this skill can get quite stuck. They may freeze up, doing nothing at all. They may continue along with their intention, like Jeremy who—despite a friend's vehement objections—grabs the orange fire engine he absolutely *must* have, and hoards it behind his back. They may turn into pint-size trial lawyers, defending their position vehemently and at length. Or they may have a full-blown explosion, like future rock and roll king Sean did before he and his family got some help. Whatever their reaction, these children show us over and over again that they don't know how to pull themselves up short, take in information that tells them their plans must change, let go of their agendas, and move on.

Getting Specific: Understanding Why Children Struggle With Flexibility and Track-Changing

There are many factors that can contribute to a child's having trouble with the sixth building block. Some youngsters experience few or inconsistent limits at home, and haven't had enough practice handling frustration to manage conflicts of interest (Kindlon, 2001; Gimbel and Holland, 2003). Some kids are born with exceptionally strong wills—they are good leaders but terrible followers and don't have an instinctive impulse to bend (Chess and Thomas, 1996). Other children have brains that get easily fixated on certain ideas that, like the scratched spots on old-style records, play over and over again in their minds.[27] Still others have experienced traumatic situations that have left them grasping for control wherever they can find it (Lieberman and Van Horn, 2004). Some children have experienced excessive bossiness or bullying from their siblings—these youngsters often behave rigidly with their friends, teachers, and parents in order to maintain a sense of power and dignity (Loeber and Hay, 1997). Then there are the kids that enter the world with a neurodevelopmental profile that makes experiencing a state of mutuality—and the flexibility that follows—particularly challenging.

Looking at Rigidity That Stems From Inborn Challenges to Relatedness

Jeremy can have trouble responding to someone else's point of view (or even their presence), especially when he's deeply interested in what he's playing or thinking; he shares qualities with the children that Greenspan describes as "self-absorbed" (see Greenspan with Salmon, 1995). With an inspired recognition of parents' and teachers' experiences—and a purposeful avoidance of diagnostic classification—Klass and Costello call children like Jeremy "quirky" (2003). The sometimes disengaged, sometimes gifted but rigid youngsters that these practitioners are referring to come by their inflexibility through their genetic make-up. Some will eventually end up with diagnoses on the autistic spectrum. In fact, although the behaviors that such children exhibit range widely (and many won't even come close to a serious diagnosis), looking to the world of theory and research connected to autism gives us a window into their constitutionally based challenges.

The idea of a spectrum is a good place to start; it helps us visualize a neurological continuum with many variations in strengths and vulnerabilities. The idea of higher- and lower-functioning children on this spectrum is helpful too—though Greenspan, in particular, is notable for his passionate emphasis on the tremendous possibilities for growth for all such youngsters when intervention is tailored to their specific profiles (1992). That said, children on the very lowest end of the continuum, many of whom don't acquire functional language, are beyond the scope of this book. Those discussed here are the youngsters who speak with some fluency (though sometimes in constricted or unusual ways), but who struggle with connection, flexibility, and emotional expression. Note that interventions for this group of children are outlined in Chapter 13.

Looking at contemporary understandings of autism, then, we find some useful concepts. First is the idea that difficulties on its spectrum involve a triad of challenges—in socialization, communication, and imagination (Wing et al., 1977).[28] The first element of this triad speaks to how autistic individuals struggle to initiate or maintain reciprocal interactions. As another way of speaking to this phenomenon—and the difficulties that ensue when it is a challenge—theorists point to the importance of "joint attention" in development, that is, the way in which two individuals connect through a state of mutual focus (Moore and Dunham, 1995).

The other two parts of the triad are important too. Some of the children whose issues connect to the spectrum we're exploring here may struggle to sequence and communicate their ideas, or have a kind of constricted, repetitive play that makes it difficult for them to embed their feelings in imagined stories (see Scarlett et al., 1998). The latter challenge is not insignificant: Such stories are not only an important vehicle for children to work through emotional distress, but are the basis of play with peers as well.

The idea of theory of mind is yet another construct that helps us understand this group of inflexible youngsters, one that refers to an individual's capacity to understand that the knowledge, beliefs, and feelings of another may be different than her own. Such a capacity allows children to imagine the experiences of others (and thus its lack may be connected to the restricted play discussed above). It is the basis of empathy for friends and family too and, perhaps, for an expansive curiosity about others' interests rather than a rigid focus on limited areas of personal concern (Sigman and Capps, 1997; Schneider, Schumann-Hengsteler, and Sodian, 2005).

Moving from theory to the experiences clinicians deal with "on the ground," it's important, once again, to emphasize the notion of a continuum. Many of the rigid or disengaged children in the category we're exploring here respond well to the kinds of strategies we'll outline later on. Others have difficulties so embedded in their neurological make-up that parents come to realize—perhaps slowly and often with deep grief—that although such strategies are a big help, life is going to be challenging for a long time to come. Jeremy is in the first category. Six-year-old Tara is in the second, and her story will help illuminate the way the constructs just described sometimes play out in everyday life.

Relating to Content More Than People

Tara's parents Marilyn and Rick are puzzled and worried. A first grader, Tara isn't doing well either at home or in school. Her teacher describes her as loveable but odd, and is asking for assistance in understanding how to help her function better in the classroom. Mr. Jackson knows that Tara has a huge fund of factual knowledge, especially about things scientific and historical. But Tara frequently refrains from participating in classroom projects, is often stiff and uncommunicative with her classmates, and can become rigidly uncooperative when expected to produce written work.

Getting Tara through everyday routines at home is as challenging as trying to teach her—she hates to interrupt the compelling things she is doing in order to take care of ordinary business. Making it to the car before school in a timely way, getting into (and then out of) the bath, successfully completing her bedtime routine, these and many other daily events can become sources of conflict and frustration for everyone, with Tara going, in her parents' words, "on strike." However, land on an activity or topic of conversation that intrigues her—and there are many—and this child becomes an engaging partner.

Tara is a prime example of a child whose inflexibility stems from a place in the middle of the continuum discussed earlier. Yet, like so many of the children on this continuum, she wasn't a difficult infant (Sigman and Capps, 1997). Far from it—she rarely cried, loved to look around, and could be held by anyone, even during the months when many kids experience intense stranger anxiety. As she got older, she'd approach and talk with countless unfamiliar people who were doing things that interested her. Both parents had seen her as a confident, outgoing girl. However, Tara may not have been as outgoing as these parents had first believed: When she'd seemed to be eagerly relating to others, *she may actually have been more engaged with content than with people*. In fact, the reasons behind Tara's early "easiness" and her later struggles are probably connected.

Tara is profoundly self-absorbed. A child who is compelled to understand how the world works and deeply interested in her own thoughts, she is constitutionally less motivated by connections to others than many children. As Tara's parents come to accept this idea, they begin to understand why she is so hard to propel through daily life. After all, much of what we ask children to do isn't inherently gratifying. Kids do what we ask in order to stay in our good graces and to feel our pleasure in their actions. Tara, unfortunately, doesn't have a strong need for either result.

In explaining the neurological profile children like Tara—and to a lesser extent Jeremy—I've found the metaphor of "deep-tracking" to be useful, an unthreatening way of conveying important information from the theoretical world.[29] When we describe this constitutionally based quality, we say something like the following: "It's like she's inside a deep track, with high sides. She knows where it's going. And she's at ease in there—she doesn't really *need* company. The reason that she's sometimes easy to connect with and sometimes so hard to manage is that when you join her 'in the track,' right where she is, she can let you into her world. But if you're 'outside the track,' she doesn't want much to do with you. She might not even acknowledge your presence. If you request that she go in a different direction, it feels awful to her. So she tries to keep what you are asking of her from happening...she protects herself. She'll go on strike, or start yelling, get incredibly stubborn or just shut you out. It feels terrible to you, but it does make sense given how she's made as a person, and where she's stuck in her development."

Getting to Work: Starting From Where a Child Is, Not Where We Want Her to Be

Whether a child in the "deep-tracked" category eventually merits a significant diagnosis, or whether she merely comes to be understood as constitutionally different, it's going to be important for parents and teachers to develop an understanding of the behaviors that puzzle them. Furthermore, they'll need to grasp the important intersection between the two developmental building blocks that most challenge these children: feeling connected to others, and being flexible. Then they can get to work on chunking down their goals for change. The work Jeremy's parents, teachers, and I do with him involves both building blocks, starting with the first. We spend weeks—at home, at school, and in my office—joining him "in the track," and strengthening his capacity to engage in pleasurable circles of connection. Tara needs the same kind of support. When we first begin our efforts with these two youngsters, we don't ask them to respond to our input. Instead, we encourage the feeling of connection by communicating interest and enjoyment in their ideas. As we often must, *we start from where they are developmentally.* Slowly, we expand the number of circles each child can tolerate before she finds it necessary to retreat to her more internal state. Then we begin "seeding" little bits of our own input into conversation and play.

As noted earlier, Jeremy responds quickly to our efforts, though he needs plenty of help. Tara's growth unfolds more slowly; her inborn rigidity is far more extreme than Jeremy's, and she has other difficulties too. Eventually, her parents opt for neuropsychological testing to help clarify Tara's learning issues, and her elementary school consequently offers extra assistance both within and outside the classroom. Even before we understand the whole picture, though, Tara and her parents make great progress together. As Marilyn and Rick begin to understand and accept the neurologically driven elements of their daughter's temperament, they began working on both connections and flexibility at home. With skill, ingenuity, and empathy, they become increasingly expert at helping her learn to be a more willing partner in family life. It is an inspiring process to witness, leading to less anger on their part and more cooperation on hers. And even with her slow progress, Tara's increased ability to be resilient in the face of the many challenges she faces is striking. It is just such resilience that lies at the heart of the final building block.

The Seventh Building Block: Feeling Capable and Confident

I really wanted to come today because there is a thing that I want to figure out and that is: What do I do when the volcano mad wants to come out and I don't know how to stop it? It's like it doesn't even feel like me and it just comes out, and then I know I shouldn't have done that but I didn't even know it was going to come out and it did.

Few second graders can articulate what troubles them in the way Eric could, even when—as he was here—they're comfortably settled in a clinician's office. But this boy's amazing capacity for introspection didn't help with self-control in the slightest. His teachers worried about his quickly ignited frustration in the classroom, and his parents were beside themselves over the venomous explosions he had at home.

I wish that when I was really mad at someone, there would be this little funny guy, not nice or mean, not on either side. And he would turn the place into a big stadium and we could have a thwack war. And I could get all the mad out, and I wouldn't get in trouble and I wouldn't feel bad that I hurt someone... In a thwack war, you hit him but you don't hurt him.

Along with these words, Eric made a drawing in which a line divided the body of a scowling boy. Thick black and red swirls covered the right half of the boy's shirt, looking like smoke as they left his body to fill the page; on its upper right-hand corner, large black letters announced the "Dark Magician of Chaos." Eric decorated the left half of the shirt with delicate circles of a soft blue, and this side sported a name too: "Gentle Blue Giant." Eric yearned to become a positive presence in his family and classroom. However, several months into my work with this boy and his family and teachers, Eric dissolved into tears, telling his parents that he *couldn't* do it, he just wasn't going to be able to get his angry feelings to stop bossing him around. One of the reasons for this, he explained, was that he loved the way "the mad" felt as it came out—it was only afterwards that he experienced intense regret.

The Place of Resilience in Early Development

Work with Eric unfolded slowly, and we won't go into its specifics here. What is important to our understanding of the seventh building block—feeling capable and confident—is that, over time, he began to feel and act less frustrated. He smiled more, could often compromise if given a little warning, and, when angry at home, used time in his room to pull himself back together. These experiences of mastery led to growing feelings of resourcefulness, competence, and optimism. Such feelings are not only the hallmarks of our last building block but also elements contributing to the resilience that is so important to children's well-being.[30]

We want children to be hardy—to be able to feel secure and capable in the face of difficulties they encounter from both the inside and the outside. When children are resilient in this way, they have a can-do approach to their dilemmas and an abiding sense of inner strength. This quality often emerges—as it did in Eric's case—through a child's hard work on the issues that challenge him. It is for this reason that we think about our last building block as resting on the previous six, and encourage its emergence through work on the others.

The Importance of Staying Upbeat in the Midst of a Child's Struggles

Skill-building assistance isn't the only element that helps kids feel more capable and confident, however. The pride children feel as they gain developmental mastery stems not only from their sense of increased competence, but also from their experiences in relationships. For example, as Eric began overcoming the two challenges he faced—regulating emotion and being flexible—his parents' increased enjoyment of his company was striking. His teacher's pleasure in his progress was clear too. These feelings had a tremendously positive impact on Eric's self-image. This shift is not unusual. When children struggle with one or more of the developmental building blocks, they aren't always fun to have around. The people they spend time with each day often feel frustrated, alienated, or judgmental, feelings that are all too apparent to the children themselves. In such situations, we often see a child's self-esteem plummet. It is because adult negativity takes this kind of toll on children's sense of inner goodness and competence that we encourage parents and teachers to remain upbeat and accepting in the face of a child's slow progress. After all, self-esteem develops less from our *telling* kids that we're proud of their good efforts—which some do so often it becomes meaningless—and more from children's *direct experience* of our pleasure in their company.

Building the Sense of a Hopeful Future

Through this joint focus on skill-development and pleasurable connection, we not only offer children opportunities for present mastery, but also the sense of a hopeful future. To help with the latter, we sometimes let them know that other kids have learned to triumph over the same struggles they currently face. Thus in my last meeting with Eric, I asked him if he'd be willing to write about what he'd learned, something that I could copy and share with other children who might need help figuring out what to do with that "volcano mad" feeling. Eric immediately set to work.

Eric's Advice for Other Kids

Hi, I'm Eric and I'm writing to any kid who needs to get better at giving in sometimes. I used to always want things to be my way and I'd get really mad if they weren't. I got a lot better at not getting so mad, that was my first improvement. What I did to not be so mad is I'd think to myself, "do the right thing." And I'd put the mad away and make myself calm down. Sometimes, I'd go into the bathroom and put water on my face, and the water would help me calm down. Sometimes I'd tell myself, "Stay cool—turn on your air conditioner!"

But still sometimes, I'd be very stubborn. My mom and dad were happy that I wasn't getting so mad, but they still really wanted me to be able to do something that I didn't want to. That was hard. Here's my advice: try letting someone else have an idea, because it might be better than yours. That happened to me with my sister once! I still really like it best if I have my own ideas though. And the hardest work is letting another person have their way if you think yours is better. Then you should think, "Later am I going to wish I didn't do that?" And jumping in the bathtub helps . . . it makes you better because it gives you a shock and makes you think. But if you can't jump in a bathtub, put water on your face or get wet. That's it . . . that's all my advice. Good-bye—Eric

Eric's writing did indeed eventually reassure some other children. After all, he sounded like a regular guy: If he'd had to contend with intense anger and had gotten the better of it, maybe they could too. But, as is so often true, Eric's journey wasn't one of nonstop progress, far from it. And along the way there were moments when his mother and father felt intensely discouraged. It was at those times that the principles we've outlined throughout this chapter kept us all afloat—we reminded ourselves to think in advance, to chunk down our goals, and to start where Eric was, not where we wished him to be. We told ourselves that kids want to do well even when they're doing poorly, and that few children get themselves on track without bumps along the way. In addition, we remembered that although Eric couldn't change his intense nature, he could learn to harness it differently. We've already noted that certain temperamental endowments can make it a challenge for kids to thrive. To explore this challenge further, the next chapter looks at the inborn qualities children bring along when they arrive in the world.

3

The Contribution of Constitution

*Understanding a Child's Temperament and
Neurodevelopmental Profile*

"NO, NO... YAYA DO IT ALL YELF!" Eighteen-month-old Sarah sits
on the hallway floor, feet stamping, eyes blazing. Her mother takes a deep
breath and tries to figure out what to do. What she really feels like doing is
crying—it's only nine-thirty in the morning and this is probably the tenth
time her daughter has shouted out the familiar command since waking
up. The problem is, much of what "Yaya" insists on carrying out herself are
things she isn't yet capable of, in this case, tying the laces of her beloved red
sneakers. Fifth percentile height, ninety-ninth percentile will, this child is a
tiny bundle of energy, enthusiasm, and stubbornness.

Sarah's disposition at eighteen months isn't a surprise to her parents; she
was an intense baby too. Wakeful, curious, unflaggingly active, she loved looking at the world around her and took every opportunity to move. By the time
she was four months old, she was trying to crawl, rocking back and forth on her
hands and knees and propelling backward a few inches before collapsing on the
floor, only to try again. At six months, she pulled herself up on every available
piece of furniture, at eight, delightedly careened around the house on two feet.
At that point, her father affectionately dubbed her the "chaos machine."

It has taken Sarah's parents a while to get used to her intensity: she's a
second child, and her sister Leah came into the world with a very different
nature. An easygoing baby, full of smiles and sunshine, Leah took her first
steps at eleven months. Wobbling unsteadily across the room, she looked at
her parents as if to say, "Okay, I did that, but crawling is a lot easier," and then
didn't walk again until she was well over a year. Even after she started toddling around, Leah loved getting a ride in the backpack her sister can barely
tolerate. As she snuggled into her favorite position, Leah would happily bab-
ble to herself, repeating the cadences of phrases she didn't yet understand, and
perking up at whatever songs her parents might sing while ambling along.
Then she'd contentedly stay put for a long, leisurely stroll.

Facets of Constitution: Temperament and Mental Processing

A child's natural style early on doesn't dictate her destiny—all kids grow and
change as they get older. Relentlessly active kids like Sarah can fall in love with

language and spend long hours writing poetry. Dreamers like her sister can become feisty, assertive teens. But this said, it's clear from both research and the everyday experiences of parents and teachers that children are born "hard-wired" in certain directions. In order to fully answer the question *What do we think?* clinicians must understand the range of these inborn possibilities.

When we first start learning about a child, our radar is up for the contribution of constitution. Walking into a classroom, observing a child with her siblings, asking questions of a concerned parent, we want to find out if she's more on the cautious or the bold side, whether she's always needed to move her body a lot or has been, historically, more visual in approaching the world. We hope to understand whether she experiences touch, smell, and taste particularly intensely, and if she's been a child who feels her emotions with great gusto. We want to see if she tends to be focused more on her inner life or the life that is teaming outside her, and if she's been flexible or somewhat rigid when it comes to change.

There are other areas to keep an eye on too. Does a youngster find it easy or hard to take in information and language? When she has something to say, does she get stuck searching for words? Can she follow multistep directions? How about her ability to run, skip, and climb: Does she have trouble getting her body to do what her mind tells it to? We watch whether she notices the expressions of others too and, if so, whether she can interpret them correctly.

The list of questions goes on. Their answers contain information about two domains that have a powerful impact on development: temperament and mental processing. In asking questions about a child's temperament, clinicians seek to understand her natural style of being in the world (Chess and Thomas, 1996). When exploring mental processing functions, they investigate how her mind carries out the many operations that allow her to take in, understand, and use information—information related to physical sensation and action, to thought and communication, and to social and emotional experience (Byrnes, 2001).

The language adults use to describe a child's struggles can convey a great deal about the contribution of constitution. In the last chapter, for example, teachers offered two striking descriptions: that one child needed to "smack into the world to live in it," and that, in the case of another, "It's as if he's listening to me but can't use what he hears." Constitutional traits don't live in a vacuum—they play out in ways we experience daily. Thus one father's description that his seven-year-old son was "like a race car engine mounted on a lawn mower" suggested that this boy's mental quickness was getting tripped up in some constitutionally determined way; later testing revealed both striking intellectual gifts and significant learning disabilities.

Getting Specific: Understanding Variations in Temperament

The division of inborn factors into two areas is, though common in the field of child development, more of a convenience than anything else: Many aspects of temperament are closely tied to how children's minds process information. That said, the distinction is helpful in both observing and understanding early childhood behavior, and will once again be used here, beginning with a look at variations in temperament. The following breakdown describes a continuum for each temperamental trait, with the first end of the range being one that more often leads to challenges in development. Note that its categories are based on the influential New York Longitudinal Study (Thomas, Chess, and Birch, 1968), the work Turecki (2000) has done to convey the importance of that study's research to parent and teacher audiences, and Greenspan's framework for categorizing types of challenging children (see Greenspan with Salmon, 1995).

Approach to New Situations and People

Range: *From* cautious, shy, or fearful *to* outgoing and bold.

Some children come into the world with an extra dose of reserve built into their genes. Others have a propensity to get easily anxious. Still others are strikingly cautious about trying new things, and balk when faced with unfamiliar circumstances. Kids on the opposite end of the spectrum feel at ease relating to others—even people they've never met—and are often adventurous in new situations.

Inner or Outer Focus

Range: *From* self-absorbed or "deep-tracked" *to* sociable and flexible.

Some children are hard to engage as infants—they seem more content attending to their inner experience than responding to the world of people. Later they may relate most easily through content that is compelling to them, and can be inflexible when asked to bend to others' needs. In social situations, their facial expressions may appear somewhat flat, and they can either avoid or hang around the edges of a lively group of peers. Children on the other end of this continuum show a strong interest in connecting with others. As infants, they tune into the faces around them and take great pleasure in sociable exchanges. They are quick to smile when approached, and initiate circles of connection long before they have language.

Level of Sensory Comfort

Range: *From* fussy and chronically over- or understimulated *to* comfortable processing wide variations in sensation.

Some children find living in the world of sensory stimulation difficult and uncomfortable. They get out of kilter in reaction to touch, taste, smell, and/or sound, and sometimes both crave sensation and find it hard to tolerate. Other youngsters handle wide variations in sensory input without missing a beat.

Emotional Intensity

Range: *From* emotionally reactive, often coupled with inflexibility, *to* easygoing.

High intensity children have big reactions to small problems. They wear their hearts on their sleeves, whether joyful or sad, anxious or furious. Paired with this quality, these children often stay stubbornly determined in their intentions far past the point when it's clear they are headed for trouble—they get locked into their emotions and then locked into their point of view. Other kids have a naturally relaxed emotional style and ride through frustration, disappointment, and changes of pace without too much fuss.

Adaptability

Range: *From* easily unnerved by changes in the environment *to* comfortable even when faced with transitions and unfamiliar situations.

Some children seem to do best when their lives are very predictable—ask them to adjust to changes in caretakers, schedules, or even food, and they lose their bearings. Others adapt easily to such changes; they travel comfortably, can handle large family gatherings without a hitch, and will deal with a new babysitter even if they'd rather have their old familiar one.

Energy Level

Range: *From* a naturally high, sometimes even frenetic, energy level *to* a slow, relaxed way of moving through each day.

High-energy kids appear born to move and are often the happiest when doing so; for some, a relentlessly high energy level is accompanied by significant struggles with attention (discussed subsequently). Children on the other end of the spectrum operate at a naturally slower speed. They don't wiggle their way through the day and settle down quickly after they've been active. Note that a subgroup of youngsters on this end of the continuum may even need some prodding to get going, and their parents and teachers can wish for a set of jumper cables to keep them moving through a day's activities.

Attentiveness

Range: *From* easily distractible and/or unresponsive to requests for attention *to* capable of harnessing attention and focus for long periods.

Children who fall on the inattentive end of this spectrum are either dreamily lost in their own thoughts, distractedly over-stimulated, or so active that they don't slow down enough to tune in. Youngsters with strengths in this area tune into outside cues quickly and easily and can stay focused for long periods even if the world around them is full of loud sounds and interesting sights.

When a child's difficulties are deeply rooted in her temperament, it's important for adults to work *with* not *against* her nature. An example of this will be seen in Chapter 8's description of a gifted teacher's classroom-based work with a shy and socially isolated four-year-old. But understanding a child's temperament is only half of the job if constitutional issues are at play; it's also necessary to get a handle on her way of processing information.

The Contribution of Mental Processing Functions

Three-year-old Antoine is tall enough to be at least five. A stocky boy with large glasses, he is frequently mistaken for an older child due both to his height and his large vocabulary. Antoine finds it hard to manage his large body through space though, and he often bumps into the classroom's furniture or stumbles while walking. Furthermore, he has a way of barging into other kids' building projects without having any idea that he is making a mess of things. Antoine's teacher Doreen knows that this boy needs help learning to play with other kids; she spends a lot of time helping him sort out his unhappy social mishaps and feels like she is doing a fairly good job of staying patient as she does so.

The thing that is getting on Doreen's nerves is that during every toileting break, Antoine can be found standing immobile in the class bathroom many minutes after his name has been called, still fully clothed. If she asks him what he is supposed be doing, he stares at her, then gravely answers, "I should pee." When told, "Well pull down your pants then," he does so immediately. But he might then stand—pants down by his feet—for a long time. Feeling that this impressively verbal, intelligent boy is seeking attention any way he can get it, Doreen is growing increasingly annoyed.

As Doreen shares her frustration during a team meeting, she acknowledges feeling guilty. "I know his mom died last year, and he's being taken care of by his aunt and grandmother. So he has a lot of reason to need some extra attention. But it seems to me that everyone is so concerned about him that they're giving him *too* much leeway at home—I don't think his cousins get away with what he does. But I can't say anything; they worry about him a lot already." Doreen is surprised to hear that, though some of Antoine's behavior could be due to family matters, he might also be experiencing vulnerabilities in nonverbal information processing. The contrast of his large vocabulary with his physical awkwardness, social struggles, and stall-outs during toileting suggests that the right side of his brain might not be functioning as strongly as the left.[1]

Doreen is especially interested to find out that kids with these vulnerabilities often have advanced language skills paired with difficulty carrying out seemingly simple routines. When asked if she's run across what we call motor planning problems before, she isn't familiar with the term. Kids who struggle with motor planning—a right brain function—have trouble getting their minds to direct their bodies through a series of physical tasks (Greenspan and Wieder, 1998). They often need help breaking the tasks down and, if strong in the verbal arena, can learn to use words rather than mental pictures to direct sequences of action. These children may also have trouble locating where their bodies are in space, and can appear strikingly clumsy. In addition, they often don't read social situations with ease, and need help learning what others intend to convey through their gestures and tones of voice.

Several weeks later Antoine's team meets again. Staff have been observing him carefully and report that the possibilities discussed in the previous meeting dovetail with what they've noticed. Doreen relates that understanding Antoine isn't being manipulative has allowed her to regain her patience. Not only that, she's realized that this boy's social difficulties stem in part from his awkward physicality, and from his difficulty understanding the social cues kids give him throughout the day. She is starting to work on helping him decode the meaning of different facial expressions and, in addition, now coaches him as he plans out how much space to put between himself and other children when saying hello or asking to play.

Getting Specific: Understanding Variations in Processing Capacities

The way the brain functions to help individuals understand and interact with their environment is complex indeed, and a book like this can't describe the systems involved in their entirety; the areas of theory and research that explore these systems have expanded exponentially in recent years. If a child experiences ongoing struggles in the classroom, there may come a time when consultation

---

Four Areas of Mental Processing

1. Processing sounds, sights, and sensations
   - Auditory processing
   - Visual/spatial processing
   - Sensory regulation*
2. Storing and retrieving information
   - Memory functions
3. Focusing in and screening out
   - Attentional functions*
4. Organizing, sequencing, and conceptualizing
   - Organizing and sequencing language and ideas
   - Organizing and sequencing physical actions
   - Building larger units of meaning from smaller ones

from the learning and pediatric specialists who know this territory best will clarify how what we refer to as his neurodevelopmental profile causes specific challenges in learning. This said, a basic grasp of variations in processing capacities allows clinicians to help parents and teachers understand puzzles in early childhood development, and a few of these capacities are outlined here. In this list that follows, which is based on the influential work of pediatrician and learning specialist Levine (2001, 2002) and that of Greenspan and Wieder (1998), starred areas highlight realms that intersect with aspects of temperament.[2]

Processing Sounds, Sights, and Sensations

Auditory Processing

All day long kids have to decode and use information that they hear. Doing this allows them to understand what people say and to respond in kind, to hear and sing melodies, even to register that a car is zooming down the street before they look both ways. Children with vulnerabilities in auditory processing can have a hard time turning bits of sound into units of meaning, and verbal communication may be a real struggle. Clinicians often advocate bringing in speech and language specialists to help with this type of challenge. However, even when such professionals enter the scene, it's crucial that parents and teachers get guidance on how to provide steady, ongoing assistance through each day; speech and language specialists have a lot to offer, but aren't around enough to supply all the support and practice a child needs.

Visual/Spatial Processing

Many of us take for granted the ability to recognize and make meaning out of what we see. We glance at a picture of a dog, and know just what breed it is. We scan a friend's face, and instantly register that he is stressed. But not everyone can quickly process what their eyes take in, and children who can't often have trouble reading social cues and negotiating space, as well as recognizing letters and numbers, drawing and building, and sorting and classifying. In addition, these youngsters may not have a visual picture of how their world fits together: where school is in relationship to home, or where the gym is in relationship to the classroom. Kids who struggle with visual-spatial processing may be so facile with language that we initially miss their vulnerabilities. It's a shame, because not only do such children often need help understanding the social world and managing their bodies through space, they may also require extra assistance as they learn to read and write later on.

Sensory Regulation*

All human beings are constantly bombarded with sensations—of touch, taste, smell, sound, sight, even the experience of movement. Youngsters who are either especially reactive to or hard to stimulate in one or more of these areas—hyper- or hyposensitive—may end up struggling developmentally. Often categorized as a temperamental trait, difficulty in the ability to regulate sensation can lead children to be chronically irritable, highly active and distractible, or somewhat sluggish and hard to engage. When it appears that a child's difficulties fall in this arena, clinicians must work to understand specifically which types of sensation pose problems. For example, some kids process sound with ease but bristle at mild forms of touch; others will wear even the scratchiest sweater but are ready to bolt if the television is too loud. Furthermore, as explored in Chapter 12, parents need to be sure that they don't get sucked into a child's response to sensory overload in a way that makes her more rather than less reactive to sensation.

Storing and Retrieving Information: Memory Functions

We use our memories constantly, as we search for words to tell a friend a story, remind ourselves not to burn the chocolate chip cookies like we did last time, or go upstairs to get the sweater we need for unexpectedly cold weather. It's when we get to the top of the stairs and can't remember what we're there for that our memory has suddenly failed us, and we retrace our steps in our mind's eye to see if we can figure out what we'd been meaning to do. It's this last experience that plagues individuals who struggle with some function of memory. They start searching for a piece of information in their mind's filing cabinet, and it's nowhere to be found.

Memory function is best conceptualized in three parts: long-term, short-term, and working memory.[3] Information stored in long-term memory is available to an individual over time. Her mother's birthday, her best friend's name—all she needs in order to call up these facts is to turn her attention toward them briefly. Short-term memory allows people to hang onto information that isn't needed for more than a little while—the two items on a mental list for a trip to the grocery store, a phone number that must be remembered briefly before it's written down. Working memory involves holding one piece of information in mind while taking in and thinking about yet more data. When preparing to answer a question with two parts, for example, a child must remember the first while listening for the second.

Vulnerabilities in memory functions impact wide-ranging areas of development. Children can have trouble retrieving the words they need to convey what's on their mind or may forget the simplest daily routines. They can struggle as they learn to read either because it's hard to hold onto the sounds that letters make, or because they forget the look of a word they've seen many times before. A boy who successfully slaves over his math facts one day only to have forgotten them completely the next may have a stronger short-term than long-term memory. A girl who loses hold of her idea for the fort she's building as she listens to her best friend's notion of what they'll do when it's finished may have weaknesses in working memory.

As seen later in Chapter 9's look at approaches to vulnerabilities in memory function, a clear "what do we see-think-do" progression can have a powerful effect on a child's development. Thus, adults first work to gain clarity about what specific challenges contribute to a youngster's struggles. Once such clarity emerges, they offer strategies that both accommodate and strengthen the area in question. With effective scaffolding—which sometimes requires the help of outside specialists—gains in both confidence and competence can be impressive.

Focusing In and Screening Out

Attentional Functions*

As any parent or teacher knows well, the ability to tune in looms large in early development. Harnessing attention requires two connected mental processes. Kids have to direct and maintain steady focus on activities that interest them and on information coming from others. Concurrently, they must screen out sights, sounds, thoughts, and impulses that aren't central to the task at hand. Whether listening to the words of a new song at group time, going down the hall to brush teeth without becoming derailed by an interesting toy on the way, or getting through a boring homework assignment without too many interruptions, youngsters have to filter out some stimuli in order to attend successfully to others.[4] Another processing function that is often categorized as a quality of temperament, attentional capacity varies widely in any group of children, and those for whom it is more difficult often require careful assistance from the adults around them. The nature of this assistance will be explored in Chapter 10. And, as first noted with Chapter 2's Gabe, we'll see how important it is that the behavioral feedback loops surrounding struggles with inattention reinforce mastery, not difficulty.

Organizing, Sequencing, and Conceptualizing

Organizing and Sequencing Language and Ideas

The ability to organize and sequence thought and language doesn't just have implications for effective communication, its impact splashes all across early development. As noted in Chapter 2, kids have to be able to connect smaller units of thought into larger and larger strings of meaning in order to play out stories of their own, and to follow and join the stories of their friends. Without this capacity, they may also have difficulty comprehending how the world works. It can be difficult for them to cope with conflicts of agendas too, because it takes them so long to compare their ideas to others', and to puzzle out a reasonable compromise. Playing, learning, and handling difficult feelings can all be at risk and, after a while, connections can be hard to keep up too. Many three-year-olds speak in simple phrases, and young pre-schoolers have a lot of tolerance for each other's hesitations and stall-outs as they communicate. But over time, it becomes harder and harder for children who struggle to organize and sequence their thoughts—or who do so very slowly—to keep up with the crowd. Not only do their friendships begin to suffer but their self-esteem does too. Frustration may soon follow.

The process of organizing and sequencing bits of language and units of meaning is, like so many other aspects of mental processing, quite complex. An easy way to visualize how it works is to picture a kind of mental overseer—someone who is good at seeing the big picture—taking in information and figuring out how it fits together. Children who can't yet perform this service for themselves need adult help in slowly learning to carry out the elements of such an overseer's job description.[5]

One of the problems for youngsters with processing and sequencing vulnerabilities is that as they get left behind by their peers, they have less and less opportunity to practice and strengthen the very skills that cause them the most trouble. In addition, siblings, friends, and caring adults may jump in to help out in an area of difficulty, often taking over the function almost entirely. *Either way, the less these kids practice such skills, the less success they experience, a cycle that quickly leads to decreased motivation in an area where strong motivation is most needed.* This is why lend-an-ally work is so important for kids who don't sequence with ease. This work is often grounded in a child's instinctive love of story, and done using naturally occurring play themes as a springboard from which to strengthen the ability to organize and connect thought.

Organizing and Sequencing Physical Actions: The Motor Planning Function

As noted in the earlier description of Antoine, motor planning is the process by which the mind directs the body through a series off physical tasks. A child's doing this requires three parts: he develops an idea of what he wants to do, plans the series of actions involved, then performs the sequence from start to finish. When kids and adults carry out motor planning functions with ease, these three steps take place not only effortlessly but also almost simultaneously. It's only when motor planning is problematic that we suddenly grasp the mental capacities behind everyday actions.

Motor planning difficulties have implications throughout a child's daily life. Kids with such vulnerabilities may have trouble with basic physical tasks: putting on a jacket, picking up a toy and placing it in its proper basket, running, climbing, or riding a tricycle. But other actions can be hard too. Youngsters may struggle to create play narratives because the physical actions involved are too hard to string together, and play can look choppy and repetitive. They may appear aimless throughout the day, or give directions to a group of buddies who then carry out a story line "on the ground." When it is time to write, such youngsters may feel quite overwhelmed: Successful handwriting (and drawing, for that matter) involves a complex and circular process of organizing and planning physical actions, attending to visual output, and getting many small muscles to perform a sometimes challengingly precise job. Note that children with motor planning problems sometimes also struggle with visual/spatial processing. Antoine has both vulnerabilities, and as he plows into a beautifully constructed block tower—to the unhappy cries of his friends—these vulnerabilities are all too apparent.

Conceptualizing: Building Larger Units of Meaning From Smaller Ones

James, a child described in Chapter 9, imitates his friends as they play with cars and trucks. But his teacher isn't sure that he grasps the overall story line they have in mind. His problems in sequencing and organizing information appear to be accompanied, as they often are, by vulnerabilities in what we call higher-order thinking. Kids who have weaknesses with higher-order thinking struggle to understand the big picture; they don't "see the forest for the trees." When a child comfortably comes up with ideas that account for a slew of smaller details, he can create increasingly sophisticated narratives of experience in both play and conversation. He can also envision structures of meaning—meaning that pertains to how people relate to each other, how ideas connect, and how the world works.

This ability to create and understand abstract concepts has broad implications for later learning but shows up early on as well. Children who struggle with the big picture often have difficulty understanding jokes and sarcasm, and can appear surprisingly literal in their reactions to friends and family. They can have trouble solving problems in new ways too, relying on marginally successful strategies they've used before rather than thinking creatively about other possibilities. Antoine has some vulnerabilities in this area: Doreen has noticed that although his vocabulary is remarkable for a young three-year-old, his problem-solving capacities are poor, and he often can't use the many words he knows to help him think through even fairly simple situations. It's an area of weakness she now understands she'll need to monitor, because as children progress through their early years, difficulties with abstract thinking can cause wide-ranging developmental vulnerabilities.

Getting to Work on Information Processing Issues

As is true in all situations when processing issues hamper growth, children can, with help, slowly strengthen areas of weakness. Youngsters whose attention is on the distractible side can learn to tune in more easily; children who get overwhelmed by sensation can come to handle variations in touch, taste, and sound. Kids who have trouble decoding auditory information can learn to make meaning of what they hear, and those who don't easily put ideas in order can be offered strategies that help them tell stories in sequence. Children with motor planning difficulties are no exception. Once there is clarity on what functions are holding them back, adults give them steady practice in planning sequences of movement. As always, it's important to "get specific" about what's going on, chunking down goals for growth, and then leaning in with a focus on one or two skills at a time. Physical and occupational therapists can be wonderful allies in this work, but teachers and parents, as always, have a large role to play too.

As Doreen and her assistant teacher embrace this role with Antoine, they begin instituting some new movement games in their classroom. These games break down a series of actions into their component parts, then slowly—and with the verbal cues Antoine needs—reassemble them into an increasingly rapid series. For example, they now play a slow motion freeze game in which, to the accompaniment of a rhythmic chant, kids pretend to get their coats, boots, and hats on, one step at a time. After a few repetitions, they start speeding up the action. Later in the day, the assistant teacher works with Antoine by his cubby, running through the same series but with the actual garments in question. Antoine loves these games, and the special attention he gets in the practice that follows, and they seem to be helping him gain the awareness and mastery he's been lacking. Once again, it's clarity in the "what do we think" category that gives a set of caring adults the specific understanding needed to help a child begin to thrive.

Armed with her new perspective, Doreen is thinking about speaking with Antoine's aunt and grandmother. She hopes to share her new picture of what might be holding Antoine back, as well as strategies they can use to help strengthen the right brain functions that challenge him. Doreen still feels that Antoine's family coddles him too much, but has a new sense of just how complicated his situation at home might be. As she thinks more about it, she wonders whether some of the leniency she's noticed comes from his aunt and grandmother's intuitive sense that Antoine is not just emotionally but also constitutionally more vulnerable than his cousins. Keeping our eyes open for such complexity is important as we attempt to understand the contribution of family life to a child's struggles. It's this challenge that we'll explore in the next chapter.

4

The Contribution of Family Life

*Understanding a Family's History and
Patterns of Interaction*

"Monica, you need to finish eating now and go get dressed." Annie delivers the familiar instruction with studied calm. Even so, seven-year-old Monica's voice shifts perilously from the sweet, sleepy timber it had moments ago as she chatted over breakfast.

Mom, you're SO UNFAIR. Liza's mother drives her to school EVERY SINGLE DAY and you make me get up SO early to take the bus. I WON'T take the bus, you can't make me!

Fearing that her daughter is going to lose control entirely, Annie suddenly feels like she's about to experience a case of emotional lockjaw. With a sigh, she crosses her arms, frowns, and responds with the exact note of irritable harshness she's promised herself she won't resort to this morning.

Monica, I absolutely can't take you—I'll lose my job if I'm late too many more times. Now you go upstairs, and put your clothes on right now. If you miss the bus again today, I'm going to be incredibly upset with you.

You're such an IDIOT mom. And you DON'T CARE about me!

Monica storms up to her room. Wandering into the kitchen near the end of his sister's tirade, ten-year-old Kenny rolls his eyes. He waits until Monica has made her dramatic exit, then grumbles his first words of the morning. "She's such a pain, mom. Why do you let her get away with it?" A shrug serves as Annie's only reply. Minutes later, Monica clomps down the stairs, dressed in yesterday's dirt-stained clothes, and she and her mother head outside for their quick walk to the bus stop. With a mix of relief that things didn't get completely out of hand, and guilt that she's sending Monica to school looking so ill-kempt, Annie offers a stiff smile and a terse "Have a good day" as her daughter grimly boards the bus.

Monica can be a challenge in school too. On hearing more about her struggles there, Annie and her husband Jack agree to the idea of consultative help—some for them about life at home, some for the school about approaches to classroom-based support. Several months into their piece of this process, Annie and Jack arrive late for a meeting. Jack walks in without a word, lowers himself onto a chair, and folds his arms over his chest. Annie slumps down in the seat next to him, and dispiritedly begins talking about the horrendous few days they've just had. "Listen, I do understand what we're talking about here and, at least some of the time, I know what I should do when she gets going. It's doing it that is the problem. I'm annoyed with her constantly. Jack is better than me for a while but then, you know, he'll suddenly lose his temper big-time." She slips in an apologetic glance at her husband, who glowers back in return. "She can be so great sometimes. But then everything just falls apart."

Getting Specific: Recognizing the Power of Family Choreography

Adult reactivity to a child's misbehavior or emotional distress. Tension between siblings. Conflict between parents. Periods of calm interspersed with significant turmoil. All of the issues seen here are common when a youngster is struggling at home. For the families in question, these issues can be truly painful. For clinicians, the job of understanding what's going on—and responding effectively—is often a challenge. Because every family is a highly complex entity, in which the business of the present is deeply affected by patterns and history from the past.

Clinicians, of course, must remain open to the countless variations in how family life is organized and transacted. One parent yells much more than she'd like, another takes care of his kids through a haze of depression. One raises her children alone, another parents alongside his own mother. Some families have an affectionate adult partnership at their center, while others, an explosive relationship that leaves everyone emotionally—and sometimes physically—weary and hurt. Families go through periods of stability and times of change, weather illnesses, financial hardship, deaths, and divorces.

All these factors are woven into the never-ending cycle of family members' responses to each other: responses between one parent and another, between parents and kids, and between siblings. These cycles often emerge out of a mix of intention and emotion, and they play a powerful role in shaping behavior. For example, parents may try valiantly to be consistent, only to realize that they've changed course midstream when they're just too tired for another scene. Then they notice how their kids complain even more the next time they say "no." Or, swearing to avoid the mistakes their parents made, they're mortified to suddenly find themselves sounding just like an unhappily remembered mother or father—with results sometimes as unfortunate in the present as they were in the past.

So with all of this complexity, how can clinicians even begin to think clearly about the contribution of family life to a young child's difficulties? Is it possible to get at the essence of family interplay with some logic, while at the same time paying attention to the thick layering of meaning and feeling that exists in every family unit? We might begin by acknowledging that all families have a way of "dancing" together—choreography that has unfolded over time.[1] While some of these transactional patterns comfortably serve everyone's needs, some most definitely do not. Parents occasionally share their awareness of the latter, describing a sudden and intense feeling of recognition in the midst of a troubling interaction: "Here we are. We've been here before, and we'll be here again. There is something about this moment that feels like us, familiar and unhappily stuck." It's precisely this kind of stuckness that Annie is describing when she says that "everything just falls apart." At such times, each family interchange can feel like it involves a set of moves that everyone knows—moves that each member, even the youngest, could pace through with their eyes closed.

Developing an Overall Picture of Family Life

It isn't within the purview of this book to take a thorough look at interventions for serious family issues; the subject requires in-depth exploration that can be found elsewhere.[2] Furthermore, the fascinating and much-explored intersection between an individual child's issues and a family's way of being has a complexity that is worth many chapters of its own.[3] That said, it's clear that the overall terrain of family functioning is tremendously important to any early childhood consultant—not only does it bear strongly on young children's behavior but, in addition, developmentally focused consultation often includes an element of conversation and problem solving with parents.[4] Thus, on the one hand, practitioners need skill in helping parents explore how a child's difficulties are nested in family interactional patterns. On the other, as they run into the all-too-common dynamics that make it hard to change the problematic aspects of those patterns, they need to understand the kinds of issues that may be at stake.

What do these facets of practice entail? First, we need a finely tuned ability to "join" families, as we adapt our style to their ways of being, stay present through periods of conflict and intense emotion, and listen to parents' stories with empathy.[5] It's only when we're successful in this kind of alliance building that we're "allowed in" enough to understand the nuances of family interplay. Second, we need creative ways to tune into the struggles (and pacing needs) of overwhelmed caregivers as we work to open up new possibilities for interaction. Finally, we must develop a sense of when and how to suggest some deeper exploration. Whether we support that exploration ourselves or make a referral, the work a family does to understand and change its process can be essential, because as families get on top of longstanding and problematic dynamics, struggling kids often benefit. Of course the reverse is often true too, and therein lies some of the power of this book's developmentally focused model: When parents discover more effective approaches to their child's troubling behaviors, a more satisfying experience of family life often emerges for everyone.

The first step in understanding a family's dynamics is to have an overview of its functioning. The following framework lays out areas for consideration.[6] Note that while clinicians who are involved in traditional family work sometimes initiate a formal assessment process that looks at these areas in detail, early childhood consultants often stay advised to their importance, yet elicit relevant information in a more flexible way.[7]

Family Functioning: Categories and Questions

Care and Connection: Is this a warm, comfortable place for both adults and children? Do the adults communicate a basic appreciation for each other? Is there a feeling of love and connection that permeates family life?

Emotional and Physical Well-Being: How do the adults feel about themselves and their lives? Is anyone especially overwhelmed? Struggling with a drug or alcohol addiction? Do any adults or kids have significant health or mental health issues?

Organization and Expectations: What is the family's overall organization? What individual or group of individuals is responsible for its decision making? Are their decisions respected by other family members? How important is extended family, and what role do they play in everyday life? Are there people outside the actual family who are, in some crucial ways, essential to its functioning? Do the adults in charge feel comfortable having reasonable expectations for children's behavior? Is the way they follow through on those expectations effective? If there are two or more caretakers at home, are their expectations similar? If not, does this result in mixed messages for the kids?

Who is aligned with whom in the family? Who is in conflict with whom? Are there subgroups within the family's structure that make it operate more or less smoothly? Are its boundaries relatively open or fairly rigid?[8] For example, how set is the family unit that lives at home? Are there many comings and goings of extended family or friends? Do children sleep in the same place each night? Are they left with unfamiliar or unexpected caretakers on a regular basis?

How does the family manage tasks like making meals, cleaning up, scheduling appointments, and paying bills? Is there an overall sense that the things that need to get done do get done, or does life feel chaotic and disorganized? Does someone keep track of bedtimes, television and/or computer time (not just *how much*, but *what* kids are watching and playing), and self-care activities like brushing teeth and bathing?

Finally, how intensely scheduled is everyday life? Is there enough time for the parent or parents to feel relaxed and in tune with their children? Do the kids feel constantly rushed, or do they have the sense that there is room for pleasurable interactions, and space for their needs to be met?

Negotiation of Needs and Conflict: How do the adults balance their own needs and the requirements of taking care of their children? How do the children respond when they must share attention or wait to get their needs met? Can the adults manage conflict without getting enraged or violent?

Do they know how to work out their differences? How do the children get along? If there is some sibling rivalry—and there often is—are there also times that the children enjoy each other? Does sibling rivalry get to the point where it feels damaging to any child?

Cultural Norms: What is the cultural background of the parent or parents? How are cultural expectations expressed throughout daily life at home? Is there more than one culture represented in the family unit? If so, how do the two sets of norms coexist? Are family conflicts partially based on their contrasts? How do family norms intersect with those of the community and society at large?[9]

Language and Immigration Issues: Do the children speak a different language in school than at home? Do the parents understand that language? If not, how does this affect the experience of comfort and empowerment for kids and adults alike? Is this an immigrant family? Do concerns about immigration status impinge on family life and stability?[10]

Resources and Support: Are there pressures about money, housing, or health care? If so, how do these pressures impinge on the warmth and ease of family interactions? Does a parent's (or parents') need to support the family require many hours away from home? Who takes care of the children in the evenings if there isn't a parent on hand? Do family members have warm connections to people outside the nuclear family, either extended family or a community of friends? In the case of a single parent, does he or she have people to turn to for help and support?

Nothing on this list is surprising. Families work best if people feel good about themselves and respect each other, if they know how to get through tough moments of conflict, and if they get support outside the family when life within it is getting overwhelming. Kids and adults all do better when there is enough time to relax and enjoy their time together, enough organization to get the basics done, and enough stability to keep things feeling safe and predictable. And without money to put food on the table and access to decent housing, a safe neighborhood, and adequate health care, no family can function with ease (Olson and Gorall, 2003).

Examining Behavioral Feedback Loops

Though consulting clinicians don't always have complete answers to the above questions, keeping their importance in mind is always useful. The elements they point to often have an impact on the moments described earlier, those during which a parent suddenly and unhappily recognizes that a certain kind of problematic interchange is happening once again. The way such interchanges unfold has been described here as family choreography, a particular version of the more generic behavioral feedback loops discussed in Chapter 2. As practitioners and families partner up to help a worrisome youngster, part of their work will involve figuring out *how a family can change its "dance" in order to foster developmental mastery.*

The process of changing family choreography relies on a clear picture of the interactional patterns in which a child's difficulties are embedded. In addition, it's important to develop an understanding of how those patterns have grown out of past interactions. In shooting for this kind of clarity, we keep in mind that while adults bring all of themselves—their histories, their emotional vulnerabilities, and their current stress levels—to their relationships with their children, those children bring things too: From the first days of life, a youngster's temperament, level of physical comfort or distress, and neurodevelopmental profile have a profound impact on interactions with caregivers. It is in the context of this intersection between parents and children—one nested within the bigger picture of family life—that the patterns which hamper development may slowly unfold. Once problematic issues emerge, parental efforts to manage a difficult behavior or developmental concern sometimes serve to make things worse.

The following questions help guide this phase of exploration.[11] Note that the first five attend to patterns in the present, while the rest tease out information about how those patterns have unfolded over time.

- When does the problem in question tend to occur?
- How do family members react to it?
- What happens when they react in this way?
- What happens next? (And so on...)
- Do these behavioral feedback loops play a role in amplifying the problem?
- How long have these feedback loops been operating? In what ways have they become nested in family life? Early on, did aspects of the child's temperament, neurodevelopmental profile, or physical well-being play a role in how these patterns unfolded?
- How did early patterns of interaction impact the child's developmental mastery? What areas of mastery were affected, and what types of behavior evidenced? Did difficult behaviors then set off further and potentially destructive family patterns?
- Have such patterns gotten so entrenched that a feeling of irritability, anger, or hopelessness has infused interactions, leaving everyone prone to quick, negative, or distancing responses to each other? What role have a child's siblings and/or extended family played in how they've been transacted?
- What impact have these patterns had on a child's experience of self and world? On her emotional well-being? On parental experiences of competence or incompetence? Have they affected the core sense of connection and disconnection between parent(s) and child? Lastly, how have such issues then contributed to further patterning?

Tracking the Intersection Between Children's Vulnerabilities and Family Dynamics

Clearly, these questions leave clinicians and families with a lot to consider. Their power is in fostering clarity in the midst of the large amounts of data—and intense parental distress—often encountered in the family-focused portion of consultative practice. Further exploration of Monica's story will illustrate how this works. Note how consultation with parents often begins with a careful look at a child's most problematic behaviors. Then clinicians help translate those behaviors into areas of developmental challenge. Next, there is some exploration of how problematic feedback loops—both past and present—have played a role in what has unfolded. Finally, all involved work together to sketch out ideas for intervention.

As Annie, Jack, and I embark on the first two steps of this process, we quickly identify that Monica's most troublesome behaviors involve difficulty keeping minor frustration from surging into major unhappiness. In Annie's words, "Monica has almost no ability to do any problem-solving when she's bothered by something...I think that's why we feel like calm in the house can be completely blown apart within seconds." Inflexibility follows quickly in the wake of these often-paired issues—kids who have Monica's trouble regulating emotion and thinking (rather than feeling) their way through frustration usually aren't able to switch agendas with ease.

Eventually, we consider Annie and Jack's earliest experiences with their daughter, and it becomes clear that the patterns underlying these difficulties go back as far as her first year of life. Jack relates that Monica was placed in the hospital's intensive care unit after birth because of breathing problems, following which severe reflux required significant extra care throughout her first year. Unlike her older brother, who had been an easy baby to take care of, Monica cried constantly, seemed, in Annie's words, "to get sick every time we went somewhere," and eventually required tubes for her ever-present ear infections. Both adults recount painful memories of how difficult it was to comfort their daughter after the procedure to place the tubes, and the way it only amplified how overwhelmed they already felt by her seemingly endless needs. This infant and her parents were, clearly, off to a rocky start.

Things didn't become much easier as time went on. An affectionate but demanding toddler, Monica had a difficult time adjusting to her baby sitter when Annie first went back to work. Separations continued to be painful, whether when Annie would leave her daughter in family childcare to head off to her part-time job or, later, when Monica got dropped off for preschool. As she got older still, Monica's needy unhappiness had an increasingly strident quality. "She had a really low tolerance level for anything that wasn't perfect," Jack recounts, "and that's still there...I feel like she can never roll with the punches."

Annie and Jack are impressively open about how Monica's early physical distress and her later emotional fragility made it increasingly challenging for them to feel relaxed in her presence, and that their growing tension probably contributed to her upsets. Monica's struggles now begin to make sense, especially as a developmental frame is reintroduced into the conversation. Children who have extreme and ongoing difficulty being comforted as infants—or whose parents can't offer the responsive care they need— sometimes don't learn how to comfort themselves. What is often called "self-soothing," an important part of the ability to regulate emotion, is something children first learn through the repetitive experience of being soothed by others (Shore, 2001a). If Monica didn't master the rudiments of this ability early on, it would follow that later, the anxiety of separation—and the experience of frustration in the face of the hurdles of daily life—would set off waves of emotion that she didn't know how to manage. Over time, her chronic physical discomfort, cranky neediness and, eventually, frequent explosions resulted in emotionally charged patterns at home, with her parents offering a confusing mix of comfort, annoyance, and guilt-laden rejection. Kenny's frustration over his sister's outbursts became part of the picture too. Now, family life feels precarious when it's calm, and full of blaming, irritation, and rage when it's not.

Noting When Intervention Is Easier to Design Than to Carry Out

Once a family and clinician have converged on such a developmentally focused understanding of a child's difficulties, in conjunction with a picture of contributing patterns of response, it's a good time to set out some initial possibilities for intervention. This work, not surprisingly, focuses on changing current feedback loops in order to foster both developmental mastery and emotional well-being. When it goes well, the results can be deeply gratifying to parents, as they take pleasure in their children's newfound abilities and confidence. However, there are many times when intervention is easier to come up with in concept than to carry out in reality, times when deep-seated issues impede a family's ability to "change its dance steps." It's just this dilemma that emerges in the work with Annie and Jack, and tracking the next stage of that work will serve as a springboard for exploring some of the complex challenges clinicians face in their consultative work with families.

After gaining an understanding of why Monica can be so trying, Annie and Jack appear eager for practical guidance about what to do at home. Thus we begin mapping out some approaches for them to try when she gets shrill and provocative. Annie develops a picture of how to be both firm and compassionate as she helps her daughter work on the important skill of maintaining composure in the face of frustration; she now sees that it only makes things worse when she defends herself against Monica's bitter accusations point by point. Jack, on the other hand, takes on the task of giving Monica more support and some warning before gruffly laying down the law, while being sure that he doesn't just avoid her outbursts altogether by letting her get her way. The latter pattern, it has become clear, doesn't give Monica the practice she needs in regulating emotion and being flexible when facing less-than-welcome expectations.

Annie and Jack embrace another developmental/emotional agenda too, that of helping Monica feel more steadily and warmly connected, so that she can trust in her parents' affection—and feel secure within herself—even when they're saying something that isn't to her liking. (At the moment, as described earlier, her first reaction when things go awry is to scream, "You don't care about me!" and it appears that she truly believes what she's saying.) In order to work on this goal, these parents agree to find as many opportunities as they can to sneak in affectionate, pleasurable interactions with their bristly girl—they've been so frustrated with her that it's been hard to offer her the steady nurturance she craves.

These ideas are all sensible enough, and Annie and Jack go home from the first few consultative meetings with the best of intentions. But not that long thereafter, Jack gruffly announces that the tip-sheets they've been taking home and posting on their dresser mirror aren't helping all that much and that—in the heat of the moment—everyone reverts to form.

Understanding and Adapting to Deep-Seated Family Issues

When parents like Monica's try taking steps in a positive direction but find themselves mired in old patterns—or want to try new approaches but are too overwhelmed to do so—clinicians need an extra dose of thoughtfulness, creativity, and flexibility. Can a limited piece of deeper exploration be contained in the consultative process? Is it time to refer out? Or, if the particular clinician's job description allows, should the focus shift to more traditional family or couples therapy? Does a family need more support and advocacy efforts in order to shore up the basics of family organization or to get help with poverty-related stressors?[12] Would it be best to start with work that only targets increased parent-child connection before laying out specific, developmentally focused strategies?[13]

There are other possibilities too. Maybe a child would be best served by a depressed parent pursuing some individual therapy. Maybe placing the child herself in treatment would serve to ease the intensity everyone feels when she's unhappy. Then again, it might be that an older sibling's issues have such a destabilizing impact on family life that it makes sense to address them above all else. Perhaps, some combination of the above is indicated.

There is, clearly, no one answer to the question of why and how a developmentally focused approach to changing problematic family patterns needs to be deepened, adjusted, or even—at least temporarily—suspended. But often, in the effort to understand what issues fuel those patterns, clinicians rely on a third set of questions, those that look to how old history can resonate in current problems, and how larger issues in family functioning thread through a particular child's struggles with her parents and siblings. Note how, once again, these questions attend to both the past and the present.

- Do the feedback loops surrounding a child's challenges connect to some painful history? For example, did either or both parents experience significant losses, trauma, and/or troubled relationships with their primary caregivers? Do they still carry some of the emotional fallout from those experiences? If so, are there old hurts or yearnings that play into what's going on now? Alternatively, does the child remind either parent of a difficult sibling or relative? What other distressing, historically generated feelings might be triggered by a child's physical presence, way of being, or problems behaving—thus fueling some of the patterns underlying current difficulties?
- Are parents and other caregivers in conflict with each other about how to handle those difficulties? Does this conflict play a part in how the family's interactive patterns unfold?
- Are there other family issues that play a role in how this problem is embedded in daily life?
- Do adult family members experience confusion about when to offer the child in question friendly support and skill-building assistance, and when to provide clear expectations and firm limits? If so, has this confusion played a part in the patterns at hand?

Answers to the first question can offer important information as to why efforts to change aren't working: Families' most problematic patterns often echo with long-familiar meaning for parents, and are laden with feeling tones connected to the past.[14] Thus while asking intelligent questions about how a family "dances" around a child's difficulties, it's important for clinicians to listen for any historical undertones. For example, a father responds with notable harshness when his five-year-old son starts to whine. Then it emerges that this youngster's behavior reminds the father of his own younger brother, a fragile individual who was chronically discontent as a child and who has never managed to create a fulfilled life for himself as an adult. The five-year-old's mother, who was often yelled at by her parents when she was young, feels she must protect her son from his father's impatience, thus leading to the boy's experience of a confusing set of mixed messages about how he reacts to frustration. The result of these old issues resonating through current ones? This child tends to get his demands met at the end of such interchanges, and thus may be inclined to whine again the next time around.

As noted earlier, clinical consultants will need to consider some wide-ranging options as they figure out how to approach roadblocks to change. Some of those options involve significant shifts, additions, or adjustments to the kind of help a family and child is offered. However, it's important to note that when a family's painful history constrains progress, there are often tremendous opportunities for growth and healing nested in the context of relatively short, developmentally focused consultation. The work of that consultation involves a delicate mix: on the one hand, a focus on practical, step-by-step strategies for changing interactional patterns, on the other, some gentle probing into the past. Let's return one last time to the work with Monica's parents, to see what such a mix looks like.

After Jack's declaration that things feel as stuck as ever, I acknowledge his disappointment, and suggest that it probably makes sense to think together about what might be getting in the way of the changes we're all hoping for. Annie stares at me sadly, then remarks, "You're telling us we're doing a bad job." Something about her statement suggests that the feeling of doing a bad job may go back a long way. It takes only a brief inquiry to elicit some relevant—and poignant—information.

Annie, it turns out, is all too familiar with the awful feeling of doing a bad job. It haunts her: at work, at home, with friends. She remembers being young and feeling squashed in between her confident older brother and her witty younger sister, feeling clumsy and stupid. Unloved too—she always had the feeling that whereas her siblings could do no wrong, she could never please. As she grew older, she grew more withdrawn, perhaps even depressed, though she didn't have words for it at the time. Her mother loudly proclaimed that she needed to pull it together, work harder at school, lose some weight, find a boyfriend.

Going back home for family gatherings is still a terrible chore; after seeing her brother with his well-behaved kids—and sensing her parents and siblings judge her as she unsuccessfully tries to keep Monica from unraveling *yet again*—Annie can feel plagued by self-doubt and irritation for weeks. And Monica's ever-present unhappiness leaves her feeling increasingly trapped. When Monica was an infant and toddler, Annie was determined to offer the comforting, steady mothering she'd never received. Now she finds herself incensed by her daughter's terrible accusations: "You never understand me. You're a terrible mom. You're an idiot. You don't love me." Annie's mind fires off a silent defense: *You have no idea what it is to be misunderstood. You have no idea what a terrible mom is like. You have no idea about not being loved.* And then its still-silent, hopeless rebuttal: *Maybe I don't understand. Maybe I am an idiot. Probably wasn't meant to have kids, at least not one like this.*

As the conversation continues, Jack has his own story to tell, one of an alcoholic, distant father, an emotionally fragile—and often physically ill—mother, and a grim, loveless household. He remembers being an intense teenager who spent endless hours in his room reading, and recounts that his friends knew him as the smart kid with the terrible temper. A number of those friends eventually pulled away, telling Jack that he'd better get some help or he'd hurt someone someday.

Jack knew they were right and, in college, determined that he'd get his temper under control. And by the time he met Annie during their senior year, he appeared to be a strikingly rational young man. "I told myself to lock up the anger, to really stuff it down. I didn't know what else to do." Annie was drawn to Jack's solid, thoughtful presence. Jack took comfort in her unassuming warmth and quiet intelligence. They began dating, and increasingly, felt they'd each found an anchor in the other. They graduated, found jobs, married, had Kenny. Life wasn't easy but it was good. Then came Monica, with her ever-present health issues, her inconsolable crying, her seemingly endless needs. Slowly, tension in the young family mounted. Jack started losing his temper again. Annie began overeating in a way she hadn't since she was a teen. Loyal and responsible, neither thought seriously about divorce. But each felt twinges of regret and confusion—what had happened to the partner they'd fallen in love with and married? Why were their old demons coming back to threaten the hard-won contentment of their new life?

Making Connections to the Past That Free Up Possibilities in the Present

It is at this point in a family's process that parents may feel ready to make connections between past and present and—with the help of our compassionate witnessing—allow the pain of history to release some of its hold on current dynamics.[15] Thus Annie and Jack have some important questions to consider: Is there any way to understand their difficulty using the strategies we've outlined in the light of the stories we've just been exploring? What happens inside each of them when their daughter's face gets red and she begins spewing frustration and accusations? Jack follows the line of inquiry with ease. "The things we need to do differently, they involve having to think before responding in some knee-jerk way. But some emotion comes up and then I can't remember what I'm supposed to do." I wonder aloud whether he can be more specific about *what* emotion gets in the way. "Well, it just seems totally illogical that she gets really angry rather than staying calm and sorting things out. I get completely frustrated when that happens." It doesn't take us long to make the connection that rationality has been Jack's greatest strength and main coping mechanism, while his pent-up rage has been a source of significant problems. Monica's inability to stay calm and think things through rubs up against his carefully contained emotional style, and sets off his own struggles with anger. Being patient with her, as a result, often feels like a sensible but unattainable goal.

Annie has her own insights to offer. "I can't stand it when she berates me. I felt so inferior growing up—it's intolerable to me that my own kid would put me down. But then, I'll doubt myself too. She's been so hard to take care of. When she was a baby and would cry and cry, I would feel like I was going to break, and I'd think that someone else could probably calm her down better than me. And now I get so furious with her for not appreciating me. Then I feel incredibly guilty for having these truly hateful thoughts about her so I bend over backward to be extra nice. And if she kind of slaps me in the face for it, I feel even more upset." As we keep talking, Annie relates that when Monica complains about her life as if it's a terrible trial, she can't stand that either. "I had to make the best of such a lousy situation, it's absolutely ridiculous that Monica is complaining just because she has to take the bus or something."

Near the end of the conversation, Annie seems particularly burdened by the whole situation. "Jack is right," she says. "We have all these new ideas of what we are supposed to do to help her learn to stay calm. But when she gets like this, she gets me going. And my rational intellect goes right out the window." The depth and complexity of this family's struggles feel like a heavy presence in the room, as I consider how to help this likeable, overwhelmed mother use some of the connections she's made about her past to free up possibilities in the present. "Annie, I'm wondering something here. You've really helped me understand what happens to you when Monica starts acting up, all the things that start running through your mind, all these feelings that come up. Can you think of anything you could say to yourself when your intellect starts going out the window? Something that would allow you to remember that you have some options right then?" Annie stares into space. Then, after a long pause, she replies. "Yeah. I think the worst of it is that Monica makes me feel stupid. I could say to myself, 'Annie you are a smart person, you can figure out what to do.'"

Helping Parents Have Compassion for Themselves and for Their Children

Though clinicians yearn to believe that conversations like this one end with parents making dramatic progress, they usually don't. More often, change unfolds slowly, as parents begin to find release from past hurts and pathways toward new ways of functioning. This is certainly true in the case of Monica's family: Annie and Jack often leave one meeting feeling inspired, only to come in for the next one appearing weary and beaten down. It's clear—as is so often true for parents who have faced great challenges in their own childhoods— that our approach to helping Monica feels daunting in its demands for time, energy, and patience. In such situations, clinicians do well to remind themselves that when parents weren't steadily loved and attended to as children, it's harder for them to feel anchored and optimistic as adults. Our job, in part, is to hold the hope for everyone.

Thus the process of helping Monica live comfortably in a less than perfect world continues to be challenging. Jack does work to separate his issues from his daughter's, noting when his temper is starting to get the better of him, and aiming for a more patient stance in the face of Monica's irrationality. Annie gets better at giving herself a quick, upbeat message when she catches herself slipping into the helpless, bitter state she felt so often as a child. We make sure to leave time in our conversations for each to explore some of the experiences they had growing up, hoping that in doing so, they'll come to have more compassion for themselves as well as for their daughter. And, slowly, their efforts begin to pay off.

Several months after Annie makes her forlorn statement about doing a bad job, Monica's tantrums are occurring once every few days rather than once every couple of hours. She still gets irritated easily, but Annie and Jack take pleasure in her more frequent gestures of affection, her newfound ability to say she's sorry, her occasional but cheerful flexibility. Later still, Annie comes to a meeting and proudly relates that earlier in the day, she was successful in walking away from Monica's strident complaints about her lack of "cool" clothes, telling her daughter that she sees there just aren't any clothes she likes this morning, that she is going to have to figure out what to wear on her own, and that there will be a special breakfast waiting downstairs once she gets the "clothes grumpies" out. We laugh about the outlandish outfit Monica wears when she arrives downstairs, and about Annie's intentionally oblivious reaction.

Kids complicate families and families complicate kids. Old issues haunt the present and the present surfaces old pains. Shame, rage, emptiness, fear— all of these feelings and more can get in the way of comfortable, sensible parenting. When history is getting in the way of growth, parents may need our help in looking inward and back, working through the stuck spots in their own development so they can free up stuck spots in their kids' lives. Doing so may be a wearying process, but it can be liberating for everyone too. Annie is beginning to understand this now and so, in her way, is Monica. At one of our last meetings, Annie arrives smiling. Monica had come in early that morning with a grin, a hug, and a question: "Mom, I think we're getting along better, do you?" Annie agreed. "Are you happy mom? I want you to be happy."

Part II
Foundations for Intervention

5

Setting the Stage for Mastery

Developing a Working Hypothesis, Goals for Growth, and a Plan of Action

Five-year-old Javier has always been challenging, but recently he's become frighteningly explosive. This intense boy with the big smile is doing so poorly that his childcare program's director has urgently assembled a meeting of all staff who work with him. Teachers jump in quickly with a range of concerns, reporting that they've had to evacuate Javier's classroom twice in the last week when he started knocking over chairs and tables, that he has to be shadowed constantly for safety reasons, and that in recent days they've been kicked and spat at in the midst of his angry episodes. Everyone involved cares a lot about Javier, whose life at home has never been easy. But they fear having to ask him to leave the program. Though they're used to youngsters from such stressed families, and committed to nurturing them through their preschool years, this level of upset can't go on much longer.

Taking a Detailed Look at a Child's Experience

The last three chapters have explored factors that may contribute to children's difficulties, and introduced some of the principles behind approaches to helping out. This one assembles that information into frameworks for observation, reflection, and intervention. These frameworks help clinicians stay focused yet open-minded through the process of gathering information about children's experiences. They provide a structure in which to organize what's been learned, thus making it easier to generate a provisional understanding of the issues at hand. Finally, they serve as guideposts in the development of practical action plans based on that understanding.

In simplest terms, we're returning to our three core questions: *What do we see? What do we think? What do we do?* This progression from reflection to action is a nuanced affair. We note the intricacies of a family's history. We pay close attention to the interplay between the way a youngster is "built" and the interactions he's had with those who care for him. We factor in issues of class and culture. We bear in mind the wide range of what's normal in a child's early years. Then, after laying out the areas of vulnerability that will guide our interventions, we take great care in coming up with strategies that will feel doable to the parties concerned.

Gathering Information and Making Meaning: Categories and Questions

The first framework used to guide this process is best outlined as sets of questions, those that clinicians hope to answer through gathering information about a child and his world:

Developmental Profile: What are this child's areas of strength? What developmental tasks challenge him?

Constitutional Contributions: How does this child's constitution play a role in his struggles? His successes? Did constitutional vulnerabilities make him hard to care for early on? Could resulting tension in his interactions with caregivers have set off further difficulties?

Relational Experience: What is the quality of his relationships with the most important adults in his life? What do we know about his early experiences of connection and disconnection? Have troubling experiences in his parents' lives—connections and disconnections of their own—made it difficult for them to be attentive, stable, and loving as caregivers? How does he get along with his siblings? With any cousins he sees regularly? With his peers? How does closeness or conflict in these relationships with other children impact his behavior? Finally, has he been cared for outside of the home? If so, what quality of care and what kinds of relationships has he experienced in those environments? Have his caretakers been steady or has there been significant turnover? Has he moved from setting to setting? How often? Why?

Overall Family Functioning: How does this family function as a unit? How organized and secure does it feel to its members? How do they express their care for each other? How do they negotiate conflict when it arises? Are there family issues that cause the child in question to feel stressed, confused, or frustrated? Does the family struggle financially? Have stable and safe housing? How has its culture, or mix of cultures, shaped this child's experience? Is the language spoken at home also spoken at school? If not, is that a factor in the difficulties we see?

Significant History: Are there recent situations that have made this child's life harder? What do we know about his earlier years, including losses, difficult experiences with siblings, medical problems, and previous developmental concerns? Is he adopted? If so, and not at birth, what do we know about his experiences pre-adoption? About the settling in process for everyone post-adoption? Is there any known trauma, neglect, or domestic violence? Has the child witnessed violence in his community? Has he been removed from the home at any point?

Emotional Issues: What is this child's inner experience of self and world? In what areas of his life, and with which people, does he feel strong, competent, and secure? Do unmet needs, grief, anxiety, anger, or helplessness play a role in his troubles?

Triggers for Problematic Behavior: Are there certain times of day, particular emotional states, or specific precipitants that set off the behaviors of concern? Are there predictable stretches of the day or types of activities during which he does well?

Behavioral Feedback Loops: What can we note about the current interplay of this child's behaviors with the reactions of parents and teachers? His siblings? Other children? How do these patterns relate to earlier patterns at home or in the world? Have behavioral feedback loops played a role in amplifying his difficulties? Are there particular people whose interactions with him seem especially helpful? What do those interactions look like?

In returning to Javier's team meeting, it becomes clear how these questions help in fleshing out the complexity of a child's situation. Much of the information discussed in the meeting isn't new to staff, but they're hoping that stepping back to reflect on it as a whole will help them understand why things have gotten so out of hand.

What Do We See?

Background Information

Javier's mother Catarina is twenty-two. Originally from Brazil—where most of her close-knit family still lives—she strains to understand and speak English. Catarina had a tumultuous relationship with Javier's father, an older Brazilian who eventually left her for another woman and who isn't currently involved in his son's life. Javier asks about his father regularly, knows he lives locally, and seems quite unhappy that he never sees him. There is no known history of abuse or neglect. However, Javier did witness some violent scenes between his parents when he was very young.

Money at home has always been very tight, and at one point Javier and his mother lived in a homeless shelter for several months. But things have recently changed for the better. Two years ago, Catarina met Elias, then twenty-one, and they now have a three-month-old son. Elias—who works steadily for a local construction company—lives with the family, and picks Javier up from preschool at least once a week. Javier adores him. He loves his baby brother too, but can be rough with him, clearly jealous of all the attention this sweet-tempered infant gets at home.

Staff describe Catarina as loving, shy—perhaps due to language issues—and very committed to Javier. Catarina has always found him to be an energetic handful though. Last year, she sought help from a local program for young parents, where she got some support for herself, and some guidance on setting effective limits. This year, she's trying harder to be firm, but still seems intimidated by her son.

School Observations

Javier thrives on getting one-on-one attention in the classroom and thoroughly enjoys his therapy hour with the program's on-site clinician. It's hard for him, though, when his therapist ends their session or teachers move on after spending time just with him. At these times, he can become increasingly frustrated and defiant, at which point the adults in question usually stick around for longer than they'd intended. Concerned about the potential for out of control behavior, they often feel there's no other choice.

This pattern is embedded in classroom life at other times too. Teachers report that they feel intimidated by Javier's terrible outbursts and, as a result, "tiptoe" around him so as not to set him off. Some of these times are predictable: Javier often has trouble during routine transitions and at naptime. However, there are also some seemingly random moments when staff wonder if this boy misbehaves in order to get attention, for example, when he crawls under the table during snack or climbs onto a dangerously high shelf when he's supposed to be waiting in line to use the bathroom. In such situations, teachers end up spending significant amounts of energy trying to redirect him.

When such redirection doesn't work and Javier gets enraged, adult responses to his outbursts range from calm to agitated. Incidents can go on for up to forty-five minutes, during which there are often two staff members working in tandem to keep Javier contained. These adults often try to reason with Javier while he's being provocative and destructive. It usually doesn't work. When he does regain control, often after he's tired himself out, he's asked to pick up any thrown or kicked items. Then he rejoins the group.

Other Information

Last year, Javier was referred for a speech and language evaluation and now receives services from the city's early childhood program. Communication is still difficult for him, but he's slowly gaining facility in both receptive and expressive realms. Language processing is not the only constitutional issue involved in Javier's struggles, however—temperament plays a role too. In addition to being emotionally intense, he has a very high-energy level and, even on his good days, finds it hard to slow down. There is an important systemic element worth noting as well: the school's policy is to never restrain children, even if they are out of control, and staff feel that this policy makes it very difficult to keep Javier and his classmates safe.

Coming Up With a Working Hypothesis

As is so often the case, the specifics of this child's life present a complicated picture. Weaving such specifics together into a meaningful whole is always the next step. In organizing our thinking about a child, it's useful to start by looking at where he is developmentally. Then, after outlining possible constitutional, emotional, and relational contributions to his difficulties, we zero in on the triggers for his behavior and the feedback loops that ensue. The result is a working hypothesis that fuels both goals for growth and strategies for intervention. Consider, for example, the way staff break down these elements as they make sense of Javier's situation.

What Do We Think?

Developmental Strengths

- Javier loves people and relates with warmth.
- He can tune and focus if he feels safe, calm, and connected. He enjoys learning.

Developmental Concerns

- Much as he seeks out connection, Javier doesn't feel secure in his relationships.
- He struggles to understand others and to express himself.
- He has trouble managing his energy, regulating his frustration, and being flexible.
- He doesn't have a competent, can-do feeling about his ability to cope.

Constitutional Contributions

- Vulnerabilities in language processing may make it hard for Javier to talk about—and work through—his emotional upsets.
- His emotionally intense and high-energy temperament probably plays a role in his difficulties managing feelings through frustrating situations and transitions. His problems staying focused and calm may have a constitutional component too.

Emotional Issues and Relational Experience

- Javier is very sensitive to rejection, possibly linked to feelings about his father's absence and baby brother's birth.
- He's also very needy. Staff wonder how capable his mother has been of being steadily loving and attentive, given how young she is, the violence in her relationship with Javier's father, how far she feels from the support of home, and how much she struggles financially.
- His early experience of domestic violence may have contributed to Javier's feelings of insecurity, and to his difficulties staying focused and calm.

- Javier's relationships with important caregivers are now fraught with tension. Adults are feeling increasingly frustrated and helpless in his presence, and he seems less and less eager to please.

Classroom Triggers for Problematic Behavior

- The loss of attention of an adult who has been spending one-on-one time with him.
- An expectation that he share adult attention with other children.
- Transitions from free play to group time and from the classroom to the bathroom.
- A period in the classroom, such as snack or lunch, when adults are busy with setup or cleanup and aren't interacting with him steadily.

Behavioral Feedback Loops in School

- Javier gets a lot of adult attention to begin with. The needier he appears or worse he behaves, the more one-on-one time he receives.
- Reactions to his upsets are inconsistent. Sometimes teachers respond with warm support, sometimes with harsh frustration. Either way, they continue to talk with him in an effort to help him calm down. Simply put, he gets a lot of attention—both positive and negative—for his escalating behavior.
- There are few negative consequences for unsafe or physically hurtful behavior. He's praised for regaining control after a lengthy upset. Then, other than having to clean up whatever mess he's made, he's free to rejoin the group.

Creative Clinical Scanning: Knowing What to Look for and How to Look for It

The clinician's role in information gathering and hypothesis building can be important: By the time a request for help is initiated, there's usually the need for both an extra set of eyes and a knowledgeable facilitator for problem-solving sessions. The consultative process often begins with careful observation. That way, it's possible to see firsthand what staff and families see every day, and hold its complexity as we come up with some initial hypotheses about what's going on. Observing with an eye to understanding isn't a simple endeavor. We need to know what to look for and how to look for it, to keep our lens wide as we engage in a thorough process of creative clinical scanning.[1] Does a child move through the room with the bravado of a teen who's had too much to drink? Like an unsteady elder? Any hunches as to whether it's emotions, temperament, or an unusual neurology driving his gait? At the odd moment, when his face is at rest, does he appear wistful, content, annoyed? What might this look tell us about his deepest experience of self?

These examples only hint at the questions explored in the course of observing preschoolers, and there's an additional set of questions necessary for work with kids in elementary school. When does a child start to doodle or look out the window? Does he ask to go to the bathroom more during spelling than during social studies? Does he call for help when he needs it? Does he call for help when he *doesn't* need it? (And why might the latter be true?) Does he appear sad, angry, or just dreamy when he's on strike while the rest of the class is hard at work on their journal entries?

Becoming a skilled observer takes time, and it helps to have a mental (or actual) list of categories and questions like those outlined earlier in this chapter. No list, however, can do justice to the subtleties of good observation. I often ask my student interns and newly graduated supervisees to go into classrooms once a week and do nothing more than observe a single child for at least an hour. Occasionally, I even observe during the same period. Then we spend a full supervision session going over what they've seen, what they've missed, and how to make sense of their observations—the range of possibilities that could account for complex units of behavior and emotion. What are the "soft signs" that might suggest an underlying neurological component to a child's dreamy disconnection? How does a youngster's explosiveness connect to his mangling the simple story of last weekend's trip to the zoo? Why does an only slightly irritated expression on his teacher's face appear to set off his newest escapade?

Functional Behavioral Analysis: A Frame-by-Frame Focus on Context and Behavior

There's another piece to good observation, a frame-by-frame focus on the feedback loops that surround worrisome behaviors. We ask: If we look *really* closely, can we discern a pattern to a child's difficulties? Is there some predictability, for example, to when a youngster explodes? Does a shy child *ever* talk when her teacher asks a direct question? When does that shy child crack a smile? Then, if we set a child's behavior in larger context, is there a pattern there too? Are Mondays harder than Wednesdays? Is it more difficult for a child to come into school after being at her mother's house than her father's? Such questions are answered through the process of "functional behavioral assessment."[2]

Functional assessments can be more or less detailed. In their simplest form, adults note, in "A-B-C" fashion, what took place just before a problematic behavior occurred, what the child actually did, then what happened in response: Antecedent, Behavior, Consequence.[3] The time of the behavior is noted too. Consultants can do A-B-C analyses while in the classroom. Teachers and parents can have a piece of paper or notebook handy and do them as well. Their results are sometimes surprising and often useful. What may be learned is that a child either *gets* or *avoids* something as the result of his troublesome behavior. (Javier hears that a favorite adult is about to move along, starts to escalate, and the adult sticks around for far longer than intended.) Or it may become clear that certain behaviors function to give children the extra stimulation they crave, or to reduce a level of stimulation that feels overwhelming. (Beyonce, who has trouble sitting in close quarters to others, is so wiggly at group time that she's asked to leave. Then she gets to play quietly at a separate table.)

Functional analyses also help interested adults see that particular times of day are more likely to end up in unfortunate crises. These adults may note, for example, that a child almost always starts misbehaving while out on the playground or during naptime. In addition, such analyses sometimes illuminate how a child's behavior is tied to specific factors at home. Thus, it may become clear that a youngster's more focused, relaxed days follow extra time spent with a parent, or the weekend-long absence of an explosive, scary sibling. Such situations are understood to be "setting events," general contexts rather than clear precipitants for behaviors of concern. Setting events can also include the overall tone of classroom life. We may note that Mei-li does worse during chaotic classroom cleanup times, better when they're calm and orderly. That she handles group time fairly well if the way kids find their seats doesn't involve a lot of jostling for position, but if pre-group tussling causes her to lose focus, she becomes—and remains—a wiggly mess.

There are far more detailed options for functional analysis as well. Charting how often and at what times of day certain behaviors occur, such options allow adults to note exactly what precipitates those behaviors, the range of what a child obtains and avoids through his actions, and the consequences he does (or doesn't) receive in response. These versions of functional analysis can be time-consuming—and initially confusing—to fill out. Wonderfully informative in their specificity, however, they work well for consultants who have the opportunity for extended classroom observations. They can also be an excellent option for teachers and parents who don't feel intimidated by their requirements.

Part of a clinical consultant's job is to figure out whether some type of functional analysis will be useful, and whether it should be done by a specialist or in partnership with parents and teachers. If the latter, it's important to think about how formal and how detailed a process to initiate, weighing the trade-off between specificity and usability. We don't want to lose too much complexity in our efforts to see clearly, but we don't want to lose the goodwill of the parents and teachers who are our partners in care either.

Whether in a highly detailed or a less elaborate form, functional analysis helps adults see a child's behavior more clearly and understand it more fully. Most importantly, it allows those involved to take stock of patterns they've probably sensed all along but haven't put center stage. ("So it looks like Javier almost always has a problem when you've been playing with him and have to go. And it does seem that he then gets you for longer, even if you're annoyed with him.") Added to the rest of our endeavors to understand, such analysis also helps us make connections between the patterns we see and the deeper meaning they have. ("Could it be that when Javier has to let go of the adults he likes, it sets off an awful feeling of neediness? And that right after that comes anger?") Finally, it encourages everyone's awareness of the connection between a child's developmental mastery and his patterns of behavior. ("Can Javier ever stay calm if he's getting frustrated? What do you do that helps? What makes things worse?")

The Power of Understanding and Empathy: Moving From Rigid Judgment to Curiosity and Warmth

We use the perspective functional analysis offers in the context of open conversation, inviting teachers and parents to bring a flexible curiosity into situations often filled with rigid judgment. The goal of all this exploration? Partly, of course, to have a clear enough feel for what's going on to be able to design good strategies for intervention. But that's only a piece of what we're aiming for. Sometimes the process of reflection itself has a remarkably positive impact on the quality of a child's relationships with the adults who care for him. This can happen as a result of school-based reflection—as it does in Javier's case.[4] Clinicians' early dialogues with parents can be just as transformational.

Chapter 4 investigated the content of these dialogues with parents, and that content won't be revisited here. Suffice it to say at this point that for clinicians, the reflective process with families can be taxing in its joint demands for clinical sophistication and personal warmth. For parents, on the other hand, it can be both freeing and energizing. Recognizing that they've been trying as well as they know how even if they sometimes feel like they're doing a terrible job, they see that if we understand together what has been going on and find some different ways for them to react to it, things could start getting much better. It's striking to note, in fact, that sometimes the most useful conversation practitioners have with families is the first or second one, when a feeling of clarity emerges from the complex web of data.

When meaning becomes clear in this way, a kind of potential may get released that allows parents to begin interacting quite differently with their youngster. Thus not infrequently, even before clinicians have begun to recommend specific strategies, parents come in saying things are considerably improved at home. There's something about the offering of insight and empathy for all the players that can be a powerful intervention all by itself. That's not to say that we don't need lots of potential strategies in our back pockets. But a clinician's overall stance—that kids have certain vulnerabilities, and that the way they interface with parents' own ways of being can play out in interactions that sometimes make things worse—can have a real impact on parents. Especially if it's experienced during friendly conversations laced with a feeling of hope. Hope rests at the center of our work as clinicians, as we encourage adults dealing with a difficult child to keep their sense of humor and their sense of perspective, and to keep an eye on the future rather than getting mired in the present. It's this looking to the future that we turn to next, in an exploration of how to formulate goals for a child's growth.

Setting Goals for Growth: Turning Problem Statements Into Teaching Agendas

The following discussion assumes that a team of concerned adults have gotten the help they need to land on a good working hypothesis—one that illuminates the reasons for a child's difficulties by integrating history, constitutional factors, emotional and relational issues, and behavioral feedback loops. The next step is to use that hypothesis to come up with overall goals for that child's growth. *In formulating these goals, we turn problem statements (Javier gets furious and explosive when staff have to leave) into pictures of a child's developmental skill deficits (Javier doesn't yet know how to regulate feelings of frustration and intense need). Then we reframe those skill deficits as positive agendas for teaching (Javier will learn to notice when he's starting to get overwhelmed, and have specific strategies to use in calming and redirecting himself).* However, goals for intervention can't only speak to skill development. They must also focus on meeting a youngster's emotional needs and changing problematic patterns of interaction. Once there is clarity about these three aspects of the work ahead, goals are chunked down into smaller units, so both children and adults can experience success. At that point, the approach's specifics are sketched out clearly. A look at what emerges from school-focused brainstorming about Javier will illustrate this process.

Overall Goals for Javier

Developmental Mastery

Support growing abilities to

- regulate emotions, frustration, anger, and intense need in particular;
- be flexible in the face of demands to share—or let go of—adult attention;
- sustain and enjoy play and conversation with peers;
- regulate energy;
- use language to get needs met, and to talk about feelings and solve problems.

Emotional Growth

Encourage feelings of

- safety, trust, and inner wholeness;
- security about getting needs met;
- pride, confidence, and resourcefulness.

Changed Patterns of Interaction

Work to offer

- less adult attention—both positive and negative—in response to inappropriate behavior and provocation, more friendly adult contact in response to competent behavior and engaged involvement;
- more clarity and effective containment throughout any process of limit setting, less adult lenience in response to intimidation or manipulation.

What Do We Do?

Core Approach

Once adults have agreed on the goals they share for a child's growth, they must develop an overall picture of the work involved, what might be thought of as a child-specific "core approach" to intervention. Consultants often play an important role at this point in the process, as they make sure that this approach speaks to the range of goals previously set out. Here is the overall picture staff come up with for their work with Javier.

- Staff will connect warmly with Javier before supporting his thinking ahead in facing predictably problematic situations, aiming to insert clear, positive choices at times when his neediness, anger, or energy is building. They'll use uncomplicated, short sentences when offering Javier help in managing frustration, because his language processing abilities, always a challenge, get weaker as his emotions get stronger. In addition—and also in response to these processing vulnerabilities—a number of the strategies used will have a visual component. When Javier is successful in using help to avoid an upset, he'll get some positive reinforcement.
- Staff will seek out frequent opportunities for enjoyable connection and conversation, thus strengthening Javier's feelings of pleasure and confidence in relationships.
- Staff will agree on a predictable plan for intervention (see below), one that involves clarity about when it's appropriate to provide Javier with support and help as he tries to think his way through an emotionally charged situation, versus when they should no longer offer extensive attention in the midst of an upset.
- Javier will understand the basics of this plan and his mother will too. Staff will stay in regular touch with Javier's mother about his successes, so that both she and they can convey to Javier their pride in his accomplishments.
- Staff will check with the state's department of early childhood services and with Javier's mother in order to get consensus on the occasional need for safe, supportive, and unthreatening holding —though only for times when they've calmly tried other options and Javier continues to be dangerous or physically hurtful to others.

Specific Strategies

Once an overall approach is in place, its specifics are teased out. It's at this point that consultants offer whatever help and ideas may be needed, while leaving plenty of room for teachers (or parents) to be creative and involved. Brainstorming rather than handing out marching orders is almost always wise. Here are the specifics designed by Javier's team at school.

- *Choice Board*: Staff will make a visual "choice board" for Javier, to be used at times when he has to let go of a favorite adult's one-on-one attention. The board will have three options of acceptable activities visualized by three separate pictures.
- *Cue*: About two or three minutes before Javier has to let go of an adult's attention, he'll get a friendly cue that it will soon be time for that adult to move along. Then he'll be offered the board and will point to his choice. After that, he'll practice his letting go ritual, described below. ("Hey Javier, that's a great choice you made! Good job! Now let's practice our good-bye with our super handshake. Then we can play a little longer before we have to stop.")
- *Ritual*: Javier's ritual will start with some simple words, *the same each time*: "Okay Javier, I have to go now. Can you say, 'Bye Karen [therapist], we'll play again soon'?" Then, Karen (or one of Javier's teachers) will say, "Bye Javier. We'll play again soon!" Following these words, a friendly handshake will mark the ritual's completion, once again the same each time. Once the adult in question has helped Javier make a choice and practiced the ending ritual, they'll play with him for another minute or two. Then they'll bring him to his chosen area and complete the good-bye routine.
- *Personalized Story*: Javier's teachers will create a simply stated, illustrated storybook about his learning to get calm in school (see Chapter 11 for more on such stories). Both his therapist and school staff will then read it to Javier on occasion, taking care to bring it out when he's doing well or before a predictably difficult transition—the best times to help easily frustrated children think out alternatives to their challenging behaviors.
- *Lending an Ally*: Teachers will offer extensive scaffolding—including modeling and supporting social scripts during play—as Javier learns to share staff attention with friends, and to negotiate with those friends in thinking up play scenarios and solving problems. They'll also support Javier's use of increasingly complex language and ideas, and give him the benefit of some friendly coaching as he works on sustaining play with friends. In essence, staff will lend an ally to support communication, attention, frustration tolerance, energy regulation, and social skill.

Behavior Management Plan

The following approach aims to diminish Javier's periods of escalating behavior, and to address problematic inconsistencies in adult reactions at those times. With clear choice points along the way, it involves quick intervention and neutral handling once Javier has lost control or become overly manipulative. The plan is broken into steps.

Step One: The whole class will do some red light/green light work. "Red light" tells children to stop what they're doing, put their hands down, and get quiet and ready to listen. "Green light" means go. (Eventually, adults use the space in between to help youngsters develop impulse control by thinking out rather than acting out the solution to a problem.) Staff will start red light/green light training with playful games at group time. Thus, kids will dance and then have to stop, pretend to play with toys and then have to stop, pretend to be angry monsters and then have to stop, and so on. "Green light" will cue them to be on the move once again.

Step Two: Once the children have gotten the hang of the game—and Javier its stop-start implications—staff will begin to use it as an intervention strategy throughout the school day. *At first, they'll follow the request for "red light" behavior only with friendly interactions with Javier.* Even after they begin using the cue to help him develop impulse control, they'll also continue using it regularly to promote friendly, nurturing exchanges—this will help the strategy stay positive.

Step Three: After Javier's response to the signals is reliable, teachers will show him that if they ask for red light behavior when he's mad, he can use their help to make a good choice, do some problem-solving, or go to his peaceful pillow to calm down. *If he does any of these, he'll get a happy face or a star on a special chart.*

Step Four: If Javier does anything unsafe—and there will be a clear, short list that he's aware of—staff will quickly remove him from activities. He'll be required to stay in a corner of the classroom away from the other children, or in the school's office. Staff will talk to him minimally when he's out of control, quietly reminding him only that he needs to calm his body and stop his words. Assuming that staff get consensus on the occasional need for supportive holding when all other approaches have failed (and they do, from the relevant state agency and Javier's mother), he may be held gently and safely until he's regained body control.

In these situations, staff again will be sparing in their verbal interactions, quietly reminding Javier every so often that he needs to calm his body and stay quiet, and briefly supporting his increasing control. ("Good, your legs are getting calm...Now your arms can get calm too...Soon I'll let go of your arms and we'll we stay here for a little while.") When he has himself back in hand, there will be a mild consequence for his lack of safety, something both neutral and boring. ("You did a good job calming your body down. Now you can sit here quietly while Dave puts out snack. In three minutes you can come back with your friends and have some fun!") Note that an important element of this plan is that Javier will learn about its specifics in advance. ("This will help you stay calm. Here's your peaceful pillow. Here's where you will sit if you hit or kick or throw.")

The Consultant's Role: Holding the Process and Staying in Touch

At the end of the team meeting, staff acknowledge feeling both energized and uncertain. Will they be able to help Javier quickly enough to keep him in the program? In the heat of the moment, how will they manage to figure out whether to be supportive or firm? It sounds great on paper to give him attention mostly when he is doing well, but he's so persistent in his demands. They can see this whole thing backfiring. And what about the needs of the other children? Is it fair to be giving Javier so much of their time when many of his classmates have troubles of their own?

As consultants, we hear such legitimate, frustration-filled questions all the time. Our job, in part, is to "hold" the process. We cheerlead and commiserate. We respect parents' and teachers' commitment and take heed of their exhaustion. Sometimes, we spend time in the classroom, offering ourselves as one of the team who will lend an ally to a child in need. It's a real plus when we're able to do this. We get to know children better, can bring our clinical acumen directly into their daily worlds, and can informally mentor and support teachers all the while.

There's another crucial element of consultative work: staying in touch about how things are going. Suppose that everyone involved has come up with a shared understanding and parents and staff have gotten to work, starting where a youngster is in his functioning, using a chunked down approach to mastery, and paying attention to the quality of interactions at home and in school. Now the clinician who has been helping with this process has the task of tracking how interventions are affecting the child's growth and behavior. We ask, over and over again: *What did he do? How did adults respond? What impact did those responses have? What should happen next?* We look at these questions both in relation to specific moments and over longer stretches of time.

If parents or teachers are trying out a strategy and it doesn't appear to be effective, clinicians might first inquire about how that strategy is actually being used. It's not uncommon to discover that adults have learned an approach's basics but not its intent: parents who, in setting firmer limits, are barking out their instructions like drill sergeants, teachers who, in offering more skill-building assistance, are approaching a child with all-too-apparent frustration. In such cases, after some fine-tuning, an approach may have a better outcome. Sometimes, though, the ideas we've come up with, even after some adjustments, just aren't working well. In these situations, it's important to keep in mind that there are many possibilities to account for a lack of success. Occasionally, it becomes clear that we're on the wrong track altogether and need to reexamine our basic understanding of what's going on. More often, it makes sense to modify the approach in question.

It might be that a team has come up with a reasonable plan, but teachers are too demoralized by a child's or classroom's demands—or by issues in their personal lives—to make use of it. It will be important to see whether further support and exploration can generate renewed energy for the hard work ahead.[5] At other times, we're dealing with a family that is far too overwhelmed or disorganized to stay focused on a child's growth. In such cases, it may be necessary to look for more resources, or to offer more support before we tackle the specifics of intervention.[6] (With families who are this stressed, clinicians also modify goals for growth, working on increased parent-child connection and the basics of family organization as important first steps toward change.[7]) Then there are the situations in which underlying family dynamics or individual parental issues are getting in the way of success. In these cases, practitioners may weave some exploration of the issues in question into consultative work, as seen in Chapter 4, or continue with practical attempts to shift patterns at home while supporting a family in seeking therapeutic help elsewhere.

A frustrating lack of progress may also emerge in situations where clinicians understand the big picture accurately, but have suggested strategies that don't suit a child, parent, or teacher. At that point, it's important to seek approaches that "click" better for everyone. Adapting consultative work to each unique situation is where the artistry of helping children, parents, and teachers comes in. We try some things, see what works, tweak what we're doing this way and that, and change gears when a particular strategy starts to feel stale for everyone. We use humor and playfulness, and sometimes just let our agendas go for a while. It's a subtle, creative, and ultimately indescribable process.

Helping Javier certainly requires creativity. Stamina too. The week after the team meets, the program's director comes close to requesting that Catarina find an alternative setting for him. He's had a big outburst in response to the firmer limits that have been put in place, and his tantrum continues in her office for a very noisy hour. She chooses to hang on a while longer, a courageous and wise decision. After that turning point, Javier's ability to handle frustration grows slowly yet noticeably, and his capacity to feel "filled up" by the attention he gets from staff does too. About three months after the team meeting, he's having an outburst once or twice a week rather than three or four times a day, and his upsets resolve increasingly quickly. He smiles more and glowers less. Staff still feel drained by him, but can see how much their efforts are making a difference in his life.

Javier's mother is relieved and pleased. She's had her own part to play in his growth. Though the family element of this work hasn't been a focus here, Catarina has returned to the local parenting support program to do some more work on setting limits effectively at home, to get help with her own feelings of helplessness in the face of Javier's demanding behavior, and to find ways to meet his need for special time with her in the midst of life with a new baby. Her partner Elias, the baby's father, joins her for a few of these meetings, and becomes increasingly committed to his role in Javier's life. Both

Elias and Catarina are excited about Javier's growing success at school, and he takes great pride in showing whoever picks him up the happy stickers he's received after that day's successful problem-solving.

Getting Stuck and Getting Unstuck: The Importance of Reflection, Support, and Self-Care

The frameworks used to observe and understand a child's challenges—and those underlying successful intervention—can be hard to hold in mind. Furthermore, families and schools are ever-changing systems that make staying grounded in our work an even greater challenge. This is why one last principle becomes, perhaps, the most important of all. We need to remember that getting stuck and then unstuck is part of the process, and that for all adults—parents, teachers, and clinicians alike—seeking out time for thoughtful reflection in the company of others is an essential ingredient of change. It's far too hard for any one person to take on a child's struggles on his or her own. The adults most concerned about a worrisome child need company, both for the support it offers, and for the wisdom found in numbers.

It's one of the problems of contemporary living that finding opportunities for such reflection is so hard-won. Parents have enough trouble managing the ups and downs of daily life and finding scraps of time for themselves. Teachers feel torn between lesson planning, mandated meetings, and in-service trainings. Clinicians bounce back and forth between crisis management and their work with a number of needy children and families. But finding time for reflection is important indeed; without it adults feel as though they're running to catch up with themselves, while with it they can find the inner resources and clarity that allow them to get in synch with the children who need their help so badly.

Children are almost always doing the best they can; parents, teachers, and specialists are too. It's important to remind ourselves of this when we're judging ourselves too harshly for a clinical error, or when we find ourselves undeniably frustrated with a family that can't seem to get unstuck. Yet we all have lots to learn. If we can keep a sense of humor, add a dose of perspective and a dollop of affection, and then take some of our principles to heart, we'll be well on the way to answering the question: *What do we do?*

Principles for Intervention: A Review

Seeking Collaborators and Perspective

Partnering Up for Change: We aim for a collaborative approach that can be shared by parents, teachers, and any specialists who are involved. When kids experience similar strategies in different places, the impact of intervention increases greatly.

Getting Specific Before Getting to Work: Before coming up with ideas about how to help a child, we develop the clearest picture possible of what is causing his difficulties.

Setting Overall Goals for Development: Once there is clarity about why the child is struggling, we develop a set of long-term goals that flow directly from our understanding.

Keeping in Mind the Importance of Connection: In the process of developing and refining approaches to intervention, we remind ourselves that warm, loving relationships between worrisome children and the adults who care for them are far more important than any specific strategies.

Chunking Down Expectations for Growth

Beginning Where a Child Is, Not Where We Want Him to Be: We begin working where the child is on a particular developmental continuum and build from there, rather than setting expectations that fit with where we'd like him to be given his age.

Choosing a Small Number of Target Areas at a Time: We don't target too many behaviors and developmental agendas at once because doing so tends to backfire. Instead, we let some of our overall goals go for a while, allowing them to become more central after there are solid signs of mastery in other areas.

Working Step-by-Step to Achieve Behavioral Goals: We break down expectations for change into little bits so that both the child and the adults who care for him can feel successful.

Cultivating a Stance of Readiness

Thinking in Advance So We're Ready in Response: We expect problematic behaviors to occur and have strategies ready for when they do. If it seems likely that a child will experience difficulty in an upcoming situation, we try to work with him *before* he gets stuck, offering the skill-building help and problem-solving assistance that will allow him to meet expectations for behavior.

Knowing When to Lean In and When to Lean Out: We shoot for a good mix of support and skill-building assistance (leaning in) and clear expectations for behavior (leaning out). Aiming for clarity in our approach, we make sure that efforts to provide skill-building help have a patient, friendly tone while limits are set firmly and clearly. Furthermore, in seeking an appropriate

TOURO COLLEGE LIBRARY

balance between leaning in and leaning out, we keep in mind that if a child doesn't have developmental mastery in a particular area, limits may help manage behavior temporarily but will only sometimes foster growth over time.

Using a Mix of Approaches to Support Mastery

Lending an Ally to Support Growth: Targeting one or more areas of mastery, we join a child in the pleasurable activities of daily living, both one-on-one and in the presence of his friends or siblings. Then, as we offer him the feeling of being in friendly company, we provide any skill-building support needed for the slow development of competency in areas of vulnerability.

Using a Child's Strengths to Work on any Challenges: When a child's motivation is high, he will be a willing partner in adult-initiated efforts to foster growth in areas of vulnerability. Capitalizing on his areas of interest and competence, we slip in skill-building support in a way that feels comfortable and pleasurable.

Setting Firm Limits on Unacceptable Behavior: Having decided what behaviors will be targeted for limit setting—and these target behaviors will change as the child changes—we set expectations clearly and follow through consistently and calmly.

Fostering Connection While Raising Expectations: Whenever the bar is raised on a child's behavior, it's also important to support his experience of increased connection both at home and in school. Thus, we "seed" the day with friendly, pleasurable interactions, seeking opportunities for such engagement when he's doing well. Parents, in particular, also try to find fifteen or twenty minutes each day to play with the child, allowing him the chance to set the agenda, and shooting for an enjoyable experience on both ends.

Encouraging the Safe and Healthy Expression of Feelings: If a child is being asked to behave more reasonably in the face of difficult feelings, we must be sure to help him find safe places to express and work through those feelings. For some youngsters, this should include regular time with a therapist. For others, such self-expression can comfortably take place at home and in school.

Supporting Opportunities for Steady Practice: Kids who face behavioral, emotional, and developmental challenges take longer than others to learn the skills that are the hardest for them. Thus, we seek out many low-key opportunities for a child to practice the skills he lacks. Whether the work focuses on building connection, effective communication, attentional strengthening, physical or emotional regulation, increased flexibility—or many of these at once—it's this practice that helps children grow.

Monitoring and Changing Behavioral Feedback Loops

Supporting Mastery Not Difficulty: We "look for the gold," the small signs of mastery that make it clear that a child is beginning to get on track. On noticing these signs, we react warmly—our pleasure will help him feel good about himself and motivated in his efforts. At the same time, we watch to make sure that the negative attention a child gets for his misbehavior isn't functioning—despite everyone's best intentions—to reinforce that misbehavior.

Shooting for an Upbeat, Friendly Tone/Diffusing Adult "Hot Spots": If a child regularly experiences heavy doses of irritation, anger, and criticism from the parents and teachers who deal with him each day, we work to shift interactions toward a more positive and supportive dynamic. And when such tension stems from troublesome family patterns and/or emotional stress triggered by a child's behavior, those adults seek contexts (e.g., therapy and/or parent support groups) in which to sort out their feelings.

Tracking and Modifying Our Approach

Paying Close Attention to Both Successes and Failures: Once we've started using a set of strategies, we watch carefully to see what is working and what isn't. We are ready to change, add to, or modify our approaches, and use both a child's successes and continuing struggles to teach us more about how to foster growth.

Making Sure That Strategies Are Tailored to the Individuals in Question: Though it's important to find an approach that meshes with our understanding, we look to implement that approach in ways that are comfortable for everyone involved. Strategies don't come in a "one size fits all" package.

Seeking Further Consultation, Testing, and/or Services: Sometimes the assistance parents and teachers have to offer isn't enough to support a child's growth. At any step along the way, testing, additional consultation, and/or direct services from specialists may be of value. When such additional help is needed, it's important to find practitioners who are a good fit for a child and his family. Such practitioners need to be easy to get to as well, particularly for busy and financially stressed families.

Accessing Additional Family Support: Therapeutic support or increased services may be essential when families are burdened with traumatic histories, domestic violence, or significant conflict. The same is true when parents are emotionally overwhelmed, struggling with substance abuse, dealing with significant medical issues, or facing serious financial and housing pressures.

Taking Care of Ourselves

Seeking Time for Reflection: Seeking out opportunities for conversation, reflection, and support is essential to staying on track with a child. No parent, teacher, or specialist should try to take on a child's difficulties without a net of connection and knowledge to buoy them up along the way.

Finding Opportunities to Get Away, Have Fun, and Regain Our Sense of Humor: Parents sometimes feel that they need a break, and rightly so. Teachers and practitioners do too. Finding time to rest, have fun, and reconnect with other adults—and to escape the anxiety and irritation that can infuse parenting, teaching, and clinical work—can be a godsend for anyone dealing with a worrisome youngster.

6

Home-Based Strategies

Helping Parents Set Effective Behavioral Expectations

Clinicians often struggle to help parents take a look at their own part in children's poor responses to expectations for behavior: There's always the danger of setting off feelings of embarrassment that then get in the way of constructive problem-solving. Using the analogy of animal training is one way to add some lightness to such explorations. Thus in parenting groups, I frequently tell the story of "Spot," a lovable charmer and inveterate beggar, though no one in his family much appreciates the latter. Of course, though the grown-ups in this family would like to think that dogs will be dogs, they and their children have unwittingly taught Spot to beg. Here's how.

> *It's close to dinnertime, and with the kitchen smelling so enticingly, Spot has been hanging around for a while. But now an adult directs him OUT in no uncertain terms—voice clear, hand signal indicating a place just outside the open kitchen doorway. The family sits down at the table and digs in happily. At first, there's Spot, lying down just where he's supposed to be. Then, while no one is looking, he makes his way toward the table. Staring at each family member longingly, his eyes seem to register every bite they take.*
>
> *"NO BEGGING SPOT . . . OUT!" Spot skulks back to his designated place, and stares at the family from there. This cycle repeats at least three or four times before dessert is finished. Five days out of six, or nineteen out of twenty, that's the end of it. But every once in a while—oh GLORIOUS day—someone relents. Spot has surreptitiously made his way almost to the table, and that charitable someone sneaks him a tidbit. The tidbit might be rather small from a hungry dog's point of view but, small or not, snap—it's gone.*

Five days out of six or nineteen out of twenty, that's how a family teaches a dog to beg. The basic principle underlying this learning process, familiar to anyone who has studied behaviorism, is one of intermittent reinforcement at variable intervals. It's a powerful way to shape behavior: If Spot has learned through experience that *at some point* the wonderful event he is waiting for will indeed occur, he'll keep on begging until it happens, even if it takes—in his doggy universe—a very long time.[1]

Describing the antics of a dog like Spot doesn't just add humor to conversations with parents, but also allows them to see what's happening at home with a fresh eye. Because moving from an understanding of why dogs beg to a feeling for why children misbehave is simple enough: It's often the same kind of reinforcement at work. Consider five-year-old Johnny's experience, for example. It's bath time and Johnny doesn't want to stop playing. He starts whining and complaining. Five days out of six, or nineteen out of twenty, his father insists that he stop anyway. After a fair amount of squawking, Johnny does just that. But once in a while—oh MARVELOUS day—Johnny gets a reprieve. He's been complaining, as usual. Dad is tired and can't stand the fuss. Or tomorrow is Saturday and it really doesn't matter if bedtime is a bit late. Dad has some work to do and Johnny is so involved with what he's doing, why not let him have another half hour—it will be good for both of them. Teaching a child to whine.

The possibilities here are many, but the underlying principles are not. Most clinicians can remember countless meetings during which a worried parent has responded to a question about limit setting with words like these: "Well, I'm pretty consistent. I have standards and she knows what I expect." There it is—"pretty consistent"—one recipe for reinforcing a child's misbehavior. The power of inconsistency is a tough reality for many parents to face. Few adults like to be consistent all the time and, to be fair, many children do just fine even though their parents waffle on occasion. But when children have less self-control than we sense they should given their age, we do well to help adults look at what behaviors they *think* they are reinforcing and what behaviors they are *actually* reinforcing.

It gets more complicated still. As just noted, some children have learned the power of negative behavior to, at least occasionally, get them what they want. Others are born with temperaments that make it hard for them to be flexible. Still more have stressful life situations that leave them feeling frustrated or angry more often that not. Whatever the reasons, once children have ongoing problems responding to daily expectations, new patterns often emerge that support the very behaviors that worry parents the most.

Johnny has had a tough month. He's balking at almost everything and getting him to bath time is now a truly overwhelming task. Dad gives him a five minute warning, then comes back to declare that bath time has arrived. Johnny balks and whines. Dad tries to stay calm, reminding his son again that he needs to stop working on his block castle. He can continue in the morning before school. Johnny starts yelling while he continues building. A few more reminders, some bona fide screaming on Johnny's part. "Johnny, if you don't stop now, I'm going to put away the blocks and you won't be able to finish your castle at all." Dad's voice is getting shrill. Johnny keeps working. Two more threats. No compliance. Now dad loses his temper and starts screaming himself. Johnny throws the block he's about to place on the castle's tower, gets up, and stamps his way to the bathroom. Cycle complete. And what's been learned here? Turning again to basic principles of reinforcement, it's clear that Johnny has learned it takes five reminders and three threats of an unhappy consequence before dad's screaming signals that he'd actually better go take his bath.[2]

Limit Setting Isn't an End in Itself

Discipline is not a magic cure, nor an end in itself, and being a consistent voice of reason at home is hard work. But parents often commit to the task of setting and enforcing reasonable expectations when they realize that such expectations have such an important impact on developmental mastery. Sensible limit setting helps children learn

- to handle frustration when something doesn't go their way;
- to tolerate other people's ideas and agendas;
- to change tracks in response to a cue;
- to control impulses—that is, to progress from feeling to thought to acceptable action rather than from feeling to immediate (and often unacceptable) action;
- to be able to wait patiently rather than insisting that most needs be met quickly.

When figuring out how to set limits effectively, adults need an intuitive sense of what's reasonable. These days, however, many parents have a hard time finding such an instinctive anchor, instead feeling confused about how many choices and how much control to give their children (Kindlon, 2001). Other issues get in the way too. When parents work long hours, they can find it hard to pick up a cranky youngster from childcare and immediately set good limits. No parent yearns to spend the small amount of time he or she has with a child by sending him to a time out chair or depriving him of long-awaited TV time. A combination of what we might think of as the "squawk factor" and guilt often trumps good sense, and children end up getting away with more misbehavior than is good for anyone.

Getting to Work: Helping Parents Set Limits Effectively at Home

Getting on track when limit setting has been on the sloppy side isn't always easy for parents. Luckily, clinicians can offer some basic guidelines that help in the process of tightening things up. As a precursor to thinking through those guidelines, it makes sense to note the following four points:

1. If a child isn't yet able think out solutions to frustrating problems, to share space and ideas with others, or to be flexible, setting limits may manage her behavior in the moment, but won't teach her the skills she needs to feel good and behave well over time. Limit setting never works as the sole strategy to help a child learn and grow.
2. The way limits are set and enforced should fit a child's temperament. Thus the approaches laid out in this chapter will need to be modified for some children. Such modifications are explored in the chapters of Part III.

3. Whenever caregivers raise expectations for a child's behavior, it's also important to ensure that they have plenty of time to connect warmly with her. This is especially important in cases where the exhausted and frustrated adults who care for an argumentative child have lost the feeling of pleasure in her company.

4. Family dynamics loom large when it comes to helping children behave reasonably; mixed messages from different caregivers—and tension between those caregivers about the nature of appropriate expectations and effective follow-through—can lead to significant problems.

Having an Overall Plan for Change

As parents embark on learning to be comfortably in charge at home, they need an initial sense of where they're heading. Clinicians can offer some version of the plan of action that follows here. Note that the steps behind this plan draw heavily on the work of Forehand and Long (1996), Barkley (1997b), Barkley and Benton (1998), Greene (1998), and Greene and Ablon (2006).[3]

Step One: Calming the House Down

Parents begin by focusing only on setting limits they're sure they want to back up. Keeping in mind that each time they cave in response to unpleasantness, they're teaching their child to be argumentative, they work to be both "softer" and "harder": giving in cheerfully if they're not going to hold the line in any event, and standing firm on expectations they do set. As part of this process, parents learn to consider their options quickly—that way, they gain needed skill in making difficult decisions in the heat of the moment.[4] In addition, they become familiar with the kinds of disciplinary strategies needed to back up expectations, while also keeping in mind the importance of seeking out pleasurable connection with their child throughout each day.

Step Two: Working on Cooperation

This step is based on the importance of cooperation as an adjunct to compliance. Parents begin by asking for small amounts of help that their children won't consider a burden and then react with real pleasure when these youngsters respond willingly—thus setting a tone of pleasure in communal responsibility. Limits are used firmly but sparingly throughout this stage of the process, and parents learn to ask for more significant cooperation in small doses.[5]

Step Three: Raising Expectations Gradually

At this point, family life should feel calmer. Children are now used to a "no" being backed up by an effective limit, and often cooperate with small requests for help. It's time to raise expectations. Parents work on figuring out what further behaviors to target, then raise the bar gradually. Pleasurable connection remains a priority through this period, as well as slowly increased expectations for cooperation.

Step Four: Building in Flexibility

Parents are rarely comfortable feeling that they can never change their minds, nor should they be. In this final step, they create opportunities for negotiation. Emphasizing that many situations are not up for discussion and that in negotiations, some "no's" change and some don't, parents set out the possibility for compromise. The important principle here is that negotiation takes place only when the parent is comfortable with it as an option, and never after a period of poor behavior. In addition, the child must be able to tolerate a less-than-welcome outcome without falling apart. If she shows that she can't, parents wait a few weeks or months before trying negotiation again.

Using a Mix of Limit Setting Strategies

Having this overview should leave parents with a good sense of what behaviors to target and how to raise expectations incrementally. Now they need help in understanding the nuts and bolts of setting and enforcing those expectations. The following points can help them stay on track:

- It's important to get a child's attention before making a request.
- Kids respond much more readily to expectations that are conveyed with self-assurance.
- Parents should be thoroughly familiar with how to use their chosen limit setting strategies so that they can react quickly when needed.

The importance of the first point can't be underestimated: A big mistake parents make is to issue requests before their child has fully focused her attention in their direction. They may yell from across a room, talk over the television, or give instructions while a youngster is busily playing with some engrossing toys. The guidelines below, based on Lynn Clark's family-friendly approach to limit setting (1996), help them to communicate expectations more effectively:[6]

1. The parent moves near the child, perhaps even crouching down to her level.
2. He calls her name and asks her to stop what she's doing.
3. Checking to be sure he has her full attention before going on, he looks for good eye contact and a calm body.
4. The parent's stance and tone of voice makes clear that he's serious about his expectations. He doesn't need to sound harsh, but does need to sound convincing.
5. He lets the child know what is expected, taking care to declare his expectations rather than framing them as a question.

As always, adults must keep a child's temperament in mind as they work on supporting appropriate behavior. Youngsters who have trouble harnessing attention will need the extra help tuning in discussed in Chapter 10. Kids with extreme difficulties managing their anger will require a careful mix of option-focused thinking, limit setting, and problem-solving, as explored in Chapter 11. Finally, the approaches offered in Chapter 13 make clear that the children this book describes as "deep-tracked" often need firm expectations along with an extra emphasis on connection. However, flexibility in response to a child's uniqueness should not be equated with an inconsistent, "sloppy" approach to limit setting, and familiarity with the following strategies can help parents stay grounded and firm in their expectations.

Active Ignoring

When parents use the technique of "active ignoring" (Clark, 1996, p. 26), they immediately remove their attention from their child's misbehavior. Active ignoring helps reduce a child's whining, crying, or complaining, and can also be used when a parent takes issue with a child's tone of voice, or in the face of temper tantrums. The technique works as follows. Once the child has been given an unsuccessful reminder that she needs to stop what she's doing, the parent turns away. He then refrains from talking or showing signs of emotion, remaining neutral and disengaged even when the child is begging for attention. (In fact, it helps if he at least looks like he's doing something important, like cooking or reading, even if his child's noisy unhappiness is actually driving him so crazy that he can't think straight.) Then, when the youngster has finally stopped behaving unacceptably, the parent reestablishes a warm connection, saying nothing, or at least very little, about what just happened.

Time Out Plans

Time out plans come in a number of versions. Each relies on the basic principle that when a child engages in a targeted misbehavior, she's quickly directed to leave what she's doing and sit in a specified spot for a set period of time. Some plans use kitchen timers to monitor the time out, others don't. Some allow the time out spot to be in a child's room while others discourage this idea. All such approaches involve adults giving a simple cue indicating that the child is expected to meet a clearly understood expectation for appropriate behavior. If noncompliance then ensues, the child is removed from the situation. In addition, there is *little talking with kids about either their inappropriate behavior or its consequences.*[7]

This last point is crucial. When parents learn to let the limits do the work—and stay calm, quiet, and firm—the quality of family life often improves quickly and dramatically. Note that clinicians may need to be quite explicit about how a particular plan will look—and to monitor how that plan is carried out over time—in order for parents to see the results they hope for. An inconsistent, frustration-filled, or inappropriately extreme use of time out often makes things worse rather than better at home.

Clinicians can consider coaching parents on how to introduce time out plans to their children; they work best when everyone is ready for what is coming. ("This new plan will help us get along better. My job will be to yell less. Yours will be to listen better.") Sometimes, it's even useful to run through some role-plays in order to help parents master their plan's specifics. Later, additional coaching can be added as well, in particular about how to support children in anticipating potential difficulties. For example, just in advance of predictably difficult situations, parents can learn to do some friendly preview- ing, reminding the child of how hard it has been for her to stay in control at such times, and how upset it's made her to have time outs. Then they help her think of alternative strategies, and let her know that they'll be very proud if she manages herself more successfully this time around.

Some parents have trouble using time out approaches because their child won't proceed to the designated seat when instructed. In such cases, clini- cians may want to suggest (for children age 4 and up) the addition of a "good time out" plan. In a good time out, the child proceeds to her spot, stays for her allotted time, and then resumes activities without further consequences. A time out is unsuccessful when the child refuses to comply entirely, doesn't go to her seat in a reasonable amount of time, or gets up once she's there. In this case—*and only after the child has previously been introduced to the fol- lowing consequence*—she loses something that is important to her: the use of a favorite toy, the ability to watch TV for the day, access to the computer. The idea is that when the child has a good time out, being in trouble passes quickly. For each time out she refuses to do successfully, she loses something she cherishes. (Note that generally only up to four privileges can be removed, one per unsuccessful time out. If the child loses all four, parents call it a bad day and leave it at that. It doesn't help young children to have consequences carried over for days or weeks at a time.)

Time Away

Time away is quite different than time out, and can be used in conjunction with it. When a child is having trouble managing herself during a particular activity, or is generally being unpleasant and cranky, parents tell her that she needs to find something else to do, usually something that she'll do on her own. Time away may mean fifteen minutes of solo play in her room, draw- ing at a separate table, or looking at a book in a cozy corner of the kitchen. Parents insist that the child take a break, then help her find an activity that is soothing for her. Clinicians who are explaining the use of time away empha- size that *it's up to the adults to decide when the child is ready to rejoin the rest of the family*, after which they may give her some friendly support as she tries to behave more acceptably.

If-Then Contingencies

If you do this, you'll get to do that. If you don't do this, you won't get to do that. These are what we call "if-then" contingencies. As seen here, they come in two shapes. One is framed positively: When your homework is done, you can go out and play. The other involves an injunction: "If you don't get in the car right now, I won't take you to the playground after we go to the post office." If-then contingencies can be very effective when offered as clear statements of intent, with outcomes that are implemented quickly and neutrally. The problem with them is that when parents are frustrated they tend to threaten such dire consequences that they can't bear to follow through when their threats aren't effective. ("If you don't leave your friend's house *right now*, I'll *never* bring you back *ever* again.") Furthermore, as we saw in the case of Johnny and the bath, parents also tend to repeat the threat of a consequence far too many times without actually carrying it out.

When parents use if-then contingencies, they must do two things: think in advance so they're ready to react calmly in response and, while doing this thinking, focus on using logical consequences. A few examples of logical consequences follow.

Positive consequences:

If you help set up for dinner, you can have a special dessert.

If you take your bath now, you can have extra time to play.

Negative consequences:

If you don't turn off the TV, you can't watch later.

If you don't put your dump truck into the shed, you won't be able to use it tomorrow.

Limit Setting Strategies in Action

We now have a full complement of limit setting strategies available to offer parents. We have a healthy respect for how useful they can be, even while acknowledging that they must remain only a part of the approach to a child's difficulties. How do clinicians help adults use them well, and what should they watch for as they do? Consider, once more, the story of Johnny and the bath, keeping in mind the importance of two, previously noted points. One, Johnny's father has inadvertently been reinforcing his son's whining. Two, as Johnny's behavior worsens, a sequence of ineffective reminders and escalating threats has taught him to ignore requests until his father's extreme anger signals that it's truly time to comply. The clinician's efforts to help such a parent must target both problems by offering a mix of strategies. Often, it's useful to begin by running through possible scenarios, and sketching out options for effective adult responses. In Johnny's case, one such scenario and its options might look something like this:

Scenario: Johnny gets a warning that playtime will soon be over. He complains that he wants more time. Dad thinks quickly on his feet. Is he going to give Johnny some extra time to play or not?

> *Option 1*: Dad decides to postpone the bath. He then immediately and cheerfully talks with Johnny about how much extra time makes sense to them both, making sure Johnny agrees that when the time is over, he'll need to end playtime without fuss.

> *Option 2*: Dad sticks with his original request, taking a moment to help his son plan what he'll do with the remaining time so that ending won't feel quite so difficult. Then he leaves.

Scenario Continues: The dreaded time has now arrived: "Okay, Johnny, time's up. Up to the bath you go." Johnny starts whining loudly.

> *Option 1*: "No whining, Johnny. It's bath time. That's one." The time out countdown begins and if Johnny doesn't head upstairs by three, he ends up in his chair for the required number of minutes. When the time out is over, dad checks in to see if Johnny is now prepared to take his bath, and the evening's routine continues. Dad doesn't remark upon Johnny's grumpiness as he finally heads upstairs, but makes sure to have a pleasant back-and-forth with his son once he's cheered up.

> *Option 2*: Dad crouches next to his son, and firmly asks for his attention. He waits until he gets it, then continues, speaking forcefully but without anger: "Johnny, if you don't come up to the bath right now, your blocks will be off-limits tomorrow. You'll be sad if you can't work on your castle in the morning! Now, I will count to five and you must be on your way upstairs." If Johnny keeps working past the countdown, dad still doesn't lose his temper. He stands in the room, not reacting to Johnny's angry remarks and insisting only that he end playtime. Once Johnny is upstairs and in his bath (or, depending on Johnny's temperament, after the bath is done), dad reminds him calmly that there will be no block play tomorrow. "That's sad. You like your blocks a lot. I hope that tomorrow night you'll go up to your bath quickly. Then you'll get to make a new castle on Wednesday."

There are a number of core principles at work here. First of all, dad is thinking in advance, considering his options carefully before responding. His requests are clear, his voice firm, and he has sensible consequences ready to back up his expectations. Then he follows through. In the midst of his son's angry distress, he stays calm and, at times, almost disengaged, letting the limits do the work. In the spirit of reinforcing mastery not difficulty, he follows up a difficult period with positive connection when Johnny is once again doing better. He also takes care to remember a crucial fact: *Kids don't learn from limits the moment they are set, they learn from their experience over time.*

If a few days after the one described here, Johnny is playing happily and dad sets an if-then contingency for stopping to take his bath, Johnny may well remember how much he regretted causing his blocks to be placed off-limits a few nights back. And that's when—we hope—he'll make a better choice.

Attending to Parents' Feelings About Limit Setting

These strategies aren't always easy to put into practice. Limit setting is not only hard work, but it may also bring up intensely difficult feelings in parents who have experienced brutality or harshness in their own lives. I remember teaching a single mother how to use time out. Marcy looked increasingly distressed and teary-eyed as she struggled to role-play the strategies in my office. We took a break. It turned out that this woman's husband had frequently become violent at home before she finally found the courage to leave him, and both she and her older daughter—who remembered some truly overwhelming scenes—were terrified of the sound of yelling. "I don't want to scare her. She gets this look in her eyes...I feel so bad." As a consequence, she had trouble setting limits with her younger daughter.

Marcy and I changed the role-play scenario. I found a doll to stand in for her rebellious younger daughter Liana and had Marcy play her older, easily frightened daughter Kate. Then I took Marcy's part and modeled the assertive, calm voice that works best for setting expectations. "No screaming, Liana. That's one." I asked Marcy if, in her role as Kate, she felt frightened. She looked confused: "No, I don't. It's not as loud as I thought." We spent some time talking about the way family violence can leave everyone feeling frightened and disempowered. Then Marcy tried playing herself again. It took a number of tries as I reflected on how she sounded and then asked her if Liana would think she meant business. When Marcy finally discovered a comfortable voice of authority, her look of triumph said she no longer needed me to ask the question.

7

Classroom-Based Strategies

*Mentoring Teachers in the Skills of Developmental
Scaffolding*

Judith is very concerned. The director of a large, urban childcare center, she
knows that the program's "Dino Room" has a particularly challenging group
of kids. As a result, she's been offering its lead teacher Rosa extra support and
supervision. But things in the classroom are definitely going downhill, Rosa's
morale has hit a new low, and Judith fears she's in danger of losing her youngest staff member within weeks. That evening, she picks up the phone to ask
for some consultation.

A subsequent observation reveals a typically busy, somewhat raucous
preschool scene.

> Four-year-old Brianna's voice rings out as, in the dramatic play area, she
> insists on being the mother and Shyang the baby. Shyang reluctantly allows
> herself to be wrapped in a blanket. Off in the classroom's far corner, a group
> of boys playing with blocks and cars are beginning to get quite silly, as whis-
> pers about pooping and farting make the rounds. Within a few moments,
> some friendly poking and pushing has broken out. The boys get louder.
>
> Rosa goes from group to group, letting the kids know that they have a
> few more minutes of playtime before cleanup. "Boys, I'd like you to calm
> down...it's getting too noisy." They do, at least while she's there. But their
> giggles start up again once she walks away, and more poking ensues. The
> noise level in the classroom amplifies. Rosa starts singing the class's cleanup
> song, and instructs groups of children about their respective jobs. Outfitted
> in high-heeled shoes, straw hat, and an over-sized dress that covers her
> jeans and t-shirt, Brianna scowls. Rosa sticks around for a few moments of
> low-key conversation, then manages to coax the girl into putting away the
> dress-up clothes before she heads to the circle area.
>
> In the meantime, the group of boys continues goofing around, their
> cleanup efforts involving a contest of speed and agility. Who will be able
> grab the "cool" cars first? Who can successfully fling the car they grab into
> the storage basket? There's some wrestling for position too and Greg gets
> hurt; he's the boy who ended up with the least interesting car, and it's not
> entirely clear if his feelings or his arm hurt more. Rosa comes over again,
> offers Greg some gentle support, then reminds the boys to calm down. This
> time, they don't even do so when she's there. Her jaw tightens as she leaves to
> join the kids who are already in the classroom's group area.

As the children gather for circle time, there is a fair amount of complaining about who will sit next to whom. The car flingers are the last to show up and, for the first time, Rosa's voice gets shrill. "Andy, sit here... no, I said HERE." Andy isn't happy with his designated spot: "I want to sit next to Patrick. He SAID I could sit next to him." Rosa glares at him. "You are going to be here next to me. And Patrick, you sit over there next to Tamar." Patrick plops himself down as asked. Andy, on the other hand, does not.

"Andy, if you don't sit here RIGHT NOW, you will leave the group." Andy stomps to the one open spot and sits down. Rosa takes a noticeable breath, lowers her shoulders, then smiles at each child in turn as she chants their good-morning song. About half the children join the singing and the rest begin to settle down. Not Brianna, however, who starts humming loudly. Andy joins in. Then, catching his friend's eye, Patrick giggles. And Rosa and her class of four-year-olds muddle their way through an irritable, fidgety group time.

Rosa is kind, dedicated, and creative. But, as in so many of the classrooms consultants encounter, her group has quite a few children who face significant developmental hurdles. Brianna, who has witnessed some terrifying family strife over the past few years, handles frustration poorly and has a huge need for control. The giggling boys know more about how to connect through being silly and rowdy than how to sustain play scenarios or conversation. In addition, many of the kids haven't learned how to stay calm and focused in the midst of distracting, noisy transitions. Rosa needs help learning to support the mastery of these individual issues, but she has another set of skills to learn too; she doesn't yet know how to keep the lid on the phenomenon of group contagion. When the three gigglers get each other going with their bathroom talk, it's this phenomenon at work. When Brianna starts humming and within seconds Andy has joined in, it's at work again. As the frustrated teacher of a very restless class of three-year-olds once remarked about trying to run group time: "One of them gets the wiggles, and it's as contagious as the flu."

After thinking about how to help Rosa, I decide to start with a focus on organizing successful transitions and managing the contagion that is taking a terrible toll on the quality of classroom life. It will be important to offer some tips on running large groups with challenging kids too. But I remind myself to tackle these goals in manageable bits because, *just like the children they care for, teachers need to learn new skills a step at a time.* Most importantly, Rosa will need support in developing a confidence essential to all teachers: that there are concrete strategies to help with many of the classroom-wide issues she faces, strategies that will allow her to take pleasure in even challenging groups like this one.

Using Transitions to Build Developmental Skill

Though not all teachers think of them this way, transitions offer excellent opportunities for developmentally focused work. We want kids to maintain an experience of internal organization when the world outside of them isn't entirely predictable. We want them to keep their frustration and energy levels low, even while they negotiate crowded, noisy spaces. In addition, when transitions go from free play to some form of classroom instruction time, children also need the ability to shift from the commotion of cleanup into the state of focused readiness that promotes successful learning. All of these skills connect to the building blocks explored earlier; as kids get better at managing themselves during these periods, they're increasing mastery in crucial areas of development.

The following list lays out the elements of developmental mastery nested in successful transition-time behavior; having them clearly outlined helps in clarifying goals for intervention.

To manage transitions from free play to cleanup to group time, kids must

- pop up and tune into signals that tell them it's time to make a change;
- change tracks flexibly—handling the frustration of having to end engrossing activities, finding a stopping point for play, and directing their focus to whatever task lies ahead;
- keep their energy and emotions regulated in the midst of increased activity levels in the classroom;
- manage their bodies and minds so that they're ready to shift into the state of calm attention that is needed during group time.

Rosa and I sit down during naptime and begin exploring this framework. Noting that a number of her children are struggling in all these areas, we come up with a plan for transition time that targets each one. Practice is at the heart of our ideas for intervention, because when children are given a ritualized structure for transitions, they have opportunities for ongoing work on the skills listed above. Not all teachers will take to the step-by-step process that follows here. Those who don't may want help finding other creative approaches to transition-time challenges. An early childhood consultant should never be rigid in offering strategies. Rather, we aim to facilitate an understanding of the developmental mastery that underlies success in a particular area, brainstorm about possibilities for intervention, and make sure that while doing the latter, we respect teachers' natural styles.[1]

Transition-Time Steps

The plan Rosa agrees to try proceeds as follows:

Step 1: *The teacher uses—or has a designated child provide—a visual or auditory cue that signals kids to freeze, most commonly, flicking lights, the sound of a bell, or a hand gesture that children copy as they quiet down.*

Many teachers, and Rosa has been one, go from group to group letting kids know what's coming next. That works fine for youngsters who are already skilled at moving through transitions, but doesn't always support growth in those who most need help. Step 1 allows vulnerable children to find and maintain internal organization in response to clear signals.

Step 2: *Children put down whatever is in their hands, stop talking and moving, and look up at the teacher. The teacher waits until all youngsters are in this state of readiness, being sure that those who have the most trouble with these expectations have responded fully.*

Here is where teachers learn to put some "muscle" into their expectations. Teachers who do use visual and auditory cues to get a group's attention often begin their instructions before the class as a whole shows solid signs of being regulated and attentive. This is frequently a mistake. In order to work on individual kids' challenges with harnessing attention and regulating energy—and clamp down on classroom contagion—it's important for an entire group to be what can be called *cue responsive*. Engaging in a quick experience of "stop, look, and listen" behavior in the midst of playtime helps kids preview the task to come and serves as a practice run at the same time, a real boost for those who need extra help transitioning.

This step sounds easy to accomplish on paper. But it's not. Some teachers find it useful to have children put their hands on their heads or in their laps. Others may choose to comment on the state of readiness they see in kids who have attended to the cue. Sometimes though, especially when a group is first getting used to a new teacher's expectations, more focused intervention is required. Then consultants may encourage teachers to initiate some playful all-group strategies that promote cue responsiveness. Here's Rosa, who has been having her group play some enjoyable freeze games. Now she's proceeding with the next step:

"Remember our freeze game? We're going to do a different kind of freeze now. When I flick the lights, this is what I want you to do. Put your toys down, put your hands in your lap, get *really, really, REALLY* quiet, and look right at my eyes. Here, I'll show you. It looks like this... Patrick, could you flick the lights when I give the signal?" (Rosa pretends to be singing and playing. Then she gives Patrick a cue for the lights, after which she quickly freezes.) "See? I put my hands in my lap and zip my lips and look up. Now we'll try it all together."

Step 3: *The teacher comments positively on some of the activities in the room. Then she informs kids that a change is coming up—in such and such a time, they'll need to stop what they're doing.*

This step is straightforward. Making sure to be both clear and positive, teachers reinforce the class's success in stopping activities and attending, convey appreciation for what's been going on, then preview the upcoming transition. Here's Rosa once again:

"Good job freezing, everyone. We've had a great morning, and I see some wonderful activities going on all around the room! Okay, it's five minutes until cleanup. Ian [assistant teacher] and I will be coming around to help you get ready. You can play now."

Step 4: Teachers find any child or groups of children who have difficulty transitioning, and offer extra support for planning out a successful ending and cleanup time.

Step 4 can be crucial for the kids who struggle the most. In between the cue that signals the upcoming transition and the transition itself, teachers find the kids who have difficulty switching gears. Beginning by encouraging kids to tune in to the adult's presence and then engaging in a few pleasurable circles of connection, the adult follows with some one-on-one work previewing the change to come, helping children plan out what they'll do, and conveying confidence that they'll be successful:

> "Hi Brianna…I was wondering, are you the mom or the big sister here?" (Rosa looks for eye contact, smiles when she gets it, and engages in a few pleasurable exchanges with her student.) "That looks like fun! Let's think a little bit. What will be a good stopping place for when I flick the lights? Do you remember yesterday how it was hard to clean up when you were sad to end? Could you try putting away two things today without getting upset? I'll be so proud of you when you do, and when you come to circle, I'll want a high five!"

Step 5: The teacher repeats the visual or auditory cue, children freeze and—after it's clear that all kids have been successful in calming their bodies and harnessing attention—gives instructions for cleanup. Before kids "unfreeze," each child and group knows their job. If there is an assistant teacher in the room, that teacher joins the child or group that has the most difficulty preparing to transition, lending an ally to support calm and focus during these instructions.

There are any number of tricks teachers can use to help kids stay focused and calm during cleanup. One preschool teacher might pick a small item from the area to which each child will be assigned, even if it's not where they've been playing, and hand the item out while naming the job in question. This allows her to separate kids who don't work well together, and keep each cleanup group to a manageable size. Another may have children gather briefly and talk about what they've been doing. Then jobs are assigned, with kids having a laminated card indicating where they'll be working. The card is returned, in exchange for a hand stamp or high five, once they are sitting quietly in preparation for group time. Yet a third will use the freeze period to read out tasks from a job board; groups of children are released from their freeze after they know what to do.

Part of the rationale behind these strategies is to make sure kids are clear about their jobs, *and to keep down the numbers of children cleaning up in each area.* There is no quicker way to ruin a transition than to have seven kids flock to the block area for an overly rambunctious cleanup, or to end up with four youngsters in a tussle over who gets to put away the fancy purple dress in the cramped dress-up corner.

Consultants can help teachers accept that not all children are able to handle the normal demands of cleanup time, even under the best of circumstances. Children who can't may be more successful if they're separated completely from their classmates and given a task with a sensory component. Some will enjoy cleaning brushes at the sink; others may like washing off the tables with a damp, warm sponge. Teachers are coached to get to these kids *even before jobs are assigned* and to let them sit or stand—in freeze mode like their classmates—in the spot where they'll begin their task. This allows easily over-stimulated kids to avoid the commotion that often starts off the cleanup period. In these cases, a small adjustment in a teacher's expectations results in a large gain in the overall calm of the classroom.

Step 6: *Children clean up, while teachers lend their presence to kids and groups that need extra support.*

This step, often missed, can be essential to effective transition-time work. Teachers predict which kids are likely to need additional scaffolding, check in with each other to make sure the most vulnerable children are "covered," and head over to lend a hand, thus preventing the escalation that leads to group contagion.

Step 7: *As children are finishing their jobs, one teacher goes to the group area to greet them. And, when needed to avoid pushing, shoving, or arguments, children are assigned designated seating with, as just as one option, carpet squares or the like laid out in advance to avoid problematic groupings.*

Part of our job as consultants is to encourage teachers to think through and "choreograph" tricky times of day. Having a teacher and her assistant work out the nuts and bolts of who will be where—so that there is someone on the spot during the predictable moments when children begin to lose calm and focus—can be a big help. In addition, we may need to offer proactive strategies for groups in which children regularly argue about their seats, helping teachers foster a group's understanding that "you get what you get and you don't get upset." (Teachers won't have any trouble knowing when they need some guidance in this direction because when they do, they'll have been irritatedly repeating some version of this rule many times throughout each day.)

Step 8: *The quality of the short period during which kids are wandering over to the group space often has a big impact on the success of circle time, and a low-key activity available to children upon arrival may prove helpful. Thus, teachers may choose to have a quiet rhythm or motion game, song, or conversational theme going as children settle into their seats.*

Step 9: *Once all the children have gathered, a quick "stop-look-listen" cue helps kids get ready for group time.*

When group contagion has taken over the feel of a classroom, some tweaking of how transitions are run is almost always in order. Whether proceeding through the above steps—or using a different but equally goal-directed approach—teachers will need a surprising amount of skill and good humor in their efforts, especially if a group contains numbers of easily frustrated or over-stimulated kids. In fact, it sometimes takes a consultant two or three observation and problem-solving sessions before a teacher lands on a comfortable, effective way to support transition-time mastery. First, we help in designing a plan. Later, we observe how it's carried out, noting which kids are still struggling. Then we brainstorm about any changes needed. In the end, teachers almost always feel that such time has been well spent.

Teaching Prosocial Behavior: Creative Approaches to Group Instruction

The next area of exploration is group time. What makes such periods feel productive to a teacher? Consider Rosa's response to a question about how circle time went last year. "Well, not perfect every day. But, I had fun and did some neat curriculum. I felt like I was doing fine really...the kids weren't so squirmy like this year and, mostly, they took turns talking. This year the kids all want to talk at the same time and they get so frustrated. They call out or else their hands are waving like if I don't call on them right away they'll explode or something. And the thing is, some of the kids who were doing well, they're acting up now too."

She knows what she's looking for. Most teachers do. *Group times go well when children are settled and focused, when content holds their interest, and when they manage the frustration of waiting their turn as they share conversational space with the teacher and other kids in their class.* Once again, we see a number of developmental building blocks at play. As usual, proactive approaches help kids develop the skills they require to show mastery. The first thing that's needed is for children to learn what adults want from them. And although that may sound easy, some youngsters find it strikingly hard. In response, as the consultant we're about to meet emphasizes in workshops for early childhood educators, teachers often end up scolding kids rather than breaking down and teaching them the skills they require. Here's Loretta, speaking with a group of teachers.[2]

> "I was a preschool teacher for many years...And when I first began teaching, I had the feeling that I kept telling these kids to be good or behave in some abstract way. But they didn't know what that meant. I thought that if I could figure out how teach kids what I wanted in a positive way, and reinforce it in a positive way, they could begin to pull themselves together."

Enter Duffy. Duffy is a large, floppy-eared dog who lives in a basket that Loretta began to keep in her classroom closet. Not a real dog, of course. A hairy puppet with a drawling voice and a quirky, loveable habit of speech: Duffy is particularly fond of words that begin with the letter "D." Duffy became Loretta's alter ego at the beginning of each school year, and made many appearances—to the delight of her students—later on. Now he accompanies her to workshops about the usefulness of puppets in teaching prosocial behavior.

Tired after their long days in school, teachers in these workshops begin perking up soon after Loretta pulls Duffy's basket from under her chair. It's the same reaction she gets from kids when she brings him to the classrooms where she now consults. Duffy, with his shaggy hair and oversize paws, is a showstopper. His job is to help groups of kids learn to sit still, attend, and get organized cognitively—to develop the skills of what we might call "ready behavior."

In order to start his work, Duffy must get the attention of the children he's about to teach. Loretta models how her fluffy assistant arrives at group time snoring in his basket. Without any lecturing on her part, the drama of the moment begins to help children focus. Then, *in response to her playful cue*, kids must count to three and call his name. Sometimes, they have to go through the steps again before he wakes up. When he does, he has goofily warm greetings for all and a question for his boss. "Hey, **D**oretta, is it okay if I tell the kids a story? I want to tell them about when I was a puppy." The heart of Duffy's teaching agenda begins, as he relates how his teacher used to get annoyed at him when he wasn't quiet at group time.

> "When I was a puppy, JUST LIKE YOU, I would be sitting in circle, and the teacher would be talking, and I was just SO EXCITED, so I'd talk to my friends, and say hello to them and tell them things and laugh and stuff. And the teacher would say, 'DUFFY!' And I'd say, 'What?' And she'd say, 'DUFFY, I CAN'T HEAR when you are talking at the same time as me …' Oh, I felt TERRIBLE. So I'd ask, 'But what should I do?' And the teacher would say, 'DUFFY, you need to BUTTON YOUR MOUTH!' "

The storytelling continues, with Duffy explaining that he'd tell his teacher he'd try to behave better if she'd show him just what to do. He demonstrates to the kids exactly how he learned to "button up," a bit dramatically of course, and then explains that he had to practice quite a bit before he got it right. Then, *he asks kids to try practicing with him.* Duffy and his willing students pretend to be talking, and then quickly button up. By the end of the first day's lesson, he's **D**elighted by their success, tells them that they've learned far more quickly than he did in his puppy days, and gives any child who wants one a good-bye kiss before heading back to his basket. In the days to follow, he comes back—at first snoring loudly—for more practice sessions.

As the workshop continues, Loretta models the step-by-step nature of this creative instruction technique. Duffy tells more stories, first about learning to keep his paws to himself, later about struggling to keep his feet folded. The stories always begin with his being in school "JUST LIKE YOU." They continue with the same scaffolding and language Loretta has used for the buttoning up lesson, beginning with Duffy's chagrin at his misbehavior, and ending with the children getting Duffy's effusive praise after they've practiced the skill of the day. As Duffy relates his experiences and works with the children on specific behaviors, teachers get a sense of how reassuringly familiar—and thus increasingly potent—his stories become. Eventually, Loretta puts Duffy into his basket and, with an affectionate pat, places him back under her chair. "After two or three weeks of Duffy being a part of my classroom, people would come in and ask, 'How do you get kids to sit like this?' Some of these kids were really challenging, so they were surprised. But Duffy had done the work for me."

The proactive stance that led Loretta to create Duffy is a tremendously important element in any approach to mastery. As explored in the last chapter, clinicians invite teachers to take problem statements, turn them into assessments of skill-deficits, then use their assessments to frame positive agendas for teaching. Once teachers have a clear sense of those agendas, they're encouraged to break down the overall skills in question and teach them a step at a time. A child has trouble paying attention? What are the elements of attention? How can those elements be chunked down and then taught successfully? A child has trouble sharing toys? How can he learn to do this? What specific words will he need to be taught? Are there simple ways to reinforce his process of learning? In essence, we ask: How can teachers, like Loretta did with Duffy, find child-friendly, engaging approaches to boosting mastery, rather than remaining stuck managing worrisome behaviors day after day?

It's not necessary for teachers to use the help of puppets in doing this proactive work. Consultants can strongly recommend they try, however, and with a little encouragement, many are willing to take the plunge. We encourage them to start with a puppet to which they're instinctively drawn. Then, either during staff trainings or in individual consultation, they begin experimenting with different voices, with how to use hand gestures to create a sense of drama, and with puppet-inspired stories and methods that teach children the prosocial skills they lack. Puppets have the power to pull in even recalcitrant children, and they bring out a sense of play in everyone. Dolls and appealing stuffed animals can be used in the same way. But, with or without the use of pretend characters, the crucial point here is that consultants help teachers find upbeat, creative ways to teach kids what Loretta calls "a set for ready behavior."

Fostering a Positive Group Climate

Clinicians regularly face two additional challenges in school-based consultation, how to help teachers create safe, caring, and vibrant classroom environments, and how to mentor them in offering individually focused skill-building assistance. We'll look at the former first, starting with a list that is merely a sensible reminder of assumptions good teachers know and share:

- Clear, positive expectations for behavior help set an overall tone for classroom life.
- Monitoring this tone—what is often referred to as a group's "climate"—keeps a lid on the contagion factor while supporting kids in remaining calm, focused, and respectful.
- Interesting activities, a lively, varied curriculum, well-designed spaces, and ample, organized, and intact play materials go a long way in preventing behavioral problems.[3]
- Predictable, well-run routines have a big impact on helping kids feel safe and organized.
- Too many transitions in a day can make life harder on everyone.
- Children who struggle in the classroom are often not responsive to directions given from a distance. Teachers may need to move in closely and support connection and focus before giving instructions.
- Limits only go so far when kids don't have positive behaviors to replace negative ones. When necessary, limits should be set firmly but calmly, with less emphasis on judgment and more on quick feedback for inappropriate behavior. A friendly focus on developmental skill-building is always needed too.
- Kids thrive on positive feedback for their successes in learning new behavioral and developmental skills, especially when they've been experiencing a lot of irritability from the adults who care for them.

When we believe that staff should attend to any one of these principles, we must think carefully about how to share our perspective. Teachers have a relentlessly challenging job, and they can get terribly worn down. Thus it's a given that we can only offer constructive feedback if they feel understood rather than attacked. An honest, friendly, and respect-filled alliance takes time to develop, and it's always time well spent, allowing for open conversations about any number of issues: how teachers' frustration with a particular child or group leads them to come across more negatively than they intend; whether it's time for a new theme in the dramatic play area; the way in which a classroom's setup promotes cruising rather than focus; ideas for beefed-up curriculum; how more age-appropriate books will help kids stay attentive during story time. If we broach these dialogues with care, leaving space for staff to express their weariness and frustration, we can often contribute to renewed energy and optimism in the classroom.[4]

One area that particularly benefits from such dialogue is group climate. Teachers know when this overall tone is positive, because their room is ordered and calm, and both children and adults feel a sense of relaxation. When a group's climate begins to get out of hand, kids become noisier, more active—and at least sometimes—increasingly rebellious and aggressive. Group contagion quickly makes its contribution once this happens. Rosa knows the terrible tension many teachers feel when a classroom's climate starts to heat up; it's when she begins thinking about quitting her job.

Classroom climates stems from four factors:

The Elements of Group Climate

1. *Noise Level*: Can children hear each other and their teachers without straining, or is the noise level starting to bounce off the ceiling?
2. *Activity Level*: When indoors, are children moving at a relatively slow pace, or are there children running, jumping, or wrestling?
3. *Level of Focus*: Are most kids absorbed in activities that they stick with for a while, or are quite a few children cruising the room?
4. *Quality of Interactions*: Do kids and staff speak to each other with respect? What is the quality of the words they choose and the tone of voice they use in their interactions?

When these elements are positive, children experience a sense internal organization. This feeling helps them learn to handle frustration, to harness and sustain attention, and to negotiate play and conversation with other kids. Monitoring and changing a group's climate is an art that good teachers know well. The most important aspect of its execution is the "eyes in the back of the head" phenomenon.

Reading the Room: Helping Teachers Watch for the Little Signals That Foreshadow Big Problems

Down the hall from Rosa's class, Stacey is teaching too. It's calm and orderly in her classroom, and there are many reasons why. Stacey has been teaching for over twenty-five years and she has an amazing ability to "read the room." No matter where she is and which child she is attending to, she manages to keep track of what's going on in every corner of her classroom. To an outside observer, it appears that she's on top of the little spikes in her classroom's climate *almost before* they happen. Two kids are starting to argue quietly? Stacey has her ear cocked; she'll be there in an instant if she needs to be. A couple of boys *just begin* poking at each other as they play? Stacey lets them know they must stop. An easily frustrated girl mutters a nasty comment about her friend? There's Stacey, telling both kids to "come sit here, we need to talk."

Stacey's is widely admired as a teacher who rarely yells. All the same, the tone of her voice modulates constantly. There's a certain quiet sternness, accompanied by "the look," that tells kids it's time to shape up. There's a way she has of pulling kids over that shows them she's not mad, but they're going to need to do some problem-solving before they can go back to what they've been doing. There's a warmth that conveys that she accepts kids even when they've misbehaved, and a goofy sense of humor she uses constantly to diffuse the little stuff. An art indeed. She practices it with great skill and creativity, and her classroom tends to be a relaxed, fun-filled place for kids to learn and grow. Rosa can learn this skill too. When her rowdy trio of boys begins whispering and giggling, that's the time for her to head over. When Shyang *just starts* to bristle at Brianna's controlling ways, that's the moment for her to lend a hand. The eyes in the back of the head phenomenon means that teachers keep one part of their mind attentive to the little signals that foreshadow big problems, and get in for some quick intervention before those problems emerge.

As consultants, we have the good fortune to be able to observe until we get a feel for what is going on with a child or classroom. Interestingly enough, many of the big upsets we see have been brewing for a while before they erupt. However, very often, staff haven't noticed tensions rising. A teacher has her back turned and is preparing an activity. Another faces the wall as she plays with kids. It's easy for us to notice, because we have a freedom to observe that teachers don't have. But, as Stacey's presence in the classroom makes clear, teachers can learn to keep their antennae up for the little signs that say: "Time to get in there and do some climate control."

Supporting Social Skill Development in the Classroom

The final element behind effective school-based consultation involves mentoring teachers as they learn to support individual children's abilities to interact successfully. Young children with poor social skills show their vulnerabilities in a number of ways. Some are explosive and grabby. Some get started on a play theme with their friends and then drift off. Others never get involved in the first place, or struggle with the basics of communication in such a way that they're left behind as their peers animatedly share conversation and story ideas. As a result, teachers are aware of social skill difficulties on three different levels:

1. A problem has just occurred and immediate intervention is required.
2. A problem is likely to occur soon, because a socially unskilled child has just joined others in play.
3. There is no dramatic problem in view, but a child is quietly unsuccessful in initiating or sustaining connections and play.

As clinicians join teachers in exploring approaches that support the steady development of social skill, the hope is to prevent difficulties in the first category, while getting to work proactively on the other two. For the latter, lend-an-ally work—to be explored shortly—goes far in offering useful assistance. For the former, a thoughtful mix of skill enhancement and limit setting is in order. Because no matter how gifted a teacher, and how strong her focus on prevention, kids with poor social skills are going to get tangled up with each other for quite a while before they develop a steady ability to be problem-solvers in the midst of frustration. Here are two principles that help when a classroom situation has already heated up:

1. Once a child has calmed down following an aggressive incident—or, even better, *after* her temper begins to flare but *before* she has crossed the threshold of unacceptable behavior—teachers work on problem-solving with all the kids involved. But teachers need to be careful. *Dictating a solution for the children, and asking the "offending" child to say he's sorry, usually doesn't get all that far.* For one thing, he's often *not* terribly sorry at all. In addition, this approach doesn't teach him the skill of problem-solving in the midst of frustration, the lack of which led him to have difficulty in the first place.

2. If a child has done something unsafe, a firm limit may be needed. Time out and time away shouldn't be used any more than necessary; that's why our work on prevention is so important. But, kids who kick or punch will need to be removed from activities, both as a way to extinguish undesirable behavior, and to give them a chance to collect themselves so they can try again. When teachers feel they must remove a child, a quick word or two rather than a frustrated lecture or "Why did you do that?" is almost always the best choice.

Effective mentoring about such problem-solving assistance can be a consultant's biggest challenge. Teachers are often justifiably frustrated with kids who hurt others when they're denied something they covet, or who start screaming and knocking toys around when they don't get their way. In the face of this understandable frustration, the clinician's job is to help teachers cultivate a patient stance, to accept that assisting a youngster in this area will take months of steady work using strategies that are quite labor intensive.[5] It's a tall order.

I've had many tense conversations with overwhelmed, angry teachers who would like nothing more than to expel a challenging youngster from their program. (And, unfortunately, preschoolers end up getting expelled from school more frequently than any other age-group [Gilliam, 2005].) Though there are no easy solutions to this dilemma in consultation, it helps to convey the following:

- Explosive or impulsive behavior is sometimes a youngster's *only* strategy in the face of social frustration. Once that child learns some new options, he'll be much easier to have around.
- Teachers who are able to "hang in" and offer effective help to an easily frustrated, socially unskilled child, are giving that child an incredible gift. One of the most important foundations for resilience in childhood is the capacity to get along with others, and to be a problem-solver in the face of difficult situations (Werner, 2000).

- The most common intervention teachers offer when children are getting hot-tempered or aggressive, "use your words," is often inadequate to the task at hand. *These youngsters often don't know what words to use or are too upset to use them.*
- If teachers intervene as soon a problematic social issue surfaces, they can slow the conflict-filled process down. That gives them space to provide children with appropriate scripts, a conciliatory tone, and problem-solving ideas that will allow for a successful resolution.
- The rule of thumb in such intervention is to *come early and stay late*, getting to a situation quickly (or even anticipating it before it starts), then sticking around past the point when the initial problem has been solved in order to support a sustained and positive exchange of ideas and friendship.
- Showing pleasure in the conclusion of the problem-solving process—supporting one child in saying "thanks" when a peer has compromised, and then having that youngster say "you're welcome" back—helps "seal the deal" and leaves children feeling proud of their successful effort to be caring friends.
- Though this approach sounds like a lot of work, it actually takes far less time (and is much more enjoyable) than intervening after things have gotten out of hand.

Lending an Ally to Support Successful Functioning: The Nature of Developmental Play Assistance

The above list serves as a foundation for classroom-based assistance in teaching social competencies. A specific version of the assistance teachers offer is what we described in Chapter 2 as lend-an-ally work. Remember that when adults lend an ally, they start by figuring out what it is about a particular building block that challenges a child. Then they provide developmental assistance by joining him while he's involved in activities that are naturally interesting to him. Whether a parent, teacher, or clinician, we lend an ally as kids play, as they talk with friends, and as they tell stories. We sit down next to them as they eat snack, or while they're building a massive space station. Bolstering their confidence through the safety of our presence, we offer "scaffolding," support for the emergence of skills they don't yet have (Berk, 2001). When we lend an ally, we stick around for anything from a minute or two to half an hour. And staying just a mini-step ahead of a child's developmental level, we foster growth in areas of vulnerability.

The lend-an-ally help teachers offer at school is useful to a wide range of children: the angry/impulsive kids who lash out because they have so little skill in solving problems; the active kids who haven't slowed down enough to learn the basics of narrative and cooperative play; the inattentive kids who need help staying tuned into what is going on around them; and the inner-focused, cautious, or withdrawn kids who don't know how to come out of their shells and engage in some give-and-take with others. It's often done in a form we'll call "developmental play assistance," work teachers do as they join a group of children as a play partner.[6] Teachers need to remember an important rule when they do this work: *When staffing patterns provide for more than one adult in the room, they'll need to signal a co-worker that they're going initiate one of these experiences.* Without that individual doing the job of "reading the room," the overall classroom climate may start to get out of hand.

Here are some questions clinicians can use to help staff offer such assistance knowledgably:

Questions Teachers Consider Before Beginning a Play Session

- Where are the targeted children in terms of strengths and vulnerabilities in their development?
- Are there other, more skilled children who might enjoy the extra attention that a play session will provide? Can they be helpers and allies in starting and sustaining a successful play experience?
- What areas will need scaffolding from staff in order for the play session to be successful? Focus? Connection? Communication? Impulse control? Frustration tolerance? Energy regulation? Flexibility? Narrative development?

Once teachers have answered these questions, they embark on the work itself, using the principles listed below as a guide:

Principles for Providing Developmental Play Experiences

- You are the ally and the "human glue." Your job is to pay attention to what kids can't provide for themselves and to offer it as much as needed. In addition, you bring cheerful enthusiasm and, if necessary, dynamic play ideas to keep things moving. However, the ideas you offer flow from the interests and materials around you, and you stay flexible as you listen and adapt to the input of the children with whom you are playing.
- Your language, tone of voice, and facial expressions help kids stay focused and engaged with the play and with each other. At first, you may be doing a lot of the work.
- Your efforts include guiding without over-controlling, modeling, supporting, and sometimes even correcting. But what you do stays playful and enjoyable, so that the play session doesn't feel like a lesson to the kids you're helping.
- You alternate between acting like a "wise child" who plays like other kids do—but with exemplary social skill—and being a friendly adult coach who stops the action, asks gentle questions, and provides options for interaction when children are stymied about how to proceed.[7]

- Each child in a group has different developmental and emotional vulnerabilities. Your job is to support them in offering what they're good at while
  you help them develop skill in areas that are more challenging.
- As children begin to master the developmental challenges you are targeting, you pull back slowly, handing over pieces of skill as they're ready.

Once teachers learn how to offer effective developmental play assistance, they
often find it a satisfying part of their job. After participating in a series of workshops on the topic, for example, teachers at one school made some changes
in the balance of running teacher-assisted projects and making themselves
available as play partners. A few weeks after they'd made the shift, Nan, the
school's most experienced staff member, found herself surprised and pleased:
"I feel like I'm starting to make a real difference to my toughest kids. We had
a meeting after the last workshop, and we decided to do two things... make
sure we each made a good connection with every kid in the class every day, and
spend a lot more time playing with groups of children. We're definitely not
doing as many interesting projects as we were before but actually, that seems
okay. I'd say every one of us is enjoying ourselves a lot more, and the whole
feeling of the classroom has changed."

In order to have a well-developed feel for the nature of developmental
play assistance, clinicians need to understand what it looks like in action.
That exploration will take place in the next chapter. For now, we'll return
to Rosa's group of challenging four-year-olds, a few weeks after she'd gone
through the initial process of observation and mentoring.

Rosa nods from across the room when I walk in for a follow-up visit. Things
are certainly different. The kids clean up without much commotion, come to
group in an orderly way, and sit down in their assigned places, ready to listen.
They even speak one at a time. But I'm almost more concerned than I was on
my first visit. Rosa is working so hard to control her class—and to jump in
quickly with social support when things get sticky—that I'm not sure she's
enjoying herself. It's also clear that the kids have lost some of the ease they
previously felt in her classroom. As is often the case, strategies that sound
good on paper have translated into action in problematic ways.

The two of us sit down for a meeting. I ask her how things are going, and she
tells me she's not worrying about the class being so out of control. But something
about this approach leaves her feeling uneasy at the end of the day. "I think they're
scared of me now, I'm being so strict." I apologize for having given her a picture
that was different than what I'd intended, appreciate her newfound ability to get
group contagion under control, and stress that her feeling relaxed and taking
pleasure in the kids is important too. Back to work we go, rebalancing priorities,
fine-tuning strategies, finding a way to use principles for intervention that fit both
the adult and kids in question. And by the end of the year, Rosa has found her
way. She's having a lot of fun with her class, but knows that she can rein things in
whenever needed. She's beginning to have an excellent set of eyes in the back of
her head too. Already a very good teacher, one day she'll be a great one.

Part III
Specific Approaches for Specific Difficulties

8

Helping the Shy, Cautious, or Withdrawn Child

*Getting to Work When a Youngster Holds Back
From Connections, Play, and Conversation*

In the process of assisting children who are strikingly shy or withdrawn, or who appear particularly cautious in the face of new experiences, we first look to understand whether their difficulties stem in part from constitutional issues. Then we consider the contribution of their experiences at home and elsewhere, whether English is their primary language, and how their families' culture compares to their schools' culture. Once there is clarity about why a particular youngster can't jump into activities and relationships, we come up with specifically tailored strategies to help out.

What Issues Might Be Contributing to the Child's Behavior?

- Cautious, inner-focused, or hard to engage temperament
- Language processing difficulties
- English as a second language
- Cultural norms/differences between cultural norms at home and in school
- Overwhelming experiences at home or elsewhere
- Little experience with relationships outside the family

Some Points to Remember

- Many children who are markedly reserved out in the world are very talkative and social with their immediate families. Some of them are even quite bossy at home, as if they spend so much time locked up within themselves that they need to make up for lost time in the place where they feel the most comfortable.
- It's common for parents to swing between overprotecting a cautious/ shy child when he's feeling uncertain—talking and acting *for* him—and pushing him to interact before he's ready. At the same time, a mix of concern about and irritation with the child's reserve may infuse parent-child interactions, leaving the child increasingly tense about the experience of connection in the larger world.

- Teachers often feel torn between asking these kids questions they regularly decline to answer and keeping pressure off by leaving them alone. Both strategies may play a part in reinforcing the experience of reserve. Finding a way to encourage interaction without inadvertently increasing the child's tendency to hold back is an important—and challenging—element of classroom-based intervention.
- Children who are particularly reserved in school aren't interesting playmates for their peers, and often end up having a kind of invisible presence in their classrooms. Some of our intervention must target this problem, helping other youngsters see a child as a potentially interesting playmate.
- Children who speak one language at home while learning a second language at school often go through a stage when they speak little if at all. This stage, though not universal, is so common as to have its own name: the "silent period." During this period, many children talk quietly to themselves as they acquire competence in the second language, venturing forth slowly as they feel growing confidence in their linguistic skill (Saville-Troike, 1988; Krupa-Kwiakowski, 1998).
- Sometimes the same reserve that worries school staff is highly valued in a child's home culture (Chen et al., 1998). At other times, a school culture that values assertive behavior is so at odds with the cultural norms of a youngster's family that he feels quite overwhelmed in the classroom. Both situations require understanding and adaptation by school staff (Lynch and Hanson, 2004; Hepburn, 2004).

Getting to Work at Home

Allowing for Dependence While Supporting Independence

Handling Separations

These children need a nonanxious parental presence before separating for school or an away-from-home visit. Parents first provide some safe, connected time at the non-home environment, *without constant reminders that the child will have to say good-bye soon.* Only when this warm-up period is almost over do they give a cue that leave-taking will take place shortly. A quick, clean departure follows.

Providing a Secure Base From Which Children Can Reach Out

Reserved kids need their parents as a home base for longer than other children do. Parents offer a safe "anchor" from which their youngster begins to relate to others, then work to slowly lessen support. Watching that they neither push independent functioning before the child is ready, nor talk/relate for him in a way that keeps him from jumping in when he's able, they seek a delicately balanced parenting style that allows for dependence while fostering independence.

Providing Skill-Building Opportunities

Fostering the Basic Experience of Connection

Some of these youngsters need to stretch their basic ability to connect, especially those who have an inner-focused, hard to engage temperament. Starting with content and experiences that are inherently interesting to the child, parents build in many short experiences of pleasurable relating, gradually supporting his ability to engage for longer periods.

Lending an Ally to Support Involvement in Play

Parents join the child in play with other youngsters, at first almost as an alter ego. Allowing him to rely on the safety of this adult-child dyad, they start by doing most of the relating. As he begins to relax, they stay put but slowly lessen their active involvement. Throughout this process, the child is not asked or forced to speak until he's ready, but is wooed into interaction through humor, interesting play possibilities, and an experience of low-key parental support.

Strengthening Communication Skill

Children whose reserve stems from language processing difficulties—and those with constitutionally driven vulnerabilities in forming relationships— need scaffolding for their attempts to communicate. Parents offer practice in opening and closing circles of communication, work that is best done when the child's interest level is high and the experience of pleasurable connection allows him to feel relaxed.

Previewing New and Overwhelming Experiences

Assuming that their child will freeze up when encountering new experiences— or when overwhelmed by the demands of familiar ones—parents preview coming events: "We're going to the bank. Here's what's going to happen. First we're going to drive there and find parking. Then we'll go inside and get in line. There might be other people in line before us and we won't know them. Somebody might say hello to you, like that lady did yesterday in the grocery store. It's okay to just smile if you don't want to say anything..."

The second step to the previewing process happens after arrival at the place in question. Parents pause before entering in order to support the child as he looks around, allowing him time to acclimate to the feared situation: "See all these people? They came to celebrate grandma and grandpa's special anniversary, just like we said. Let's stay here for a minute to see whom we recognize. Oh, there's grandma...and there's Uncle Bill! Do you remember that you can sit in my lap until you feel like visiting with your cousins? And here's your bag of things to do for when I want to walk around and talk to people. Should we find a cozy place for you to play if you get tired of all the noise? Then we'll sit down."

Working on Family Issues

Taking a Look at Family Stress and Family Dynamics

Sometimes a youngster's inability to feel confident in the bigger world is a sign that family issues have become overwhelming. When a child's difficulties engaging stem from significant stressors at home, parents consider what they can do to make things better for everyone.[1]

Finding Time for Fun

Parents monitor whether they have enough time to feel in synch with their children and—even if it means that certain chores or errands have to wait— find opportunities for relaxed, playful, and connected experiences for all family members.

Watching for Emotional, Physical, or Sexual Harm

Youngsters who are profoundly withdrawn are occasionally reacting to some kind of physical, sexual, or emotional mistreatment. Thus parents watch carefully, taking action if they sense that such a situation is occurring, whether within or outside of the family.[2]

Getting to Work in School

Increasing Safety, Reducing Stress, and Encouraging Confidence

Choreographing Separations

Because so many parents have trouble handling separations with their reserved children, teachers offer a clear model for letting go. Emphasizing that it's better to "be here when you're here and leave when you leave," teachers invite concerned parents to come into the classroom for a warming-up period. During this time, parents offer their friendly presence, help their child look around, join in an activity with or near the youngster's peers, and *don't mention anything about needing to leave.* After a period of such support—usually no more than five to ten minutes—parents tell the child that leave-taking will take place shortly. Teachers encourage parents to react to any protest without appearing upset themselves and to come up with a brief daily ritual to mark their exit. After leaving, parents *don't return or stand at the doorway to watch their child struggling.* If it's clear that a child will need help when parents are ready to go, a teacher stands by to offer comfort.

Monitoring the Greeting Period to Avoid Pressure

Parents and teachers refrain from behavior that leads a child to feel on the spot first thing in the morning. Teachers encourage parents not to talk with their child about participating in school, and design a morning ritual in which he feels comfortable *not speaking if he's not ready.* If the youngster covers his face or hides shyly behind a parent's legs, teachers engage in some friendly, adult-focused conversation; hear about the child's morning; and offer a warm hello without expecting a reply. They then talk to the child in a way that doesn't require a response—even a nod of the head—and find friendly, nonverbal ways to offer connection too.

Offering a Home Base for Exploration

These children may need a particular adult to provide safety, a staff person (or two) to whom they go when their caution gets the better of them. This teacher will be the preferred "handoff" person when the parents leave and may also be the best choice to offer the lend-an-ally assistance outlined in the following section.

Reducing Overly Solicitous Responses to Reserved Behavior

Shy youngsters often invite a kind but almost infantilizing response in their caregivers. Teachers look to provide a good balance between gentle support and a matter-of-fact, upbeat style that conveys confidence that the child may communicate and get involved at any moment.

Providing Skill-Building Support

Fostering the Basic Experience of Connection

See similar section under "Getting to Work at Home."

Strengthening Circles of Communication

Children whose temperament makes it hard for them to relate warmly—and youngsters with language processing issues—often need support and scaffolding as they learn to participate in and extend circles of communication. When a child can't yet respond verbally, teachers offer opportunities for nonverbal engagement that woo him into classroom activities.

Offering Second Language Learners Relaxed Opportunities for Listening and Speaking

Scaffolding language development helps young kids learn a second language comfortably, even if they aren't yet doing much talking themselves. Teachers slow down their pace of speaking, emphasize important words—using nonverbal cues to help children understand—and provide plenty of opportunities for relaxed experiences of hearing and trying out simple language. If a child is silent as he takes in the new language, teachers look for the signs of understanding and involvement that suggest that solid learning is taking place all the same.[3]

Lending an Ally to Support Connection, Involvement, and Social Skill

Cautious, shy children often end up shadowing their adult caretakers, playing mostly by themselves, or hanging around the edges of peer play without entering. Teacher support for involvement, offered in small increments over the course of months, can provide a huge boost to growth. Such lend-an-ally work relies on a few basic principles:

1. Minimizing pressure to speak while offering possibilities for involvement
2. Employing humor and playfulness to encourage interest
3. Keeping motivation high by using intrinsically interesting play themes
4. Preparing children before inviting them to respond verbally
5. Using dramatic play characters to invite connection
6. Offering themes involving roads, bridges, tunnels, pathways, journeys, and visits, to create possibilities for safe engagement through play

Previewing the Content of Group Time

Reserved youngsters often feel frozen when asked questions during group discussions. Once a child is showing small signs of readiness, teachers can go to him *before* group time starts and give an upbeat "heads up" about the upcoming discussion topic, including advance warning of any questions to be posed. ("I'll bet you will think something interesting about that!") If the child is already talking one-on-one with his teachers, this advance warning can include some brainstorming about answers he might have in mind. *As long as it doesn't convey any expectation that the child speak up,* such previewing—sometimes over many months—contributes to the feelings of comfort and belonging that lead to eventual success.

Monitoring and Modifying Classroom Routines and Organization

Cautious children thrive on a calm, organized classroom atmosphere. When teachers maintain a relaxed and orderly tone throughout the school day—through the use of well-organized transitions, effectively run group time, and classroom-wide climate control—these kids gain a sense of safety that allows them to participate more easily.

Respecting and Adapting to a Child's Home Culture

Teachers work to educate themselves about the cultural norms of a child's family, including having respectful conversations with parents (Sturm, 1997). If a child has learned that asserting his needs boldly, making eye contact with adults, or speaking loudly to make himself heard are not valued behaviors, teachers find ways to foster involvement within the child's frame of reference. When the tone of classroom life is overwhelming because it is at odds with a more restrained, orderly atmosphere at home, some adaptations may be in order as well (Leung, 1990; Chang, 1993; Dilg, 2003).

Watching for Emotional, Physical, or Sexual Harm

If teachers suspect that a youngster's reserve stems from serious mistreatment, they watch carefully, consult with colleagues and/or clinical staff, and take action when appropriate.[4]

Seeking Outside Help

Considering the Possibility of Testing, Consultation, or Therapy

Some of these children will benefit from testing and/or specialized help for language processing issues, while others may need mental health services for themselves or their families. When teachers and parents are not sure whether either type of help is indicated, early childhood consultants can often offer some needed perspective.

Watching for Language Processing Issues With Second Language Learners

Sometimes, a child's bilingual status masks language processing difficulties. If a youngster continues to looks mystified even after a period of learning, it may be time for a specialist to check for vulnerabilities in language processing functions. It is often useful to find out how the child is faring in his native language; bilingual kids who will benefit from specialized intervention often have trouble with the language spoken at home too (Genesee, Paradis, and Crago, 2004).

Accessing Pharmacological and/or Cognitive Behavioral Intervention

Most children respond, even if slowly, to the strategies outlined in this chapter. But when a child's extreme inhibition doesn't lessen even slightly after three or four months (excluding situations involving second language learning), or if a youngster has been selectively mute for an alarming period, a referral for cognitive behavioral work and/or a medication consult may be in order.[5]

Strategies in Action: Supporting Children Who Feel Overwhelmed Socially

Getting to Work With Caroline—Helping in the Face of Temperament-Driven Reserve

The following vignette tracks the process of understanding and helping an intensely shy preschooler. The approach that was so helpful to this child can assist a wide range of reserved youngsters and is sometimes also effective in targeting selective mutism. When a child's reserve has resulted in this extreme state of social inhibition, consultants may choose both to mentor teachers in the lend-an-ally strategies described in the following section and to provide ongoing classroom-based assistance. The latter gives a silent youngster the benefit of extra clinical expertise and helps teachers maintain a patient and upbeat stance in the face of what is sometimes very slow progress.

What Do We See?

Gathering Information Through a Detailed
Classroom Observation

Staff are feeling increasingly alarmed about four-year-old Caroline. Almost always late due to her intense resistance to going to school at all, she is painfully withdrawn once she gets there. Because things have only gotten worse since the school's winter break, Virginia and Michael, Caroline's parents, have agreed to some consultation. Late as usual, Caroline isn't there when I arrive for an initial observation. Soon, however, she comes in clutching her mother's hand. Heading straight to the book corner, she leans into Virginia's side while they read, then says a quiet, sad good-bye. Lead teacher Leroy walks over to ask what she might like to do. With a whispered "I don't know" and a frown, the short, slender girl eventually heads over to the science table to see what has been put out for the day.

Throughout the free-play period, Caroline gravitates toward activities that she can do without interacting with other kids. She assembles a challenging puzzle, makes a collage in the art area, then stands by the sand table where some children are setting up a desert scene with an array of plastic lizards, rocks, and sticks. Though these kids are amiably chatting together, and clearly notice Caroline's presence, not one child speaks to her. I wonder if—as is so often true with reserved children—she hasn't made herself available as an interesting playmate during the year and has consequently become an almost invisible presence in the classroom.

Caroline looks on attentively for almost five minutes, but shows no signs of attempting to join in. Moving on, her face lights up for the first time that morning. Keisha—an outgoing three-and-a-half-year-old—has set out some blocks and plastic animals and is in the midst of building a zoo. Caroline plops herself down on the floor and starts humming. Keisha looks up. "Caroline! Wanna make this?" Caroline looks straight at Keisha, giggles, then makes a noise that sounds like a car honking. Keisha starts laughing, and the two girls poke at each other playfully. They trade a few honks before Keisha returns to her half-made zoo. "Wanna Caroline?" Caroline shakes her head, stands up, and walks away. Keisha doesn't follow.

When consultants note a striking change in a child's usual behavior in the classroom, it's important to consider what accounts for the shift. Interested in why Caroline seems far more engaged with this friend than others, I seek out Leroy to ask whether the two girls interact like this often. He replies that their mothers are good friends, and that they play together regularly outside of school. He makes clear that moments like the one just observed are rare, however, a fact that is confirmed by Caroline's behavior for the rest of the morning: She remains a stiff-looking observer at circle time and later roams the playground away from the fray. That said, her playful moments with

Keisha—and the impish smile that peeks out when someone says something particularly funny—suggest that underneath her frozen demeanor is a girl with a delightful sense of humor, one who would be happy to connect with friends if she only knew how.

What Do We Think?

Checking for the Possibility of Language Processing Difficulties

One of the first hypotheses to entertain in a case like this one is whether a child is struggling with communication skills: Caroline has said hardly a word throughout the morning. But a subsequent meeting with her parents reveals that this girl talks volubly at home—the problem there is that they can't get her to be quiet. It isn't just at school that Caroline clams up, however; with relatives, family friends, and neighbors, she barely speaks and interacts. Virginia and Michael recount that their only child has always been reserved and had even more difficulty than most kids during the period when babies typically get alarmed around strangers. They think of her as shy, and figure she'll grow out of it eventually.

Considering Whether Temperament Plays a Role in a Child's Struggle to Connect

The idea of Caroline being shy by nature fits the information gathered thus far—it appears likely that she was born with an extra load of caution built into her system. Research suggests that about 10% to 20% percent of kids come into the world with such a temperamental bias (Kagan and Snidman, 2004). These children are prone to react to unfamiliarity with vigilance or apprehension; they may withdraw in new situations or with new people, cling to their parents at family gatherings, or refuse to let their mom or dad leave when being dropped off at a birthday party attended by children they see every day.[6] Kids with this temperament not infrequently have a parent who reacted similarly when young, and Caroline is no exception: Michael mentions that he was very reserved as a child and hopes Caroline won't have to endure the painful struggles he experienced all the way through elementary school.[7]

Noting Behavioral Patterns That Amplify Cautious Behavior

When a child's temperament lies at the root of her troubles, any strategies used to encourage growth will need to work *with* not *against* her nature. These strategies often support a change of course because, as noted in this chapter's "points to remember" list, the existing feedback loops surrounding a young-ster's reluctance to connect may have become part of the problem. This seems to be true in Caroline's case, at least at school. Observation of her reactions in the classroom has revealed that on the occasions when someone tries talking directly to her, she quickly withdraws. In fact, during the entire morning's visit, she doesn't once respond to a direct, verbal overture with openness. It seems likely that as her teachers have continued to ask her friendly questions she's too paralyzed to answer, and encouraged her to connect with other kids in ways she can't, Caroline's withdrawal has just gotten more extreme. Trying as hard as they can to keep the window to connection open, these adults have inadvertently been slamming it shut.

What Do We Do?

Lending an Ally to Support Connection, Involvement, and Social Skill Development

In a post-observation team meeting, staff easily embrace the hypothesis that Caroline's difficulties stem mainly from an intensely shy temperament. They ask about how to support her more successfully: This girl is more imprisoned in her reserve than any child their program has served in recent memory, and they're well aware that what they're doing isn't working. We begin by exploring the kind of lend-an-ally assistance that often helps kids whose shy temperaments have propelled them into frozen, nonverbal states in their classrooms. An outline of this assistance is offered in the section "Getting to Work in School."

Mentoring teachers in this approach isn't easy. Its mix of factors—patience for a child's cautious pace; nonverbal "wooing"; regular, unthreaten-ing invitations for involvement; and upbeat confidence in a child's eventual ability to get engaged—is difficult to learn. Teachers are trained to make ongoing eye contact with kids, to ask questions and enjoy their answers, and to help children use increasingly complex speech patterns with their peers. It's challenging for them to invite a child into interaction, refrain from insist-ing on eye contact and verbal responsiveness, and, at the same time, avoid an overly solicitous stance. Furthermore, there's an art to sensing when to move in with a direct question because a youngster is finally ready to break out of his shell, especially when teachers' reactions to that child's successful involve-ment should be so matter-of-fact as to suggest the change isn't even remotely momentous.

Due to these challenges, clinicians may find it useful to begin the con-sultative process with some classroom-based work. We join the child with her peers as we offer some lend-an-ally support, both checking out the viability of this approach and asking teachers to keep an eye on what we're doing. We follow with a training session in which teachers explore the nuances of such support. Only then do we suggest that they try out these new strategies in the classroom. It's almost always important for us to return for follow-up observation and feedback sessions. With particularly challenging children, we often continue to offer classroom-based assistance ourselves as well.

Supporting a Sense of Safety and Nonverbal Participation

Let's examine how Leroy works with Caroline after he's become familiar with the strategies in question—work observed in a follow-up observation. Doing so will illuminate how teachers and clinicians can support social engagement with reserved children and also provide an example of the developmental play assistance introduced in the last chapter. Note that while he proceeds with his own unique flair, Leroy is actually following a clear protocol, important elements of which will be highlighted in italics.

The work begins with Leroy cheerfully remarking on Caroline's place as an observer, thus making it clear that she is a presence in the circle of play. Then, inserting her name into the conversation regularly—and slipping in quick moments of relatedness that don't require a verbal response—he offers her a safe experience of connection and belonging. As he continues to shape this experience so that the other girls stay open to Caroline's potential as a playmate, he uses her enjoyment of silly humor to gently encourage involvement.

Here's what this process looks as Caroline hovers near the block-building area where Keisha and four-year-old Angie are building homes for the room's collection of plastic animals. Leroy ambles over to the large, circular rug where the girls are playing and leans down.

"Hello girls! Angie and Keisha, you two are building animal houses! *And Caroline is watching!* Is it okay if I help?" Receiving enthusiastic nods from the two builders, Leroy lowers his large frame to the floor. "I think I'll make a place for the pigs...Is that okay if I do that?" More nods and a cheerful "Do it!" from Keisha. "I'm going to take some of these purple blocks for the fence...Do you like purple, Keisha?" " I love ORANGE!" Keisha replies with a grin. "Oh yeah, I see your house has some orange blocks. And Angie, yours has green and blue and brown blocks. Is one of those your favorite color?" Angie answers definitively, "Nope, I like pink, but no pink blocks." Leroy nods. "Yup, no pink blocks here...I bet you wish we had some!"

Leroy sits quietly for a few moments as he constructs a pigpen. "So Keisha, you love orange, and Angie, you love pink. *I'll bet Caroline has a favorite color too*...and so do I. I LOVE red...red, red, RED is the color for me!" *Leroy glances up at Caroline, makes a goofy face, and points to his red shirt. Then he points to the red stripe on her pants.* Though her face stays impassive, her eyes meet his. *He smiles before looking down again.*

Leroy is wooing Caroline. Having offered himself as a play partner, he's light-heartedly insistent yet not overly intrusive as he uses humor and warmth to catch her attention. In addition, throughout his chatting with Keisha and Angie, he weaves in Caroline's name, never speaking in such a way that she'll need to respond. Then, as illustrated shortly, he proceeds with the approach's next step. Continuing to engage with Caroline through brief moments of friendly eye contact, he expresses an upbeat curiosity about the play in a way that supports her in letting her guard down. Note how he does this by making comments and asking questions that appear to be coming from both of them. Then he transmits the other children's answers to Caroline, even though she doesn't yet say a word. We might think of this as developmental play assistance's "we" stage. In it, Leroy provides Caroline with the sense that they're a duo, offering her the security of his presence in order to help her feel connected to her classmates. At this point, he does the work of connecting for both of them:

> "Caroline…" Leroy sneaks in a quick glance in her direction before going back to his building project. *"I bet you see what I see!* Keisha is making a really tall wall around the giraffes. I wonder if that's so they can't get out…I think I'm going to ask her…Keisha, is that so they can't get out?" Keisha nods. "Cause they could scape." *"Yeah Caroline, that IS why she made it so high. She thinks they could escape if it's too low! Maybe you wondered that just like I did, and now we know."* He looks up at her, smiling once again. The two builders start making a huge enclosure for the horses, after which Leroy gathers up a small collection of blocks and sets them not too far from Caroline's feet.

Helping Children Shift From Observers to Players

Now Leroy works to help Caroline shift from observer to nonverbal player. He does this by gently offering her a potential role in the goings on, and by asking questions and getting answers from the "we" stance. As is standard in developmental play assistance, he builds invitingly on a dramatic play theme that's already unfolding and, without being obvious about it, uses Caroline's friends as collaborators in encouraging her growth. He continues to do most of the connective work himself, again refraining from asking this child any direct questions. As seen here, the result of these efforts is that Caroline feels safe enough to make a small step toward active participation:

> *"Hey Caroline, you might feel like building in a while, so I'm putting these here in case you do.* See Keisha and Angie? There is a place for Caroline right here…. I don't know if she'll want it, but she might. I think I'll put some elephants there in case she wants to make their home. *Caroline, I'm going to ask them if it's okay if I do that.* Is that okay if I put some elephants there Keisha? How about with you Angie? It is? *Great—Caroline, they say it's fine.* Keisha, could you just hand me those two baby elephants and I'll put them over here next to the mama elephant?" Keisha complies and calls out happily, "Caroline, elephants for you!" Caroline cracks a quick smile and sits down, though she doesn't pick up the animals.

It's been over five minutes and Leroy signals his assistant teacher to see if he can continue with what he's doing; as we've noted in the last chapter, she'll need to keep monitoring the rest of the room to be sure that other children are getting the help they need. Then, once he gets her assent, Leroy proceeds with the protocol. In following its steps, teachers stay alert to the possibilities of the moment, and continue to build on the interests of the particular children with whom they're interacting. Having successfully woven the targeted child's name—and presence—into the ongoing dialogue, they now look for a theme that will inspire a particularly high level of interest. (Ice cream flavors, as seen shortly, are almost always a hit.) Then they ask the more outgoing children their thoughts about the topic at hand. After hearing and enjoying these youngsters' replies, teachers wonder aloud whether it would be a good idea to find out the reserved child's opinion on the same subject. Assuming that the other youngsters agree to this idea, and they almost always do, the teachers gently inquire of the shy youngster *whether it would be okay to ask a question.* It's only when they get a nod or a yes that they actually ask that question.

If a teacher—or clinician doing this classroom-based work—doesn't spring such an inquiry too early, the shy child often signals his assent. By that time, he's already had two warnings that a specific question is coming, and a chance to prepare his response. Sometimes, it helps to have a pretend character or puppet serve as the questioner: The natural appeal of imaginative play leads shy children to respond to such characters more easily than they do to adults' direct inquiries. Leroy employs this strategy to great effect here:

> "Hey Angie, One of my pigs is getting hungry. He thinks he wants to leave his house to find some food. Do any horses want to come too?" Angie nods. "Mine too!" adds Keisha as she grabs two tigers and brings them to the pig-pen." Leroy's face takes on an amused expression. "What do they want to eat, ice cream? Mmm Mmm Mmm!" He rubs his stomach. Leroy looks over at Angie. "What do you think, Angie, do you think the horses want to try some ice cream? They might like it!" Angie brings two horses over and places them next to the tigers. *"Hey, Keisha, Angie... I'm wondering if the elephants might want some ice cream too. Do you think I should bring my pig over to ask Caroline if the elephants want to come?"*
>
> The girls agree that this is a good idea, and Leroy turns to Caroline. *"Caroline, is it okay if the pig comes over to ask a question? Because we have a question for the elephants."* Leroy lowers his voice's naturally loud volume, and when he glances at his shyest student, has a gentle, almost shy expression himself. Caroline nods her assent. The pig trots over to where the elephants are standing. *"Hi elephants! I was wondering if you might like to come get some ice cream. The horses and the tigers and I really want some, and we're going to the ice cream store. Do you elephants want to come too?"* Caroline nods again.

Fifteen minutes into the play, the elephants have joined the crowd, and Leroy is inquiring about what kind of ice cream the animals would like. When it comes to asking Caroline, he goes through his routine again.

"Keisha, Angie, should I ask Caroline what kind the elephants want? I should? Okay…Caroline, is it okay if I ask you something?" Another nod. "We're wondering what kind of ice cream the elephants might want to have. Do they know what kind they want today?" "Chocolate Chip." Caroline's answer is quiet but clear. "Chocolate Chip it is…the store has lots of that! I like chocolate chip myself. How about you, Angie, do you like Chocolate Chip?" "Nope, but my brother does."

"Chocolate Chip." When Caroline dares to answer Leroy's carefully staged question, he uses his gifts as a teacher to downplay the moment's importance. Quickly turning the spotlight away from her, he seamlessly brings in another child, thus supporting his student in a quick circle of language and engagement. With play as his medium, and conversation as his tool, Leroy has just successfully lent an ally to support safe connection in a situation where temperament has gotten in the way of development.

The Stages of Developmental Play Assistance

Leroy's efforts offer an excellent example of the early stage of developmental play assistance. During this "we" stage, the teacher, parent, or clinician models much of the work herself. Then, as the youngster develops more confidence and skill in the targeted area, that adult begins to pull back slightly. She will remain ready to offer help when needed, but will leave room for the child to do whatever he can on his own. We might think of this second phase as the "you…we" stage of the work. Later, as the child has developed yet more skill, adults start leaving him on his own for brief periods, returning regularly to offer support. Farther along still, they'll merely keep an ear cocked for times when the child needs a more active partner: the "you…me (if needed)" stage.[8]

Lend-an-ally assistance works particularly well in the midst of unfolding play narratives. As adults offer support in building on open-ended scenarios as Leroy does here, they also watch for opportunities to insert journeys, visits, pathways, roads, and bridges. Such themes and construction items allow shy children to have separate, safe space within a communal story line while remaining connected to the other players. As seen in the next chapter, lend-an-ally work can also be used to support children's successful involvement in conversation as they eat, draw, or build near more socially confident classmates.

Monitoring Family Interchanges

As is so often the case, Caroline's natural reserve has been amplified through ongoing experience. This is just as true at home as in school: Michael and Virginia have realized that they spend too much time either shielding their daughter from anxiety by speaking for her, or unsuccessfully pressuring her to interact when she is clinging to their side. They need to begin previewing new situations with her, then providing a relaxed and secure base of operations as she takes the time she needs to venture out into the social world. Thus Virginia has a new approach to her daughter's arrival at school. Now, before she and Caroline enter the room, they stop in the doorway. As Virginia crouches down, arm encircling her daughter's shoulders, they look to see who has arrived, and talk together about what kids are doing. After they enter the classroom, they no longer head directly to an isolated spot in the book corner. Instead, Virginia seeks out Leroy for some conversation, regardless of whether Caroline is making every effort to appear invisible. She makes sure to weave Caroline's name into the morning's check-in, at the same time reminding herself not to pressure her daughter to speak up. Eventually, Virginia sits down at a table with a few other children and, much like Leroy, connects with the group in such a way that Caroline has room to join in if and when she's ready.

Two months after we begin working with Caroline, I get a call from Leroy. "It's pretty amazing... she's chatting nonstop now. And she's so much happier! Yesterday, she even came up to give me a hug. But I'm a little worried. All she talks about is stuff from home, things she's done with her dad, or funny jokes her mom tells. The kids are okay with it for now, but they're looking a little mystified. She doesn't seem to know how to bring up the things most kids talk about at school. I'm afraid that they're going to tune her out again if she doesn't figure out what else to do pretty soon."

After some conversation, Leroy decides to sit with Caroline and her friends and model other possibilities; this girl has just come out of hiding and probably doesn't know what else to talk about. And it takes some time, but Caroline does eventually find a comfortable place for herself in the group. Walking into the room in early June, it takes me a while to locate the child everyone has been so worried about. Smack in the middle of a throng of girls who are getting their dolls ready for a picnic, Caroline is chatting animatedly with Keisha and another child. Then she and her buddies start giggling hysterically as she places her doll's underwear on its head as a hat.

9

Helping the Child With Language and Information Processing Issues

Getting to Work When a Youngster Struggles to Understand and Be Understood

When children struggle to understand the world around them, or to let others know what they feel and think, we may see signs of withdrawal, frustration, or anxiety. The first step in helping these youngsters is to figure out what elements of information processing are problematic. Then we offer scaffolding to promote skill building in areas of difficulty. Understanding the three-part nature of language processing explored in Chapter 2 and the elements of information processing covered in Chapter 3—and consulting language or neurodevelopmental specialists when needed—allows us to get specific before getting to work with these kids.

What Issues Might Be Contributing to the Child's Behavior?

- Inner-focused, hard to engage temperament
- Challenges in harnessing attention and maintaining focus
- Challenges in decoding auditory or nonverbal information
- Challenges in storing and retrieving information
- Challenges in organizing and sequencing language and ideas
- Challenges in building larger units of meaning from smaller ones
- Difficulties with articulation
- Overwhelming experiences at home or elsewhere

Some Points to Remember

- Vulnerabilities in language processing are often masked by frustration and impulsivity. Thus when children act rashly or angrily, it's important to think about whether difficulty communicating is at the root of their problematic behaviors (Cohen, Davine, and Meloche-Kelly, 1989; Gilliam and de Mesquita, 2000).
- Children who have a hard time understanding and responding sometimes become increasingly inattentive, disengaged, or withdrawn. Before

working successfully on communication issues, we need to bolster their experience of tuned-in connection.

- The linguistic pace of their world often doesn't allow these children enough opportunity to build competency in areas of vulnerability. Part of supporting mastery involves regularly slowing conversation down so that they can develop new skills.
- Siblings, friends, and caring adults often jump in to provide words for these youngsters. As a result, the feedback loops surrounding communicational difficulties can exacerbate both their feelings of inadequacy and their inability to get needed practice.
- Children with language processing issues are often compelled by television, DVDs, and computer games—all of which don't require verbal interaction. Parents need to monitor their family's use of such entertainment: These kids need plenty of time for the creative play and verbal interactions that help increase communicational competency.
- Second language learners may appear to be having processing difficulties when they are merely taking the time needed to master a new language. See Chapter 8 for more information on what we often call the "silent period," on ways to support such children in classroom settings, and on how to determine when a child is in fact experiencing vulnerabilities in language processing.

Getting to Work at Home and in School

Offering Skill-Building Opportunities

Strengthening the Experience of Tuned-In Connection

Parents and teachers slip in opportunities for pleasurable connection, making sure to first support the child in the effort of harnessing attention. In the beginning, fostering these increased circles of connection may involve simple or nonverbal content, so that the child's ability to connect isn't hampered by her processing challenges.

Expanding Circles of Communication

Parents and teachers seek to understand the specific nature of a child's processing difficulties, then work on expanding her ability to engage in successful circles of communication. Offering an easy-going pace for these exchanges, and providing any necessary scaffolding, they slip in such practice regularly. Throughout this process, adults pay attention to the child's strengths and areas of interest, building on both as a way of making these opportunities for communication pleasurable.

Providing Opportunities for Supported Conversation and Play

Children with these vulnerabilities often struggle to talk and play with siblings and friends. Parents and teachers watch to make sure that other children aren't speaking for the youngster in question and then scaffold her efforts to communicate. If she's become a child whom others leave out because it's too frustrating to have her join in language-based play, they also help siblings and peers experience her as a more viable participant by offering, when possible, their presence as her play partner. These opportunities not only foster increased skill, but also boost the child's growing sense of competence and confidence.

Assisting with Healthy Problem-Solving

Kids who struggle to communicate may either allow themselves to be taken advantage of by siblings and peers, or lash out in frustration when they can't communicate their needs effectively. Adults keep an eye out for such situations, and move in quickly to support the child in communicating her point of view. Providing this problem-solving support helps reduce aggressive, impulsive, or quietly frustrated responses, while increasing the child's skill in healthy self-assertion.

Working on Family Issues and Modifying Family Routines

Monitoring and Changing Family Patterns

Parents watch for how family patterns have unfolded in relationship to the child's processing vulnerabilities. Are family members speaking for her when she's struggling? Does she feel able to assert her needs in a positive way? Working to change any feedback loops that may be depriving a child of the practice she needs, they do whatever is required to give her more space and time to communicate, thus allowing her to feel like a full player in family life.

Monitoring Use of Television/DVDs and Computer Games

Parents make sure that they restrict the amount of time their child spends on entertainment that doesn't require verbal responses, and work to provide alternatives that strengthen vulnerable processing functions.

Watching for Emotional, Physical, or Sexual Harm

Children who struggle to communicate are sometimes showing the cognitive effects of physical, sexual, or emotional mistreatment. Thus parents and teachers watch carefully, and take action if they sense that such a situation is occurring.[1]

Seeking Outside Help

Considering the Possibility of Consultation, Testing, and/or Speech and Language Services

Concerned adults need detailed information about a child's challenges communicating, information best gotten through consultation and testing with specialists—those who look specifically at speech and language issues and/or those who assess overall neurodevelopmental functioning.[2] Once diagnostic work is completed, and any outside services put in place, parents and teachers keep in mind the importance of ongoing consultation for themselves: While an hour or two a week with a specialist can benefit these youngsters greatly, the work parents and teachers do—when well thought out—is just as important, and available whenever needed too.

Looking for Help With Emotional and Family Issues

Some parents will benefit from professional assistance that targets how a child's processing vulnerabilities interact with life at home. Furthermore, if after getting some help from teachers, parents, and specialists, a child still feels overwhelmed by her frustrating attempts to communicate, she may profit from time with a child therapist. Note also the importance of seeking such help if a child's difficulties stem from traumatic experiences, including witnessing violent conflict at home.[3]

Strategies in Action: Supporting Children Who Struggle to Communicate

Getting to Work With James—Helping with a Mix of Processing and Family Issues

When children struggle with language and information processing, their difficulties are, by definition, woven into the fabric of family life. Thus a consulting clinician's job is often to help parents understand how a child's constitutionally based vulnerabilities may have been aggravated by their experiences at home. The following case examines this kind of interplay and offers an example of how intervention targets both strengthened processing capacities and healthier family dynamics.

What Do We See?

Considering Information From Teachers and From Direct Observation

It's early October, and Barb has called to ask for some consultation about four-year-old James. An experienced teacher, Barb states that she believes that "something is off" but she doesn't know what:

> He's a happy kid, and he comes in without a problem. But every single morning he forgets to take his picture card and put it up on the chart to show he's here. If I ask him what he's supposed to do, he gets this totally blank look. I can't decide if he's just spaced out or if he really can't remember the routine. Actually, I get that blank look a lot... sometimes I call his name and start talking with him, and I'm really not sure he's with me at all.

Statements like Barb's —"He gets this blank look... I can't decide if he's just spaced out... I'm not sure he's with me"—aren't unusual when a child is experiencing processing issues. Thus clinicians listen closely to teachers' questions, and mine their descriptions of life at school for clues about possible areas of vulnerability. Such descriptions often include information about how children interact with their peers, as is true in this teacher's further account of James's situation:

> There is something about the way he plays that concerns me. He hangs around the fringes of what's happening and then imitates what other kids are doing. Ben is great with him—they're good friends and Ben kind of takes him under wing and shows him what to do. But if Ben is absent, James seems pretty lost.

Barb relates that Ben is a highly verbal child with a disquietingly unsettled home life, and that all through last year, he relied on James's loyal, upbeat presence to help him feel secure at school. She's not worried about the friendship being one-sided, but she is concerned that Ben's almost constant presence at his friend's side has kept staff from realizing just how much James is struggling to keep up with his age-mates.

When considering the possibility of vulnerabilities in language processing functions, consultants often find it useful to observe a child first hand, and I soon spend some time in James's classroom. He's an outgoing, endearing boy, and other kids seem to enjoy his presence. However, his behavior does suggest that he has trouble understanding much of what goes on around him and, as a result, isn't experienced as an equal player in the classroom scene. At one point, for example, a classmate inadvertently calls James by her two-year-old brother's name, with a tone of voice that suggests she's talking to someone much younger. In addition, the blank look Barb has described crosses James's face worrisomely often. I wonder whether trouble comprehending what's going on around him has propelled him into a habitually tuned-out state.

A post-observation conversation includes more astute observations on Barb's part:

> Sometimes I feel like James can only manage one simple idea at a time. Or he'll start telling me a story in the middle as if I already know the beginning. There's another thing too—recently, he's been getting incredibly frustrated. He had a huge tantrum last week when Ben wasn't here. We've never seen that from him before.

In response to a question about James's home life, Barb relates that James's mother left her alcoholic husband two years ago because of his violent behavior. Patricia seems to be managing fairly well, even with financial pressures a continual worry, and James's relationship with her appears warm and stable. He may have witnessed some scary scenes between his parents when he was a toddler though. Furthermore, Barb guesses that he spends a lot of time in front of the television: Patricia has mentioned that she's so exhausted from her job as a home health aide that she doesn't have much energy left for either James or his six-year-old sister Mandy. The energy she does have tends to go to her daughter, a high-strung child who is still contending with the emotional aftermath of her parents' stormy relationship.

What Do We Think?

Identifying Specific Areas of Processing Weakness

Vulnerabilities in information processing lead to a particular diagnostic challenge. It is certainly important to zero in on a youngster's specific areas of weakness. But at the same time, we must be sure to factor in relevant emotional issues and any feedback loops that keep the child from getting the practice he needs to gain skill. In considering the information processing piece of this diagnostic triad, Barb and I agree: James seems to struggle with memory functions, has trouble generating and managing sequences of information, and—a connected problem—has difficulty organizing ideas. These three vulnerabilities would account for his inability to follow the morning routine without a daily reminder, his difficulty keeping up with classroom play, and his habit of relaying information in a seemingly illogical fashion. They'd also explain why James's language development appears to be delayed; problems with memory and sequencing make it hard for children to communicate with increasing complexity (Greenspan and Wieder, 1998).

Attending to the Intersection of Processing Issues With Experiences at Home and in School

Moving to the triad's other elements, we wonder to what degree James's processing issues have been exacerbated by his friend Ben's constant presence at his side in school. There are also questions about how much these issues connect to inborn traits, and how much they hinge on experiences he's had at home. Children who have witnessed overwhelming situations in their families or communities can end up with learning issues that stem from emotional rather than constitutional sources (Van der Kolk and Streck-Fischer, 2000; Cole et al., 2005). It's possible, for example, that James's blank looks stem from a coping mechanism he developed in his earliest years. Realizing that James's mother is needed in order to answer these questions more fully—and to consider what to do—Barb calls to arrange a meeting.

Patricia, it turns out, feels badly that she hasn't brought up these issues before: She's well aware that her son's language and play aren't nearly as accomplished as his sister's had been at that age. "He's just such a great kid," she relates. "He'll go with the flow almost all the time. I guess I'm so relieved that he's happy that I ignore the things that aren't going well. Mandy is tough and takes up a lot of my time, and James just takes care of himself when we're arguing, which helps a lot. And my mom hasn't been well either. I usually bring the kids over to her place on the weekends, and they zone out on the TV while I help her. He probably needs me more than he gets me." As the discussion continues, Barb, Patricia, and I mark weaknesses in language and processing functions while keeping in mind James's warm, loving manner. We think about the chaotic nature of family life when he was very young. Then we compare notes on his habit of blanking out, realizing that it happens as much at home as in school.

Patricia offers a window into what goes on at home—and how she compensates for James's vulnerabilities—when she starts talking about how hard it is for her son to stay focused and clear-headed. "I do a lot for him, because it goes so much faster. I'll lay out his clothes at night, and get his stuff together for him in the morning. And I talk for him when Mandy is angry with him. He just can't keep up on his own, not with her anyway." Barb tells her that James is having the same problem at school, though kids aren't frustrated with him all that often.

The three-way conversation allows for just the kind of meaning-making consultants hope to facilitate. By its end, the scattered observations that have nagged at both Patricia and Barb have coalesced into a coherent picture of James's difficulties—difficulties that stem from a complex mix of processing issues, family dynamics, and the usual problems kids like James have in keeping up with the crowd. The next step will be a follow-up meeting with the intent of developing an initial plan of action.

In fact, however, the process of change has already begun. At the second meeting, it's clear that paying closer attention to James's experience has left

Patricia both increasingly concerned and more motivated to offer help. This mother relates that as she's observed her son and his sister carefully, she's become aware of just how domineering Mandy can be. Patricia thinks that James is quite intimidated by Mandy and believes that he may be confused by what he feels as well. For example, she's noted that her son looks quite spacey when Mandy goes on the offensive. Patricia relates that she gets like a mother lion when that happens, and thinks James has been relying on her too much to smooth things out. She now believes that she should give him more support in solving these sibling issues himself but acknowledges that she doesn't know how.

What Do We Do?

Developing Precise Goals for Increased Processing Competence

As always, the initial stage of strategizing involves sketching out hoped for areas of mastery, with overall goals for each. In situations like James's, it's important to tease out goals for specific processing vulnerabilities, as well as those for emotional support and for modifying feedback loops that have hampered growth. Note that in the list that follows, problem statements (e.g., James spaces out a lot) are turned into goals for skill-development (e.g., he needs help strengthening his ability to tune in).

Overall Goal #1: Strengthening Weak Areas of Mental Processing

Intervention will work to

- strengthen James's ability to tune in and stay focused on conversations, play, and learning;
- strengthen his capacity for organizing and sequencing his thoughts, and for understanding sequences of ideas that he hears or sees;
- strengthen his ability to use memory functions—to develop strategies for remembering things from day to day and for holding his thoughts in mind as he takes in new information;
- boost his ability to process information more quickly, and to ask for help when he's getting lost;
- strengthen his capacity to engage in increasingly elaborate two-way conversation, and to create more complex narratives in play.

Overall Goal #2: Working on Emotional and Familial Issues

Intervention will also

- help James become more assertive about his own ideas and more confident of his importance at home and in school;

- shift dynamics at home so that the balance between attention to James's and Mandy's needs is more even;
- help Patricia develop an easier relationship with Mandy, so that family life becomes calmer and more enjoyable for everyone;
- help James deepen his experience and understanding of emotions;
- help James learn to use play and conversation to express and resolve troubling emotional issues.

Targeting and Strengthening Mental Processing Functions

Barb stands at the classroom door as James approaches with his mom. "Hi James!" She kneels down directly in front of the youngster and smiles. "You've got your *teddy* shirt on, the *orange* one . . . I *like* that shirt James. Look, I have some *orange* on too!" Barb has spoken slowly, and carefully emphasized a few choice words. But she notices James's dazed look, realizes she's overwhelmed him with her flood of language, and tries a new tack. She pauses for a moment, then quietly claps out a simple, repeating rhythm. James perks up at the sound and, eventually, gazes straight at his teacher. *"Good-morning,* my friend!" she says. "If I move my fingers, will you move yours back?" Barb makes a silly face as she wiggles her fingers. James continues to stare at her, now with the hint of a smile crossing his face. After another prompt, he mirrors her gesture.

"James, our fingers said *hello!* Hmmm . . . there is something to do now." She pauses again before continuing. "Can you think of what you do when you come in?" James's blank look makes its second appearance of the morning. Normally, Barb would now direct James to his picture and then to the chart, worriedly cueing him through the routine. But this time, as planned, she proceeds differently. "I know. Let's look." Barb moves so that she and her student are now gazing into the classroom together. Motioning Patricia toward the "Who's Here" chart, she asks James to look at his mom and begins to sing a simple, repetitively worded song about putting his picture on the chart. Patricia holds up the laminated picture for him to take, and James places it correctly.

Using Connection and Attention as a Springboard for Skill Building

If having James perform his job independently were the measuring stick, Barb and Patricia would be disappointed in the initial outcome of the new plan. But, in fact, their consultation-inspired goals for this first morning have been met: James has started his day with some tuned-in circles of connection, and Barb has introduced a song that she'll use each morning over the next few weeks, in the hope that its melody and rhythm will help her student encode the words for and actions of his job.

When working to strengthen mental processing functions, adults keep in mind a crucial point: *vulnerabilities in these functions often lead a child to feel out of synch with what's going on around him and, consequently, both disengaged and unfocused. And without the grounding presence of connection and attention, any efforts to support growth won't get very far.* Therefore, the first element of intervention involves using a youngster's strengths to invite him into a state of pleasurable, focused interchange. Over time, this connection becomes a springboard for his attention to the world around him and to the skill building he'll be asked to do.

Offering Sound, Movement, and Relational Cues to Foster Growth

Barb's work relies on an educative aspect of the consultative process: Part of our previous discussion highlighted the fact that *chants, songs, and movement games can help kids get themselves organized mentally.* We also talked about how an extra emphasis on nonverbal relational cues can help; adults may need to make their tones of voice and facial expressions more exaggerated and friendly with these children than they do with others. Barb capitalizes on what she's learned as she uses some repetitive clapping to capture James's attention in the first place, wiggles her fingers rather than speaks her greeting, looks at him in a strikingly animated way, and finds a song—one that repeats its simple, chanted instructions several times—that reminds James of his job in a way that his brain may be trained to remember. She's using his strengths to work on his weaknesses, one step at a time.

Expanding Circles of Communication

Over the next weeks, Barb and Patricia work hardest on the task of helping James stay more connected to and focused on his relationship to both of them, using his good cheer and desire to please to support quick, enjoyable interchanges. Reminding themselves not to try for too much too soon, they keep their words simple. Only after they feel that James is more adept at engaging in circles of connection do they focus on expanding circles of communication. At that point, they add ongoing lend-an-ally work in the classroom and at home, the specifics of which will be explored shortly.

Supporting Sequencing and Organization

Both adults know that, in time, they'll need to help James elaborate upon and vary the stories he plays out; at the moment, he's stuck in some repetitive, choppy tales about cars, trucks, and police chases. Helping him learn to create the kinds of longer narratives that most kids his age enjoy will strengthen his capacity for organizing and sequencing his ideas, give him a place to work through any feelings that are troubling him, and allow him to find a more comfortable niche in the social world at school too. This work will rely on an understanding of how organization and sequencing connect to two important areas of development: a child's ability to play out the stories that most concern him and his capacity to think through—and then to share—ideas about himself and his world.

Chapter 2 explored how kids learn to string together small units of ideas into large, cohesive sequences. Through the creation of such logical progressions, they conceptualize cause and effect, understand and represent the passage of time, and bridge actions and feelings. Such sequencing also allows them to both understand themselves and be understood by others. It's this ability that kids like James find so difficult; as Barb has accurately noted, James is most comfortable managing single ideas. His play is choppy, his thoughts are brief, and, as a consequence, he has little ability to create or express complex ideas about himself and his world. No wonder that he's showing signs of frustration.

Patricia and Barb hope that their efforts to support increased skill will help lessen this frustration, as they offer James what might be thought of as a workout for his weak "mental muscles"—after all, it won't be that different than what adults do when they lift free weights every morning to strengthen their arm muscles. In providing this kind of skill-building assistance, adults use their growing understanding of what specific processing functions are hard for a child and then offer "intervention at the breakdown point" (Levine, 2002, p. 282). To this end, Patricia and Barb watch for single units of meaning as James plays with cars and trucks. Before he repeats a unit too many times in a row, they initiate some friendly circles of connection. Then they ask questions and model narrative development. Lending an ally as they meet him in the story lines that interest him, they push for the extension and deepening of both content and emotion.

Monitoring and Changing Feedback Loops

As she does this work in the classroom, Barb attends to the quality of Ben's involvement in James's everyday activities. Gently supporting Ben in giving James more space to articulate his ideas for himself, she helps the boys recalibrate their contributions to play scenarios so that James has opportunities to practice new skills. But Barb has to be careful—the friendship has been operating this way for a while and is very important to both boys. She needs to watch that her efforts don't sour either child on the depth and pleasure of their bond.

As Barb and Patricia offer James the support he needs, they remember the importance of paying close attention to a child's strengths, not just his vulnerabilities. After all, this boy demonstrates not only a flexible temperament, but a natural warmth and empathy too. It's on both of these qualities that they'll rely as they work to help him remember, sequence, and organize information more capably. Their efforts involve the specific strategies already mentioned, as well as some others. Listing those efforts in their entirety will illuminate the kind of incremental and multifaceted approach we take to processing issues.

Getting to Work at Home

- Patricia will support many quick, pleasurable interchanges with her son, encouraging him to make eye contact and stay focused as they connect. She'll remind herself to initiate such interactions when she can reward James's attention with a pleasant back-and-forth; at the moment, she often leaves him alone until she wants something about which he won't be happy.
- Patricia will refrain from jumping in when James is struggling to express himself. Helping him stretch his ability to connect single ideas into longer sequences of meaning, she'll also insist that Mandy give James more space to speak. In addition, she'll spend ten to twenty minutes a day giving James her undivided attention as he plays or talks with her, thus encouraging the development of longer play narratives.
- Patricia will make a picture chart of the morning routine, thus helping James both remember the order of activities and take more responsibility for getting himself ready.
- Once Patricia feels that she has a better handle on her relationship with Mandy, she'll work to help James assert himself more effectively with his sister.
- Patricia will occasionally take time to help James notice and understand the different kinds of emotions that everyone feels at home, including her own.

Getting to Work in School

- Staff will also initiate frequent, pleasant interchanges that support focus. Using humor, playfulness, and animated facial expressions, they'll make sure to keep motivation for connection high and overwhelming verbal input low. Then, as he develops a stronger ability to attend while interacting with staff, they'll begin helping him open and close increasing numbers of circles of communication.
- Lending an ally, teachers will join James in play and conversations, both on his own and with friends. Keeping interest level high by focusing on activities and themes that are compelling to him, they'll help him connect small units of meaning into larger and more organized sequences. When this work takes places alongside his classmates, they'll gently encourage all kids, but especially Ben, to give James the time and space he needs to offer input. In addition, if James begins telling a story in the middle of the action—or misses a crucial element of description—staff will respond with interest and scaffolding, thus helping him consider and order his ideas.

- Through the use of songs, rhythmic games, visual aids, and rhyming poems, staff will work to strengthen James confidence in and ability to use his memory. When he's struggling to remember a word, fact, or experience, they'll take care not to jump in to rescue him from discomfort, instead offering supportive cues. Then they'll praise James for his success in helping his mind become "like an elephant's."
- Staff will watch for times when James is unhappy with what his friends are doing yet unable to speak up for himself. Helping him find words for his experience, they'll encourage him to articulate his needs and feelings.
- Using children's literature and a "feelings picture chart," staff will help James begin to understand and put words to different emotions.[4] In addition, they'll do a unit on feelings for the whole class, using art, drama, puppet play, and books to encourage discussion and understanding of the range of emotions children and grown-ups can feel. Following this unit, they'll occasionally help James identify the range of emotions he feels himself, and those he sees other kids experiencing.

Seeking Outside Help

- Barb and Patricia will initiate a referral to the city's early childhood program, in the hopes that a speech and language evaluation will lead to James getting some specialized help. If this process is successful, they'll also ask for ongoing consultation to support their home and school-based efforts.
- Patricia will get some help from a child guidance specialist. With the goal of decreasing the number of stormy interchanges between herself and Mandy, she'll work on developing more effective limit-setting strategies and a more steadily positive, warm relationship with her high-strung daughter. As part of this effort, she'll try to better balance the amount of attention she gives each of her children.

Six months later, James looks quite different. He's long since mastered the early morning routine, and happily places his picture on the "Who's Here" chart as he enters the classroom. James still struggles to put his ideas in order, but tries much harder to do so. He's been getting plenty of help at home and at school, and now participates in a twice-weekly speech and language group through the city's school system. In general, he appears both happier and more tuned in. Barb tells me that he and Ben are still best friends, though both feel comfortable letting go of each other to find other connections in the classroom.

James has made a new friend, Jenny, who speaks mostly Chinese at home. Another child who struggles to communicate, Jenny often looks for James as she heads toward the housekeeping corner. Shortly after arriving for a scheduled observation, I see them there, laughing and talking as they set out a lunch of pancakes and pickles. Barb stops by for a chat. "Oh Jenny, did you ever eat pancakes and pickles? Are those pickles very sour?" Barb's face takes on a crinkled, unhappy look, and James begins to laugh. "I *love* pickles! Mom loves pickles! She puts too many pickles on her hot dogs and they fall out!" With a huge grin, James picks up the plate with its unlikely combo. "Want some Barb?"

10

Helping the High-Energy and/or Inattentive Child

Getting to Work When a Child Has Trouble Slowing Down or Tuning In

Children who struggle to harness attention can be divided into two basic groups: the spacey dreamers who seem to float through their days, and the "wiggly ones" whose activity levels are so high that it's hard for them to stop, look, and listen. With the first group, we mostly look to support increased focus. With the second, we target a combination of strengthened attention and body state regulation. This chapter explores approaches to both sets of children because the strategies used to address their vulnerabilities blend together.

Due to the complex neurodevelopmental factors involved for some of these youngsters—especially those who struggle with a combination of inattention and impulsivity—the strategies that follow may come across as confusingly detailed. However, they are more cumbersome to explain than to implement. Once parents and teachers understand what to do and why to do it, they're often surprised by their comfort levels in "getting to work."

HELPING CHILDREN LEARN TO TUNE IN

The first stage of these explorations looks at how parents and teachers foster a child's ability to focus successfully, an ability that connects the four elements of attention discussed in Chapter 2: popping up, tuning in, taking in, and popping down. It's the mastery of these elements that helps children follow directions, take in new information, learn new skills, and participate successfully in play and conversation.

What Issues Might Be Contributing to a Child's Inattention?

- Struggles with language and information processing
- Inner-focused temperament
- Problems regulating sensory experience
- Vulnerabilities in executive function (see next section)

- Difficulties regulating energy (see next section)
- Poor muscle tone and/or difficulties with motor planning
- Inconsistent limit setting at home or in school and/or a chaotic home life
- Conflict-ridden interactions with parents or siblings
- Overwhelming emotional issues/trauma
- Lack of sleep

Some Points to Remember

- Adults often make requests or give instructions before these children have successfully harnessed attention. Non-compliance frequently follows.
- Parents and teachers often ask for distractible children's attention only when they feel it's absolutely necessary. Consequently, these youngsters pop up and tune in mostly to requests they'd prefer not to hear. Over time, they become increasingly unmotivated to attend.
- In the effort to get a distractible child's attention, parents and teachers may—with increasing annoyance—repeat his name, the requested behavior, or the unpleasant consequences that will ensue if he doesn't respond. When their frustration reaches its peak, these adults often resort to yelling, the intensity of their reaction finally breaking through the child's lack of focus. This unfortunate but understandable pattern results in the child learning to wait until adults have become angry before, finally, tuning in.
- Changing these three patterns is at the heart of the work we do to strengthen the capacity for focus.

Getting to Work at Home and in School

Providing Skill-Building Opportunities

Working on Tuning In When the Child Is Doing Well

An important step in strengthening attention involves joining a youngster in activities he enjoys. Helping him pop up and tune in for moments of enjoyable connection and attention, we make eye contact (if he allows it) and convey a sense of pleasure once he's tuned in successfully. This reinforces a positive experience of focus.

Working on Tuning In Incrementally

Rather than initially expecting long periods of focus, we support growth a step at a time. First, we help the child stick with us for moments of pleasant interaction. Later, we start raising expectations, asking for longer stretches of connected, attentive interchange.

Chunking Down Goals for Behavior

Breaking down the elements of mastery, we make small, manageable demands at the beginning of this process. For example, a parent might ask a youngster to head upstairs, then go up and give him one task at a time as he gets ready for bed. (After all, these are the kids who head willingly to the bathroom to brush their teeth and are later found happily playing with a toy truck halfway there.)

Using a Child's Strengths to Support Mastery

We help children stretch their capacity for focus in vulnerable areas by playing to their strengths. For example, if a child easily attends to things he hears but has a harder time with things he sees, we pair something he can listen to with something he needs to look at.

Lending an Ally—Lending Some Focus

Throughout the day, adults offer their supportive presence to encourage focus—as a child dresses, does a project, or plays out a story. Even short, scattered periods of this scaffolding at home and in the classroom can make a big difference.

Setting Effective Expectations

Moving Close to the Child When Asking for Attention

These children don't respond well to requests for attention given from a distance. Moving next to the child—or, in school, giving him a one-on-one heads up that a class-wide request for focus is coming—helps facilitate success in tuning in.

Making Sure That the Child Has Successfully Harnessed Attention Before Issuing Instructions

Refraining from repeating a child's name or our instructions, we first take time to support the effort of tuning in: "That's great—you've stopped what you are doing. Now can you look here? Good job."

Making a Pleasant Connection Before Asking for Compliance

Underneath everything, these children want to please the people who care for them. When parents and teachers initiate positive moments of tuned-in connection before asking for attention to a request, things go far more smoothly.

Setting Consistent Limits at Home and in School

Clear and reasonable limits—set quickly and firmly—are an essential part of our efforts. In combination with the supportive strategies listed in this section, such limits add to the clean mix of leaning in and leaning out these children sorely need.

Monitoring Feedback Loops

Following the 90-10 Rule

As noted earlier, adults often "reward" the eventual focus of inattentive children with a less than welcome request or some criticism. To shift the unfortunate consequence of this pattern, we initially follow about 90% of our requests for focus with a wholly positive experience of connection (see earlier section). In only about 10% of cases do we use such requests to deliver a message that's less pleasurable.

Cutting Out Irritability

Once requests for attention become fraught with adult irritation, these kids begin tuning out partly to avoid unpleasantness. Therefore, parents and teachers seek a friendly style with which to use the strategies listed here. In response, children's inattention often lessens.

Modifying Family and Classroom Routines and Organization

Shooting for an Organized, Predictable Home Life

Children who have trouble harnessing attention do better when their families function with predictable routines. (Conversely, when life at home is on the chaotic side, distractibility often worsens.)

Using Well-Organized Transitions, Effectively Run Group Time, and Classroom-Wide Climate Control to Support Mastery

Children whose inattention stems from a high sensitivity to stimulation benefit from a calm, organized classroom atmosphere. Teachers will find the strategies outlined in Chapter 7 to be a big help in supporting increased focus.

Watching That Bedtimes and Bedtime Routines Allow Children to Get Enough Sleep

When children are overtired, their ability to focus often suffers. Yet inattentive kids can have trouble moving through evening routines, resulting in a later bedtime than parents intend. Parents set a consistent bedtime, back up routines so there is time for a little dawdling, then use the strategies listed here to help kids get to sleep at a reasonable hour.

Watching for Emotional, Physical, or Sexual Harm

Inattentive children may be reacting to physical, sexual, or emotional mistreatment, or to frighteningly violent conflicts at home. Thus parents and teachers watch carefully, taking action if they believe that any such situation is occurring, whether within or outside of the family.[1]

Seeking Outside Help

Attending to the Constitutional Factors That Make Paying Attention Difficult

Children with language processing issues—and those who have sensory issues, low muscle tone, or poor motor planning—may need extra help from parents, teachers, and outside specialists. If such help is indicated, parents contact their child's pediatrician and/or the local school department to initiate appropriate consultation or evaluation.

Seeking Additional Support if a Child Is Inattentive Because He's Overwhelmed

If a child appears too preoccupied with his feelings or too vigilant about his or family members' safety to focus successfully, consultation with and/or ongoing help from a child or family therapist may be essential. In such situations, advocacy and support services for the family are often important too.

Having Hearing Checked

Occasionally parents discover that a child's inattention stems from hearing difficulties. Major hearing loss is usually picked up before the preschool years, but hearing loss due to illness or chronic ear infections is not as easily noticed.

Consequently, a trip to the pediatrician's office for a screening is a sensible precaution.

Considering the Option of Medication

It's usually wise to refrain from considering pharmacological intervention for a young child before there are significant opportunities for focused, skill-based work at home and in school. But when a child is not responding to such help—or is so unregulated that he can't use the help he's offered—it may be time for a medication consult.

HELPING CHILDREN LEARN TO SLOW DOWN AND STAY CALM

These explorations now turn to strategies for supporting body state calm. Note that explaining and/or using these strategies effectively requires a familiarity with the constitutional factors connected to challenges in energy regulation (see Chapter 2). One such factor involves difficulties with sensory regulation. Another has to do with vulnerabilities in executive function. A number of the vulnerabilities in the latter category are reviewed in the "points to remember" listed shortly.

What Issues Might Be Contributing to the Child's Behavior?

- Constitutionally based high energy level
- Difficulties regulating sensory experience
- Vulnerabilities in executive function
- Hard to adapt temperament
- Inconsistent limit setting at home or in school and/or a chaotic home life
- Conflict-ridden interactions with parents or siblings
- Overwhelming emotional issues
- Lack of sleep

Some Points to Remember

- Children who operate at a consistently high energy level have trouble focusing on what is being said to them or asked of them when they are in their high-activity mode. They need to "slow down their motors" before they can take in information from the adults and kids around them. However, their skill in doing this is often poor.

- High-energy youngsters with executive function weaknesses have trouble using their minds to oversee their activities and monitor their performance. As a result, they may experience a range of challenges. It can be hard for them to think about future consequences in the face of present impulses. They may have trouble staying organized, and struggle with time management. It can be truly difficult for them to screen out interesting but irrelevant stimuli too, leading them to cruise the house or the classroom. Academic productivity is frequently at risk as well.
- As a result of the factors listed here, these youngsters may look chronically disobedient and impulsive. Not surprisingly, their caretakers tend to get highly frustrated and may end up doing a lot of nagging.
- It's common for such children to develop very oppositional habits as they begin to tune out such ever-present reminders to slow down and listen.

Learning to Slow Down and Sustain Focus—Stages of Growth

The strategies we use to support increased mastery require an understanding of how highly active children learn to manage their energy. Conceptualizing the growth process as unfolding in stages helps us remember that chunking down our overall goals into smaller units is the best route to success. Once we have a handle on these conceptual stages, however, it's important to acknowledge that work on this issue is rarely so orderly—attention to stages one and two melds together, and focus on stages three and four does too.[2]

Stage One: Achieving Adult-Supported Calm

In this stage the child learns to use his mind to direct his body to slow down; by its end, he is able to identify what slowing down feels like and, *with help*, can get himself to "coast down the energy highway."[3]

Stage Two: Achieving Adult-Supported Focus

Now, still with adult assistance, the child calms his body and then finds a settled activity on which to stay briefly focused. At the end of this stage, he competently uses adult lend-an-ally support to accomplish both tasks and is able to sustain attention on his chosen activity for at least ten or fifteen minutes.

Stage Three: Achieving Limited Independence in Maintaining Calm and Focus

At this point, the child can comfortably use adult scaffolding to slow down and find a settled activity. In addition, after remaining focused with this support in place, he sustains a state of calm attention while the adult leaves for short periods. Later in this stage, in response to increased mastery, the adult leaves for longer and longer periods.

Stage Four: Achieving Extended Independence in Maintaining
Calm and Focus

The child still requires support to slow down and focus. Now, however, he
can do more of the work himself. Using adult scaffolding as a signal to rely
on his own increased competence, he sustains attention on a settled activity
for twenty minutes or more. During this stage of growing independence,
adults watch carefully for signs of backsliding: Few children progress
through these stages in a linear fashion. Thus when a youngster is under
stress, feeling sick or tired, or working hard on other issues, his level of mastery may slip. In response, adults provide support and scaffolding typical of
stages one through three.

Getting to Work at Home and in School

Clarity about the nature of these four stages , in combination with an understanding of how to help children tune in, assists parents and teachers in doing
the multifaceted work active/inattentive children need. This work includes a
focus on changing patterns of irritability at home and in the classroom, and
relies on a mix of clear limits and extensive skill-building support. It requires
a big dose of patience on the part of adults too.

Fostering the Experience of Connection

Offering Support, Hope, and Warmth

High-energy kids need time to develop new skills, and along the way they'll
require plenty of firmness. But such children can be in danger of feeling unlovable, both at home and in school. Though it can be a tall order for parents and
teachers to stay upbeat and positive with these impulsive whirlwinds, cherish-
ing them even in the midst of their difficulties is the first step toward change.

Providing Skill-Building Opportunities

Progressing Through the Four Stages, Starting with
Stages One and Two

In school, teachers support increasingly independent focus as best they can,
given the overall context of classroom life. At home, by the end of two or
three months, the child is spending at least fifteen to thirty minutes a day in
an expected "quiet time." Many parents call this time by the child's name,
that is, "Billy Time," and find a consistent spot for it in the day's schedule.

Throughout this process, it is important for both parents and teachers to set limited, reasonable goals and to remember that the process of growth may be slow and unsteady. Each bit of progress leads to the next; every time a child is able to calm down and focus, even if briefly, he's made some movement in the right direction. Possibilities for supporting growth during this period include the following:

1. *Using imagery to support new learning*: "Slow down the beat;" "Be like a sea turtle, swim steady and slow;" "Your engine is running fast—let's slow it down;" and so on. Children like to help generate these.
2. *Encouraging mind-body awareness*: Adults help the child notice which parts of his body are still on the speedy side, for example, "That's great, your arms are quiet, but your legs need to slow down now too."
3. *Modeling targeted skills*: In the process of supporting mind-body awareness, adults model the "slow motor way," speaking quietly and pacing their words.
4. *Playing action games that support mastery*: "I'll meet you in the wiggles, you meet me in the slows;" speedy driver—gentle driver; slow motion baseball—these games can be as creative and varied as adults care to make them.
5. *Developing a code phrase to reinforce new skills*: The child comes up with a descriptive label for a calm body state. The label is paired with the state each time the child successfully settles down, and eventually the phrase itself helps the child achieve body-state regulation.

Note that as adults help children progress through these first two stages, they often encourage activities that take place with the child either sitting in a chair or, even better, on the floor—"bottom on the floor" play helps kids stay calm.

Strengthening the Ability to Harness Attention

Children who have trouble regulating energy often have difficulty harnessing attention too. Thus the previous section's strategies for supporting focus are frequently used in conjunction with those listed here.

Lending an Ally—Lending Some Calm

Parents and teachers join the child in conversation and play, scaffolding experiences of calm, organized activity. Then, as he becomes more able to settle into group play experiences, they model appropriate interchanges, lending support as necessary. Even short periods of this assistance will help the child interact more successfully with peers, especially when paired with "slow motor" work throughout the day.

Offering Opportunities for Physical Containment

Physical touch and visual images can help a child slow down—an adult's hands on the child's shoulders; nonverbal cues during transitions (hands by sides, body in a body bubble that doesn't touch anyone else's bubble); placement in smaller groups during classroom hand-washing; a special rug, pillow, or contained place for the child during group time in school or playtime at home, and so on.

Providing Physical Outlets and Sensory Stimulation

Making Sure There Is Plenty of Time for the Child to Play at a Comfortable "Motor Speed"

Noting when the child needs opportunities for physical discharge, adults offer them regularly. Otherwise, it's going to be even harder for him to do the work of staying calm.

Offering Individually Tailored "Sensory Diets"

Parents and teachers note whether a youngster craves additional stimulation or feels overwhelmed when sensory input is too much. Then they figure out how to help the child regulate sensation more comfortably. With some kids, this will involve adding sensory experiences to a child's routine: time at the water or sand table, hugs that offer deep pressure, the opportunity to carry a heavy object on an errand or in a game. With others, it will require cutting down on a home's or classroom's overall level of stimulation. Either way, adults attend to the importance of sensory regulation both when the child is revving up in a troublesome way and as part of providing a steady sensory diet throughout the day. (See also "Getting to Work when a Child has Sensory Sensitivities" in Chapter 12, which addresses strategies for handling family patterns in relationship to these issues.)

Strengthening Executive Functioning and Problem-Solving

Helping the Child Learn the Skills of "Self-Talk"

Offering the skill-building work that allows children to better monitor their behavior, adults teach them to control their impulses by being a STAR: to Stop, Think, Ask, and Respond.[4] First, a youngster stops himself from acting before reflecting. Then he tells himself to think: What will happen if I do this? Is there something else I should do instead? After he engages in such self-monitoring, he learns to ask: How did I do? Did it work? These questions point to one version of the "self-talk" that helps children control their impulses through complex situations.[5]

Helping the Child Understand What the Faces and Voices Around Him Are Conveying

Parents and teachers help the child pay attention to social cues: "Do you notice what my face is doing? Do you know what it means? It means that I've had enough questions (or enough play time) for now... What should you do now?" First helping the child regulate his energy, then directing him to focus on such nonverbal information, adults encourage him to use his growing understanding of social cues to shape his responses.

Supporting Problem-Solving

High-energy children often react impulsively to frustrating situations they're experiencing with siblings and friends. Moving in quickly when a problem has just emerged, adults first support the child in slowing down his body and mind. Only then do they help him articulate his dilemma and think out a response.

Setting Effective Expectations

Moving Close to the Child When Making Requests

High-energy youngsters often don't respond well to instructions given from a distance. When parents and teachers move nearby, ask for a child's attention, and only then issue a clear request, they go far in supporting good behavior.

Setting Effective Limits While Avoiding Negative Interactions

Adults avoid chronically negative interactions between themselves and a child by finding a good mix of leaning out and leaning in. Settling on a calm, effective approach to limit setting, they modify the number of demands they make throughout the day, then remain consistent about the limits they do set. As part of setting clear expectations for behavior, they also clamp down firmly on the relentless negotiating that some of these kids do so masterfully.

Using Behavior Charts and Token Systems Judiciously

Some active youngsters respond well to token systems and behavior charts. Parents and teachers must beware, however. High-energy children tend to get bored quickly. In addition, such systems are often instituted with overly vague goals ("has a good morning") or with dauntingly long periods for good behavior ("has a good day"). Instead, reward programs should be used over short time frames, then ended before they wear out their welcome. They must offer incentives for compliance to clear, limited expectations ("puts on shoes by himself;" "asks and waits nicely during breakfast"). Expectations are raised slowly as the child gains mastery and, to alleviate boredom, rewards are changed frequently.

Making Sure That Feedback Is Given Directly at the "Point of Performance"

We know that these children struggle to remember the future as they live in the present. This "in the moment" quality means that adults must give positive feedback quickly when a child is successful in meeting goals.[6] At the same time, all limits should be delivered directly following noncompliant behavior. This kind of steady, immediate feedback slowly fosters a child's ability to control impulses by self-monitoring.

Planning for Predictably Difficult Situations

Setting Expectations in Advance

Parents think out how to handle predictably stressful situations: birthday parties, family gatherings, trips to the grocery store, and so on. The first step in such planning is to come up with a sensible picture of what a particular child can handle and to define reasonable expectations for behavior. A high-energy child, for example, will not be able to sit still through a long family wedding, or behave himself with ease through a birthday party in which other children are calmly doing a long art activity. Parents do what they can to refrain from bringing children into situations where they'll be set up to fail, then come up with an "exit plan"—a clear picture of how they'll respond when a child needs a break or is misbehaving—for places they do go.

Exit plans are based on the assumption that high-energy kids won't be able to remain completely settled even when they're trying their hardest. They operate best when parents find time for breaks *before* significant misbehavior happens. Older children are informed of these plans in advance: "If you start to get restless, we'll go outside and take a break. Maybe we'll even play tag! Then you'll come back in for some more time with your cousins. It's okay if you need a break, but if you hit or don't listen, we'll sit in the car for fifteen minutes."

Teachers can also think proactively about how to handle stressful, over-stimulating situations: all school assemblies, classroom presentations to parents, and so on. After developing reasonable expectations based on a particular child's level of mastery, they share those expectations clearly. It's in response to such a focus on incremental success—rather than on expectations for perfect behavior—that active children come to feel that they're positive members of their classrooms rather than their teachers' biggest headaches.

Using Visuals to Support Self-Control

When a child regularly struggles at certain times of the school day, he can be given visual assistance in knowing what's expected. For example, a teacher might make a chart for math time. With stick figures going through a five-part progression, the chart would show the following: (1) a child sitting quietly in a group as his teacher explains the lesson; (2) that youngster walking to his seat; (3) his sitting concentrating on work; (4) his raising his hand for help; and (5) his smiling as he brings his paper up to the teacher's desk. Once such charts are shared and understood, teachers can use nonverbal cues to give the child a thumbs-up when he's following the progression, while offering friendly and equally silent reminders when he's off task.

Some teachers even offer an active youngster one or two non-punitive "I need a break" tickets that can be cashed in during group times. The child is expected to show up and remain in group at first, then has a designated place—set up with a quiet activity—where he can go for short periods before returning. Parents may find visual aids useful too, especially for morning routines, bath time, or bedtime.

Starting Small

When a child is predictably difficult during everyday routines, we start with clear but lowered expectations and build from there. For example, a child never sits through meals at home, and his irritated parents have allowed him to hop in and out of his chair to cruise the kitchen. The new plan begins with a timer set for two minutes, during which the child is expected to sit calmly and eat. If he doesn't sit for that period, he'll be asked to leave the kitchen entirely or to sit in a nearby time-out chair. If he does, he's allowed to get down, though he can't take food with him. To make things easier, there are some special activities he can do at a table or blanket in a corner of the kitchen. Once the child has gotten down, he's free to play quietly, but not to disrupt the family's mealtime. If at any time he decides he's still hungry, he's welcome to come back to the table.

Parents always lay out such plans in advance with the child. Then, after the plan fosters some initial success, the timer is set for increasingly longer periods, with the end result that the child can join a family meal—if he's four or five years old—for perhaps ten to fifteen minutes.

Doing "Practice Runs"

When routine, away-from-home activities are particularly difficult, parents consider doing practice runs. For example, a child is regularly hard to manage on trips to the grocery store. Dad sits down with him to lay out expectations. "You have to sit, not stand, in the cart. We'll talk in soft voices. You *can* pick your favorite box of cereal, but you *can't* touch other things in the aisles. If you follow the rules, you'll get a special treat that you can have in the car! If you don't, we'll leave the store and I won't play with you when we get home." Dad may choose to make a pictured list of these expectations as he and his child discuss them; he can later use this visual reminder just before they enter the grocery store.

Puppets or stuffed animals can be used to run through both the "happy" and the "unhappy" grocery trip scenarios, with some playful dramatization of the latter. Then, *the parent plans one or more unnecessary trips to the grocery store in which he assumes things won't go well. He is ready to leave with his child after just one reminder of what's expected, and does so quickly when the child isn't compliant.* Such dry runs, though time-consuming and annoying for parents, often have a powerful effect on children's behavior over the long haul.

Modifying Family and Classroom Organization

Shooting for an Organized, Predictable Home Life

Kids who have trouble regulating their energy do better when their families function with predictable routines. (Conversely, when life at home is on the chaotic side, a child's frenetic energy level often worsens.)

Using Well-Organized Transitions, Effectively Run Group Time, and Classroom-Wide "Climate Control" to Support Mastery

Children who have trouble regulating their energy benefit greatly from the classroom-based strategies outlined in Chapter 8.

Decreasing Reliance on TV, DVDs, and Computer Games

Many parents of active kids rely on screen-time activities to keep their children out of mischief. Such activities appear useful because they allow youngsters to slow down. Unfortunately, screen time does little to help a child attain mastery in regulating energy and maintaining focus.[7] Consequently, parents slowly decrease their reliance on these activities, at the same time increasing expectations for the child to slow down and focus on his own. Eventually, a gently enforced quiet time (the "Billy Time" mentioned earlier) replaces the frequent use of screen time in promoting calm in the house and in the child.

Finding Time for Fun Even When Things Are Busy

Parents monitor whether they have enough time to feel in synch with their children and—even if it means that certain chores have to wait—find opportunities for relaxed, playful, and pleasurable experiences for everyone.

Watching That Bedtimes Allow Kids to Get Enough Sleep

When children are overtired, their ability to stay calm and focused can suffer. Yet high-energy kids often have particular trouble making the shift from the active mode of the daytime to the sleepier, slower mode of pre-bedtime. Parents set a bedtime, back up routines so there is enough time for their child to make the switch and then, if possible, reduce lighting. They insist on quieter voices and set a consistent routine of stories and quiet play—often in a child's room—to help him get to sleep at a reasonable hour.

Watching for Emotional, Physical, or Sexual Harm

Children who are both highly active and inattentive are sometimes reacting to physical, sexual, or emotional mistreatment, or to violent conflict at home. Thus parents and teachers watch carefully, taking action if they sense that such a situation is occurring, whether within or outside of the family.[8]

Seeking Outside Help

Considering the Possibility of Consultation, Evaluation, or Specialized Services

If it appears that a child is struggling to regulate sensation, an evaluation for sensory integration issues may be in order. Outside treatment and/or a clearly planned out "sensory diet" may have a very positive impact on a child's ability to stay calm and focused.

Thinking About Therapeutic Help

Sometimes a child or family has gotten so entrenched in difficulties connected to a constitutionally based high activity level that help from a family or child therapist can be useful. When a child's frenetic activity level is connected to overwhelming experiences—and the overwhelming emotions that result—therapy may be a necessity.

Considering the Option of Medication

See "Seeking Outside Help" under "Helping Children Learn to Tune in."

The Challenges of Elementary School: Helping High-Energy Kids Participate in Calm, Focused Learning in the Classroom

In addition to the strategies just outlined, it is important to take note of the challenges of working with high-energy, distractible children beyond the kindergarten year. Because while many preschool and kindergarten teachers feel relatively free to concentrate on children's developmental needs, first- and second-grade teachers often feel pressured to stay focused on academic progress. This pressure translates into a tough road for everyone, since such youngsters can struggle mightily to remain attentive, calm classroom members. Part of the challenge often stems from the vulnerabilities in executive function explored earlier; these weaknesses make it hard for children to plan out, sequence, and then monitor schoolwork. In response, teachers need to target not just academic but also developmental goals; if they don't, these children may begin to feel defeated and inferior. In the most dire cases, they come to hate school, hate themselves, or both.

Having a Joint Academic and Developmental Agenda

What additional principles help teachers work with these kids through their elementary school years? Let's add the following list to those we've come up with earlier[9]:

- We need a learning profile—what is easy, what is fun, what is harder, what is hardest? *Why* is this so?
- We try to *teach* rather than *manage or correct* in the developmental realm, becoming positive allies in supporting growth.
- We *isolate agendas*, so that a child can attend to each task without getting overwhelmed: First a slow body—then attention—then connection—then planning—*then focused learning*—then reinforcement through positive attention.
- We monitor challenges and track success, so that while kids experience their "smarts," adults stay a step ahead of the game.
- We anticipate difficulties and stumbling blocks, staying clear but positive: "Today was a day that . . . Tomorrow we'll try . . ."
- We *explain learning and developmental challenges to children*, helping them understand the way their minds work: "You're the kind of kid whose mind does 'x' easily. It's harder for your mind to do 'y'."
- We keep motivation high, using our connections with children and our pleasure in their accomplishments as a primary reinforcement. When needed, we use concrete reinforcements too.

- We use a mix of support, firm expectations, and accommodations in our approach to a child's challenges.
- We try not to personalize.

Approaches to Intervention in the Upper Grades: Targeting a Mix of Classroom-Wide and Individualized Strategies

The strategies consultants help elementary school teachers put in place for these youngsters always involve a mix of classroom-wide and individualized approaches, and can be as creative as teachers wish to make them. They include attention exercises and getting to work games, random checks for classroom-wide focus, and ample breaks for kids to move around. Teachers look at how their rooms are set up too, make sure that there are non-penalizing places for kids to work by themselves, and then take care that those places aren't just used by the class's most inattentive kids. In addition, they have periods of well-enforced, classroom-wide quiet, so that children who have trouble working in the midst of conversation experience the climate they need to succeed. Finally, teachers find creative approaches to *isolating skills*, and check in with individual children about the following questions[10]:

- Are you ready? What does it look like? How will we know?
- Are you attending? What does it look like? How will we know?
- Are you planning? What does it look like? How will we know?
- Are you staying on task? What does it look like? How will we know?

Strategies in Action: Helping Children Stay Calm, Organized, and Attentive

Getting to Work With Adam—Creative Approaches to Supporting a High-Energy Kindergartener's Growing Skill and Self-Confidence

At the point that consultation was requested for five-year-old Adam, he was full of both motion and mischief, and alternately delighted and incensed his single mother Lisa and his kindergarten teachers. It quickly became clear that while it would take some time to unravel the reasons for this boy's relentless energy, distractibility, and defiance; helping him was certainly going to require some changes in family dynamics: Lisa was so chronically upset with her son—and he with her—that life at home had a distressingly negative tone. But the first step would have to be some support, because by the end of my initial conversation with this young parent, it was clear that she felt profoundly alone in her struggles.

When families or teachers arrive in a state of intense distress, clinicians don't always wait to get a full picture of what's going on before getting to work. Instead, they often begin by offering a feel for how the process of change will unfold, and a sense of optimism about where things will end up. Thus, not long after our first conversation, I sent Lisa a letter:

> Hi Lisa—I wanted to drop you a note about what we're trying to do over the next couple of weeks. I know life with Adam has been really difficult, and that it can be hard to calm things down when you feel so discouraged. But it will be a great start if you can...
>
> 1. Focus on the "big stuff," the really unmanageable issues, for now. If you can, let the lesser problems go for a bit. For these few weeks, make as few demands as you can, then stick to them in the way we talked about. This should help cut down on your and his feeling of constant battle.
> 2. Leave out as much of the talking and lecturing as you can, so that mostly Adam gets clear expectations for behavior and quick consequences when necessary. It will help if you stay firm without getting annoyed, even when he's pushing. That's easy to say but hard to do, so just do the best you can.
> 3. When Adam is getting testy, try to ignore how he's attempting to get you going. Take a minute to relax before seeing if he'll let you give him some friendly redirection away from the hole he's starting to dig himself into. Once he's dug in, he doesn't always believe that he can get out, nor that you can help! (And by the end, you probably feel like you're in there with him too...)
>
> Don't worry too much if all you're doing for now is just calming things down a little. If there are times you can enjoy him, that's great. But if not, that's okay too. We'll get there soon! Most of all, try to be gentle with yourself—I sensed in our meeting how much pain this situation is causing you. I know Adam has been very tough. But he's also a terrific kid and we can make lots of headway, slowly but steadily, so that he'll feel better about himself and be easier for everyone to be with. Hang in there, and I'll talk with you soon...

What Do We See?

Offering Support and Hope During Information Gathering

The intent of this note was to give Lisa some support while starting work on the harmful interplay between parental frustration and child defiance that's often a part of the mix when a high-energy youngster is acting up. In addition, it conveyed a few important ideas—that the work of helping Adam would proceed step-by-step; that I understood that Lisa yearned to feel more loving as a parent;

and that underneath his difficult behavior, Adam was a delightful boy with many strengths. Most of all, I hoped to give this discouraged mother a sense of hope.

Taking Stock of Family Dynamics and Family Stress

Hope was going to be an essential ingredient of change. In our second meeting, Lisa spoke of experiencing such distress watching her dynamo of a boy blast his way through birthday parties and family gatherings that she quickly became critical. She talked of feeling intense shame when her son's behavior was out of synch with that of cousins and friends, and of how this shame led her to try "to fix Adam's problem and fast." As a result, the interchanges between her and her son could quickly escalate into yelling, rough physical contact, and mutual antagonism, and this youngster had become practically immune to his mother's constant admonitions to stop or slow down. I soon learned that Adam's teachers, too, noticed themselves giving him copious, irritation-laced feedback. At the end of a particularly trying day, they realized that he probably hadn't learned about much other than their annoyance with his relentless activity level.

What Do We Think?

Noting the Intersection of a Child's Hard-Wiring With His Ongoing Experience

Of course, this letter was just the beginning of a long process of understanding and intervention. Soon after it was written, Lisa, Adam's teacher, and I talked about how this child's hard-wiring often undermined his efforts to do well. Because Adam, it became clear, was a youngster with a full set of the constitutional vulnerabilities connected to harnessing attention and regulating energy. Poking at his kindergarten buddies, listening only to directions delivered with frustrated sternness, highly intelligent yet in danger of becoming the school's newest "bad boy," Adam struggled with many issues: impulsivity, inadequate problem-solving skills, difficulty slowing down, difficulty paying attention, limited organizational competence. Picture the challenges of a child who has weak executive function and poor body state regulation, mix those difficulties into a chaotic, stressed family life, and you might meet a defiant whirlwind like Adam.

What Do We Do?

Targeting Incremental Goals for Mastery

Following some initial consultation, Adam's mother and teachers quickly agreed on some basic ideas: that Adam was starting out with little skill in slowing down, that at first we'd mainly target increased skill in this area, and that it would be a while before we could reasonably expect him to stay at activities for prolonged periods. In fact, the home-school team didn't ask this boy to play peacefully on his own for many months after initiating initial strategies. Since Adam had considerable difficulty harnessing attention as well, these "partners in care" also supported little, pleasurable moments of tuning in long before expecting him to remain focused through a long set of instructions.

It took Lisa a while to develop the patience required for this work. Initially, as she tried to help Adam slow down, she'd wait until he was terribly wound up, then sternly use the cues we'd devised together. Resulting in a shouting match more often than not, these efforts were frustratingly unsuccessful. Eventually, she came to see that she needed to offer help *before* she was completely fed up. She learned to be careful, too, that she didn't rev up along with her son when things got intense. The process of her gaining these new skills required close attention on both our parts; sometimes we spent our consultation meetings teasing apart Lisa and Adam's interactions as if we were looking at the individual frames of a home movie. After a while, however, Lisa started to feel great pride in her ability to help her son find "the silky feeling"—her son's code phrase for the calm, relaxed sensation that signaled his success in slowing down. Here's an example of this skill-building assistance in action:

> Lisa is sitting on Adam's bed. Covering one of her hands is "Marvin," an impish-looking monkey puppet. Resting in the other is Adam's favorite stuffed animal, a scruffy-haired cat he's named "Keeka." Marvin has been gleefully jumping around on the bed. Adam's face wrinkles in delight. Suddenly, Keeka's soft voice asks Marvin if he can stop. "You're making me nervous," she purrs. A discussion between the monkey and cat ensues. "Can you slow down a little? Here, pat my fur, it will help." Eventually, Adam plays Keeka, giving clear instructions to Marvin the monkey on how to calm down.

In addition to his high energy and trouble with attention, Adam tended to act before thinking, impulsively grabbing a coveted toy from a buddy or knocking over a juice pitcher in the effort to snatch the first drink at school. He certainly needed help in all three areas, each of which maps onto one of this book's developmental building blocks. However, once again, it was going to be important not to ask too much of this child at once. Consequently, Adam's mother and teachers agreed to manage his impulsivity as best they could until he had his energy level and ability to focus more in hand, and to do so—as far as humanly possible—without losing patience. After all, despite his frequent mishaps, much of Adam's misbehavior came from a lack of mastery rather than willful disobedience.

Early on, these approaches were hard to implement in school. One stumbling block was that Mrs. Donovan, Adam's teacher, had been applying a

common standard to all the youngsters in her typically energetic classroom.
During circle time, for example, "Mrs. D" called on children when they were
sitting calmly and raising their hands. This expectation, of course, was tremendously difficult for Adam, who would squirm his way through such group
activities, poking his classmates, fiddling with whatever objects might be
within reach, and calling out with glee when he had something he wanted to
say. In response, he was given endless reminders, called upon near the end of
such activities, or, not infrequently, asked to sit in a chair behind the group.

Following a consultation session, Mrs. D began working on simple body
awareness coupled with the task of harnessing attention. Her efforts included
setting a different standard for Adam, one that supported an only rudimen-
tary ability to slow down and focus. Thus she started giving Adam a job until
just before group time was about to start. In addition, she allowed him steady
access to the group space's prized corner seat, one that would support his back
and help him refrain from leaning on other kids. Then she would watch for
brief moments of connection and attention, calling on Adam often when he
was having some success in meeting her now chunked-down expectations. At
this point in the process, Mrs. D would compliment him on his demeanor,
give him some additional, specific instructions to encourage increasingly
focused behavior, and then invite him to contribute to the discussion at hand.
The flexibility to do all this without worrying that she was lowering the bar
for other children was a crucial ingredient of her efforts.

Strengthening Executive Function

Preschool and elementary school teachers may need help in understanding
the idea of executive function. One way consultants can support such learning is to provide a visual image for this element of mental processing. Thus
we paint the picture of a mental "boss," a chairman of the board who sits at
the head of a hypothetical table in the brain, monitoring behavior, noting
time, and reminding children to stay focused and on task. This executive also
helps kids envision the future as they operate in the present—offering steady
advice to behave well in the face of impulses to do the contrary by predicting
unfortunate consequences for children *before* they do something unacceptable. (Part of helping children develop a metaphorical chairman of the board
is supporting the self-talk defined in Chapter 2.)

Once teachers picture how a weaker element of brain functioning causes
so many of the problems they encounter, they're more likely to be both understanding and proactive. The strategies they use in their efforts can then be as
varied as their teaching styles. What such strategies share is the intention to
support stop–look–listen and stop–think–act progressions. These are objec-
tives that Mrs. D demonstrated as she worked to support impulse control
and self-monitoring. Let's look at several moments from a period toward the
end of Adam's kindergarten year. Note how this teacher uses cues that she
and Adam have practiced many times before, how she makes sure to insert

moments of connection before delivering any necessary course corrections, and how she reinforces Adam's success through the warmth of her responses to his efforts. The result is a boy who is motivated to do the hard work that is being asked of him:

> Adam is pacing back and forth in the construction corner, directing his two buddies not to take down the spaceship they've all been building.
> Mrs. D heads over. "Adam, red light." Adam looks up, and stops cold. "Good job! It looks like you've been doing some great building. What have you made?" As Adam explains that the spaceship has room for three astronauts, Mrs. D is duly impressed. "I'm wondering, did you hear what I asked a minute ago, Adam?" He shakes his head in the negative. "I thought maybe you'd missed it … it's time to clean up. Can you help put things away?" Still standing still, Adam nods. Mrs. D gives him a warm smile, then says, "Okay, green light Adam. Thanks for your help!" As she leaves, Adam kneels down and gets to work.

Adam has had a rough morning. Now it's circle time, a point in the day that's a challenge even on his good days. Mrs. D. calls him over and asks him to bring a note down to the school nurse. When he gets back, kids will be getting ready for some full-group math instruction. Can he come in *really* quietly and sit on his mat? She'll be so proud if he can stop at the door, give her the "I'm ready" sign, and then tiptoe to his spot. He takes the note and skips out of the classroom.

Setting Effective Limits

The strategies illustrated in these vignettes emerged out of Mrs. D's stance of readiness, as she set expectations and offered developmental scaffolding throughout Adam's day. Unfortunately, as we've noted, such a healthy mix of leaning in and leaning out can be especially hard to maintain in the face of a child's impulsive behavior. At first, Adam's mother found herself stuck in a much messier version of these two elements, yelling at her son to stop jumping on the couch, then giving him a hug when she saw his look of pained mortification at being scolded once again, or acquiescing with irritation to his request to run round the house after bath time. Lisa needed more clarity about when to offer the skill-building assistance that would target mastery, when to provide consistent limits that would support containment and safety, and how to do each comfortably.

Lisa had little practice setting effective limits. She hated the way she sounded when she was being stern; it reminded her of being screamed at by her forbidding parents. In order to help her master effective approaches to setting limits, we spent a number of meetings sketching out firm responses to Adam's predictably difficult behavior. At the same time, she began seeking out times to enjoy her son, noticing with increasing pride his endless curiosity, his love of the natural world, and his surprising ability to create complicated structures out of simple materials—if he could only stick around long enough to do so. Lending an ally to support his growing ability to focus, she and Adam started making a town out of cardboard, a little bit each day. And the pillow fights they started having a few times a week seemed to go far in helping him see that he could find a playful place to put both his intensely competitive spirit and his deeply-felt frustration.

Throughout this period of growth, Lisa needed help remembering that Adam would require both practice and time to make steady gains. In fact, it took many months for this child to learn to slow down and even longer to comfortably pop up and tune in to cues and requests. It was well into our work when Lisa came in excitedly, reporting that she'd squatted down next to Adam, gently called his name (only once!) and Adam, engrossed in the midst of a building project, looked up with interest. Behind this seemingly effortless exchange was months of skill-building assistance targeting both energy regulation and the four elements of attention.

Considering the Option of Medication

The slow development of more affectionate family and classroom interactions had a very beneficial effect on Adam's development. Even so, his progress wasn't linear, and during Adam's third grade year, Lisa decided that a medication trial might be wise. Because with that year's increased academic demands, her son was having a much harder time remaining focused. As he labored unsuccessfully to stay on track, he seemed to feel increasingly discouraged, and his teachers saw him retreating to the role of class clown. Lisa had been approached about the idea of medication before. She also knew that the factors leading to an attention-deficit/hyperactivity disorder (ADHD) diagnosis meshed closely with Adam's challenges. But she'd always thought that she and teachers could give Adam the help he needed without having to fill his body with medicine that had effects she didn't entirely trust. Yet after all their efforts, Adam was still struggling and it seemed time to consider medication.

Entertaining the possibility of pharmacological intervention can be a big step for some parents. Others jump at the chance. As they consider their options, parents are often deeply affected by their own histories and cultures. They're impacted by mainstream culture too: We live during an era in which sustained therapeutic and developmental help is hard to access and pay for, while medication may be quickly suggested as an important—and reimbursable—intervention. There is no easy answer to when a medication trial is indicated. With young children, it often makes sense to start with a period of emotional, behavioral, and developmental assistance, both at home and in school. The consultant's job, over this time frame, includes supporting parents and teachers as they take a second look at a child's struggles, think about how their reactions may be playing a role in his difficulties, and offer steady help in the midst of his predictable ups and downs. After providing such guidance, clinicians sometimes end up in a perplexing bind. We may believe that, in ideal circumstances, a child could get the help he needs without the addition of medication. At the same time, it may appear that the youngster's family is too overwhelmed to provide an adequate version of that help. In such situations, medication may give the child enough of an emotional or behavioral boost that his family becomes more able to offer him at least some of the support he needs.

At other times, even with steady, collaborative efforts between parents and teachers, a child seems buried under his own nature. Staying afloat in the classroom or at home is a terrible trial and, on occasion, the very experience of walking through a school's doors—or struggling with family realities day after day—sets off intense feelings of failure. In these situations, too, a medication trial may make sense. As responsible clinicians, we keep our eyes open for how a child is responding to such a trial, noting whether the medication in question seems to be helpful, whether there are notable side-effects, or whether the match of medication (or dosage) to child may be poor. In the last two cases our role is, in part, to advocate for responsible care, especially if a child's family is too overwhelmed to stay on top of the situation by themselves. In addition, when caregivers do choose to go this route, we encourage them to see medication as one element of an overall approach to a child's difficulties.[11]

All this said, for Adam, who'd worked so hard, and whose mother and teachers had worked so hard with him, the decision to try medication was a good one. Adam himself was a partner in the decision to give the idea a try and, after a few weeks of dosage-tinkering, was clear about his feelings. Though he disliked taking pills, his "attention medicine" did help him stay on track in school.

The last I time I heard about Adam, he was in seventh grade. He continued, of course, to be very active, but was negotiating the challenges of middle school, had some good friends, and was far easier to parent. A gifted athlete, he was—to everyone's surprise and pleasure—showing signs of the talent and focus it takes to become a skillful chess player. It all sounds a bit magical, but as we've seen, the process of change had been far from straightforward. Lisa had indeed become a more patient and skillful mother, but still had a dangerously hot temper, and still lashed out at Adam more times than she wished. Adam's teachers would just be celebrating a period of wonderful progress when he'd go through a patch of restless inattention that really worried them. Medication had helped, but wasn't a panacea. Though far happier than the kindergartener I'd met long before, Adam could still be impulsive with friends, and his teachers could never get him to slow down quite enough to take full advantage of his impressive intelligence. No longer in danger of being his school's "bad boy," Adam was now known as a delightful underachiever whose addition to a class list would make for an interesting but exhausting year. And as for Lisa? She had become the increasingly proud mother of a child who told his friends, "Let's go to my house. My mom is great!"

11

Helping the Easily Frustrated, Impulsive Child

Getting to Work When a Child Doesn't Calm Down and Think Before Acting

Parents and teachers often feel overwhelmed by easily frustrated youngsters. Such distress isn't surprising: Once these children have gotten upset, they don't think before they act, often lashing out at those around them. Classroom and family life quickly suffer. In order to function more successfully, these children must learn to tolerate frustration, to develop problem-solving skills, and to find safe places to express and work through their feelings.

The first task in helping an easily frustrated youngster is to understand why she loses composure so easily. Because when approaches to intervention are based on mistaken ideas, things may become more rather than less stressful for everyone. For example, if teachers wrongly interpret the frustration of a child with subtle but significant language processing difficulties as coming from an inability to handle limits, they may end up using "time away" as a core strategy when a primary focus on communication might serve her better (Gilliam and de Mesquita, 2000). On the other hand, when a youngster's behavior stems from inconsistent limit setting at home, clearly enforced expectations, in combination with supportive lend-an-ally work, may be just what is needed (Barkley, 1997b).

What Issues Might Be Contributing to a Child's Difficulty Managing Frustration?

- Inconsistent limit setting at home
- High intensity temperament and/or constitutionally based low adaptability
- Struggles with language and information processing
- A disorganized or chaotic home life
- Conflict-ridden interactions with parents or siblings
- Overwhelming experiences, including domestic violence, and/or physical, emotional, or sexual abuse
- Feelings of confusion or inadequacy in the classroom
- Exposure to violent material in the media
- Insufficient sleep

Some Points to Remember

- Children who struggle to manage frustration can get stuck in an escalating pattern with their parents: The child begins to lose control, a parent threatens consequences, then the child's behavior escalates. At some point, the parent loses his temper, screaming at the youngster to stop what he, the parent, is now doing as well.
- It's not uncommon for parents and teachers to change their expectations midstream if an easily frustrated child looks like she's about to lose control. As a result, the child is inadvertently reinforced for explosive behavior.
- Kids who have gone beyond a certain emotional threshold can't think clearly enough to reason their way through their dilemmas. Past this point, they've also lost their ability to take into account how badly they'll feel about an outburst after they've calmed down. However, children in this state of agitation often appear to make sense. As a result, adults sometimes continue efforts to help these kids see reason long after such efforts only enflame the situation further.[1]
- If a child is in this state of emotional overload, her only job should be to regain composure. Once she does, problem-solving assistance may be useful.
- Children who lose control frequently often have only marginal problem-solving skills, even when they're calm. In addition to any necessary limits, they also need help learning to evaluate and choose alternatives when situations aren't to their liking.
- Easily frustrated youngsters are hard to be around and they know it. They often begin to see themselves as not only unpleasant but also unloved.
- Research tells us that exposure to on-screen fighting and violence can significantly increase aggressive behavior.[2] Aggressively themed toy choices can also have a negative impact.[3] Some of our work with families may involve education about the impact of what children see and play with, and encouragement of healthier options for home-based activities.

Getting to Work at Home

Supporting Connection

Making Time for Relaxed Contact

Parents look for regular opportunities to connect with their youngster and work to avoid irritability through effective limit setting. They also make time to join the child in play, shooting for mutually enjoyable experiences during which she gets to be in charge.

Connecting Warmly Before Expecting Compliance

Handling everyday requests they don't like can be truly hard for these kids. When caregivers initiate positive moments of tuned-in connection before asking for compliance with a less than enjoyable expectation, things go far more smoothly.

Setting Effective Expectations

Enforcing Consistent Limits

Parents plan out when to ignore their youngster's misbehavior and when to stand firm. Then, when the child exhibits a targeted behavior, they act quickly, hanging on for the ride if she reacts angrily. The disciplinary strategies they use must be strong enough that the child learns from her mistakes but moderate enough that she can continue to have a reasonable day once consequences are over.

Considering the Judicious Use of Behavior Charts and Token Systems

Not all parents like using charts and tokens and not all should do so; such systems are not only time-consuming, but require neutrality, consistency, and steady vigilance. That said, there are times when codified behavioral monitoring can help easily frustrated children gain self-control. However, parents must beware: Setting out a plan's expectations too vaguely (has a good morning), or asking for long periods of positive behavior (doesn't hit all day) won't work. Children with short fuses need systems with clear, reachable goals (keeps her hands to herself) and short time frames (during breakfast; in the car). It's important, too, that these systems are left in place only briefly. Later, parents find other ways to build on a child's growing mastery.[4]

Providing Skill-Building Opportunities

Offering Communicational Scaffolding if Language Processing Issues Are at Play

See Chapter 9 for more information on this strategy.

Fostering the Capacity for Problem-Solving

Parents look for moments when the child is just beginning to get frustrated, then move in quickly to offer effective support and step-by-step problem-solving assistance.

Supporting the Skill of Thinking Before Responding

Parents help the child self-monitor by using a cue that tells her to stop, calm down, and reflect before acting. The STAR system first outlined in Chapter 10 is one useful version of this. The child learns to *S*top, *T*hink, *A*sk (Is this really worth a huge fuss? Can I make this big, angry feeling get smaller?), and *R*espond. Another possibility in this vein is the use of a red light cue, first introduced in Chapter 5. The cue signals the child to freeze and think, with an adult-dictated green light once she's figured out what to do next. Learning the skills of impulse control and self-talk takes a while; progress is helped along when adults respond appreciatively after a child has been successful in backing off from a big scene.

Helping the Child "Read" Faces and Voices

Children who get easily frustrated don't always read the nonverbal cues that say trouble is imminent. Thus parents support the decoding of such cues: "Do you notice what my face is doing? Do you know what it means? It means that I'm starting to feel frustrated. What do you think my face will look like if you don't stop?" When adults stay calm while supporting a child's ability to understand and think about such important social cues, she can sometimes redirect herself.

Lending an Ally—Lending Self-Control

On their good days, these kids get a lot out of parental support and modeling as they learn to play and share successfully with their siblings and friends. During rockier periods, such support is essential. Parents, of course, can't offer this help all the time, but five or ten minutes here and there will go a long way toward helping a child behave as well as she's able.

Recognizing Emotional Overload

Parents take note of when a child has gotten too frustrated to be able to think her way out of a problem. Then they firmly direct her to a predetermined place where she can collect herself. Some children do well in their rooms. Some require an adult-dictated time out. Still others need physical contact to calm down.

Fostering the Ability to Understand, Express, and Work Through Feelings

Supporting Acceptable Outlets for Anger

As parents raise expectations for behavior at home, children need safe places to express and work through their feelings. Drawing, storytelling, narrative play, and safely-monitored wrestling and pillow fights can help kids channel their aggression.

Using Children's Literature and Adult Storytelling to Communicate Acceptance and Hope

Highly frustrated children often feel comforted and understood when adults read them illustrated children's books with themes of anger and resolution. Books which speak to specific issues in their lives—loss, illness, family conflict, sibling rivalry, etc.—may be beneficial too. Parents can also tell stories of their own childhood experiences handling frustration or—if they're comfortable doing so—make up narratives about animals or people who struggle to cope with strong emotions. All of these strategies communicate to children that their feelings are legitimate, and that finding alternatives to explosive behavior is hard work for everyone. (See also the section on personalized narratives under "Fostering the Capacity for Problem-Solving" in "Getting to Work in School.")

Emphasizing Prevention

Offering Breaks Before Things Get Out of Control

Break periods—times when the child is not being punished but goes to a cozy spot to calm herself—can be an excellent prevention tool.

Shooting for an Organized, Predictable Home Life

Children who have trouble managing frustration do better when their families function with predictable routines. When life at home is on the chaotic side, anger and irritability often worsen.

Watching That Bedtimes and Bedtime Routines Allow Kids to Get Enough Sleep

When children are chronically overtired, their ability to handle difficult emotions almost always declines. But, like all kids, easily frustrated children are often exhausted at the end of a long day, leading to argument-filled evening routines, and less sleep than they need. Parents set a bedtime, back up routines so there is time for a few mishaps, then use a good mix of support and limit setting to help kids get to sleep at a reasonable hour.

Reducing Exposure to Violence in the Media and Computer Games; Rethinking Toy Choices

With an eye to minimizing exposure to violent content, parents pay close attention to what children view during "screen time." They also consider whether to allow access to aggression-focused play materials.

Working on Problematic Family Dynamics

Monitoring Parental Hot Spots

Parents avoid a climate of intense frustration, irritability, or hopelessness by keeping an eye out for how a child's behavior sets off issues of their own.

Taking a Look at Family Issues

When a child's frustration stems, at least in part, from larger issues in the family, parents take a close look at what they might do to make things better for everyone. Sometimes a child's inability to handle the minor bumps of daily life is a sign that problematic family dynamics are too much for her to handle.

Support, Support, Support

Parents remind themselves that it will take their child time to become less volatile. After all, if a particular youngster knew how to control herself, she'd probably do it. Easily frustrated kids need the safety of firm limits, but limits go only so far in supporting frustration tolerance. When there is an over-emphasis on discipline—coupled with a lack of friendly skill-building support—an unhappy family life is often the result.

Watching for Emotional, Physical, or Sexual Harm

Easily frustrated children may be showing the effects of physical, sexual, or emotional mistreatment. Though there are many other reasons to account for explosive behavior, parents watch carefully, and take action if they sense that such a situation is taking place, whether within or outside of the family.[5]

Getting to Work in School

Supporting Connection

"Feeding" the Relationship When the Child Is Doing Well

Many easily frustrated children have trouble enjoying relationships, and even more can't take help when they're angry. That's why it's so useful for teachers to initiate frequent experiences of affection-filled contact when a child is doing well. Firstly, she'll feel cared for and may be more inclined to use teacher assistance when she's about to lose control. Secondly, many of these kids have parents who are enraged at them for being so difficult. The experience of feeling cherished helps them turn around their image of being bad and unlovable.

Connecting Warmly Before Expecting Compliance

See similar section under "Getting to Work at Home."

Setting Effective Expectations

Providing Clear, Positive Standards for Behavior

A classroom approach that emphasizes positive expectations is a real boon for these children. As teachers find ways to reinforce such expectations, they keep in mind that their response to a child's actions should be in synch with her level of mastery; some youngsters may benefit from a teacher's warmth or praise for behavior that is a big success for them but wouldn't be for others.

Enforcing Limits

Some of these youngsters need occasional "time away" to help them with impulse control and emotional regulation. The idea is for the child to have a place to go to quickly, somewhere that she can calm down and regain self-control. This place may be a time out chair, but can also be a seat at a table where she draws or reads a book. (Some classrooms have a "take a break basket" on hand to support self-soothing after an upset.) Such children also need a quick, warm welcome back into classroom activities once they've calmed down.

Using Behavior Charts and Token Systems Judiciously

See similar section under "Getting to Work at Home."

day. For over a month, whatever cookies I presented, hurriedly pressed from play dough, weren't acceptable. The king would roar in outrage (no overstatement here) and then inform me that I would have to have my head chopped off. King Sean would instruct me to moan over this verdict disconsolately. But despite my desperate pleas, the dire punishment would be carried out, immediately after which I was required to become yet another, soon-to-be-beheaded servant. (In my early meetings with Sean, I had the interesting opportunity of living at least nine or ten lives per therapy hour.)

About two months into our work together, as Sean's intense rage began to lessen, a new character appeared. This boy would be presiding over my imminent demise when his voice would change timber. The good king had taken over, he would tell me, and all was forgiven. This gentle ruler also requested cookies and, upon on their receipt, made it clear that I really hadn't done a very good job baking them. But it was okay, he would declare, he'd eat them anyway. Usually I was offered some too, and as we munched away, his highness would tell me that they weren't so bad after all.

What Do We See?

Looking at the Interface Between Child Frustration and Family Functioning

Sean's experience in therapy undoubtedly helped him feel steadier and happier. But attention to family issues was needed as well, and his parents and I met regularly to sort out what might be making him feel so angry. In such situations, it's particularly important to explore the interface between a youngster's struggles and her family's dynamics. We think about the child's temperament. We note her family's history and culture. We track the feedback loops that surround her difficult behavior, paying special attention to those related to her parents' approach to discipline. In addition, we take a close look at underlying tensions in the family as a whole.

Being a naturally intense child born into a staunchly religious family hadn't been easy for Sean: By the time he was two, he'd been expected to behave far better than he was able. Most of his days were spent with his mother and sister. Sam worked many hours each week to support the family, and Carla faced long, lonely stretches of solo parenting. A soft-spoken, contained woman, Carla felt overwhelmed by her two rambunctious children. Having been brought up in a strict family, she was torn between her parents' firm childrearing style—one she'd found oppressive—and the more permissive attitude she observed in the families of her children's friends. With Sean, she found herself bouncing back and forth between the two approaches. One day, she'd swear that she was going to stay patient and flexible. The next, she'd decide that she was going to show him who was boss. Whatever she did wasn't making things any better. Both at family gatherings and at the Sunday lunch

Providing Skill-Building Opportunities

Offering Communicational Scaffolding if Language Processing Issues Are at Play

See Chapter 9 for more information on this strategy.

Fostering the Capacity for Problem-Solving

Easily frustrated children will need step-by-step help with the basics of problem-solving. (As noted in Chapter 7, a simple "use your words" is generally insufficient.) Some classrooms use group-based social skills curricula to lay the groundwork for such help; others use occasional group meetings and/or puppet play to reflect on common classroom tangles; yet others have a special table set aside for conflict resolution.[6]

Problem-solving can also be encouraged through the use of personalized narratives, stories that address a particular child's challenges and support positive outcomes. The most well known examples of such narratives are the Social Stories™ first developed by Carol Gray for children with autistic spectrum disorders—her clearly structured story protocol is now used extensively to help young children master common challenges both at home and in school (Burke, Kuhn, and Peterson, 2004; Brody and McGarry, 2005). With an introduction that sets the stage, a short, neutrally described center that lays out both a child's dilemma and some friendly solutions, and an upbeat conclusion that predicts success, these simply illustrated stories work wonders in supporting emotional regulation.[7] They're just one of many visual, story-rich approaches to fostering children's capacities for problem-solving. All such approaches, over time, help children be ready for predictably difficult situations and have strategies on hand to handle those situations successfully.

Lending an Ally—Lending Self-Control

On their good days, these children benefit greatly from a teacher spending time with them as they play with friends. On their rough days, they may not just benefit from but require such support. Either way, as potentially frustrating conflicts emerge, teachers model the skills of sharing agendas, problem-solving, and communicating interest and pleasure in others' contributions. Teachers can't offer such help all the time, but five or ten minutes here and there can help the child steady herself and get involved in constructive activities.

Other Skill-Building Strategies

See similar sections under "Getting to Work at Home" for these strategies:

- Supporting the Skill of Thinking before Responding
- Helping the Child "Read" Faces and Voices

Recognizing Emotional Overload

See similar section under "Getting to Work at Home."

Supporting the Safe Expression of Feelings

Finding Acceptable Outlets for Anger

These youngsters need a way to express intense feelings. Teachers may offer an "angry book" in which a child can draw and write, support storytelling and narrative play, and provide acceptable physical outlets for aggression.[8]

Helping Children Channel Superhero Play Constructively

Aggressive children may spend inordinate amounts of time engaging in dramatic play filled with violent content. Teachers often feel stymied by such play, finding that banning it often results in themes of battle becoming all the more compelling, as well as secretive efforts to keep such intriguing story lines alive but out of view. As an alternative, teachers take an active, interested part in redirecting such play, thus allowing children to embrace their interest in issues of power and control while developing positive pictures of self-assertion and community responsibility.[9]

Emphasizing Prevention

Supporting and/or Cueing the Child When She's Close to Losing Control

Over time, these children can begin to take help *before* they lose control. Teachers spend some friendly, one-on-one time with a youngster, brainstorming about "how to keep that angry feeling from bossing you around."[10] Laying the foundation for self-talk, this work often includes the child and teacher coming up with a code phrase or nonverbal cue. Whatever the cue, teachers do some problem-solving and/or role-playing with the child, *giving her specific ideas of how to help herself calm down when she sees or hears the cue.* Then, throughout the day, teachers watch for moments of deepening frustration, offering the cue as needed. When the child is successful in maintaining self-control, a quick high-five, or a star on a behavior chart can foster her sense of pride and accomplishment. Then, supporting the final stage of the process, teachers stay with the child in order to help her work through whatever situation set off her feelings of frustration.

Allowing the Child to Take Some Constructive Time Away

If an angry, impulsive child is having a rough day, she may benefit from downtime when she's looking particularly overwhelmed. The offer to run an errand, to assist with chores, or to sit in a comfortable beanbag away from the fray can be a great way for the child to regroup. Time with a favored adult can help too. Some teachers even talk about taking "a good time out," one the child asks for when she feels close to losing control. It's important to note that teachers sometimes allow a child to reenter a frustrating situation before she's actually regained composure. This usually backfires.

Using Touch to Help With Self-Control

An arm around the shoulders or a firm hand on the back sometimes provides a frustrated child with a feeling of containment. These youngsters can feel as if their bodies are about to explode and for some, touch helps support a growing sense of calm.

Using Well-Organized Transitions, Effectively Run Group Time, and Classroom-Wide "Climate Control" to Support Mastery

Children who have trouble regulating their emotions benefit greatly from the strategies outlined in Chapter 8.

Other Strategies

See similar sections under "Getting to Work at Home" for these strategies:

- Monitoring Teacher Hot Spots
- Support, Support, Support
- Watching for Emotional, Physical, or Sexual Harm

Seeking Outside Help

Seeking Consultation, Testing, and/or Speech and Language Services

If a child's frustration appears to stem from vulnerabilities in language processing, a consultation, assessment, and/or specialized help may be in order.

Accessing Therapeutic Help

When overall family dynamics play a large role in a child's difficulties, family or couples counseling may be indicated. (Note however, that when home life includes domestic violence, individual help for the victimized partner—as well as therapy for any child witnesses to this violence—is often more appropriate.) Another possibility is for the youngster to get some individualized help. Sometimes both are in order. It can be hard to decide if a child should get one-on-one help quickly, or if she'll improve once adults have developed a better approach to her difficulties. At times, we take a wait and see attitude. But if her behavior is extreme, it may be a good idea to connect her up with a good child therapist quickly.

Considering the Option of Medication

Many children will respond well to the mix of strategies listed here. But occasionally, despite an ongoing mix of effective limits, skill-building support, and family-focused work, a youngster still struggles mightily to manage frustration. That's when a medication consult may be in order.

Strategies in Action: Helping Children (and Parents) Learn to Manage Frustration and Control Impulses

Getting to Work With Sean—Exploring the Mix of Practical Approaches and Emotional Support for an Easily Frustrated Child and His Family

By the time he was four, Sean was in danger of seeing himself as both overly powerful and essentially bad. In his deeply religious family, the moral overtones of these judgments carried an especially hefty weight, and Sean's despair after one of his many venom-filled outbursts was noticeable to parents and teachers alike. But the intensity of his anger overpowered his desire to do well, and the "Dr. Jekyll–Mr. Hyde" quality of his days struck everyone as particularly noticeable given his young age.

Sean is the boy, first introduced in Chapter 2, whose dream was to become a guitar-smashing rock and roll king. Sean's behavior was so extreme, and his words so full of the desire to hurt those he loved, that his parents Sam and Carla had agreed that intervention should include some play therapy. Soon after arriving at my office, Sean would push together two large armchairs, quickly assemble a makeshift crown, and hold court. I was King Sean's servant, my job to bake and serve the particular cookies that he requested that after church services, Carla felt miserably aware that her son was leaving hurt feelings and bruised limbs wherever he went.

Carla didn't know what to do and felt her husband didn't help. Sam had a more relaxed manner than she and, at and least sometimes, seemed to get more of the response he wanted from Sean. But Sam was tired from working such long days and when he finally arrived home, radiated a quiet annoyance that things in the house weren't more peaceful. Carla felt that he faulted her for Sean's difficulties and in some ways she didn't blame him: It had been a joint decision that she would stay home full-time. Even so, she felt deeply frustrated that instead of supporting her attempts to set limits with Sean and his sister, Sam would subtly communicate to both kids that since their mom wasn't strong enough to manage them, he'd have to take over.

Carla and Sam had strong feelings about the nature of marriage. Both had grown up in religious homes with little overt conflict between their parents and both felt it was wrong for husband and wife to argue. Thus the tensions they experienced with each other remained undercurrents to a partnership that looked strikingly unruffled on its surface. But tensions there were all the same. Sam came home to a house full of conflict and a wife whose brittleness bore little resemblance to the warm, loving manner he'd always counted on. Carla felt increasingly isolated from her husband and from her family and friends as well. She worried that everyone was judging her, and she may even have been right. She got more and more desperate about having control over her son, and more and more in conflict about whether to discipline him with a vengeance or to love him into compliance.

By the time this family sought help, things were in terrible shape. Carla felt she had tried everything, even, once or twice, washing Sean's mouth out with soap when he was rude. She didn't like herself for doing this, but it had been done to her and her siblings when they were young and had worked back then. She would send Sean to his room for long stretches too, then listen to him slam his toys against the bedroom wall. After such incidents both she and Sean would feel remorse and things would often be easier. Not for too long though. Soon enough, the cycle would start again. Sean would begin getting testy. Carla would remind herself to stay calm and in control. Eventually, Sean's defiance would get to her and she'd begin threatening terrible consequences if he didn't behave.

What Do We Think?

Noting Conflict and Emotional Depletion in Adult Partnerships

It wasn't just Sean and his mother who were stuck in a demoralizing pattern, Carla and Sam were too. As life in the household became more difficult, both parents found themselves increasingly exhausted and scarily distant from each other. In the midst of their deepening unhappiness, this couple experienced few options. Brought up in families whose cultures placed a high value on coping, neither would even consider bailing out on the marriage. Sharing their feelings with each other wasn't comfortable either.

These descriptions just skim the surface of this family's experience. Even so, we can see that family history, powerful cultural norms, and habitual patterns of interaction affected Sean's difficulties. As noted in earlier chapters, family life is a potent mix of past and present, driven by themes of intimacy, power and, frequently, money. The tensions about what aspects of life men are supposed to take care of and what women are responsible for can be there too, often with collisions of old and new norms about gender. When a child is having trouble managing frustration, whatever fault lines there are in a family often come to the surface. Sometimes the child's temperament is what sets off the troubles in the first place; sometimes a parent's own emotional difficulties or a family's way of functioning lie at the heart of the matter. Whatever the cause, and frequently it's a mix of all three, family dynamics can be at their most problematic when kids are inflexible and explosive.

What Do We Do?

Processing and Alleviating Family Tensions

Sam and Carla were experiencing just this phenomenon, and our early work partly focused on their acknowledging some deeply painful feelings. Carla let Sam know that his habit of summarily taking over when he got home made her feel both worthless and angry. Sam shared his intense humiliation over his earning power and its impact on his limited presence at home. Carla communicated how ashamed she was of her part in the problem and spoke of her need to feel that Sam understood rather than judged her. Sam told Carla that the troubles at home left her so preoccupied that he felt she had no energy left over for him. Both vented their despair over Sean's situation. And slowly, life at home started to improve. Sam began trying to support rather than undermine Carla. She, in turn, made sure to communicate appreciation for the work he did to support the family. As they came to see that with support, Carla could learn to manage Sean successfully, they reaffirmed their decision to have her stay home with the children. Eventually, they began setting aside needed time just for each other. That helped too.

Working on Effective Discipline

Our conversations didn't just concentrate on these issues, of course. Over time, we also explored specific strategies that Carla and Sam could use to help their son. Early dialogue focused on the threats Carla used to try to control Sean's behavior. We looked at how extreme they were and how Carla often backed off from carrying them out once she realized what it would take to do so. Like so many parents of explosive kids, Carla was engaged in a destructive pattern: She threatened limits that Sean knew she might not back up, Sean's behavior escalated, and she threatened some more. Not infrequently, she lost her temper, muddying the situation even further. Sometimes, against her better judgment, she harshly asked him why he couldn't behave as well as his sister did. Sam threatened dire consequences less often, but also had a habit of changing his expectations midstream if Sean looked like he was about to blow. Using terminology defined earlier, behavioral feedback loops were amplifying rather than diminishing problematic behavior.

When families are stuck in such destructive patterns, effective limit setting is an important aspect of intervention. Thus, Carla and Sam had a lot to keep in mind. First, they needed to think proactively, to assume that Sean would have many difficulties throughout the day, and to be ready for those difficulties when they occurred. "Being ready" included chunking down expectations so that Sean could begin to learn the basics of self-control. In addition, Carla and Sam had to plan out when to ignore their son's misbehavior and when to clamp down on it. They had to make rapid decisions about when they were going to set a limit, then stay steady when Sean got angry at its enforcement. Furthermore, they needed consequences that Sean could learn from: meaningful consequences that weren't so extreme as to leave no options for enjoyment once he'd dug himself out of trouble. Because despite their feeling that Sean's behavior was utterly unacceptable, he couldn't help himself. He hadn't yet learned to control his temper, nor to soften the words coming out of his mouth when he was furious. If he was to learn how to do both, he'd need steady practice, without feeling that one mistake would not only ruin his entire day but destroy his parents' opinion of him as well.

Providing Skill-Building Assistance

Easily frustrated children need sensible and consistent limits, but they also require skill-building assistance: We must lean in as well as lean out. When we lean in with kids like Sean, we find situations—often in their play—in which they can happily boss us around. We support them in finding means of self-expression that don't get them in trouble. We sit with them and lend an ally as they slowly learn to tolerate their siblings' and their friends' ideas. In addition, we help them preview situations in which they might get frustrated so that they can think out and even role-play reasonable responses *before* they get consumed with anger.

The meetings with Sam and Carla included attention to all of these areas. We worked on cleaning up the sloppy mess of threats and cave-ins, of angry diatribes and distressed apologies. We outlined the nature of lend-an-ally work and highlighted the importance of finding many moments of pleasurable connection with Sean. In addition, we discussed the fact that, however unacceptable Sean's behavior, talking about the importance of being good and kind when he was thoroughly enraged just wasn't going to get through.

Understanding That When Emotions Run High, Clear Thinking Runs Low

One day when Sean was in my office, we took a break from our adventures at court to talk about handling tough situations without exploding. "It's hard Sean, because sometimes your feelings get really big really fast, and they can stay big for a long time." He knew just what I meant. Children who have feelings that get "really big really fast" face a daunting challenge. *They can't think straight once they've hit a certain emotional level, and they hit that level without much warning.*[11] As noted earlier, one of the most common mistakes that parents and teachers make is to try to reason with children once they are past this point.

Understanding this phenomenon is a crucial element behind parents' and teachers' proactive approaches to easily frustrated children. Clinicians can foster such understanding by offering the visual image of an "emotional thermometer."[12] This thermometer goes from one to ten—one is very calm while ten is terribly out of kilter. A child who regulates emotion easily will slowly head up toward a three or four when she's getting frustrated. She may whine or bang her hand on the table, using predictable signals to convey that she's getting flustered. Then she'll sort her way through what's bothering her on her own or, conversely, ask for some adult assistance. If it's the latter, caring adults will have time to lend a hand before she loses control.

As we help parents and teachers picture what a specific child looks like as her emotional temperature increases, we emphasize that problem-solving help is most useful when she's in this two to four degree range on our imaginary thermometer. Beyond that point, it's harder for her to think clearly because her emotions begin to get in the way. By the time she's reached a six or so, we explain, she may still sound like she's thinking straight, but she isn't. It's at this point that a child will say the same things over and over again, no matter what response she's getting. Parents may reason with her, teachers may try offering support and solutions to her dilemma, but nothing seems to have an impact.

Reading the Emotional Thermometer

Talking with concerned adults about a child like Sean builds on these ideas. We describe how such a youngster may start out at zero on the thermometer. Then, some seemingly small frustration sends her emotional temperature straight to a four. If a parent or teacher steps in to help but says something that's not to her liking, she instantly heads up to a six on the scale. At that point, she's no longer accessible for problem-solving at all. However, it's all happened so quickly that the kids and adults around her are left trying to work out whatever has gone wrong. As she gets increasingly upset, kids may well get out of her way. (Except those who have trouble regulating feeling in their own right—these children seem unfailing in their ability to find each other.) Adults, though, often keep trying to make a child see reason. Unfortunately, we explain, with these children, the more adults try, the higher on the scale the child is likely to go. Kids like Sean occasionally rage around at a nine or ten for an hour or more.

After Carla and Sam learned about this phenomenon of emotional overload, it didn't take them long to understand that they only enflamed the situation by appealing to Sean's higher instincts when he registered an emotional temperature of six or above. The trick would be to learn what they could do to help their son in that brief moment after he shot up to a four. Up to this point, their tendency had been to urge him to calm down so they could help him but, in truth, that rarely worked. Helping parents and teachers learn to read a child's emotional thermometer—and to have strategies on hand that can be matched to her temperature at a particular moment—is an important element of consultative work. As these children head up the scale, there is an art form to figuring out whether they're still accessible for problem-solving assistance, or whether *they've shot up so high that intervention should only target regained control, control that will allow them to manage their bodies and use their minds.*

Once parents and teachers have a handle on these ideas, clinicians can help them find a good balance between setting limits and offering support. If they do too much of the former, they may not be teaching a child the skills she needs to think out rather than act out her dilemmas. If they focus mainly on the latter, they may be giving the child's emotional outbursts far too much space. Landing on the best mix for a particular youngster usually comes from a combination of thoughtful reflection and trial and error. The work we do with families and school staff often involves such reflection, as we track a child's growing ability to manage her emotions in the face of frustration.

"Trumping" the Child When She's About to Lose Control

As Carla and Sam sought the right mix of strategies for Sean, I shared with them one of the strategies some parents have found useful: *compassionate "trumping" of a child's feelings.* (Trumping, for readers who aren't card players, is when one plays a card in a suit that tops other cards on the table, thus winning the round.) Compassionate trumping looks something like this:

Carla's voice, both loud and sympathetic: "Sean, you're *very* frustrated!! Something must be going on that you *really* don't like!" *Sean responds angrily, but with some information.*
Carla: "Well, I can *see* that got you upset! You don't like that! *Sean reiterates his unhappiness, a little more calmly.*

Carla's voice, this time more calmly: "I'm glad you told me what's bothering you…Hmmm, this is a real problem, isn't it? We'll have to think about this…Do you think you could calm down a little bit so I can try to help?" *Carla is lucky: Sean complies.*
"Okay, now let's see, here is what seems to be bothering you…*A more detailed description of the dilemma, including the other child's point of view if another child is involved.* Hmmm…Do you have any ideas of what you can do?" (Alternatively: "I have an idea for you. I'm not sure if it will work or not. Do you want to hear it?")

There are a lot of words here and they have one intent: to help Sean calm himself enough to do some problem-solving. Trumping a child communicates that her intense feelings are understood rather than judged. Once she experiences this kind of witnessing, along with some gentle help in slowing things down, she may regain the ability to think clearly. Having access to rational thought will allow her to figure her way through whatever has set her off. Learning to think out rather than act out is a skill she doesn't yet have, one that must be a major focus of intervention.

Combining Problem-Solving With Limit Setting

As we coach parents and teachers on the subtleties of this work, it's important to emphasize that setting limits with easily frustrated kids sometimes takes place in tandem with problem-solving. A child is becoming volatile over something that adults have decided she can't do or can't have. They're clear about their decision yet hope to avoid a full-fledged blowout. Thus in their efforts to foster problem-solving, they decide not to set a limit immediately. Instead, as the child starts to lose her temper, they "trump" her feelings. Then, if they're successful in forging an alliance with her in the midst of her distress, they sympathize briefly with her fury before setting expectations. Here's what this process might look like as Carla works to support Sean in regaining self-control:

"Oh Sean, I see how mad this makes you! You really want pizza for lunch, don't you?" *Sean responds, still very upset.*

Sean, we have a hard problem here. Because you so want pizza, and you're angry that I won't go out and get some! *More upset and yelling.*

But, Sean…here's our problem. If you scream or hit me, you know what will happen. The rule is that you'll go to your room. Then you won't get to watch [favorite TV show] later. "Do you remember how that happened yesterday and you felt so sad about it?" *A defiant "I don't care" from our volcanic child, but with enough calm that he appears to be listening.*

Sean…"I'm going to try something. I'm going to be quiet for two minutes and fold some clothes. And I'm wondering if you can work hard so that you don't miss your show. Here's what you need to do…you need to be able to choose either peanut butter and jelly or grilled cheese, even though you don't want to. And, you need to stop talking about there being no pizza. When the two minutes are up, I'll decide if you need to go to your room. I think you can do it!"

In providing guidance about this mix of firmness and compassion, clinicians emphasize that when consistent limits do the work of enforcement, parent and teachers are freed up to offer support. Part of this guidance relies on a principle nested in the work just outlined: Weeks earlier, during a period of calm, Carla and Sam held a family meeting in which they laid out expectations and consequences. Thus, Sean has already experienced the consequences in question. Furthermore, he's learned that he'll experience them again if he doesn't pull it together. Such consistency is very reassuring to easily frustrated children. They also find it comforting to know that they'll receive the same kind of adult coaching each time they're losing control, and that this coaching can really help.

In fine-tuning these opportunities for practice, we work with parents to figure out which children benefit from revisiting an unhappy situation later on in the day. Not all do. When a child is responsive to the process of review, it takes place long after an unhappy explosion is over. A parent or teacher sympathetically asks if they could help plan what the child can try the next time she's feeling so angry, so that she won't again be faced with an unpleasant consequence. Maybe there will even be some practice with puppets or stuffed animals playing both child and adult. At home, the addition of milk and cookies sometimes sweetens the deal.

This principle of *reflecting about a child's difficulties when she's doing well* is another important piece of our approach. It allows us to avoid unhelpful moralizing in the midst of a child's breakdown, or trying to get her to see the folly of her ways immediately after she calms down. Generally, when an easily frustrated child has just made her way through an unhappy outburst, the last thing she's ready for is a long conversation about what she's done wrong. If parents and teachers are going to revisit anything about what just happened, they need to make it quick. Mostly, it's important for them to welcome her back into family or classroom life, and to communicate that they're as glad as she is that trouble has passed.

Helping Kids Regain Self-Control if They're Past the Point of No Return

The next piece of consultative work helps parents and teachers understand when it's sensible to offer problem-solving assistance, and when not. Trumping a child's emotions, for example, is worth a try when adults believe there's a chance of helping her lower her emotional temperature. But if they sense that the child has lost control, keeping discussion minimal is going to be important. Sometimes adults walk away or firmly inform the child that they're not going to say much until she's less upset. Sometimes, they send her to a previously chosen spot to calm down. This spot may be her room, a place on the stairs, or a playroom's designated "cozy corner." It may be the classroom's "peaceful pillow" or time out chair. What's important is that the youngster knows that this is the place she goes when her feelings have gotten too big to handle, and that her job is to stay there while she settles down. Adults then wait until she's quite calm before talking with her, and keep things simple and friendly once they do. Parents and teachers may react to these explanations with skepticism. Their faces, if not their words, convey disbelief: "*Yeah sure, that sounds great, but I'd never be able to get her to go there, much less stay put if she did.*" If such adults are feeling powerless to enforce reasonable limits, they'll need help understanding the strategies laid out in Chapter 6.

Throughout this process, everyone involved remembers that finding the right balance for a particular child is an art, not a science. Sometimes it works better to start almost entirely with clear limits and to wait until things have settled down before there is work on the problem-solving end of things. (If parents and teachers choose this route, they make sure to build in positive times for connection each day, at home and in school.) Conversely, there are situations in which it makes sense to focus on support and problem-solving first, leaning out toward effective limit setting only after a child shows increased self-control.

Working on Connection, Containment, and Problem-Solving in School

The work explored to this point has focused on Sean's home life because it was at home that his issues began and were the most extreme. Some explosive children, and Sean is one, do better in school, where they get a break from painful family dynamics and where expectations for behavior may be clearer. Others feel relatively contained with their families only to blow fuses during their long days in a bustling classroom. Whatever the balance, the strategies explored in this chapter apply equally well to intervention in both places. How these strategies look in school is fleshed out more fully in Chapter 5's explorations of the classroom-based work with another explosive boy, Javier.

Of course, teachers must offer their help in the context of overall teaching agendas and large groups of children. That's why classroom work with kids like Sean and Javier must have a predictable quality and a proactive thrust. Without both elements, teachers don't have the time to offer a child adequate help. An important piece of this help is developmental play assistance, especially in the free-play-friendly preschool and kindergarten years. One of the biggest challenges of dealing with easily frustrated kids in school is that they grab, hit, kick, and yell at classmates who won't bend in the face of their demands. With their poor skills in tolerating frustration and limited capacity for problem-solving, such children don't understand the basics of sharing toys, space, and ideas. It's for this reason that the phrase "use your words" can be so ineffective in promoting mastery. Explosive children can't use those words in moments of conflict because their emotional intensity gets in the way. The words they *do* use at such times often get them in trouble.

In the developmental play assistance that focuses on frustration tolerance, teachers offer extensive scaffolding when conflicts arise; each step of negotiation is supported warmly and clearly, with language the child can try out herself. Most importantly, this work is not done *for* but *with* her. Note that staff stay put throughout this process, and then stick around to make sure any agreed upon resolution holds. If they leave too soon, they'll most likely hear a new conflict emerge almost instantly. Even better, teachers show up before anything has gone wrong, and support positive play experiences from start to finish. When adults don't just arrive to support calm in the midst of conflict, but join children as this kind of play partner, they provide even more opportunities for mastery. As noted in Chapter 7, the play partner role involves two elements: a "wise child"—who plays like a child but with admirable warmth and flexibility—and an adult coach who offers the targeted youngster, sotto voce, ideas for socially skilled, inviting contributions to the play scenario at hand.

Supporting Safe and Acceptable Expressions of Feeling

There is another element to our work with easily frustrated children: In order to develop skill in emotional regulation, they need to know that their feelings are legitimate, and that while it's not acceptable to unleash those feelings in hurtful ways, there are places to express and work through them. Parents and teachers may not initially be comfortable with this idea. One of the problematic aspects to Sean's situation, for example, was that Sam and Carla had communicated that—in the context of their family's deeply felt religious beliefs—anger itself was unacceptable. Eventually, these parents and I had a fruitful discussion about how conflicted Sean was about his rebellious feelings, and about how much he judged himself on moral grounds. We began thinking about places he could express these intense feelings at home, places that they could respond to with understanding. At first, both parents communicated reservations about this idea, especially about sitting with him while he used his beloved superhero figures to play out narratives of revenge and annihilation. They feared that providing Sean this support would encourage him in unkind thoughts and actions. Talking about the importance of play as a place for kids to express and work through feelings helped them agree to give the idea a try.

Sean was delighted, particularly as both parents learned to show real interest in his tales of war and conquest and, eventually, to convey a genuine acceptance of his aggressive impulses in play. He took special pleasure in inviting his mother into his narratives, and even more when she eventually surrendered to some positively demonic portrayals of the "bad guys." In addition, Sam began initiating occasional pillow fights with his son. During the giggle-filled ruckus, Sam used cues to stop and start the action, thus helping Sean experience self-control in the midst of expressing aggression. Both parents started telling Sean stories of their own childhood frustrations, including some of the things they'd done that had gotten them in trouble. In addition, they tried to avoid invoking themes of religious judgment when they were especially frustrated with their son.

Helping Children Work Through Troubling Feelings: The Question of Therapy

Some aggressive youngsters need only a combination of this kind of support with good limit setting and friendly skill-building help. But some, Sean included, profit greatly from the extra assistance clinicians can offer. In order to understand whether to suggest therapy, it's important to think about how young children work out the emotional dilemmas that disturb them. Children, after all, experience many of the same upsets and confusions that adults do. They feel great loss and great anger, intense jealousy and terrible worry. They react to financial woes and serious medical concerns, and also to the everyday tensions of family life. In the midst of such experiences, they often demonstrate a natural ability to sort out their confusions. They plop themselves on the floor and play out stories of separation or envy. They play out hospital scenes, going to school scenes, scenes of birth and scenes of death. They use their growing ability to use words—in combination with the expansive language of symbols—to create long narratives of woe and redemption, and to relate the intricate details of their dreams. They draw vivid pictures of family breakups, and gleefully squish the clay monsters they've just made.

An overwhelmed child often gravitates toward a few forms of expression, and uses them to work through the problems she faces. As Carla and Sam learned, parents and teachers may keep a youngster company as she finds such vehicles for self-expression, encouraging exploration through gentle comments and questions. Often, with or without adult help, this "work of play" allows children to feel more at peace.[13] There are times, however, when a child's difficulties have gotten lodged deep within her sense of self and world, and in such cases, therapeutic help may be in order. Therapy offers children a safe place to express overwhelming feelings and opportunities to work through those feelings with someone who has specialized skill in helping untangle the emotional jumble. Parents often request advice about whether they should seek therapy for their youngster—it's often hard to fit into a crowded schedule and can be hard to pay for too. Our response includes that therapy should be considered when the outlets a child has found for expressing and working through her feelings—even after parents and teachers have supported her doing so—don't adequately address her need for emotional release and resolution.[14]

12

Helping the Anxious Child

Getting to Work When a Child's Worries, Fears, or Sensory Sensitivities Take Over Daily Life

When a child struggles to keep his worries in check, the feedback loops in a family and classroom can become quite problematic. It's not hard to understand why. Anxious children repeatedly check out their concerns with the adults they trust. Feeling increasingly hemmed in by the need to provide constant reassurance, these adults often try to organize the world in a way that allows a youngster to feel more at ease. Unfortunately, such efforts often end up with the child learning to avoid the things that frighten him, and to check in with adults even more frequently. Figuring out the right balance between leaning in and leaning out—giving a youngster the support he needs while also setting expectations for self-soothing—is a challenging but important task.

What Issues Might Be Contributing to the Child's Behavior?

- Cautious, shy, or fearful temperament
- An overscheduled, pressured, or chaotic experience at home
- Parent or parents working long hours, with little time for family members to get in synch with each other's needs
- Other family stressors including parent or sibling conflict, divorce, financial and/or housing issues, illness or death of a family member
- A difficult experience of school life
- Overwhelming experiences, including domestic violence and/or physical, emotional, or sexual abuse
- Insufficient sleep

Some Points to Remember

- There are four kinds of anxiety that we tend to see in young children[1]:
  1. Social/relational anxiety—fears and/or reluctance about connections
  2. Performance anxiety—fears about being in the spotlight
  3. Generalized anxiety—worries and fears about many things
  4. Phobias—worries and fears about very specific things
- Some youngsters appear to have a predisposition toward anxiety and have been on the fearful side for a long time. Others experience a period of

anxiety that's set off by a stressful experience, a rough patch at home, or an aspect of classroom life that feels overwhelming (Morris and March, 2004).

- Anxious children often:
  1. attempt to avoid uncomfortable feelings by avoiding the things—or places—that trigger those feelings
  2. look almost entirely to others to soothe their fears
- As a result of the above, one of the features in the lives of these children is that the adults around them often get "pulled into" their struggles. It's not uncommon for these youngsters to get far more attention during their periods of worry than during stretches when they are doing well, with the unfortunate though unintended result that difficulty, not mastery, is being reinforced.
- Youngsters who struggle with a constitutionally based tendency toward anxiety often have a parent or two with similar vulnerabilities (Hettema, Neale, and Kendler, 2001). Such parents can find it especially hard to avoid the pattern just described.
- Our goal in helping anxious children is *hardiness*, that is, resilience in the face of both internal and external stressors. Thus, over time, we want to help these children learn to soothe themselves, to be able to "ride the worry wave down."[2]

Getting to Work at Home and in School

Supporting Mastery Not Difficulty

Offering Extra Attention When the Child Is Doing Well

Parents and teachers note when the child is at his most relaxed and respond with interest, pleasure, and nurturance.

Avoiding Constant Reassurance

Adults provide friendly, sensible support without getting into the habit of constantly reassuring the child that things are safe. When parents and teachers reassure kids over and over again, children don't learn to manage their fears.

Providing Skill-Building Opportunities

Having a Plan for Responding to Worries

Adults think in advance and come up with a plan for when they'll actively discuss the child's concerns, when they'll offer brief support, and when they'll convey that—even if the child is feeling uncomfortable—it's time to stop talking. The plan will involve some mix of the following:

1. **Acknowledging the Child's Distress:** Parents and teachers respond empathically when the child first approaches them in an anxious state. "Oh, do you have that worried feeling again? I bet you don't like that."
2. **Responding to the Content of the Child's Worry:** *If the child hasn't brought up his specific concern recently,* and if there is time available, adults ask about what is bothering him. They then convey that they understand what he's worried about and, when indicated, offer reassuring information about the situation in question.
3. **Helping the Child Do Some Problem-Solving:** After attending to child's distress, parents and teachers support him in coming up with a plan for how to deal with (rather than avoid) the anxiety-provoking situation. ("So you want to hold my hand for a while after we go into grandma's house? You'll tell me when you're ready to go down to the basement to play with your cousins? And I should come downstairs for a couple of minutes until you're ready to play on your own? That sounds like a good plan!")
4. **"Capping" the Discussion:** Even after such a friendly conversation, the child may remain concerned. Letting him know that it's now time to stop talking, adults make clear that he's welcome to stay with them. However, they have things to do and won't answer more questions. When he's ready, they'll be happy to help him find something to do. (One way of thinking about this strategy is that the adult offers him or herself as a boring but safe home base.)
5. **Asking the Child to Manage His Concern Without Conversation:** *If the child's worry is a familiar one,* parents and teachers acknowledge that he's feeling nervous. They offer some gentle physical or nonverbal support, at the same time emphasizing that they're not going to talk about what's on his mind. Then, as above, they allow the child to stay with them without much interaction. They do, however, respond with interest and support *when the child is ready to reengage in a pleasurable activity.*

Offering Support as the Child Learns to Approach Rather Than Avoid Stressful Situations

Adults offer a feeling of safety as the child works to master his fears. Staying with him as he observes an overwhelming situation, they comment on what he sees. For example, as the child stiffens upon seeing the dog in a neighbor's fenced-in yard: "Hey, let's stop for a minute. There's Zeke and he's barking and running around! Let's watch him while we hold hands. He's so loud when he barks, isn't he? I wish he understood people language and we could tell him, 'BE QUIET ZEKE!'"

Supporting Involvement and Social Skill Development

Anxious children aren't always comfortable playing with peers—the content of play often scares them. Lending an ally, adults offer themselves as a play partner, thus providing a child a secure base as he ventures out socially. Doing this for even ten or fifteen minutes a day at home and in the classroom can make a huge difference.

Teaching Relaxation Techniques

Adults offer techniques to relax both mind and body, including child-friendly breathing exercises and guided imagery. (In the latter, the child relaxes his body as he imagines a pleasurable scene.) Teaching these techniques when the child is doing well, parents and teachers then encourage their use in periods of distress (March, 1995; Goldstein, Hagar, and Brooks, 2002). Note that parents sometimes need guidance in learning how to help children use these strategies. In the classroom, it's often best to teach these approaches in a large group, something which many students enjoy.

Demystifying Anxiety

With older children, parents and teachers can offer a simple explanation of how anxiety works: First, the mind has a scary thought. Then, it sends messages to the body, causing the body to feel jittery, get stomachaches, and so on. As the body gets tense, the mind notices, and its ideas get even more frightening. (Note that in the clinical world, this pattern is often described as the "fear of fear" spiral [Chambless and Gracely, 1989].) Once children understand this progression, they can be taught to come up with *other, less overwhelming ideas,* thus calming themselves down: "What could your mind say when it sees our neighbor's dog? How about, 'That dog is behind a fence! He sounds scary but he can't get out!'"

Providing Opportunities for Expressing and Working Through Feelings

Finding Occasional, Relaxed Times to Discuss the Child's Concerns

Some of the best opportunities to help a child work through anxiety come when he's not in the midst of distress. When directing a child to contain feelings during a difficult moment, parents and teachers emphasize that there will be a specific time to talk over concerns later on. Then, when the designated time arrives, these adults listen carefully. In response to what they hear, they offer any explanations or support the child finds useful, often in reassuring terms they've used before. (Kids experience repetition as useful when they're feeling anxious, finding it easiest to take in—and eventually use on their own—simple explanations offered in familiar language.)

Entering the Child's Symbolic World to Help Him Master Anxiety

Parents and teachers offer art materials, create stories, and engage in dramatic play in order to help the child master his worries. Sharing stories about their own childhood experiences of overcoming worry can also be useful. In addition, adults can locate some of the excellent children's books on this topic, many of which recount engaging stories of children and animals facing down their fears.

Setting Effective Expectations

Sometimes anxious children are not only overly vigilant but whiny and demanding too. Adults make sure to set clear expectations for behavior, then follow through effectively when a child is acting unacceptably.

Modifying Family and Classroom Dynamics and Organization

Monitoring the Contribution of Family or Classroom-Based Stress

It's not unusual for a child's anxiety level to stem, at least in part, from difficult experiences at home. In such cases, parents strive to change the quality of family life, watching for the impact of parental and sibling conflict, slowing down the pace of activities, and shooting for an organized but not overly pressured set of daily routines. In other situations, a child's anxiety level emerges out of stress he experiences in school as he struggles to separate from his parents, to manage difficult experiences with peers, or to deal with curriculum he finds overwhelming. Depending on the situation, teachers work with parents on a plan for successful separation (see Chapter 8), monitor and help with social dynamics, and/or offer support for learning challenges.

Using Classroom-Wide "Climate Control," Well-Organized Transitions, and Effectively Run Group Time to Support Mastery

When classrooms are calm and orderly, anxious kids feel more secure. As a result, children who have trouble managing their worries and fears benefit greatly from the teaching strategies outlined in Chapter 7.

Reducing Irritability

Kids who get overly worried can leave their parents and teachers feeling highly frustrated. Shooting to avoid irritability whenever possible, adults aim for a tone of low-key friendliness.

Finding Time for Pleasurable Family Time

Parents monitor whether they have enough time to feel in synch with their children and—even if it means that certain chores have to wait—find opportunities for relaxed, playful, and connected experiences for everyone.

Watching That Bedtimes and Bedtime Routines Allow Kids to Get Enough Sleep

Tired children often manage anxiety poorly. This is a particular problem for overly anxious youngsters, who may feel especially burdened at bedtime. Extending evening routines into a seemingly endless series of requests for company and attention, these children often end up getting less sleep than they need, leaving them even more vulnerable to evening fearfulness. To break this cycle, parents set a reasonable bedtime, come up with a relaxing but not unusually long bedtime routine, then stick to both.

Watching for Emotional, Physical, or Sexual Harm

Highly anxious children are sometimes reacting to physical, sexual, or emotional mistreatment, or to frightening violence at home. Though there are many other reasons that a child may feel overwhelmed, adults watch carefully, and take action if they sense that such a situation is taking place, whether within or outside of the family.[3]

Seeking Outside Help

Getting Therapeutic Help

When family dynamics play a significant role in a child's difficulties, family or couples counseling may be a boon for everyone. Another possibility is for the child to get some individualized help. Sometimes both are indicated. When domestic violence and/or abuse have contributed to a child's anxieties, such help can be crucial.

Accessing Clinical Support for Cognitive-Behavioral Approaches

Parents and/or kids may need assistance in learning relaxation and desensitization techniques. The clinicians involved should have expertise in cognitive-behavioral work, and specifically in anxiety-reduction techniques. (One reason for this is that, carried out improperly, desensitization protocols can increase rather than decrease children's stress levels.) Since only certain professionals are knowledgeable in this area, consulting clinicians may need to help families locate appropriate practitioners.

Seeking Consultation, Testing, and/or Specialized Services

When a child's anxiety stems from his feeling overwhelmed as a learner, parents and teachers may find it useful to get further information about what's getting in his way. Pediatricians or school personnel can help get such a process started, with the possible outcome of school-based or outside help for the challenges in question.

Considering Pharmacological Intervention

Many young children respond well to the approaches outlined in this chapter. However, if parents and teachers have offered steady assistance and the child continues to be highly anxious, a medication consult may be in order (Kutcher, Reiter, and Gardner, 1995).

Strategies in Action: Helping Kids Manage and Overcome Anxiety

Getting to Work With Rachel—Targeting a Mixture of Constitutionally Based Anxiety and Problematic Patterns of Interaction

Four-year-old Rachel's intense fearfulness has her teachers stymied, and they want some guidance about how to help her feel more at ease. As I enter the classroom, the director points out a lanky child contentedly chatting with some friends at the art table. But a few minutes into the observation, Rachel's face draws taut as she spots a monster-filled adventure unfolding in the block area. She freezes in the middle of her art project, then runs to her favorite teacher to ask her to "tell those boys with the monsters to stop their game." The pattern continues throughout the morning's free play period: This youngster is happily occupied in one part of the room, only to be jolted by the need to ward off imagined danger in another. As a result, both of the classroom's teachers spend far more time than they'd like with a worried Rachel clutching their hands and asking questions about the threats she perceives surrounding her. At the end of my time in the classroom, I find myself thinking about how tiring it must be for a child to worry so intensely and so often.

What Do We See?

Noting Family Issues and Patterns of Reassurance-Seeking or Avoidance

When children are particularly anxious, it's important to pay close attention to patterns of avoidance and reassurance-seeking. In addition, we gather information about a child's family. In Rachel's case, there is important information to be learned in both areas. Rachel's teachers, for example, relate that they don't know how to respond to her mother Stephanie. Stephanie is the only parent doing drop-offs and pick-ups, and she has many questions about classroom safety. Not unlike her daughter, Stephanie fails to get comfort from the teachers' patient responses, bringing up her uneasiness over and over again. In addition, it becomes clear that each member of this nuclear family wrestles with bouts of worry: Rachel's older sister Tanya is getting some help with difficulty separating to go to elementary school, while each of her parents acknowledge that they too have struggled with anxieties for a long time.

When anxiety appears to be embedded in a family system, it's useful to find out whether there is a history of such patterning going back over years. This turns out to be true in Rachel's family: Anxiety has reverberated through the generations on both sides. Barry, Rachel's dad, mentions that his mother and grandfather are known as his family's "big league worrywarts." Stephanie recounts that an older brother suffered from panic attacks throughout his adolescence, and tearfully reveals that her fretful mother offered little comfort to any of her kids as they were growing up. Stephanie is adamant that she is going to do better with her own children and bends over backward to offer support when they feel unsettled.

However, Barry responded to the fear-filled atmosphere of his childhood home by trying to keep his own anxieties in check, and he sees things differently. Often feeling that his wife overreacts in the face of their children's worries, he can become coldly critical, and a fair amount of marital tension now surrounds family episodes of escalating anxiety. Adding to the stress from these ever-present patterns are feelings related to a current situation: Barry's mother has recently become very ill. Both girls are aware of his sadness about her prospects and Rachel, in particular, has been asking her parents many uneasy questions about both her grandmother's and their health—questions that they can't answer in a way that comforts her.

What Do We Think?

Considering the Intersection of Constitutionally Based Anxiety, Family History, and Current Patterns of Interaction

By this time, there is a lot of information to consider. First of all, the obvious: Rachel isn't coping successfully with her fears. She has a lot of them, they have an intense grip on her, and these two facts cause real problems in her four-year-old universe. These struggles, of course, need to be kept in context. Many young children have fears—monsters under the bed, scary-looking dogs, robbers lurking in the dark of basement or closet. But Rachel is the only child in her classroom who, more than just occasionally, holds back from activities that bring her pleasure in reaction to the fears that plague her. The normal anxieties of early childhood have amplified to cause intense and worrisome distress.

In the process of understanding children like Rachel, it's important to consider the intersection of genetics, history, and behavioral feedback loops. We ask whether a youngster was born with an extra dose of sensitivity. We wonder if experiences at home have left him emotionally off-kilter. We factor in family history—the stories parents have lived, and the ways those stories echo through the present. We look at the relationships between anxious children and anxious parents, and ask whether they're caught in a subtle tangle of worry and love. Then, whatever the original reason for a child's vigilance, we think about how parents and teachers may be making it worse rather than better. Are they continuing to answer the child's ever-present queries with comforting explanations, even when those efforts only result in more nervous questioning? Are they teaching him that scary feelings must be avoided at all costs by distracting him constantly?

Through the process of considering these questions about Rachel, a picture takes shape. The anxiety running through the generations in Rachel's family suggests that she has an inborn tendency to get anxious. Then, when she starts feeling overwhelmed, Stephanie gets very involved in a loving but tense way and Barry often becomes short with both of them. This unhappy family choreography—driven, in part, by painful experiences from the past—causes Rachel further distress in the present: Neither parent is able to offer the easy-going support she needs to calm down. Thus, her worries amplify, taking over not only her inner experience, but the air in the household too.

The fact that Rachel's grandmother is so sick is probably contributing to the mix as well; Barry is not only deeply saddened by his mother's failing health but is also spending many hours by her side, and a feeling of imminent loss permeates daily life in the household. The idea of serious illness and death is scary for any child, most especially one who gets easily overwhelmed to begin with. Having parents who have trouble handling their own anxiety only makes such a situation more alarming. Moreover, if a child is in the habit of asking about her worries over and over again, leading to increasingly irritated answers, it's hard for anyone to regain a sense of calm.

Then there are the interactions at school. From the best of intentions, it looks like Rachel's teachers are repeating her mother's pattern: responding to Rachel's continuing questions long after it's clear that no comfort is to be found in their answers, and inadvertently reinforcing the idea that the thing to do when you are worried is to flee the situations that scare you. Unfortunately, when a child's primary strategy in the face of unwarranted anxiety is to avoid the things that trigger it, the world tends to feel less and less safe. Rachel needs help, and much of that help will involve her parents and teachers learning different ways to react to her distress.

What Do We Do?

In designing a set of strategies for Rachel, our goals are to help her worry less often, and to encourage her to ride out the fears she does experience as quickly as possible. The plan we come up with targets the feedback loops noted earlier, and works to shift attention away from times of difficulty toward periods of mastery. In addition, it offers Rachel space for working through worries, while giving her parents opportunities to reflect on problematic dynamics at home. Here is its overview:

At Home

- Barry and Stephanie will offer extra attention when Rachel is feeling calm and at ease.
- They'll set aside one period a day, after dinner, to have a supportive conversation about worries. At other times, they'll give Rachel some friendly physical comfort if she's anxious, and ask her if she wants them to write her worry down (one time a day per specific worry) to put in a "worry box." Then they'll remind her that they aren't going to talk about her worry any further right then. Instead, going about their day, they'll offer themselves as boring but secure anchors, with an emphasis on helping Rachel get re-involved in pleasurable activities.
- At an agreed upon time, the worry box will be opened so that Rachel can ask any questions she might have about what is troubling her. During this conversation, Rachel's parents will patiently talk over her concerns, even if how they respond involves a repeat of previously discussed content. In

fact, Barry and Stephanie will try to use the same soothing language each time they talk with their daughter about her fears.

- Barry and Stephanie will try to avoid being in conflict with each other about how to handle Rachel's anxieties, especially when she's in the room. They'll meet with me every few weeks, so that we can keep an eye on how things are going for their daughter, and also talk about some of the family issues that are making life difficult for everyone. As part of these meetings, we'll discuss how they react to Rachel's sister's anxieties, to see if there is a way to make the household approach to anxiety consistent for both girls.

- Rachel's parents will, through the use of children's literature and conversation, help her feel less overwhelmed by her grandmother's illness. Barry, especially, will offer some perspective on how his mother's situation is both sad and a part of life. In addition, both he and his wife will, during their evening "worry talks," remind Rachel that "we are planning on being around for a long, long time."

At School

- Rachel's teachers will give her extra attention and nurturance when she is contentedly involved in classroom activities.
- When Rachel becomes fearful and requests help, they'll briefly acknowledge her feelings, then offer some low-key physical reassurance. Letting her know that she can stay with them until she's ready to rejoin play, they'll then attend to other children. When Rachel is ready, they'll offer warm support as she begins to engage in an enjoyable activity, and remain with her until she's comfortably involved.
- If Rachel is frightened by something in the room, her teachers will invite her to approach the scary situation. Then they'll quietly observe with her, commenting on what's going on, but not trying to explain that there isn't anything to be afraid of.
- When Rachel seems interested in but afraid to join an activity, her teachers will—time permitting—lend an ally, becoming her play partner as she dares to participate.

Rachel starts calming down soon after her parents and teachers begin using these strategies. She makes progress most easily at school, where staff are delighted at how quickly she finds a more relaxed approach to classroom life. It's not hard to understand why things take longer to improve at home—Barry and Stephanie have their own demons to battle in order to help Rachel with hers. But eventually family life, too, begins to have a lighter tone. A wonderful side benefit of our work together is that Rachel's sister Tanya also begins to be less plagued by anxiety. By the time Barry's mother passes away, the foursome has some newfound resources with which to face their loss.

Step-by-Step Intervention for Anxiety

The plan above allows for this progress. But as the big picture gets better, Barry and Stephanie bring up other concerns. Like many anxious children, Rachel fears that an unnamed threat might be lying in wait anywhere in the house. As a result—to the great inconvenience of her parents—she refuses to go upstairs to the second floor unless accompanied. Furthermore, bedtimes feel like they go on endlessly. Rachel wants to have many stories read. A glass of water. Numerous lullabies followed by a special backrub. Then, finally ready to close her eyes, she insists that someone stay with her until she falls asleep, a process that can take well over an hour. Should the adult on hand try to tiptoe out precipitously, Rachel's eyes fly open and she cries out for company. They come back.

Barry and Stephanie ask for help in addressing these issues. Before considering the specific approaches they embrace, it is worth considering two important points. First, they only embark on this new work after Rachel shows a better ability to cope with anxiety in general. Second, and this is often true, *they need precise and ongoing guidance in order to understand and follow through on the strategies they use.* Note how the following strategies reflect core principles for working with anxious children: They target amplifying feedback loops, change those loops a manageable step at a time, and are set out in advance so that children can prepare for what's coming.

Tackling Bedtime Difficulties

- It's bedtime. Rachel now knows that two stories are the max—she's heard about this in a short talk she and her parents had a few days ago. She's not pleased that things are going to be different, but her parents have been clear, saying that everyone will be a lot happier when the new plan does its job. The plan starts like this: Rachel gets a nice snuggle and two stories. She can have a glass of water by her bed, but mom or dad sets it out before they settle down together. She has her last pee just before they read together too. Then, after the second story and a song (only one), it's time to turn out the light. After that, for now, mom and dad stay like they always have. However, after lights out, *there isn't any talking even if Rachel wants to tell them something. Whatever is on her mind will have to wait until the morning.*
- It's week two and now, after fifteen minutes of lights out, mom or dad takes a two-minute break, and sits in the hallway just out of sight. There still won't be talking, even if Rachel complains that she wants them to stay. When they come back in, a quick pat will signal their support, but they won't say a word. Then, if she's still awake ten minutes later, they'll leave again. And so on.
- During week three mom or dad stays for ten minutes. After that, they go out for five minutes, after which their return is signaled by the usual quick

pat. This time they only stay for five minutes, however. Then they come and go in the same way until Rachel falls asleep.

- By week four, Rachel's parents stay for five minutes, come back after ten, check in with a pat, and then leave for fifteen. That's how things will remain until Rachel is comfortable falling asleep on her own.

At first glance, the timeline here may appear laboriously slow. But the routine in question has been going on for almost a year. Altering it gradually over the course of a month makes more sense than asking Rachel to adapt to a large change all at once. The plan's success—and it is successful—relies on this incremental quality, on Barry and Stephanie's skill at preparing Rachel for each of its steps, and on their ability to withstand her distress when they don't respond to her wish to keep talking.

Tempering a Child's Anxiety-Driven Need for Constant Company

At the same time that these parents tackle bedtime behavior, they begin helping their daughter get used to going upstairs on her own. Like the process described above, their approach works step-by-step, in this case starting with Barry and Stephanie working merely to *reduce the irritability that surrounds Rachel's lack of independence.* Thus throughout the first week, they willingly accompany her upstairs when asked. Weeks two and three involve their going upstairs with her, but waiting at the top of the stairs while she's busy, first counting quietly so she can hear their voices, later staying quiet. By week four, these parents wait midway down the stairs and by weeks five and six, at the bottom. During week seven, Rachel gets some quick support, hears where her parents will be while she heads upstairs, then goes independently. Week eight? An ice cream party to celebrate her bravery.

Staying Flexible When Initial Approaches Don't Work

Plans like those outlined for Rachel work well for many children, especially if adults stay relaxed, remain consistent, and allow a child to master one stage before moving on to the next. Occasionally, though, an initial set of strategies doesn't work. Then it may be necessary to bend more in the direction of a child's anxiety. The trick in these situations is for parents to offer further support *without reinforcing anxiety with extra attention.* For example, if a bedtime plan like Rachel's is backfiring, consultants can suggest a slightly altered approach. Note that, once again, nighttime plans like the following are only implemented once parents have noticed the child mastering anxiety more successfully during the day.

The plan starts as in Rachel's case. But, when it's time for the parent (for ease of explanation: dad) to leave, the child can, if he'd like, go along and sit in the room where his father will now be reading or doing chores. They won't talk together at all, however. Neither will the child be permitted to play or read, though he may have his special "blankie" or comfort object on hand. When the child is ready to lie down and go to sleep (and he won't be allowed to fall asleep except in bed), he can tell his father. Then he'll be tucked in and the original plan will move forward just as it used to.

There is an art to knowing when a bedtime plan hasn't been given enough time to work, and when a change of direction is in order. Kids occasionally do need a shift like the one just outlined; their initial anxiety at bedtime is too extreme for them to tolerate even a graduated plan involving separation. Often, with the addition of the steps above, parents can soon return to the more conventional approach used by Rachel's parents. As we coach parents in this minor change of pace, we make clear that they'll need to tolerate a ghost-like partner through the evening for a number of days (occasionally even weeks) before things begin to turn around.

Supporting Children With Situation-Specific Anxiety

Our approaches to children with sudden-onset anxiety are often different from those just explored. The youngsters in this group may need help in understanding what has set off their unhappiness, and support in mastering their overwhelming feelings. Sometimes, as in the case that follows, it's initially hard to find the source of a child's growing turmoil. At other times, adults are well aware of what is going on: a death in the family, an imminent family breakup, a sudden change in housing. Of course any time a child is looking uncharacteristically anxious, we also look carefully at his world, watching for signs of trauma, neglect, domestic violence, severe bullying, or parental substance abuse.

Getting to Work With Justin—Targeting a Mix of Situational Overload, Temperamental Self-Sufficiency, and Long-Standing Patterns of Interaction

Four-year-old Justin has always been an easy child. His parents have relied on his good cheer, his ability to play contentedly by himself, and his willingness to go with the flow when life at home gets stressful. Which it often does: Justin's older sister is autistic. Justin has been easy at school too. He'll play with almost anyone, smiles easily, and almost never resists the classroom's routines. Things aren't going quite so smoothly of late, however. Suddenly, this boy is balking when his mom brings him into the classroom. Looking panic-stricken, he stands immobile near the doorway as his mother prepares to say good-bye. When she tries to give him some attention before she leaves, he only appears more overwhelmed. After she's gone, he doesn't move. Then, though he makes no noise, tears begin rolling down his cheeks.

Justin's teacher Karen now goes to him soon after he and his mom come in, but neither adult can get him to say what's wrong. Though Karen can usually help him find something to do once his mother leaves, his frightened expression always appears close to the surface. He now spends much of his time alone at the drawing table, not a place that used to be of interest. Then, when it's time to transition from free play to group time, he'll stand frozen and overwhelmed once again, shedding more quiet tears if a teacher comes over to offer support.

What Do We See?

Carefully Examining a Child's Experience

Karen requests an observation and follow-up consultation, explaining that neither she nor Justin's parents understand what has gone awry. Then she relays some information she's learned about from Liza, Justin's mother. About a month ago, Justin gave up his pacifier. A week later, Liza was in a car accident, experienced some whiplash, and consequently wore a neck brace for a few days. Justin's dad had been out of town at that time, and taking care of the two kids had been trying. Liza has mentioned that she probably hadn't been herself emotionally either—the accident had been scary though thankfully not serious. Justin, as usual, had been a rock through the whole thing, though perhaps a little more quiet than usual. It was after his dad got back that he started acting differently. Now things seem to be getting worse.

During a post-observation conversation, Karen relates that the thing she's most aware of, in addition to Justin appearing so frightened, is that he's lost his sense of humor. "He used to just bounce around the class with an impish look on his face, and almost anything could get him to start giggling." Her remarks confirm what I had noted while in the classroom: These days, even when Justin looks relatively calm, his face has a grave, sad expression. Karen goes on. "I just can't figure it out. It's really odd for a child to go from being so content to being so scared and unhappy when nothing terrible seems to have happened."

What Do We Think?

Considering Specific Triggers, Children's Coping Mechanisms, and Family Dynamics

Karen's concerns lead to a set of questions consultants often ask in the face of sudden-onset anxiety: What might have set off the child's current stress level?

How might that "triggering" event have intersected with his temperament, way of coping, and place in his family? These questions have a particular thrust in Justin's case. When this boy was doing well, I inquire, did the teachers feel deeply connected to him? Not really, they reply. He was certainly a likeable, happy child, but on the self-sufficient side, not the sort who would come to them to proudly share his accomplishments. And if he got hurt, would he approach them then? Rarely, they answer. They might have gone to him when they'd noticed he'd stumbled, but he wouldn't want to be comforted. On the other hand, he tended to bounce back cheerfully right after a fall or scrape. In response to an inquiry about Justin's family, it becomes clear that school staff see his parents as wonderful, warm people though, understandably, they sometimes appear to be deeply tired in the face of Justin's sister's many needs.

It's an intriguing puzzle. Could Justin be one of those kids who come into the world with both a natural flexibility and a kind of comfortable inwardness? If so, did these qualities end up being especially helpful to his family given his sister's difficulties? Staff and I wonder whether he ever learned to seek support when overwhelmed, and if giving up his pacifier has left him without an important source of comfort. Then we think about his mother's car accident. How might she have appeared to Justin as she moved around the house, stiff and uncomfortable, a large white brace around her neck and a distracted, perhaps frightened, expression on her face? Did she seem almost foreign? Scary? We also consider the question of how Justin's autistic sister reacted to the change. Had things gotten fairly intense over the few days that Justin's dad was away?

Eventually, we come up with a tentative picture of what's been going on. Perhaps Justin never fully learned how to seek comfort. Perhaps, in the aftermath of his mom's car accident—and without his trusty pacifier—he became truly overwhelmed. Maybe he remains quite stuck emotionally, feeling frightened and, given his temperament, uncertain both about what he's experiencing and about how to reach out. That would account for his frozen behavior in the classroom and his tears when adults try to comfort him. The team decides to try some new strategies, understanding that if this hypothesis is wrong, or the strategies off-base, they probably won't make things any worse. Karen agrees to ask Justin's parents to set up a consultative meeting as well; it will be important to brainstorm about how to help this boy at home too.

What Do We Do?

Offering Emotional Support While Fostering Connection, Containment, and Involvement

Consultation with Justin's parents leads to a coherent approach that spans both home and school. In the outline below, that approach is presented with school strategies first—because Justin is so overwhelmed, the school team starts using those strategies even before his parents get a chance to join the conversation.

In School

- A teacher will go to Justin when he looks overwhelmed. Rather than asking him what's wrong, they'll kneel down and try a version of the following: "Justin, you look unhappy... maybe you're feeling scared. I'm going to stay here, because sometimes it's nice to have someone around when you feel that way!"
- After a period of keeping Justin company, the teacher will note what's happening in the room. ("Hey, I see Jack playing with blocks. And Miranda is looking at a book. And she's grinning, that book must be funny!") The teacher will ask if Justin would like to come with her and find something to do. If he declines, she won't press him, instead conveying appreciation for how he feels, and a heads up that she's going to attend to some other children. ("You know Justin, *it's okay to feel unhappy or scared*. Sometimes it takes time before people feel better. But, don't worry, because *you'll feel better after a while!* I'm going to go help some other kids now. Soon I'll come back to see how you're doing.")
- After about five minutes, the teacher will come back to check in. She'll once again kneel down and comment compassionately on how he's feeling. She may well repeat that it's okay to feel unhappy or scared, and that sometimes it's nice to have someone with you when you feel that way. Then she'll continue to come and go in this way for as long as needed.
- When Justin is ready, the teacher will join him in watching a group of kids who are playing. She'll stay with him as he looks on, using humor to help him reengage with both her and his buddies. Eventually, she'll see if she can help Justin join in, *staying for a little while if he's able to do so.*
- At times when Justin looks relaxed, teachers will seek him out and, relying on his wonderful sense of humor, initiate moments of pleasurable interaction. *Aiming to stretch his ability to participate in extended circles of connection, they'll find many moments a day to help him find this more engaged and enjoyable experience of relationship.*

At Home

- Justin's parents will note times when their son looks like he may be feeling overwhelmed. Going to him when they can, they'll gently tell him that "it's okay to feel unhappy or scared" and that it can feel good to have someone with you when you have those feelings.
- They'll also note times when Justin is playing on his own and take time to join him in what he's doing, shooting for eye contact, warmth, and pleasure in his responses to their presence.

- In addition, these parents will sneak in more moments of physical contact—Justin is a little stiff when it comes to hugs and snuggles. Trying not to overwhelm him with their affection, they'll work to help him tolerate and enjoy this kind of connection. As they do, they'll make statements that let him know that such contact can feel good: "Ummm...I like having my arm around your shoulders! It feels good to have you close to me!"
- Though they do want their son to be self-directed and self-sufficient in the face of his family's situation, Justin's parents will remind themselves to keep an eye on his needs, and to refrain from expecting him to be more grown-up than he can handle.

Happily, these strategies have a wonderful impact on Justin. Though he continues to experience moments of intense panic for over a week, he seems to appreciate his teachers' reassurance that it's okay to feel unhappy or scared. As these episodes diminish in frequency, Karen also notes that he looks relieved when teachers tell him that people often like having others around when they don't feel good. Most importantly, after he regains a more solid footing in the classroom, his teachers remind themselves not to leave him quite so much on his own. This is a child who needs help learning that close connections are important, sustaining, and pleasurable. Justin's parents see a big change too. And they are a bit humbled by the whole experience. "We'd been asking more of him than we realized," Liza reflects in a follow-up meeting. "He's been such a pleasure to us both, so much fun and so together. We just hadn't noticed that he needed more support than he let on. I don't think we'll forget this and, in a way, I'm almost glad it happened."

Getting to Work When a Child Has Sensory Sensitivities

There is another group of children whose difficulties parallel those of typically anxious children, those who find it hard to tolerate certain sensations. (We might think of these youngsters as experiencing a kind of *sensory anxiety*.) Parents sometimes find themselves tremendously challenged by these youngsters who, usually from birth, are highly reactive to sensory experience. It can feel as though months worth of meals are organized to avoid foods that taste or smell "yucky," a list that appears to grow daily; morning routines may revolve endlessly around locating shirts that are neither too tight nor too loose. These patterns are common but worrisome. Children with sensory challenges can and should gradually learn to tolerate at least some of the sensations that feel uncomfortable to them, even as they are offered real accommodations for their vulnerabilities. Monitoring the feedback loops that surround their reactivity—and cleaning up the sloppy mix of frustration and compassion in parental behavior—is essential. Otherwise, family interactions become increasingly fraught with conflict and kids end up having trouble regulating emotions as well as sensations.

This sounds great on paper. But how do we help parents figure out when to give in to a child's need to have a different pair of socks on and when to ask that child to deal with some discomfort? It helps to remember that these children engage in the same kind of avoidance that anxious kids do. Something doesn't feel good (in this case an unpleasant physical sensation rather than an unpleasant emotion) and *they try as hard as they can to escape the feeling by escaping the stimulus that triggers that feeling.* Just like anxious kids, they then look to others to soothe their discomfort. The result of all this is that parents try to organize the worlds of these youngsters so that they experience a minimum of discomfort; it seems logical that doing so will make life far less stressful for everyone. But, unfortunately, such efforts sometimes backfire. Children end up learning that the main way to deal with physical discomfort is to get away from it, and everyday experiences of taste, smell, and touch become harder and harder to tolerate. All of this may be happening with a fair amount of whining and crying to boot.

The remedy relies on the principal of clarity in leaning in and leaning out. Clinicians begin by helping parents accept that their son or daughter truly does experience the world differently than many. Thus, we encourage them to look for clothing that is reasonably comfortable for their child, and to provide foods that go down easily. If a youngster hates the feeling of sand, parents have beach sandals on hand. If he doesn't enjoy bare feet on the grass, they relax about letting him keep his shoes on. For children who get easily overwhelmed by noise, the radio stays on low, everyone makes an effort to keep their voices down, and community fairs and parades are no longer considered a requirement for a successful childhood. There are other proactive ideas consultants support too. When it's time to use bleach on the laundry or a strong cleaner on the floors, the smell-sensitive youngster is now told in advance. He's welcome to some help finding something to do in a different part of the house. All of this is done with good cheer or, on difficult days, with as little irritation as a parent can manage. Leaning in.[4]

However, once there are some socks around that are reasonably comfortable—or shirts with a decent approximation of what the child likes—consultants guide parents in leaning out. No, the *perfect* shirt is dirty and will stay in the laundry hamper. Here are the other three that feel okay though not quite as good. Dad is going downstairs and Thomas will have to figure out which one to wear. The trip to his favorite park will have to wait until he's dressed, and no TV will go on until he's ready either. Yes, dad really understands that it doesn't feel good and he knows it's not fun. But, Thomas will be able to make do if he tries hard. His favorite shirt will be clean in a couple of days. Leaning out.

This leaning out sometimes moves into the arena of limit setting. Thomas refuses to put on his second-favorite shirt? The trip to the park is regretfully cancelled and that evening, dad reminds him of what happened so he can try again tomorrow. As we coach parents in this ongoing work—and ongoing coaching can be essential in the face of a child's sensory intensity—we emphasize that the first step in leaning out is a clear but friendly expectation. The second is some quick problem-solving or a brief reminder. The third—without extended lecturing—may be some mild discipline.

Parents often struggle with this process, because helping these children get used to the sometimes-uncomfortable world in which they live isn't easy. In addition, children whose challenges in processing sensation have a profound effect on many areas of development need a more sophisticated approach than the one just described. Some in this group have challenges like those discussed in the next chapter. Others look like the most extreme children discussed in books devoted solely to sensory integration. But, as any parent knows who hears that their very picky youngster has enjoyed chicken nuggets at a friend's house when chicken is an absolute no-no at the family dinner table, many children have more of an ability to tolerate uncomfortable sensations than they realize. When the feedback loops surrounding a child's sensitivity are really out of hand, everyone may end up deciding that a child *can't* deal with a situation that, in other circumstances, he might actually be able to manage fairly well.

13

Helping the Disengaged, Offbeat, or Gifted but Rigid Child

*Getting to Work When a Child Has Trouble
Relating With Interest and Flexibility*

This chapter looks at children struggling with a range of interpersonal difficulties. Some have trouble establishing and maintaining a basic sense of relatedness. Others are interested in connecting but do so too much on their own terms. Experiencing profound discomfort when faced with demands for sociability, children in the first group appear emotionally unavailable. Without an easy ability to share ideas, space, and materials, children in the second seem unaware of the nature of social interchange.

A significant number of these children have powerful gifts and, in part due to the strength of these gifts, appear more compelled by content than by people. If an adult or child wants to discuss a topic that intrigues them both, that's terrific. Should that individual have an agenda that's outside the child's interest of the moment, disengagement, frustration, or rigidity may follow. At their best, these kids are our future scientists, mathematicians, and historians. At their worst, parents worry that they'll become eccentric social isolates.

Youngsters who experience such challenges have been called "quirky" (Klass and Costello, 2003) and "self-absorbed" (Greenspan with Salmon, 1995). Another phrase to describe them, first introduced in Chapter 2, is "deep-tracked." Visualizing these children as traveling along a deeply compelling but internal track allows us to think about "joining a child in her track," helping her "widen the track" to include another person's presence, and supporting her as she works to "change tracks"—three experiences that increase her basic sense of connectedness and allow her to gain skill in social exchange. Providing such experiences lies at the core of the work we do with these children. This work may be slow; the difficulties described here often stem from powerful hard-wiring. But it can be tremendously exciting too, as we watch a socially awkward or unresponsive child emerge into the world of pleasurable relationships and mutuality.

Note that the following material is not adequate for understanding and helping children with extreme relational and developmental difficulties. It's not that the strategies here don't apply to such youngsters, they often do. However, there is far more to understand about them than can be covered here, and any number of books devoted solely to their issues.[1]

What Issues Might Be Contributing to the Child's Behavior?

- An inner-focused, inflexible, and/or hard to engage temperament
- Difficulties harnessing and maintaining attention
- Difficulties processing sounds, sights, and sensations, including challenges in sensory regulation, auditory processing, and/or visual-spatial processing
- Vulnerabilities understanding and processing information, including challenges in motor planning and/or organizing, sequencing, and conceptualizing language
- A complex neurodevelopmental profile involving a mix of vulnerabilities in right hemisphere brain function
- Chaotic or overwhelming experiences at home

Some Points to Remember

- Deep-tracked children often have difficulty joining others in a state of what we call "joint attention." When in this state, two people *notice and respond to each other's presence* (Moore and Dunham, 1995). Initial work with these children targets joint attention as a primary goal; once youngsters become more able to take part in moments of mutuality, other developmental growth follows more easily.
- Parents and teachers often feel frustrated by the challenge of initiating or maintaining periods of joint attention with a deep-tracked child who fends off invitations for connection. Similar feelings emerge in the effort to ask a gifted but rigid child to share conversational space. Over time, adults may resignedly leave such youngsters to their self-absorbed states (Greenspan with Salmon, 1995). Other children may also leave a deep-tracked youngster to herself, or cave into a gifted but rigid youngster's need for control. These common but unfortunate patterns tend to amplify a child's natural tendencies.
- Children who have trouble experiencing a basic sense of intimacy and mutuality struggle for a variety of reasons. Thus, before getting to work, parents and teachers need to gain clarity about the nature of a child's challenges. Looking to discover what issues contribute to her struggles, they must ask: What's hard? What's easier? What strikes her interest? What input can she tolerate? What part of this is about her temperament? Her ability to process information? How should life at home and in school be factored in?
- Concerned adults often decide that an assessment is necessary in order to answer such questions, and some (though by no means all) of these children will eventually be diagnosed with a nonverbal learning disability, Asperger's syndrome, a pervasive developmental disorder, or an autistic spectrum disorder.[2] These diagnoses can be helpful in establishing a

youngster's eligibility for needed services. However, such diagnoses are only sometimes coupled with understandably written test results and friendly, intervention-focused follow-up. In addition, they occasionally leave parents and teachers underestimating a child's capacity for growth.[3]

- Some of the children who first appear to be demonstrating neurologically based struggles to connect are actually showing signs of early trauma, neglect, and/or severe difficulties with attachment. Though such children may respond to some of the strategies that follow, the work of helping them feel trust and openness in relationships is based on a different understanding and thus has a different thrust (Groves, 2002; Lieberman and Van Horn, 2004).

Learning to Connect With Others—Stages of Growth

In order to support a deep-tracked youngster's growth, it's necessary to understand the stages through which she'll move and the skills she'll learn along the way. The following progression won't look this orderly in day-to-day life, but keeping it in mind allows all involved to have an overall picture of what progress will look like. Then, with a start point that reflects the child's current level of mastery, she's offered help, one step—and one level—at a time.[4]

Over time, the child will learn to...

1. respond to (and later initiate) invitations for joint attention
2. engage in one or two circles of communication[5]
3. expand the number of circles she can sustain at one time
4. communicate in ways that others can understand: finding words, organizing and sequencing ideas, and building larger units of meaning from smaller ones
5. use language and symbols to express feelings, convey increasingly complex ideas, and play out imaginary scenarios

As a child is supported in progressing through these stages, she will become able to...

1. share thematic agendas with others
2. respond flexibly to requests for track-changing: ending activities or conversation; moving through family routines; leaving the house in a timely way; transitioning from one period to another in school
3. develop skills in social pragmatics—how to initiate or join ongoing play; how to suggest rather than insist upon play ideas with peers; how to initiate conversation yet leave space for others' ideas; how to note and understand facial expressions and tones of voice

The strategies used to support growth through these stages often involve parents, teachers, and specialists offering themselves as partners in play, conversation, and problem-solving. Then, as seen below, those adults provide the kind of developmental scaffolding that fosters the capacity for intimacy, mutuality, and flexibility.

Getting to Work at Home and in School

Providing Skill-Building Opportunities

Encouraging the Experience of Tuned-In Connection

Parents and teachers pay close attention to what intrigues the child, what "track" she likes best. Then they *join her in the track*, thus helping her participate in brief moments of joint attention. Finding creative ways to encourage eye contact and doing what they can to make these experiences pleasurable, they look to increase the number of times a child pops up and tunes in for such moments of connection.

Supporting Circles of Communication

Remaining within areas of interest and high motivation, adults work to help the child open and close one or two circles of communication, encouraging her to respond in a way that connects to what they've said or done. (Otherwise, though it may look like there's been an exchange, the child actually remains in a self-absorbed state.) As the youngster gets better at engaging in such interactions, adults seek to increase the number of exchanges she can sustain at one time.

Strengthening the Ability to Take a Break in Order to Listen

This step takes place after there has been progress in the two just listed. Parents and teachers first support moments of connection and interchange. Then they help the child take in information from the outside. Sticking with the principle of chunking down goals for growth, these adults start by offering information that stays within the child's area of interest, and focus on two agendas: assisting the child *as she stops her forward motion "on the track,"* and helping her *"widen the track" so that it includes another's input.*

Lending an Ally—Working on Expanded Content

Some of these children speak in short, seemingly unrelated units of meaning. They need help sticking with a topic, then organizing and expanding their ideas. Adults join the child as a conversation or play partner, and then offer the scaffolding she needs to successfully sequence and communicate more complex thoughts.

Lending an Ally—Targeting Mutuality

As the child gets better at widening the track and communicating ideas, adults continue to join her in play and conversation, during which they shoot for more mutuality during exchanges. Asking questions, offering ideas, and gently blocking the child's quest for complete control, they encourage her ability to remain connected through mild experiences of frustration, all the while keeping interactions playful and pleasurable.

Lending an Ally—Building a Narrative World

Many of these youngsters have a hard time understanding and expressing their own emotions. Making sense of the emotional experiences of others can be hard too. Parents and teachers help the child put words to what she and others feel, and encourage her in capturing emotionally laden experiences in stories, play scenarios, and drawings. Staying with her as she plays, draws, or talks—and relying on her increasing ability to sustain focus, develop content, and experience depth in her relationships—they help her connect the things she sees and does to a growing understanding of human nature.[6]

Reducing "Self-Stimulating" Behavior

Some of these children flap their hands, rock, or spin to soothe themselves. Others find different ways to experience the calm they need, for example, humming or whistling constantly. While understanding a child's need to engage in such self-soothing behavior, adults work to gradually decrease the behavior's "hold" by intervening with opportunities for engaged interchange.

Emphasizing Prevention While Promoting Mastery

Supporting Awareness and Flexibility in Response to Outside Cues

Adults work to help the child pay attention to outside input, and to respond flexibly and compliantly to expectations. This work often involves some limit setting, but progresses in a way that takes into account her deep-tracked nature. Thus, using the following steps, adults help the child *slow down her forward motion "on the track" so she can "change tracks."* Note that teachers, especially those who are alone in their classrooms, have less time for the one-on-one nature of this work; they'll keep in mind the principles behind these steps and modify them as needed:

1. The adult takes time to get the child's attention, after which he initiates a pleasurable exchange.

2. He previews the upcoming situation, giving the child some friendly information about any expectations for flexibility or track-changing.
3. He helps the child plan how to make the adjustment needed, assisting her in figuring out what she can reasonably do in the period before she must shift agendas.
4. Before giving the child a chance to go back to what she's been doing, the adult reminds her of any consequence for non-compliance, and offers encouragement about her ability to follow through on what's expected.
5. The child returns to her activity for a previously determined period.
6. When that period is over, the child is told that her time is up and she must stop what she's doing. Offering her some low-key support, the parent or teacher rewards success in track-changing with a few moments of warm exchange. However, if the youngster isn't able to do what's required, the adult follows through with the preset consequence. (Note that at a later point during which a similar problem is likely to emerge, the adult previews the new situation using these same steps, but adds a friendly reminder of how badly the child felt the last time she experienced the consequence in question. Encouraging her to work as hard as she can, he lets her know that he believes in her ability to do the track-changing needed so that *this time* her behavior won't result in unhappiness.)

Using Visual Aids to Support Track-Changing

As part of the previewing process, adults use picture charts, handmade countdown clocks, "my turn" cards, and other visual aids to help a child respond to expectations.

Providing Expectations for Reasonable Behavior and a Mastery-Focused Environment

Setting Effective Limits

Adults avoid irritable or angry interactions by shooting for a good mix of leaning in and leaning out. Previewing upcoming situations so that the child knows what is expected, setting clear expectations supported by reasonable consequences, then following through calmly, these adults use failures in compliance to help the child plan for flexible and appropriate responses in the future.

Shooting for an Organized and Predictable Home Life

Parents keep an eye on the chaos level at home. Deep-tracked children do best when life is calm and predictable without being rigid.

Using Well-Organized Transitions, Effectively Run Group Time, and Classroom-Wide Climate Control to Support Mastery

Teachers remind themselves of the teaching strategies outlined in Chapter 7. Deep-tracked children function best in classrooms that are relaxed, calm, and predictable.

Monitoring the Use of TV, DVDs, and Computer Games

Adults monitor and, if necessary, restrict the amount of time deep-tracked youngsters spend engaged in screen time. Such time offers little opportunity for the kind of practice these children need in relating, developing play narratives, and staying attentive to and engaged in the world of people.

Accepting the Need for Practice and the Slow Pace of Change

Because constitutional issues often lie at the heart of a deep-tracked youngster's struggles, parents and teachers remind themselves that it will take the child time and practice to show steady signs of mastery. Then they watch for subtle indications of progress, remembering that growth doesn't happen in a linear fashion and that many small successes can make for a big change over time.

Support, Support, Support

Deep-tracked children can be delightful and interesting family and classroom members. But they're almost always frustrating too. Parents and teachers remember to seek out support from friends, relatives, and colleagues, to take time to relax and regroup, and to stay patient with themselves as well as the children they're trying to help.

Seeking Outside Help

Getting Assistance in Understanding a Child's Profile

Parents and teachers may need outside consultation and/or evaluation in order to fully understand what issues drive a child's struggles. For some of these youngsters, a full evaluation will be helpful, with attention to speech and language issues, sensory vulnerabilities, gross and fine motor challenges, and emotional and neurodevelopmental factors. Once there is a clearer picture of the child's strengths and vulnerabilities—what we call an individualized profile—concerned adults will find it far easier to sort out what kind of help she'll need at home, in school, and from any specialists who will become involved.[7]

Finding Someone to Keep an Eye on the Big Picture

When a child's issues stem from a complex set of factors, parents will often benefit from having someone on hand to help them oversee how things are going. This person—a professional whose specific credentials are less important than his or her accessibility, knowledge base, and extensive experience with significant relational difficulties—helps monitor the child's progress; facilitates contact between specialists, families, and teachers; keeps track of the need for additional services or a shift in approach; offers guidance for home and school-based strategies; and is available to discuss concerns.

Setting Up Extra Supports for the Child

Many deep-tracked youngsters benefit from extra assistance, and one or more of the following may have a role to play in overall approaches to intervention: work supporting sensory integration; occupational or physical therapy; speech and language services; and/or developmentally oriented therapy. Medication is sometimes useful too; parents may want to consider a medication consult if their child is getting good help but isn't as responsive as had been hoped.

Considering the Possibility of Therapeutic Help and Guidance for the Child's Parents or Family

Deep-tracked children can take a toll on a single parent's piece of mind, the good will of a marriage, or the overall quality of family life. Finding a place where parents can get the help they need to support the child—while they and their other children find ways to stay buoyant and connected—can be a real boost to a weary family.

Strategies in Action: Supporting Increased Connection and Flexibility

Getting to Work With Jeremy—Step-by-Step Approaches to Helping a Gifted but Rigid Child

These explorations now return to Jeremy, Chapter 1's creative, inflexible "royal racer." Here, we'll take a close look at the mix of clinical intervention and home-school efforts that help this child become more responsive to adult requests and more capable of the give-and-take required in friendship. An exploration of the elements involved in this mix will illuminate the subtle combination of leaning in and leaning out required to support increased relatedness and flexibility in deep-tracked children.

What Do We See? What Do We Think?

Identifying Vulnerabilities in the Capacity for Joint Attention and Flexibility

Jeremy's parents have agreed that it may be useful for him to have some meetings with me. It's not that this boy has deep-seated unhappiness to sort out: He is a joyful and well-loved child. However, we've come to believe that Jeremy's deep-tracked temperament has gotten in the way of his development. Thus, in addition to help from his parents and teachers, he'll now have some one-on-one time focused on two interconnected skills: tuning into the ideas of others, and responding with both interest and flexibility.

What Do We Do?

Fostering and Practicing New Skills

A close look at the nuts and bolts of Jeremy's individual meetings will illustrate the step-by-step nature of the assistance many deep-tracked children need. Note that although such skill-building support may be easiest to provide in a clinician's office, where there is no need to balance the input of other children, consultants also sometimes offer it in a child's classroom. Furthermore, it parallels the help parents and teachers provide at home and in school. Whatever the work's context, the adults on hand set out a series of incremental goals, target one at a time, and provide plenty of opportunities for practice. Here's how efforts to achieve the first goal unfold with Jeremy.

Developmental Goal 1: Taking a Break in Order to Listen

At the beginning of his first meeting, Jeremy jumps into one of what will be a series of wonderfully inventive stories about monsters, prisons, and escape attempts. After he's had some spacious time to play, we talk about how hard it can be for him to take a break from the "neat stuff" he likes doing in order to listen if somebody wants to say something. Sometimes when we're together, I explain, we'll practice the "stopping thing" so that it will get easier for him. When asked what word or phrase he'd like to use for that practice, his response, as usual, is unequivocal: " 'Stop' of course. Just say 'stop!' "

So "stop" it is. Jeremy learns that directly following the stop cue, he'll need to put down whatever toys he's using, cross his legs, lay his hands in his lap, and get quiet. Then we'll look at each other. We practice the cue and response six or seven times as Jeremy pretends to be busy with something and I call out. Jeremy seems to find the whole thing a bit ridiculous, and at first balks at the expectation to get fully still, but eventually he responds well to the cue. Finally, he gets the go ahead to get back to his prison tale. I warn him, however, that I'll probably call out "stop" a few times while he is busy, to see how it goes. It goes well.

Several weeks later, another story is underway on my office floor. I give the stop cue and Jeremy glances up, gives me a mildly annoyed look, then puts down the block he's carefully placing on an elaborate prison gate. "Don't forget the hands in your lap," I whisper. He sighs loudly and places his hands on top of his crossed legs. "This is such a neat prison! I have a question, can you look here?" Jeremy looks toward me momentarily, then gazes longingly at his building project. "Could you look up Jeremy? I know you wish you could keep building." Finally, Jeremy's eyes meet mine. "Oh, thanks! I'm wondering about this gate. You said there's a monster that guards it…what's his name?" "It's Slabkirk, Deborah, I *already told you that*." "Oh yes, of course…. Could you look up again? Because I have another question." He does, more easily this time. "Where will Slabkirk go when you finish the gate?" "Right next to it, and he has *huge* feet that can squash people if they try to escape." "Oh! Do you think his parents will try?" I ask. Jeremy stares at me intently. "They might. But it's *really* hard to get out of here. See how thick this wall is?" He looks back down, and resumes building as I watch.

Developmental Goal 2: Sustaining Circles of Connection

This work on cue responsive behavior is often the first step of the goal-directed process described earlier. Adults join the child in his play, give him a clear prompt for the cue in question, then provide ample opportunities for friendly practice. At first, as seen above, *the cue is only followed with quick, positive feedback*. Eventually—and the timing depends on the pace of progress—parents, teachers, and clinicians (if involved in the direct work) begin to support an extended experience of mutuality. For Jeremy, the second step of this process starts about a month into our meetings. That day, he comes in and begins setting up a corner of the office as the home of "Uncle Drawer"—a newly created character that ordinarily resides in my dollhouse's desk.

Upon hearing that it's time for some "stop" practice, Jeremy's dour look communicates his displeasure in the now familiar undertaking—Uncle Drawer is far more interesting as he prepares to fight off a band of thieving scoundrels. But our drills go smoothly after I remind Jeremy that once we get some good practice time in, he can go back to the adventures of this interesting arrival. In fact, it doesn't take long for him to demonstrate his now quick, steady response to the prompt. Then, as Uncle Drawer commences his attack, I call out "stop" on a number of occasions. This time though, instead of just asking Jeremy to pause and focus, I aim for more sustained contact, asking about what is happening in the battle, the specifics of Uncle Drawer's brave exploits, and so on. Keeping the spotlight on his story, and interacting with him about what he is doing, I try to ensure that *his success in taking a break from the action will be rewarded by pleasurable connection.*

Keeping this skill-building work enjoyable is at the heart of our work with deep-tracked children. We convey genuine interest in their detailed stories and topics of conversation, and regularly use the stop cue to help them take a break from their inner experience in order to connect. We engage in some back-and-forth, and then relax the pressure as they return to their more natural inner focus. Sometimes, when a child is having an especially hard time shifting attention from within to without, we go back to our basic "practice runs," often making them funny to keep the work light.

Developmental Goal 3: Sharing Space and Ideas

"NO, THE SHIP CAN'T HAVE A FLAG THERE. IT HAS TO GO HERE!" It's three months into our work, and Jeremy is far better at stopping for some conversation as he plays. He can look at me, smile, answer questions, even tolerate some of the "stupid" things I seem to want to know about. Now, I often call his name rather than use the stop cue, and he'll usually come up for air and contact. This progress isn't just a result of the incremental work we've been doing in my office; Jeremy's parents and teachers have been using similar approaches at home and in school. Jeremy still can't bear sharing ideas in his play, however, and the adults on hand have agreed that it's time to set some new goals.

"Jeremy, stop." Jeremy glares at me as he grabs the flag and places it where he wants it. I try again. "Jeremy, stop!" He bangs an extra block down next to the flag, checks to be sure it isn't wobbling in its proper spot, and balls his fists into his lap. "Thanks...it was hard for you to stop, because you feel mad!" "But don't you see? The flag HAS to go there! It's dumb to want it on the back of the ship!" "I know, you *really, really* want that flag in front!" I pause for a moment. "Jeremy, I know this doesn't feel good. But can you keep your hands from building while we figure out what to do?" A low, unhappy "yeah" tells me he's with me, though barely.

As we ramp up our expectations for cue responsive behavior and mutuality, we need to ensure that a child feels understood. Deep-tracked youngsters find it truly challenging to attend to others' needs, and we get much further if we witness their distress. It's only after experiencing our compassion that they can continue to do the hard work ahead. It's this mix of empathy and expectation that infuses the next interactions with Jeremy, interactions intended to stretch his capacity for sharing space and ideas. "Jeremy, you have such great ideas, and you like those ideas a lot! But I have some ideas too. And people like when some of their ideas get used." Jeremy appears bored—he's heard versions of this lecture many times before. It's clear that I need to be much more concrete.

"What should we do? I want the flag in back, and you want it in front. Two ideas and one flag...how can we work this out?" "It should be IN FRONT...that's just the RIGHT THING!" Jeremy puts his hand on the flag. "Woops, back in your lap, remember?" His hand balls up again, almost slamming into his body. "Okay Jeremy, here's an idea. You *really* want that flag in front. And I don't. But maybe I could say it's okay if you agree that when we put the treasure chest in the boat, *I'll* get to decide where it goes. That way you can have an idea, and I can have an idea. Could we do that?" Jeremy agrees, and we shake hands on our compromise. I compliment him on stopping what he was doing to figure out our hard problem.

Developmental Goal 4: Negotiating Play Through Asking Questions

Though a more productive exchange would have been wonderful, Jeremy is demonstrating—as is so often true with deep-tracked kids—just how slowly adults will have to proceed through this next stage of mastery. Later that day he does, in fact, let me place the treasure chest, though it takes an unhappy interchange before he's able to do so. There are many more negotiations to come in future weeks, though all the adults involved try not to overload his capacity for learning. Eventually, his parents, teachers, and I get to work on the next step of our work, the "How Abouts." Once a deep-tracked child has developed a beginning ability to tolerate conflicting ideas, we ask him to pause when he is about to make a unilateral decision during joint playtime. Then we encourage him to phrase his idea as a question. Were Jeremy farther along in his growth, I might have given him the stop cue, complimented his building, and then encouraged him to say something along the lines of "*How about* if the flag goes in front?"

As we support a child like Jeremy in learning the nature of give-and-take, we're not only targeting flexibility in general, but also the specific skills he'll need to play successfully with other youngsters. We want to help him tolerate the idea that sometimes he'll be able to have his way entirely, sometimes he'll need to find a middle ground, and sometimes he'll have to bend to someone else's agenda. Five months into my work with Jeremy, we've stopped work on a building project for some collaborative planning. I'm quietly stating that I *really* wish the doghouse could go next to the palace door, when he looks at me with a kind of stern affection: "Oh, ALL RIGHT.... You can have it there!" It was the kind of moment the team would celebrate: Jeremy was learning to share space and ideas.

Supporting Track-Changing With Deep-Tracked Children

As is true in Jeremy's case, work with deep-tracked children often begins with leaning in. Once they get skilled at connecting with us "in the track," we try widening it a little, still staying within their range of interest. Later, once their capacity for connection has increased, work on flexibility can begin. But this work has a particular progression. Deep-tracked youngsters often balk when asked to adapt to adult requests, even after they've gotten more comfortable connecting in basic ways. Therefore, we add an extra piece to the usual way of asking children to shift what they're doing. As noted in our list of strategies, this work involves a combination of leaning in and leaning out. If guided by Jeremy's mother Cassie, it might look something like this:

> "Jeremy, could you look up?" *Jeremy meets her eyes.*
>
> "This is a super fire station. Would you show me its rooms?" *Cassie gets the grand tour. Then they chat further as Jeremy keeps building.*
>
> "Jeremy, I have something to tell you, can you look up?" *Jeremy needs a little help tuning in, but eventually does.*
>
> "Thanks! I want you to know that there's five minutes until we have to pick up Laura at school. Let's plan a good place for you to finish up so you'll be ready . . . ." *They discuss what he realistically has time to complete.*
>
> "That sounds like a good ending spot! Jeremy, you're getting really good at finishing up when you need to. But remember that if you can't stop on time, you won't get to build later. Do you remember last week when we put your ship away because you kept working on it after it was bath time?" *With a last, interested question about his fire station, Cassie goes about her business.*

Note what is happening here. *Leaning in*, Cassie joins Jeremy in his "track," supporting him as he shifts his attention from his building project to her. Then they share some pleasurable circles of connection. After a few easy circles, she gives the stop cue—now more loosely offered since he's used to it—and gets Jeremy to pause his forward motion. Previewing what is to come, she helps him plan his change of track. Finally, *leaning out*, she gently reminds him of what will happen if he can't meet her expectation. This kind of friendly previewing helps deep-tracked children learn to exit their agenda in order to join someone else's.

When consultants first describe this kind of chunked-down work, parents and teachers frequently respond with skepticism. The child in question requires so much effort already. How can they find the extra time needed to go through such a long ritual of connection and previewing in order to get her to do something that most kids do without blinking? It's often only after an acknowledgement of their exhaustion that these adults agree that once this child goes on strike, she's very time consuming. If such work will allow her to change tracks without a fuss—and help build skill at the same time—it may be more efficient than it appears.

Using an Understanding of Temperament to Think in Advance

Deep-tracked youngsters often pull the adults around them into irritable and inconsistent responses to their behavior. That's why proactive thinking is such an important element of our approach, as adults work to avoid any feedback loops that amplify rigidity. Paying attention to how such feedback loops play out in school is just as important as looking at those nested in family life, something that is certainly true in Jeremy's case: At the point of initial consultation with his preschool teacher Pat, her patience has reached an all-time low. Worn out by Jeremy's constant interruptions during discussions, his ongoing scuffles with friends, and his chronic inability to end activities he's enjoyed, Pat has little tolerance for his behavior and she knows it. Her desire for help is impressive, however, and after exploring the interface between Jeremy's make-up and his troubles at school, she becomes an enthusiastic partner in supporting his growth. She starts initiating circles of connection throughout the day, and she and Jeremy begin warming up to each other. Pat comes up with some terrific strategies to help him learn to change tracks too. The chart she makes to help him successfully end free play periods is only one.

Helping Inflexible Children End Activities and Share Conversational Space

Jeremy adores playing in the block corner. The problem is that he always has "just one more thing" to add to his elaborate creations, and often continues building even after the rest of his class has finished cleaning up. Pat makes a chart with removable numbers from one to five. Then she orders them—five at the top, one at the bottom—on a rectangular board. Before ringing the bell for her "five minutes until cleanup" announcement, she finds Jeremy. First she connects with him. Then she tells him that the warning is coming and helps him make reasonable plans to finish up. Showing him the chart and pointing to the five, Pat reminds Jeremy that he needs to stick to his plan so he'll be able to build again the next day. "I know you can do it Jeremy, but try to remember that if you don't stop, you'll have to find somewhere else to play when you come in tomorrow . . . ."

Pat returns with the chart and takes off the numbers over the course of the five minute period—no lectures, no threats, just a quick point to the board to show how much time is left. And Jeremy responds with a greatly improved ability to change tracks at this time of day. He loses a few block-building sessions early on, but then shows himself able to benefit from Pat's combination of leaning in and leaning out. Later, she uses a similarly visual approach to helping him rein in his compelling need to call out at group time. She has Jeremy decorate a sturdy cardboard square with a picture of someone talking. She makes sure to have some positive back-and-forth with him before the start of circle time. Then, during the meeting, kids pass the "my turn" card to the person whose chance it is to speak. Jeremy has to work especially hard at this task, because he seems to feel that when Pat talks, she's addressing only him. But the visual cue—along with some time away from the group if he's lost all motivation to give others space—supports learning in this area as well.

Jeremy makes steady progress as Pat offers many opportunities for growth at school, I see him individually, and his parents offer support, modeling, and limits at home. Insisting that he leave room for others to speak at the dinner table, lending an ally to help him play with more give-and-take, Cassie and Howard assist Jeremy in becoming more responsive to the needs of others in the family. They even set some periods for quiet in the house, because Jeremy's desire to talk and hum nonstop sometimes drives Cassie to distraction. By the time he creates the royal racer story, this boy has come a long way. He continues to need help with social issues for the next few years, and his elementary school teachers occasionally seek outside consultation to deal with backsliding in the classroom, but he's increasingly able to handle himself as a friend and as a student. And he keeps his zest for living and learning all the while.

Getting to Work With Nicky: A Year in the Life of a Disengaged Four-Year-Old

Though deep-tracked, Jeremy never struggles in such a way that leads to testing or diagnosis. Nicky, a child with a different neurodevelopmental profile, has more extreme difficulties. Looking at how adults come to understand this girl—and at her parents' eventual decision to seek testing and services—will highlight the particular dilemmas that emerge in the face of conflicting points of view, kinds of diagnoses, and approaches to intervention with neurologically complex children.

What Do We See?

Listening Carefully to Teacher Concerns

Lead teacher Pippa has requested some consultation. "I'm not sure why," she begins, "but I'm worried about this girl Nicky. She seems withdrawn and out of synch. It could be that she's just shy, but I'm not sure that's all it is . . . something is making me uneasy." In response to a question about who lives at home with four-year-old Nicky, Pippa explains that she lives with her mother, father, and an older brother, and adds that she recently spoke with Nicky's mother Phyllis about some of her concerns. Apparently, Phyllis had appeared relieved to have the subject broached, and hinted at the fact that Nicky can be far more challenging to parent than she is to teach.

When a child has significant neurodevelopmental challenges, a clinician's conversations with teachers or parents sometimes start like this dialogue with Pippa. Something is odd. A boy seems withdrawn but his reserve doesn't feel like run-of-the-mill shyness. Eye contact is difficult. Sharing even more so. Whatever the description, we often get a sense that there's something unusual going on. It's almost always important to observe firsthand. Thus, I return for an observation that begins in the program's "big room," a large activity space where most of the children are playing tag or gleefully avoiding near crashes as they pedal around on tricycles. Nicky is doing none of these things. Instead, she's wandering through the room as she talks to herself. She keeps glancing uneasily in my direction too, and it's clear that having a newcomer around makes her nervous.

Scanning for Signs of Neurodevelopmental Vulnerability

Nicky has the part to a plastic marble chute in her right hand and jiggles it as she mumbles. In a response to a question about what she's doing, Pippa has a lot to say. "That's part of what worries me," she starts out. "She has this wand at home she calls her 'wiggler.' Her parents won't let her bring it to school. So, she always wants that marble thing. Once we said no and she got unbelievably upset. She holds it all the time and shakes it, at group and at lunch and everything. Even when she's doing a puzzle . . . she has this one puzzle she likes to do over and over again. I keep asking her if it wouldn't be easier to do her puzzle if she put it down, but she won't."

When we sense the possibility of a neurologically driven difficulty with connection, it's important to watch for such signs of self-stimulating behavior. We also assess a child's level of self-absorption, her capacity to engage in relationships, her ability to sequence language, and any rigid areas of interest. Thus, after further observation, I have some more questions. Does Pippa, for example, know what Nicky is saying to herself? "I think she's acting out the story from this one movie that she likes" Pippa responds. "But it's hard to make out what she's telling you when you ask her about it—it's like she's still talking to herself. She kind of jumps around so you can't follow her." In response to an inquiry about this girl's language, Pippa emphasizes that Nicky has a large vocabulary. "And she knows some incredible stuff. When we were talking about dinosaurs the other day, she knew a huge amount. The kids got really interested. Usually, they don't pay much attention to her."

This last piece of information is of interest. When a deep-tracked child is especially motivated in a subject area, we often see her most accomplished level of functioning. Therefore, it seems important to find out whether Nicky made sense when she was talking about the dinosaurs. Could she speak in full sentences and stay on topic? Pippa responds affirmatively, adding that she'd been surprised. The next question addresses whether Nicky ever plays with other kids, and its answer is different: "Well, sometimes she'll wander near them, but no." I ask whether Pippa ever feels like *she's* got something going with Nicky, that she and this girl are relating warmly. Pippa replies that it sometimes feels that way, but then, "just when it seems like we've started a friendly conversation, Nicky turns away." She adds that Nicky does seem close to her mother Phyllis. They'll snuggle up before saying good-bye and Pippa can tell they love each other. She wonders whether I might like to meet Phyllis, and her idea makes sense as a next step. Though the information gathered so far suggests that Nicky's inborn nature makes it hard for her to be an engaged member of the classroom, it seems wise to get more information from the family before sharing ideas with school staff.

Gathering Information About Life at Home

When parents have a child with notable neurodevelopmental challenges, they often have a disturbing sense that something is amiss long before they figure out why. Thus, in sitting down with Phyllis and her husband Jim, it feels important to proceed gently in asking about what Nicky is like at home. Phyllis and Jim don't hesitate to jump in, however, relating that their daughter can be terribly difficult, and always wants things just so. In response to a question about what happens when things don't go her way, Phyllis worriedly states that "things get messy very fast." Nicky, it turns out, has intense tantrums and gets so stuck on what's bothering her that both parents try not to force issues that aren't important. It's not that they don't set limits, they explain. The problem is that while Nicky's brother learns from his mistakes, Nicky doesn't. The threat of a consequence—even though Nicky must know that her parents mean business—doesn't have much impact. She spends more time in the time out chair than they feel good about, but they don't know what else to do.

The patterns here confirm that this is probably a child for whom relating is deeply challenging, and who isn't naturally motivated by outside cues. In such situations, it's important to seek information about how a youngster's challenges have played out within her family: Youngsters like Nicky are strikingly hard to parent. I ask if there are areas about which Phyllis and Jim disagree and hear that there are indeed. Phyllis is quite worried about there being something wrong with Nicky. Jim, on the other hand, thinks his daughter is merely stubborn and will outgrow her difficult behaviors if they hang tough.

When asked what daily life looks like at home—and what Nicky likes to do for fun—Jim relates that she gets really excited about science books, especially about astronomy, and that there are a couple of videos and a particular computer game that his daughter asks for over and over again. She hates being asked to turn the game off, however—that's one of the times she'll blow a fuse. Nicky spends a lot of time wandering through the house with her "wiggler" too, contentedly telling stories to herself. Jim and Phyllis ask if I can explain why her wiggler is so important to her—her attachment to it both puzzles and alarms them.

What Do We Think?

Developing a Shared Understanding of a Child's Strengths and Vulnerabilities

The question ends up being a good entry point for some initial meaning making, and I share my hunch that Nicky is built in a way that involves a particular mix of intellectual gifts and developmental vulnerabilities. If this hypothesis is correct, it would make her particularly compelled by certain areas of interest yet "closed up" when faced with other possibilities for involvement. More generally, she would find it hard to exit her inner experience to engage with others, to have easy access to the relational give-and-take involved in everyday life. I ask whether this idea makes sense to them: Could it be that Nicky's inborn nature is contributing to her social isolation at school and her inflexibility at home?

As the discussion unfolds, we talk about how hard it is for Nicky to make eye contact, how sensitive she is to noise and to visual stimulation, and how vigilant she becomes around new people. We note the variation in her ability to express herself; when a content area is of interest, she sometimes talks in logical paragraphs. But she can also be very hard to follow as she jumps from idea to idea with few links in between. I mention that she may have some problems sequencing information. Another possibility—and the two aren't mutually exclusive—is that she doesn't have an intuitive grasp of how others experience her. If this is the case, the effort of making sense to anyone but herself won't feel like a high priority. (Note that the ability to conceptualize the feelings and thoughts of others is sometimes called a "theory of mind" [Schneider, Schumann-Hengsteler, and Sodian, 2005]. Deep-tracked kids don't always have such a theory, and the work we do on social pragmatics can help them develop one.)

What Do We Do?

Supporting Relatedness and Track-Changing

After listening intently, Phyllis remarks that these new ideas make more sense to her than just thinking that Nicky is shy and stubborn. Jim is intrigued too, and mentions that he finds himself thinking about one of his uncles, a highly intelligent but odd man who's historically had a lot of difficulty dealing with people. He asks whether Nicky is destined to be like this isolated relative or whether there is something he and Phyllis can do to turn things around. It's a great question, one clinicians hear over and over again in conversations about deep-tracked children. We talk about how there are no guarantees, because the kind of hard-wiring we're discussing can make it a real challenge for kids to engage with others. But I emphasize that having watched Nicky, it seems very possible that, with help, she'll be able to connect with other adults and kids far more successfully. We agree that they and Nicky's teachers will continue with some ongoing consultation. In addition—given that Nicky's school has access to the services of a gifted speech and language specialist—we'll set up some extra classroom-based support as well.

By the end of the meeting, we've mapped out the things Phyllis and Jim can begin doing at home. Emphasizing the importance of keeping the work manageable and success-oriented, I encourage them to take things slowly. Our first two goals are simple. The first involves increasing Nicky's experience of pleasurable connection; as her ability to feel comfortably engaged increases, everything else will become easier. The second focuses on developing Nicky's ability to comply with some basic expectations for track-changing. The strategies Jim and Phyllis will use to support these goals go home with them on a brief "tip sheet," which emphasizes that, for now, they'll support connection independent of expectations for compliance. ("Try to have it feel good for her and you…and don't worry about the content—anything is okay if she sticks with you!") The sheet also walks them through the earlier-described protocol for supporting track-changing (connect→preview and plan→finish up→connect→change tracks).

Tracking Progress and Slowly Adding Goals for Growth

The process of change has begun. And Nicky, it turns out, is a terrific partner in our efforts. When Phyllis and Jim show up for their next meeting, they are far more upbeat than they'd been only two weeks earlier. It's not that life has changed dramatically, but they feel that something is starting to shift. Nicky has been smiling a little more. There have been a few times when they've done "that track-changing thing" and she's responded to what they've asked without a fuss. She even came up to Phyllis the other day and said, "I love you mom." She's certainly never done *that* before. Of course, she's had her share of tantrums too, and had one monumental meltdown after they asked her to leave her wiggler at home. They've both lost their tempers a few times as well, even though they know they shouldn't. Working to find ways to connect with her is quite a challenge. But things are heading in the right direction.

Exploring the Possibility of Testing and the Potential for a Diagnosis

It's no surprise that as Nicky's year unfolds, questions about assessment emerge, and that Phyllis and Jim eventually seek further information about their daughter. Decisions about whether to pursue a formal assessment can be stressful, as they were for this family, and not just in the case of children like Nicky. Whatever the issue at hand, parents often yearn for the clarity that an assessment can offer. At the same time, they may be concerned about their child receiving a diagnosis when she's so young. They may also worry that such a diagnosis will follow her through her school years, yet be aware that without one, she could be deprived of badly needed services. In addition, they may assume, sometimes rightly so, that assessment will be followed by the suggestion of a medication trial, an intervention some are not sure about pursuing.

To complicate matters, different testers and different programs may come up with varying results. In the case of youngsters like Nicky, one tester may diagnose a pragmatic language disorder, while another points to sensory integration dysfunction. One may end up stating definitively that a child has a pervasive developmental disorder, while another suggests that, while there are some right hemisphere vulnerabilities, a child is far too young to assume anything other than the need for thoughtful help.[8] Our role as educators, guides, and—sometimes—questioners of our medical model culture can be very supportive to worried parents. We offer information about the assessment process, keep parents company as they consider its implications, and provide direction as to what kinds of assessment may be useful. Then, if parents decide to proceed, we stay posted throughout the process, and discuss any results if they have questions. They often do. It's not uncommon for parents to initiate an assessment, only to find themselves confused by its jargon-filled write-up. That said, there are many cases in which a thorough assessment carried out by a competent team offers great clarity about a child's challenges, and allows for the possibility of state and locally funded services to support growth.

The Clinician's Role—Supporting, Monitoring, and Guiding

In Nicky's case the assessment process is, ultimately, a positive one, resulting in both increased clarity for her parents and teachers and increased services for her. But the need for such an assessment—and this family's readiness to embark upon it—doesn't emerge right away, and this formal process is only a small part of Nicky's year. It is a year full of trial and error, progress and backsliding, and hope trading off with discouragement. It's a time full of conversation and questions too. We have a lot to figure out together as we keep a step ahead of Nicky:

Early November: Nicky now often responds to Phyllis and Jim's requests—if they remember to go through our steps. She's a lot more affectionate too, though they have to be careful not to ask too much of her. They have a question, however. Should they ban the computer game that their daughter is so obsessed with? Because even when she's not playing it, she's wandering around the house pretending she is. We decide to limit her access to the game. In addition, an adult will keep her company when she plays—building in moments of connection by doing some stop and go work in which Nicky takes a break from the action to explain what's going on.

Mid-December: Pippa is torn. Should she insist that Nicky put down her plastic chute? It feels as though it's an impediment to involved play. We decide to set short periods during which Nicky will be asked to place her wiggler close-by. The strategy seems to work. She still relies on the chute, but begins to use it less. Phyllis and Jim start doing the same thing at home. Soon she'll take her bath without asking for it at all, which is a first.

Late January: Nicky has a friend! Johnny looks for her when he arrives in the morning, and they quickly jump into their ongoing pirate saga. Pippa now looks for the chance to sit with the children in lend-an-ally mode—supporting Nicky in sticking with what she and Johnny are doing together rather than drifting off in her own direction. And slowly, Nicky's ability to engage in mutual story-telling is improving.

Late February: Phyllis has a question. Does her daughter have Asperger's disorder? A lot of what she's been hearing about Asperger's sounds like Nicky. The question doesn't come out of the blue: We've talked about the possibility of significant neurodevelopmental vulnerabilities from the start. But, it's not clear whether it makes sense to seek out a full assessment right now. Nicky is young, and she's making progress so quickly that none of us know where she'll be even six months from now. The team decides to consider the possibility of an evaluation in a month or so if, as seems likely, we feel that Nicky will benefit from more services in her last year of preschool than she's been getting in this one. At the moment, everyone agrees, she couldn't be progressing any more quickly than she is.

Late March: Nicky and her brother Daniel have been getting along much better. Daniel likes pretending to be an astronaut, and Nicky is now willing to be his second in command. Daniel has been a lot nicer to Nicky since she started joining him for some planetary exploration, and Phyllis and Jim feel like their family is starting to look more like those of their friends. If they get too ambitious, though, or forget to spend time every day working on connection, Nicky starts balking.

April: About this testing—what should we do? School staff sits down with Nicky's parents. Acknowledging that it's been a great year, we flesh out our concerns: Nicky still gets lost in herself, still relies on her wiggler, and still requires support to connect with her friends. There's the question of sequencing problems too. It's not yet clear whether she just needs more practice, or if there's a neurodevelopmental issue nested in her difficulty telling stories in order. It seems clear that testing could prove illuminating, and might give Nicky access to more support than she's currently getting. Phyllis and Jim hear an advance warning, however: If Nicky gets overwhelmed during the evaluation process, her testers may come up with a more dire picture than the team now has.

Early May: The head of the town's early childhood program comes out to take a look at Nicky as the first step toward evaluation. Unfortunately, though not surprisingly, Nicky not only notices the somewhat formidable looking newcomer, but also seems to be aware that she's the one being watched. Her wiggler is out in force, and she's back to mumbling and wandering around the room. She looks more like she did early in the fall although, everyone admits, she still has days like this even when nothing new is going on. The administrator pulls Pippa aside. "Have you asked the parents about applying for a spot in one of our special needs classrooms?"

Late May: There's been a lot of conversation and some real confusion too. Would Nicky get better help in a classroom with more kids like her? She'd certainly have access to additional specialized services, because her test results do point to a neurological component to her struggles. But she's doing so well where she is. She has some budding friendships, and she's learning to play. In addition, the staff is incredibly invested in her and her family. It's a tough choice. Phyllis and Jim share the same initial instinct—to keep Nicky in the place that's been so important to her growth. After some soul-searching, they come to a decision. They'll take Nicky to one of the school system's twice-weekly social skills groups. That will get her started on an individualized educational plan (IEP), something that will be needed when she gets to kindergarten. But they'll keep Nicky at her current pre-school for her last year. They can't imagine asking her to leave a place where staff have worked so hard to understand and support her.

June: I come in for my final observation of the year, back to the program's "big room" for one last visit. And there's Nicky, standing next to Johnny and Samantha, who are on the floor building with the big cardboard blocks. "Hey, what are you doing? Can I do it too?"

Nicky has a long way to go, and her parents don't yet know if she'll continue emerging into the world of pleasurable connections, or if she'll hit some daunting roadblocks along the way. Perhaps by middle school, she'll be thriving as a slightly offbeat, science-oriented girl surrounded by a group of like-minded buddies. Maybe she'll end up needing extensive help throughout her childhood and adolescence. But for now, Phyllis and Jim couldn't be happier with her progress. Neither could Pippa, who tells me that she'll miss Nicky terribly when she heads upstairs to the pre-kindergarten class. It has been, truly, a wonderful year for Nicky.

Part IV

Questions and Conclusions

14

Additional Issues

*Addressing Trauma and Loss, Monitoring Media
Choices, Providing Guidance During Crises,
and More*

Adaptations to the strategies explored thus far are often needed in the face of situations that cause children and families extreme distress: abuse, domestic violence, serious illness or death of a family member, divorce or separation, homelessness, parental substance abuse or incarceration, community violence, significant parental (or sibling) mental health issues. The list is long and sobering. Added to it are the complexities of living in a culture that is saturated with violence, violence children hear about and see in the world around them, and watch on film, television, and computer screens. One book can't explore all these issues in depth without becoming encyclopedic. This chapter takes a brief look at how clinicians address a few of them, including how we help children deal with trauma and loss, death and serious illness, and separation and divorce. It also explores how to support parents in making healthy media and entertainment choices for their children. Lastly, it discusses the importance of having resources on hand for times of crisis and stress. None of these topics are covered thoroughly; clinicians in need of more extensive information will find additional resources listed in this chapter's endnotes.

Before turning to specifics, it's important to note that the principles laid out in previous chapters apply to children across a range of stressful situations. We offer many chances for safe, warm connection. We encourage children to let us know what they're feeling, and support them in understanding and working through their experiences. We provide stable, calm classroom environments with the rich opportunities for learning and exploration that they may not have encountered at home. We try to ensure that overwhelmed youngsters feel contained by firm limits while, at the same time, they get the skill-building support they need. We work to reach even our most challenging families, understanding that, underneath it all, parents almost always want to give their children a better life than they've had themselves. We support such parents in connecting with their children even in the midst of difficult circumstances, and encourage them to establish some basic, reassuring routines for family life. Finally, we stay alert to the nuances of culture, working to make the help we offer sensitive across a range of expectations, norms, and experiences. Then, while relying on all these principles, we seek the knowledge needed to understand and support children experiencing specific stressors.

Helping Children Cope With Trauma

Four-year-old Bethany arrived at her new preschool with two previous school expulsions and a reputation for aggression. As they braced themselves for the challenge ahead, her teachers were worried yet sympathetic. Bethany's foster parents had recently initiated adoption proceedings; they'd been caring for her since the state intervened in response to severe neglect at the hands of her teenage mother. Bethany was eighteen months old when placed in Mary and John's home, an engaging toddler who thrashed her way through each night's sleep and who, when hungry, would open the refrigerator door and insist on finding her own food. Mary and John adored Bethany yet despaired over the trials of raising her—she desperately wanted control of even the tiniest details of daily life, and her angry outbursts riled the household all too regularly.

It was an intense year. Lead teacher Lynn and her assistant Andrea started out by giving Bethany extra leeway and support when she refused to comply with basic requests, knowing that her willful inflexibility emerged from an adaptation to deeply painful experiences. This approach had worked well with other traumatized children, allowing staff to raise expectations after a youngster felt more trusting. Not this time. Bethany responded with increased rigidity, and showed a complete inability to make up her mind when given the space to exert some control. Hoping that she just needed some time to settle in, the teachers stuck with this approach for a very trying month. Then, after some consultation, they decided to try something different: giving very few choices at times of stress.

Lynn set up a "cozy corner" where Bethany would be able go when she wasn't able to comply with their expectations. Then, though it made them uncomfortable, she and Andrea started to set limits on even small infractions of classroom rules. At the same time, they began taking extra care to connect warmly with Bethany throughout the day. Bethany's parents, who had been terribly confused about when to be firm and when to give in, agreed to take a similar tack at home. They needed regular support in order to do so, because riding out Bethany's fury when they set sensible limits was a real challenge; they felt deeply for their daughter, hated to cause her more distress and, in addition, had a hard time tolerating the intense anger she directed at them when she felt crossed. To help Bethany work through some of her confusion, anger, and distrust, they also began bringing her to a play therapist. These new approaches needed plenty of tweaking, and Bethany's progress was slow. In time, however, she began to blossom. This was a girl who was so utterly conflicted about issues of control, and so in need of secure, loving relationships, that a combination of friendly strictness, warm connection, and therapeutic help worked well.

Providing Safety and Opportunities for Healing to Traumatized Children

Bethany's story is a hopeful one. Her foster parents had tremendous love and patience to offer, her teachers hung in through a very difficult year, and everyone involved was able to keep the lines of communication open. Helping this resilient but troubled girl required a flexible approach to intervention. This is often the case: There is no one way to work with traumatized children, each of whom finds his own way to cope with unimaginable suffering (Groves, 2002; Osofsky, 2004).

Childhood trauma refers to a range of overwhelming situations, both acute and chronic, both within the family and in the wider world. It applies to youngsters who have been abused by a parent or relative and those who have suffered at the hands of a stranger; children who have experienced a natural disaster, fire, or terrible car accident and those who have witnessed domestic violence; kids who have lived in war zones overseas, and those who face life in the inner city communities that can feel like war zones of their own. Children who have experienced significant, painful, and ongoing medical problems—as well as those in circumstances of serious neglect—may show signs of trauma as well. While the impact of trauma may be emotionally and developmentally worrisome, even devastating, it's important to remember how resilient children can be in response to sensitive help (Cole et al., 2005). Understanding the nature of that impact and of that help is crucial. Moreover, we need to recognize and appreciate that children's seemingly negative responses to trauma almost always reflect their struggles to adapt and cope, both physiologically and psychologically.

Any of this book's seven building blocks can be compromised as a result of traumatic experience. Children can have difficulty feeling safely connected and may withdraw from contact, appearing emotionally flat or relationally unreachable. Alternatively, they may become so needy that they seek out contact with almost anyone, even those who may not be entirely trustworthy. They can struggle to attend, have trouble using and understanding language, or lag in the ability to sequence and organize information. They may have problems regulating their energy or emotions, appear rigid and inflexible, or feel incompetent and insecure. In particular, traumatized children often exhibit difficulties with aggression, difficulties that are often understood as an adaptation to overwhelming feelings of fear and vulnerability. Separation anxiety is common as well: These youngsters can experience tremendous panic in response to their understandable fear that they and their parents aren't safe.[1]

In sum, a child's abilities to feel close to others, to be calm and organized, to play and make friends, and to communicate and learn may all be at risk (Koplow, 1996; van der Kolk and Streck-Fischer, 2000). Whether any—or even all—of these areas are affected depends on a number of factors: the nature of the trauma, the age and temperament of the child, the quality of his ongoing relationships with those who care for him, and the support he gets through and after the experience or experiences in question (Linares et al., 2001; Groves, 2002). In most cases, the strategies previously offered in regard to specific difficulties—for example, those supporting increased attention and body state regulation—apply to children who are experiencing developmental vulnerabilities as a result of traumatic exposure. But there is additional information to hold in mind as we support such children.

Part of what has been discovered in recent years, for example, is that traumatic experience can have a powerful impact on brain function. Fear activates certain neural pathways, and chronic fear can result in those pathways remaining activated (Siegel, 1999; Shore, 2001b). Thus parents, teachers, and clinicians may note a kind of unrelenting vigilance in a traumatized child—what we call hyperarousal—or, in contrast, a detached, numb quality of dissociation. Sometimes both are in evidence. Our responses to traumatized children thus target the emotional and behavioral issues we see so readily, at the same time that they take into account the brain functions invisible to our eyes: We focus on connecting with, soothing, and supporting the child emotionally, containing and redirecting him behaviorally, and helping his brain "re-wire" or recalibrate physiologically.[2]

The Clinician's Role in Trauma-Focused Intervention

The clinical consultant's role in supporting such assistance often involves keeping an eye on the overall process—coaching teachers in the mix of warm support and friendly containment that is so important to these children; working with parents on a child's need for steady, safe connection and as calm and organized a family life as is possible; helping connect a child and family with the appropriate therapeutic services; staying in touch with any therapists who get involved; and working with teachers, directors, and/or family members on contacting the appropriate agency if abuse is suspected or disclosed. It is a complex role that may also include, when warranted and logistically possible, some classroom-based support for a child. In addition, clinicians often help parents and teachers understand a child's need to play out his experiences, and provide suggestions on how to accept and support such play, while also offering the containment necessary to keep things safe. We make sure to encourage caregivers in facilitating other kinds of pleasurable, calming, and normative activities as well.[3]

Helping Children Cope With Death and Serious Illness

Alexander came back to preschool a week after having witnessed his mother's death from sudden cardiac arrest. Never an active child, the four-year-old now sat in a quiet corner, carefully arranging a set of crayons in a straight line, abruptly sweeping them away with his hands, then lining them up once again. His favorite teacher sat with him for more than half an hour as, over and over again, he mutely ordered and destroyed his crayon world. It wasn't until six months later that he began dictating stories about animals that couldn't find their parents and traveled long and far—sometimes even to other planets—to be reunited.

Julia was brought to therapy shortly after her father learned that his cancer was not responding to aggressive treatment. Knowing that he probably had less than six months to live, Ed and his wife Jan worried tremendously about their four-year-old daughter's well-being. When should they tell her that he was going to die? What should they say? Julia's way of expressing her feelings about her father's illness had thus far focused on the blue baseball cap he wore to cover his now-bald head. Her comment: "I don't like it when dad takes off his hat." Her question: "When will dad's hair grow back?"

Katya's mother Elena couldn't figure out why her five-year-old daughter was suddenly being so difficult. Usually an even-tempered child, Katya had started screaming and kicking when asked to do the simplest things, then crying when reprimanded even mildly. Katya's grandmother had died three weeks earlier after a long illness. During the two months before her mother's death, Elena had had to be away from home on many an occasion. Katya's favorite aunt had pitched in though, and the girl had seemed to be holding up well. One evening, after a particularly trying day, Katya finally began talking. It was her fault that "Baba" died, did her mother know that? One day she'd wanted her mother to come home so badly that she'd wished that her grandmother were dead. It was the day after that that Baba had died. Did her mother think she could make other people die too? She thought maybe if she got punished enough she'd never think a bad thought like that again.

Lizzie's mother Marie had recently found out that she had breast cancer. Her prognosis was good but in addition to a mastectomy, she was going to need chemotherapy. Lizzie had just turned three. Her favorite form of comfort was to snuggle in her mother's arms and stroke her long, thick hair. What, Marie wondered, should she tell her daughter about why she was going to lose it?

Providing Information, Support, and Comfort in the Face of Illness or Loss

As these vignettes illustrate, a wide range of issues can emerge when a family member has died or is seriously ill. The same is true when the individual in question is a community member, a classmate, or a teacher. In order to understand how to help a child and family cope—or how to support a school community—clinicians need to look carefully at the specifics of the situation at hand. How old is the child? What do his level of development, the things he says, and the way he behaves tell us about how he understands illness or death? About how he's feeling? With what kind of illness or death are he and his family contending? Will the person who is ill get better? Has there been a long process of decline? Or, conversely, has there been a sudden and tragic loss? And what, specifically, has a child seen? Hair loss? Growing physical debilitation? Dementia? If the last, what might this look like to a young child and how might he understand it? When children are dealing with illness or death, we must put ourselves in their shoes enough to imagine how they might experience and make sense of the confusing or painful world in which they live.

As he ordered and swept away lines of crayons, Alexander conveyed that the world as he knew it had, in an instant, fallen apart. He had no words to speak of his bewilderment and shock, and no way as a four-year-old to understand what had happened. His teacher, wisely, sat with him as a caring witness, not trying to fix anything, yet offering her loving presence as a reminder that he wasn't alone. Alexander's later stories of planetary exploration and parental reunion spoke of his yearning for his mother, and of his growing cognitive and emotional reorganization following the overwhelming experience of witnessing her death.

Julia, in contrast, watched her father decline slowly. Through a gradual process of acceptance, and with support from the many adults who cared for her, she worked to understand her father's illness and to make sense of the fact that doctors—who are supposed to be able to help people get well—could not find a medicine to cure him. Part of the work we did with this young girl was thus to clarify the difference between the "sick" her father was, and the "sick" she sometimes got. There were other clarifications made too: that not all cancers make people die, that going to the hospital—though not in her father's case—can be just what someone needs to get better. In fact, Julia's mother, father, and I spent a good part of one of our conversations trying to figure out what issues we needed to emphasize so that this young girl didn't walk through the next number of years more frightened than she needed to be.

Throughout the process of helping young children cope with loss, we listen for the language and symbols they use to express their feelings and make sense of their experiences. For Julia, baldness was the most vivid image of a changed world: "When I was little and dad had hair, he used to let me stand on his feet and we'd dance." Hair loss loomed large for young Lizzie's mother too. Losing her hair was a terrible blow to Marie's own experience of femininity, and connected to complex feelings of loss about her upcoming mastectomy. Her imminent hair loss was not only hard for Marie, however. It had implications for her daughter as well. Marie knew that Lizzie's way of stroking her hair was woven into the texture of their deep connection with each other; when she wept about how to explain that it would be cut off—as is true for many cancer patients, Marie didn't want to wait for it to fall out in clumps—she was expressing a many-layered sorrow.

There are other issues we attend to, too. Knowing that young children don't distinguish well between fantasy and reality, nor between destructive feelings and destructive potential, we listen for how they understand their part in the situation at hand. Katya, for example, had constructed a narrative in which she killed her grandmother. Severe punishment was the only way to ensure that she didn't think such dangerous thoughts ever again, and the way to be punished was to behave intolerably. Of course, this youngster's misbehavior may have been multi-determined. Her mother had been very sad, and not as available emotionally as Katya might have needed. Her beloved "Baba" was, before she was too sick to play, a favorite companion. But after Katya informed her mother of her murderous nature, and her mother comfortingly explained that kids' feelings don't kill people, she was greatly relieved. Better behavior soon followed.

It's a given that while we attend to children's feelings in the wake of loss or illness, we stay responsive to the experiences of their caregivers and teachers as well. In fact, the most important feature of good clinical consultation in the face of illness and loss is often flexibility. Does a teacher need support and guidance before talking with a class about the fact that a child's mother has just died? What does this situation bring up for the teacher? How is the class's community of parents coping? Are there other children who may have particularly strong reactions based on their own life experiences? What kind of support does a mother need when her mother is dying? And how is a child's caretaking world changing as a result of his grandmother's illness? Is his mother away from home a lot? Who takes care of him when she is? Is there any predictability to the schedule of baby-sitters, relatives, and friends who are helping out? Would a weekly calendar help him feel more secure in the midst of the unavoidably cobbled-together caretaking schedule? Finally, if there is someone in the family who is chronically ill or disabled, how is family life structured? How might a clinician be able to help the family attend, as best as possible, to the different needs of all its members?

Identifying Concerns About a Child's Process of Grieving

There are no hard and fast rules that define when grief has become overwhelmingly debilitating: The behaviors which signal that a child's way of grieving has become problematic can also be part of a normal—and essential—process. That said, we keep an eye on children who seem particularly withdrawn from family and friends, who are unusually and persistently aggressive or anxious, or who show an ongoing desire to be reunited with the person who has died. We pay close attention if a child becomes notably accident-prone, complains regularly of feeling ill, or behaves as if nothing at all has happened. If such behaviors don't decrease in frequency and intensity or, over many weeks, continue to interfere with a child's ability to feel pleasure at home or in school, we ask ourselves whether he needs additional help. Furthermore, as we watch to see how a child is handling his grief, we remember a few important points:

- Children grieve in many different ways. Some begin showing signs of grief right away. Others begin to grieve fully only months after an important individual has died, appearing almost unfeeling beforehand. Some children do their deepest grieving after the adults around them—who may have been profoundly sad and overwhelmed themselves—appear more available for emotional support.
- Consultants may want to remind parents and teachers to be ready for the fact that children often want to talk about a loss at unpredictable times, not necessarily when an adult is "ready" for a big conversation.
- Some of the losses that children experience are in relationship to individuals about whom they had very mixed feelings. Most children's books written about death assume that the featured child has lost a beloved animal, friend, or relative.

As we keep these points in mind, we also remind ourselves that, just as with trauma, our focus is jointly on the child and those who care for him. When death or illness strikes a family and community, our role is to keep our lens wide and our support and consultation available to all who are affected.[4]

Helping Children Cope With Separation and Divorce

Five-year-old Nell has always been an intense child. Her parents are intense too, and have never found it easy to get along. Now their strife-filled marriage has unraveled and Nell's mother Tammy has moved to a small apartment. Money is tight, tempers flare easily, and the scene when it's time for Nell and her younger sister to shift caretakers is often fraught with tension. Nell and Suzanne have spent a few days with their father, after not having seen him for almost a week. When Tammy arrives to pick them up, Nell is nowhere to be found. Eventually, her father Jim finds her hiding under a bed. As her parents begin arguing about what to do, Nell rolls into a ball and refuses to come out. Tammy and Jim look at each other across a chasm of hostility, and finally decide to let Nell stay for an additional few hours. The following week, she does the same thing at her mother's place.

Billy has appeared to be coping well with his parents' breakup. Seemingly relieved that he no longer has to contend with their endless arguing, he's been less anxious than he was during the period before his father moved out. Now, however, Billy's kindergarten teacher has contacted both parents. Billy has stopped interacting with other children at school, and seems notably unhappy. It's a puzzle. Kate—who was initially quite overwhelmed and withdrawn post-separation—is much happier. Billy's father Rob is more relaxed too. The only change, Kate notes, is that she and Rob have recently changed their parenting schedule, and Billy now has to make an extra switch each week.

In the course of one of Billy's occasional therapy sessions, he begins talking about all the houses he spends time in over the course of a typical week: mom's, dad's, mom's new boyfriend's, dad's new girlfriend's. And, of course, grandma and grandpa's house too. When asked how many different beds he sleeps in, Billy is clear. He visits five houses, but only sleeps in four beds. That's because they never sleep at dad's girlfriend's house, though Billy wonders if they might start doing that soon too. Billy nods sadly when I remark, "that's a lot of houses and a lot of beds!"

Understanding Children's Reactions to Separation

It's a given that living through the dissolution of an adult partnership can be hard on children and grown-ups alike. But there is, of course, no one version of separation or divorce that applies to all families. When couples have been in steady or explosive conflict with each other, children sometimes experience a breakup as a relief. At other times, the end of a seemingly friendly marriage can come as a complete and unwelcome shock. Children of all ages may feel angry or deeply upset. Young children, in particular, may mostly be bewildered, not understanding exactly what is happening nor why. Kids may adjust easily or, like Nell, experience great difficulty shifting from one household to another. Then, of course, come legal questions concerning custody, practical questions concerning money, and emotional questions having to do with how each parent is holding up. The last two sometimes get intertwined; when money is very tight, life can feel terribly stressful. Layer that stress on top of an already overwhelming change, and there are often unhappy implications for a child's life at home. In addition, some children find that one parent becomes, over time, a significantly less important presence, perhaps even absent altogether. Others, even very young ones, end up being required to see each parent over long stretches while the remaining parent is far away. Then there are those who find themselves in arrangements that involve shifting from household to household many times a week. The possibilities are as varied as the different kinds of partnerships and families in question.

When parents are contemplating separation, they may turn to clinicians with questions about when and how to inform their children about what's to come. In general, we help parents keep their explanations simple; young children only have limited abilities to listen to and understand discussions of complex adult issues. We encourage them to emphasize that their children aren't responsible for what has happened, even if often-overheard arguments have involved conflict over childrearing. We support parents in accentuating the fact that though they no longer want to be together, they'll always love their kids. In addition, we prepare them to answer very concrete questions about schedules, housing arrangements, and school drop-offs. As we help parents get ready for these important conversations, we also predict some of the ways that children react to separation—with anxiety, frustration, regression, or withdrawal. Just as importantly, we work to help these adults keep their children out of the middle of whatever unhappy conflict is still to come.

Encouraging Moderation and Child-Centered Decision Making

This last point is not always an easy one for parents to hear, nor to carry out. Conflict-ridden divorces and separations are all too common; toxic custody battles are too. Our job as clinicians may be to help mediate such situations—to encourage parents to put their children's well-being over their need to battle out every issue. This role may require us, at times, to be as forceful as we are compassionate. Because if embattled parents turn to clinicians for guidance about their children, those clinicians may be able to infuse some good sense into situations in which other involved parties feel they must either take sides or remain silent. Thus, after acknowledging parents' intense anger, we may decide to emphasize that when previously partnered adults don't refrain from heated arguments over custody, or continually complain about each other in their children's presence, kids suffer far more than they would otherwise. Co-parenting doesn't end when a separation begins, we stress. As one distraught mother put it, after she'd had yet one more unhappy phone conversation with her ex: "I hadn't realized when we got divorced that, in some basic way, we were in it for life all the same."

As part of these efforts, we also work to help parents devise a structure for switching homes that puts their children's developmental needs over their own convenience. As we see in the stories of both Nell and Billy, the transition from one household to another can be highly stressful, and an overly chopped up schedule, at least for many children, even more so. Once again, we may find ourselves shifting from offering support to providing psychoeducation and even, on occasion, moral guidance. It can be a complex and difficult balancing act, one whose goal is to help parents stay focused on their children's well-being even in the midst of conflict-ridden negotiations and emotion-filled days.[5]

Helping Families Make Healthy Decisions About Media Exposure and Entertainment Choices

A few days after the first "Spiderman" movie came out in 2002, teachers in a Boston-area childcare program became aware of increasing aggression in their four- and five-year-old classrooms, especially among the boys. At the same time, they overheard numerous conversations among children who had already seen the PG-13-rated film. These children appeared intrigued but also over-stimulated and even frightened by what they'd seen. Concerned, the teachers contacted both their clinical consultant and their director. Was there anything they could do to prevent other kids from seeing a film that was so inappropriate for preschool-aged youngsters?

The consultant and director conferred, then phoned a few colleagues at nearby centers. Other programs were also beginning to worry about what they saw as a lack of parental discretion. That evening, the consultant drafted a letter to parents, which the local early childhood association's board quickly approved and signed. Emphasizing that with a PG-13 rating and significant on-screen violence, the movie was not appropriate for three- to six-year-olds, the letter was disseminated to parents in most of the town's preschool and childcare programs within days. A number of parents later reported that it helped them hold the line when their children were begging to see the movie that "everyone is going to."

Addressing Concerns About Culturally Based Trends

As seen here, the partnerships between early childhood educators and clinicians can be an important force in addressing worrisome developments in a particular community. They can have an impact on troublesome issues in the culture at large too. For example, there is now ample data to suggest that violent imagery in the media—on television, film, and in computer games—has a significant impact on some children (Bushman and Anderson, 2001; Singer and Singer, 2002). Research shows that thoughts, feelings, and arousal can all be affected, children may become more aggressive and/or fearful, and that—as a group—boys behave more aggressively in response to on-screen violence than girls. (Rideout, Hamel, and the Kaiser Family Foundation, 2006) Other research suggests that early television exposure may result, at least in some children, in later difficulties with attention (Christakis et al., 2004). Add to this what we know about families' viewing habits and there is grave cause for concern. A few statistics from a 2006 Kaiser Foundation report help illuminate the scope of the problem.[6] In the large group surveyed:

- Four- to six-year-old children spent, on average, about two hours a day on "screen time," including TV, DVDs, and computers. However, some children were permitted far more exposure: There were reports of those who spent up to twelve hours watching TV alone.
- Nearly a third of children six years and under lived in a home where the TV was on all or most of the time.
- In homes where parents watched their own TV shows, 61% of children were in the same room some of the time, and 29% were in the room all of the time.

- The number of parents who had rules for how much TV or computer time their young children were allowed had dropped significantly from previous studies. For example, 61% of parents reported that they had rules setting a limit TV screen time in 2003. By 2005, that number had dropped to 49%.

These statistics give us an empirical backing for concerns that are widely shared in the early childhood community. Anecdotally, for example, consultants hear that teachers are struggling to cope with increased aggressive and inattentive behavior in their classrooms. Though such behaviors stem from a multitude of factors, the above-mentioned research certainly gives cause for concern. Furthermore, some parents report that they feel uneasy with how much time their children spend watching TV and playing computer games, and are worried about effects they may not intend (Rideout, Hamel, and the Kaiser Family Foundation, 2006). Those who have older children may fret that it will only get harder to pull back later on, and worry that their children will become teenagers who can't be pulled away from their computer screens—and violent games—to socialize with friends.[7]

In the face of what is undoubtedly a media and electronics-focused shift in family and community life, clinicians have a potentially important role to play. How can we encourage reflection and thoughtful responses to what many of us see as destructive cultural phenomena? How can we invite teachers, directors, and parents into community-wide discussions and commitment to change? When, on the other hand, should we broach these touchy subjects in individual meetings with parents? In addition, whether we hold community meetings, have private dialogues, or choose some combination of the two, what perspective can we bring to bear on the problems we see? Can we raise these issues in a way that doesn't come across as judgmental or preachy? After all, parents often turn to TV and DVD watching in order to maintain order and peace in an overly stressful life. They see many others doing just the same. Furthermore, the media-driven, violence-saturated world in which we live makes it hard for parents to even know what it would look like to make different choices.

Our stance in relationship to these issues will be deeply personal. But keeping an eye on the culture at large, understanding its impact on children and families, and being willing to consider a kind of compassionate activism when we see trends that are of grave concern, is an important option. We can partner with programs and call community meetings. We can offer user-friendly trainings about media violence. We can hold informational sessions about toy options—another area in which parents are inundated with commercially-driven choices—and emphasize the importance of open-ended, creative play in fostering healthy development. We can initiate safe and respectful dialogue, then help it deepen again and again. It's through such ongoing connection and community-building that clinicians, parents, and teachers can take a stand against the destructive yet powerful cultural forces that shape—and burden—children's lives.[8]

Having Resources on Hand for Times of Crisis and Stress

When unavoidable crises leave children and parents overwhelmed and reeling, teachers often feel uncertain about how to be useful. It's in such situations that consulting clinicians may provide badly needed calm and perspective. At the same time, they can offer concrete resources to help everyone cope. For example, an early childhood consultant at one program in the Boston area has assembled a set of "resource bags" on a wide range of topics (Roznowski, 1999). Teachers can request bags for families just having learned of a cancer diagnosis, for families with a newly incarcerated parent, on the topics of hospitalization and death and dying, and for families expecting a baby, to name just a few. Inside the cloth bags, concerned adults find a short set of tips on helping children with the issue in question as well as a list of books—some for adults and some for children. Several books from the children's list are included too. Another Boston-based clinician has developed annotated bibliographies of children's books on a similarly wide range of topics; these bibliographies are easily accessed through local preschool programs, the city's early childhood program, and local libraries.[9] The common thread here is that resources are collected *before* a crisis hits, and thus available quickly when everyone's ability to think is dulled by shock or unhappiness.

Some crises, however, can't be prepared for. In my hometown, for example, a group of early childhood directors called an emergency meeting on the evening of September 11, 2001. The conversation was full of emotion as we brainstormed about how to help teachers and parents support children when they, themselves, were having trouble coping with such unthinkable tragedy. As we conversed, we agreed that one major concern was how young children would decode the endlessly repeating, televised pictures of the towers burning and collapsing. The next day, in preschool and childcare programs all across town, teachers came in early and spent some time processing their concerns. Then, with signs taped to their shirts, they greeted parents and children. The signs read: "We know you're worried. But don't turn on the TV while your kids are up." Teachers also handed out a one-page letter we'd drafted offering parents some simple answers to children's questions, encouraging them to keep routines steady and calm, and suggesting that, when needed, they reassure children that adults were working hard to keep them safe. Several nights later, we held an open meeting during which parents could ask questions about how much to tell their kids, how to respond to their concerns, and how to provide a sense of safety in the midst of such uncertainty.

In the case of unexpected crises, our role as clinicians can be tremendously important. We gather information quickly, and find the other caregivers and professionals with whom we'll need to collaborate. We scan the kids, parents, and teachers in our communities to see what help might be most useful. Then we offer that help in the places where those individuals spend time, and do our best to make it compassionate, flexible, and practical. Depending on the situation, we may be reeling ourselves. But our unique training, at least some of the time, allows us to think on our feet, and act promptly to provide much-needed guidance and support.

15

Elementary School and Beyond

Perspectives for the Long Haul

As kids proceed through latency and adolescence, they don't become different people—only, we hope, more comfortable versions of themselves. And, not infrequently, the issues that plague them in their earliest years resurface in various ways as they mature. Children who struggle to attend can get much better at sustaining focus yet, at times, will still need scaffolding to stay on task. Youngsters who used to lose their tempers many times a week may need help staying steady during later periods of stress. Kids who are on the reserved side may look increasingly confident, only to lose ground amidst the social complexities of middle school. Fortunately, the work we do to understand young children stands us in good stead as they grow older. The approaches we come up with to help them often still apply as well, with additions and adaptations as circumstances change and development unfolds. Throughout children's growing up years, we return to our three-part process over and over again. We look carefully: *What do we see?* We reflect fully: *What do we think?* We muster up as much patience and skill as we can: *What do we do?*

Honoring Children's Gifts

The progress of royal racer Jeremy is a case in point, and his story continues here in order to illustrate the perspectives adults need over the course of a child's development. Helping Jeremy become more responsive and flexible was a challenging endeavor—in large part because along with his incredible zest for learning and living came a constitutionally based rigidity. Thus, he and his parents and teachers had a lot of work to do before he was able to be a good friend, a cooperative family member, and a productive student. Luckily, he was an eager partner in doing that work—children who are offered compassionate and sensible help usually are—and the adults who cared for him were too. In considering how that work proceeded over the years, we should note how important it is to honor a child's gifts even as we seek to understand his difficulties: It is those gifts, after all, that often point the way toward mastery.

Jeremy's giftedness as a thinker and questioner was especially apparent in his storytelling. As a preschooler and kindergartener, for example, he played out richly detailed sagas that addressed some of the biggest questions faced by both children and adults—questions about good and evil, about grief and loss, and about the conflict between doing what one wants versus what will be best for those one loves. Jeremy's understanding of human nature, in fact, often appeared almost adult-like in its depth and sophistication.

Accepting That Progress Is Rarely Linear

There was a problem for Jeremy at this stage of his development, however: The gifts that allowed him to imagine the experiences of his pretend characters were far more developed than his ability to empathize with the real people he encountered every day, most especially those in unhappy circumstances he had some large part in creating. As a result, his preschool and kindergarten teachers spent many a conversation trying to help their recalcitrant student understand and apologize for the upsets he set off when he grabbed toys or knocked down friends' buildings that were—in his forcefully announced declarations—improperly designed.

The early, step-by-step work Jeremy's team did to address such difficulties—described in earlier chapters—allowed him to do much better by the end of kindergarten. At that point, he no longer needed the kind of skill-building support he'd experienced in our individual meetings (described in Chapter 13). After those meetings ended, however, his parents and school still required consultation, though not regularly. Because, as is so often the case, Jeremy's progress was not linear. He'd show signs of increased cooperation, of growing empathy for his buddies, and of a willingness to do schoolwork that was, in his eyes, truly boring. But then, at some point, he'd start balking, playing the class clown, or being particularly domineering at home. Eventually, I might get a call.

By the time Jeremy was in third grade, those calls came few and far between. When they did, I'd usually go in to observe him in his classroom. Later, I'd sit down with his teachers for some conversation and problem-solving. The themes were familiar, but their iterations were different each time. Often, I'd write a note to his teachers and parents after my visits, as a way of reminding all of us about how far we'd come and where we still had to go. The one after my sole third grade visit discussed his difficulty slowing down his mind in order to do more careful work, his struggles to sequence and organize his ideas in a way that would make sense to others, and the need to make sure that a good home-school partnership was in place to support growth.

Celebrating Progress While Recognizing Challenges

Two years later, I was back for another observation. Jeremy had made some wonderful gains in fourth grade and, until recently, had been doing fairly well in fifth grade too. However, now he was fooling around a lot and doing a sloppy, disjointed job with many of the longer assignments required of the class. These were undoubtedly important concerns. But my visit also revealed wonderful signs of growth. For example, Jeremy clearly had some good friends and, as he helped a struggling classmate with a difficult math problem, showed tremendous compassion. After he'd spent a good five minutes patiently walking this girl through the problem, it was time for recess. Their lockers were across the hall from each other and as they got their coats, Jeremy overheard her telling a friend how bad she was in math, and that she'd done a lousy job with the assignment. He crossed the hall, voice booming with confidence and affection. "No Mizuki, you didn't. There was just that one little part that wasn't right, and it made everything else go wrong. When you figured that out, you did it perfectly!" It was a lovely moment—Jeremy's empathy for those he knew was beginning to catch up to his deep understanding of the human condition.

In a follow-up meeting, Jeremy's teacher Lois and I talked about fifth grade as one in which educators help children get ready for the middle school experience and, at the same time, keep an eye on preparation for the eventual demands of high school. Watching this big picture would be particularly important for Jeremy, we agreed. His preschool-era issues resonated through the conversation as we discussed how to help him develop better access to a fifth grade version of ready behavior. In addition, Lois noted that Jeremy had difficulty remaining focused on a full set of directions and that, though he was doing better than he had in third grade, he still didn't always write his ideas in sequence nor in logically flowing paragraphs.

As children grow, we take what we know about them from our earliest attempts to help out, then add any additional perspectives that flow from their current stage of development—whether those perspectives involve changes in academic expectations, social complexity, or emotional challenges. In Jeremy's case, this process led us to brainstorm about some additional scaffolding teachers could provide to help with previewing, organization, and production. We reminded ourselves of what had been observed a few years back, that Jeremy was a child whose mind liked to make big leaps but didn't always proceed logically. Once again, his "hard-wiring," something that had come up in every school visit from preschool on, was center stage. We finished by thinking about the kinds of proactive work that could be useful to Jeremy—graphic organizers, preview-focused conversations before project time, check-ins about focus, production, and quality control, and more. Then we agreed to stay in touch. Jeremy had always been wonderfully responsive when the adults who cared for him kept the lines of communication open and when the help they offered was skill specific and consistent.

Staying Tuned to the Uniqueness of Each Situation

In Jeremy's case—as in all cases—there was always more to learn and think about. That's true in regard to the overall approaches offered throughout these pages as well; they are just one element of a larger picture. For example, this book has only touched upon the nature of therapeutic work necessary for some children and families. The same holds true for questions of medication and testing, and for the importance of parenting groups, advocacy efforts, and systemic change. What the book has done in some depth, on the other hand, is to place development—and the ongoing relationships that shape its course—at the center of its explorations. In addition, it has highlighted two ideas: that the mix of strategies used to help a child should always be particular to his situation, and that early childhood work relies on the joining together of "partners in care," a "we" of parents, teachers, specialists, and clinicians.

As such partners, we take into account a youngster's temperament, the culture in which he lives, and the way his family dances together. We look at family tangles with both compassion and clarity. We try, as best we can, to get the worst of those tangles unknotted so that there is room for a child to grow. We track the feedback loops that have surrounded the child's problematic behavior, and we look at whether the use of limits has been consistent or inconsistent, sensible or extreme. Then, we think in advance, not in response. We chunk down our goals for growth and start working on them, one or two at a time. We try to be ready for what is coming, and respond with help that meets the child right where he is in his development. We shoot for a mix of leaning in and leaning out, supporting him when he can't do any better, but setting the bar on his behavior high enough that he is learning new skills all the time. We lend an ally in the areas that are the hardest for him, giving him the sense that we are right there to offer the help he needs, and modeling the specific skills he can't yet use on his own.

We rejoice when he shows little signs of growth, and we let him know, by our pleasure in his success, that we believe in him. But when he stumbles, and he will, we go back to our slow work. We remind ourselves that we knew another trip-up was coming, and that we have an approach that will keep such trip-ups from eroding his sense of self worth. We remember, too, that all of us—kids and adults alike—need to express and process our troubled feelings. We make sure there is room at home, at school, and with a professional if need be, for that expression to take place freely and safely. We keep talking to the other adults who are our collaborators in helping the child, continually leaning on our partnerships in care for ideas, support, and hope.

As we do this labor-intensive work, we remember, most of all, that it is in the context of feeling accepted and cherished that children grow. Our work as clinicians must always keep this fact in mind, adapting to the particulars of a child's world, and looking to foster experiences of adult-child connection, understanding, and pleasure. Such experiences allow children to feel fully alive, deeply loved, and loving in return.

A month after my visit to Jeremy's fifth grade classroom, his mother called to say that her father had died. Jeremy was devastated—his grandfather had been an extraordinarily important presence in his life. Jeremy had actually spoken at the funeral, she told me, would I like to have a copy of what he'd said? A week later, an incredible eulogy arrived in the mail—loving, wise, funny, and in the nicest way possible, offbeat. Class clown and class math tutor, gifted yet struggling writer, and now, an orator who could bring a group of mature adults to tears, Jeremy continued to be, ineffably, himself.

> *I am reflecting on the happiness and joy that continually filled him up.*
> *I remember his smile, his big wide smile, I'll never forget that. Grandpa shined*
> *in uncountable lights, and somewhere out in this vast and terrific world, his*
> *spirit continues on. In the grass, in the trees, in the earth, and in every nook and*
> *cranny around.*

When children feel appreciative of themselves, their worlds, and the people who care for them, they are free to be curious and open. They can tell us how they feel and what they wonder about. They can play with freedom, befriend with confidence, and learn with zest. These are the treasures that our royal racers seek and that we can help them find.

Notes

Introduction

1. For an overview of the systems in which early childhood consultation is embedded—and of the frameworks on which such consultation is based–see Donahue, Falk, and Gersoney Provet (2000), and Perry, Kaufmann, and Knitzer (2007).
2. Although these issues are not explored in depth, the question of pharmacological intervention is briefly addressed in Chapter 10, while concerns about when and why to refer out for psychotherapy are covered in Chapter 11. A limited discussion of parental feelings about the process of assessment and diagnosis can be found in Chapter 13.

Chapter 1

1. See Boyce (1996) and Campbell (2002, pp. 65–72) for further explorations of this dilemma.
2. For a cogent set of essays examining the interface between cultural trends, diagnostic questions, and pharmacological intervention, see Diller (2006).
3. In addition to the previously referenced work of Stanley Greenspan and Melvin Levine—both of whom have made seminal contributions to our understanding of the power of such individualized profiles—see also, Nelson (2007), who in discussing individual pathways of development writes:

The important point is that each individual child develops in terms of particular experiences (which are conditioned on inheritance as well as experiential history and social and cultural conditions), and that the result is differences in patterns of development as the individual, self-organizing system puts together its puzzles in its own sequences and with varying components. (p. 14)

Chapter 2

1. See Nelson (2007, pp. 1–28), "Modern Metaphors of the Developing Child," for a cogent exploration of some of these paradigms.
2. For excellent overviews of child development literature, see Campbell (2002), Landy (2002), and Berk (2005).
3. The notion of developmental "building blocks" has been used in various ways over the years. Shonkoff and Phillips (2000), for example, state that "human relationships, and the effects of relationships on relationships, are the building blocks of development" (p. 27).

4. For further information on the connection of attachment issues to children's responses to trauma, see Groves (2002). Vis-à-vis the ramifications of healthy attachments in supporting resilience, consult Werner (2000). For issues related to attachment difficulties and learning, see Shonkoff and Phillips (2000).

5. For overviews of attachment research and theory, see Siegel (1999), Cassidy and Shaver (1999), and Grossman and Grossman (2005). See also, the National Scientific Council on the Developing Child's Working Paper #1 (2004), "Young Children Develop in an Environment of Relationships."

6. See Siegel (1999) for an elaboration of theoretical categories of attachment.

7. Note the importance of cultural variation in children's ways of experiencing and expressing closeness and distance. For further information on understanding and working with such normative variations, see Lynch and Hanson (2004), Rowena (2004), and Rhodes, Ochoa, and Ortiz (2005).

8. Note the important work of Trevarthen (1980, 1993) and Tronick (1989) in investigating the finely tuned exchanges between babies and their caretakers.

9. The discussion here is necessarily brief. For conceptual overviews of the complex nature of attention, see Shonkoff and Phillips (2000), Barkley (1997a, 2005), and Schneider, Schumann-Hengsteler, and Sodian (2005). See also, Levine's (2001) discussion of saliency determination, and useful visual representations of both attention control and phenomena related to weak attention control.

10. As noted, this is an overly simplified distillation of the intricate process of communication. See Bonniwell Haslett and Samter (1997) and Buckley (2003) for thorough overviews of this complex process, as well as Nelson (1996), and de Villiers and de Villiers's classic *Early Language* (1979).

11. See Buckley (2003, pp. 57–59) and deVilliers and deVilliers (1979, pp. 31–39) for explanations of the phenomenon of overextension.

12. See Buckley (2003, pp. 71–73), Landy (2002, p. 271), and Gopnick and Meltzoff (1988) for information on what we sometimes refer to as a "vocabulary (or naming) explosion."

13. For more on the important interrelationship between cognitive development and language development, see Bonniwell Haslett and Samter (1997, pp. 14–16).

14. Note this chapter's earlier explanation of the idea of opening and closing circles, as well as Greenspan and Wieder's (1998) discussion of how a child's increased capacity to engage in numbers of these circles develops over time (pp. 76–82).

15. See Bishop (1997) for a thorough look at communicational difficulties.

16. Note also—in addition to Vygotsky's (1978) contribution of the idea of developmental scaffolding—his important, related concept of the "zone of proximal development." See also Berk's (2001) thoughtful discussion of these constructs and their implications for practice (pp. 37–64).

17. Note that this image draws from the work of Williams and Shellenberger (1996), who both explain and depict it visually in their "Alert" program Leader's Guide (p. 1/8).

18. Note the important research of Christakis et al. (2004) which suggests that early television exposure can contribute to later attentional problems.

19. Credit, again, to Williams and Shellenburger (see endnote 17) for this imagery.

20. Note Brazelton's (1983) important contribution to our understanding of the unique relational issues that can emerge between parents and active babies.

21. See Turecki (2000) for the additional construct of "wear and tear," an apt description of these problems.

22. The proactive approach described here owes a debt both to Barkley's (2000) useful way of conceptualizing intervention for parents of children with ADHD, and Greene's (1998) family-friendly approaches to inflexible children. See also Faculty of Tufts University (2003).

23. See Greene and Ablon (2006) for an exploration of the importance (and challenges) of problem-solving in childhood development. Note also the discussion of this developmental skill as explored in Bilmes's (2004) classroom-focused, developmental framework.

24. Note the importance of emotional regulation as an underpinning to successful peer interactions. See Fabes et al. (1999).

25. Note the important work of the early family therapists and systems theorists in fleshing out how behavioral feedback loops can serve to solidify or even amplify a problem of concern. See Watzlawick, Weakland, and Fisch (1974) and Haley (1977), as well as Hoffman's (1981) discussion of the ideas behind strategic family therapy (pp. 271–278).

26. The language here is mine; the idea of leaning in versus leaning out is based on the work of Barkley (1997b, 1998), Turecki (2000), and others who look at the ways in which behavioral feedback loops may be reinforcing unwanted behavior while, at the same time, a child is left with such irritated caretakers that he doesn't get the nurturance he needs.

27. Note the connection of children's obsessive tendencies and/or OCD and the experience of frustration. See Rapoport (1991), March and Mulle (1998), and Chansky (2000).

28. For a more thorough discussion of what we call "Wing's triad," see Happé (1994) and Sigman and Capps (1997).

29. Although the idea of deep-tracking is my own, it draws liberally from the work of Greenspan (1992), Greenspan with Salmon (1995), Greenspan and Wieder (1998, 2006), and Szatmari (2004), and from the family-friendly explanations of Klass and Costello (2003).

30. In addition to the earlier referenced work of Werner (2000) and Masten and Coatsworth (1998), see Garmezy and Rutter (1983). Note also the contribution of Brooks (2001) and Brooks and Goldstein (2001), most especially the important idea of "islands of competence."

Chapter 3

1. For simple, parent- and teacher-friendly explanations of right hemisphere vulnerabilities, see Thompson (1997).

2. In addition, see the texts of Byrnes (2001) and Hale and Fiorello (2004) for comprehensive explanations of neurodevelopmental issues.

3. See Schneider, Schumann-Hengsteler, and Sodian (2005), Levine (2002), and Shonkoff and Phillips (2000) for more thorough information on the complex mental processes involved in memory function.

4. See earlier discussions of attentional issues in Chapter 2, as well as Levine (2002) and Barkley (1997a).

5. See Bishop (1997) for more on how we support children by using such scaffolding

Chapter 4

1. Note that the term "family choreography" originally comes from Papp (1976), who built on Duhl, Duhl, and Kantor's (1973) idea of sculpting the family as a therapeutic intervention. Whitaker and Bumberry (1987) also worked with the concept of choreography—or in their case, dancing—and the metaphor remains alive in more contemporary literature as well (Knapp and Womack, 2003).

2. For recent overviews of family systems thinking and the practice of family therapy, see Goldenberg and Goldenberg (1996), Nichols and Schwartz (2004), and Gladding (2006).

3. Ellen Wachtel (1994), whose work of integrating both individual and family systems perspectives has influenced so many clinicians, writes about this intersection as follows:

One can think of individual concerns and difficulties as *influencing* and being *influenced by* the system yet having a separate and distinct existence. Symptoms in both adults and children are therefore partially autonomous from the system in which they flourish and which, in fact, they may play a role in maintaining. Like the ocean and the bay, the tides and currents in the larger system influence those of the smaller, but the smaller nonetheless has its own identity. (p. 14)

4. For more on this issue, see Donahue, Falk, and Gersony Provet's chapter, "Engaging Families" (2000, pp. 101–132) and Pawl and Milburn's "Family and Relationship-Centered Principles and Practice" (2006).

5. See Minuchin, Colapinto, and Minuchin (2007, pp. 42–45) for an explanation of the idea of "joining," a core concept in the family therapy literature. Note also the importance of being attuned to a family's culture (or cultures) of origin: see McGoldrick, Giordano, and Garcia-Preto (2005).

6. For further exploration of the important factors we consider when thinking about the context of family life, see Wachtel (1994). Note especially the section, "Gathering information for systemic, psychodynamic, and behavioral hypotheses" (pp. 30–41), and its excellent list of frequently omitted questions. See also, Kaiser and Rasminsky (2003, pp. 35–42), and Minuchin, Colapinto, and Minuchin's (2007) "Suggested Questions for a Family Intake" (p. 84).

7. For a cogent exploration of the importance of family assessments, and the evidence base supporting their therapeutic usefulness, see Lawrence (2006).

8. See Minuchin, Colapinto, and Minuchin (2007) and Minuchin, Nichols, and Lee (2007) for an elaboration of these concepts.

9. See Lynch and Hanson (2004) for an exploration of cross-cultural issues and practitioner competence.

10. For an exploration of the unique issues involved in understanding and working with immigrant and refugee families, see Rowena (2004).

11. See Chapter 2's endnote 25 for the references on which these questions are based.

12. For extensive exploration of elements involved in work with families facing poverty-related stressors see Aponte (1994) and Minuchin, Colapinto, and Minuchin (2007). For more, specifically, on the coordinated systems of care that may be so useful to such families, see Pumariega and Winters (2003).

13. The parent-child work touched on here owes a great debt to Selma Fraiberg's influential idea of "ghosts in the nursery" and the ways she and her colleagues framed a parent-friendly model that promotes increased connectedness between children and their emotionally fragile caregivers (1980). See also, Costa's (2006) treatment of "infant as transference object" and Lieberman and Pawl's (1993) discussion of parent-child psychotherapy.

14. For an excellent exploration of this issue, see Siegel and Hartzell (2003).

15. See Siegel and Hartzell (2003) again for concrete and well-illustrated examples of how to help parents with this challenge.

Chapter 5

1. See Boehm and Weinberg (1996) for more on the skills of astute classroom observation in early childhood settings. See also Brassard and Boehm (2007) for a comprehensive overview of preschool assessment.

2. Although this book offers an overview of functional assessment, it does not explain the process in depth, nor provide adequate specifics. See O'Neill et al. (1997), Kaiser and Rasminsky (2003), and/or Watson and Steege (2003) for further information on how to understand and carry out such assessments. For an analysis of how to pair functional analyses with preschoolers' natural preferences in order to improve behavior, see Blair, Umbreit, and Bos (1999).

3. The following explanations draw on Kaiser and Rasminsky's (2003) thorough information on this topic (pp. 195–210).

4. For important material on the power of reflective practice to foster effective intervention, see Parlakian (2002) and Shahmoon-Shanak (2006).

5. See Donahue, Falk, and Gersony Provet (2000) and Johnston and Brinamen (2006) for important explorations of the common and sometimes complex challenges of working with stressed, overwhelmed teachers .

6. See Minuchin, Colapinto, and Minuchin (1998), Walsh (1998), and Kaufmann and Wischman (1999) on working with overwhelmed and/or underorganized families.

7. Note Fraiberg and colleagues' (1980) seminal work on supporting stressed parents—and nurturing parent-child connection—in order to foster healthy child development.

Chapter 6

1. For an overview of behavioral principles, see Chance (2003). For explanations and examples of how reinforcement principles play out in family life,

including the way such principles in action may serve to amplify rather than extinguish undesired behaviors, see Barkley (1997a).

2. Barkley (1997a) offers a striking flow chart which illustrates "the sequencing of interactions between parents and defiant children during a command-compliance encounter" (p. 28). Note that this chart can be used to great effect in either individual parent meetings or parent groups.

3. While very useful to clinicians, a number of the publications referenced here are written directly for parents, and are an excellent resource for parents who use reading as a way of gaining new skills.

4. See Greene's family-friendly exploration of "basket" thinking" (1998, pp. 133–172), on which this chapter's idea of option-focused thinking is based.

5. See Barkley (1997a, pp. 112–114) on "compliance training."

6. Note the power of Clark's humor-filled and cartoon-illustrated *SOS for Parents* (1996)—an excellent resource for parents looking to master the nuts and bolts of effective behavior management.

7. See Barkley (1997a), Forehand and Long (1996), Phelan (2003), and Clark (1996), all of whom offer sensible, clear versions of time out plans.

Chapter 7

1. For a more through exploration of the importance and implementation of developmentally supportive classroom routines and transitions, see Malenfant (2006). For concrete, creative ideas for supporting transition-time success, see Larson, Henthorne, and Plum (1994).

2. This section is appreciatively based on the work of Loretta Wieczner, early childhood specialist with the Newton Community Partnerships for Children; quotes with permission.

3. For information on effective classroom design, see Curtis and Carter (2003) and Isbell and Exelby (2001). For more on possibilities for enriched curriculum, see Redleaf Press's *Creative Curriculum* series, accessed at www. readleafpress.org

4. See Donahue, Falk, and Gersony Provet (2000), Johnston and Brinamen (2006), and Shahmoon-Shanak (2006) for more on the delicate process of forging constructive, trusting alliances with weary teachers.

5. For a wonderfully upbeat, suggestion-packed publication that helps teachers cultivate this stance, see Bilmes (2004).

6. Note Scarlett's (1998, p. 25) important notion and description of "co-play," which bears a strong relationship to the lend-an-ally work so essential to this model.

7. Thanks to Loretta Wieczner (see this chapter's endnote 2) for the idea of the wise child.

Chapter 8

1. For further exploration of the family-related issues that can take a toll on a child's ability to engage comfortably, see Chapters 4 and 5 in Campbell's comprehensive *Behavior Problems in Preschool Children* (2002).

2. This issue requires much more intensive treatment than can be undertaken here. See Chapter 14 for a brief introduction, as well as Groves (2002), Lieberman and Van Horn (2004), and Osofsky (2004).

3. Clinicians do well to understand the issues involved in bilingualism and second language learning. See Tabors (1997), Roumaine (1999), and Genesee, Paradis, and Crago (2004).

4. Once again, this is a far larger issue than can be explored here. See this chapter's endnote 2 for further information on this complex topic and, by way of an introduction to intervention, Fitzgerald Rice and Groves's excellent *Hope and Healing: A Caregiver's Guide to Helping Young Children Affected by Trauma* (2005).

5. For an overview of the phenomenon of selective mutism, see Black (1996). For information on pharmacological treatments for this problem, consult Golwyn and Sevlie (1999) and Dummit et al. (1996). See also, Kumpulainen (2002) for a discussion of the place of medication in overall treatment approaches, including an advisory about turning to pharmacological alternatives only when other treatment methods have not been helpful.

6. See Kagan (1997) for descriptions of the temperamental bias that causes some children to react to unfamiliarity with marked caution. Note also that the figures mentioned here, drawn from Kagan and Snidman's seminal *The Long Shadow of Temperament* (2004), refer to "high reactive infants." This treatise notes that about 60% of these infants become very shy toddlers, while by school age only a third can be designated in this way. It is important to be aware of a culturally based variability in this phenomenon: The authors highlight that these figures are lower for Asian children.

7. Research suggests moderate heritability of this temperamental bias toward caution in the face of novelty. (Robinson et al., 1992; DiLalla, Kagan, and Reznick, 1994) Note, however, that there may well be a mix of constitutional factors and relationship-based learning behind a child's behavior when both a child and parent have such an inborn bias.

8. Note the relationship of these stages of lend-an-ally assistance to Pearson and Gallagher's (1983) influential approach to teacher-initiated academic scaffolding: the "gradual release of responsibility" model.

Chapter 9

1. See endnote 2, Chapter 8.
2. See Braaten and Felopulos (2004) for a straightforward approach to talking with parents about educational testing.
3. See endnote 4, Chapter 8.
4. For further information on how teachers can help children understand and put words to their feelings, see Fox and Harper Lantini (2006).

Chapter 10

1. See endnotes 2 and 4, Chapter 8.
2. The stages are my own, but build on the family and classroom-friendly work of Barkley (2000) and Greenspan and Wieder (1998).

3. This imagery is based on descriptions and concepts in Williams and Shellenberger's "Alert" program Leader's Guide (1996).
4. For creative strategies to help children with self-talk and impulse control, see Caselman (2005).
5. See Barkley (2000, pp. 54–56) on the importance of self-directed speech.
6. Ibid. pp. 149–150.
7. See Chapter 14 for further information relating to media exposure, as well as Christakis et al. (2004).
8. See endnotes 2 and 4, Chapter 8, for further information.
9. This section owes a great debt to the influential work of Levine (2001, 2002). See also Barkley's (2000) fourteen guiding principles for the parents of children diagnosed with AHDH, three of which highlight keeping a "disability perspective," not personalizing a child's difficulties, and "practicing forgiveness" (pp. 152–153). In addition, note Brooks's (2001) emphasis on keeping a child's strengths in mind while supporting growth in areas of vulnerability.
10. Note the following parent- and teacher-friendly information that can be easily accessed online: the Chesapeake Institute's *Attention Deficits: What Teachers Should Know* (available: childrendisabilities.info), and the Boston Medical Center Developmental Assessment Clinic's "Resources for Parents, Teachers, and Caregivers"—*Tips for Teachers of Children with Attentional Problems* and *Examples of Adaptations for Children with Attention and Organization Problems* (available: bmc.org).
11. The question of psychopharmacological intervention for young children is a hotly debated one, with strong arguments on both sides. For a reasoned discussion of the issues at stake, see Diller (2006). For a cogent defense of a conservative approach to medicating young children—and excellent questions about current cultural trends—see Willis (2003). For information on positive outcomes in response to medication trials for inattentive, impulsive children, see Monteiro Musten et al. (1997). For an overview of psychopharmacological intervention for children, see Brown, Arnstein Carpenter, and Simerly (2005). For a discussion of the challenges of studying medication trials for young children (many of the medications given to young children are prescribed "off-label"), see Greenhill and Blumer (2003). Finally, for straightforward, demystifying, and medication-friendly explanations that can be offered directly to parents, see Wilens (2004).

Chapter 11

1. This point and the following three are based on the influential model of Greene (1998; Greene and Ablon, 2006).
2. See Landy (2002, pp. 244–245 and 538–539), Bushman and Anderson (2001), Singer and Singer (2002), and Gentile et al. (2004) for explorations of this complex, troubling issue. Note also further explorations in Chapter 14 of this book.
3. One of the best sources of material on children's toy choices is the Web site of TRUCE, Teachers Resisting Unhealthy Children's Entertainment (online: www.truceteachers.org).

4. See Barkley (1997b, 1998) and Barnett, Bell, and Carey (1998) for thorough discussions of token systems and other forms of codified reinforcement.
5. See Chapter 8, endnote 2.
6. For examples of well-respected social skills curricula, see *Second Step: A Violence Prevention Curriculum* (available through cfchildren.org); *The Incredible Years: Dina Dinosaur Classroom Curriculum* (available through: www.incredibleyears.com); and *Al's Pals: Kids Making Healthy Choices* (available at: wingspanworks.com/alspals). See also NAEYC's (November, 2006) web-archived *Young Children,* "Building Social Skills in the Early Years and Beyond" (online: journal.naeyc.org—go to "Beyond the Journal").
7. For more on Social Stories™, see Gray (1994) and Gray and White (2003). See also the Gray Center for Social Learning and Understanding (online at www.thegraycenter.org).
8. Note the importance of Vivian Paley's work on storytelling in the classroom (1981, 1983, 2004).
9. For a powerful exploration of children's violent play, see Katch (2001). For a creative approach to channeling such classroom-based play in constructive ways, see Hoffman (2004).
10. Note the usefulness of the approaches pioneered in narrative therapy when adapted for classroom use. See Freeman, Epston, and Lobovits (1997).
11. Note the tremendous influence of Greene's (1998; Greene and Ablon, 2006) work in the conceptualizations and discussion which follows here.
12. Merrell (2001) clearly explains the functions of an "emotional thermometer" in helping children be aware of and regulate emotions. Greene (1998, pp. 216–218) also offers a compelling, color-coded emotional rating scale to be used by children in the process of learning to remain calm.
13. See Bettelheim's (1987) influential article, "*The Importance of Play.*" See also Paley (2004).
14. See Boyd Webb (2007) for an exploration of therapeutic work with children in crisis. See also Gil (1991) and Bromfield (1992).

Chapter 12

1. Note that this chapter does not explore the issues faced by young children with obsessive tendencies. Youngsters who become increasingly compelled by ritualized behaviors—or besieged by unpleasant, repetitive thoughts—require a type of intervention that parallels some of what is discussed here but is beyond the scope of this book. See Chansky (2000), March and Mulle (1998), and Rapoport (1991) for more information.
2. For other images that can be used with anxious children, see Goldstein, Hagar, and Brooks (2002).
3. See Chapter 8, endnotes 2 and 4.
4. See the suggestion-packed work of Stock Kranovitz (1998) for further elaboration and ideas for intervention.

Chapter 13

1. See Greenspan and Wieder (1998, 2006) for an elaboration of the approaches offered in relationship to severely challenged children. Note

also the debt this chapter owes to Greenspan's career-long focus on the children described within; much of its foundational understanding—and many of its practical strategies—grow out of the perspective he offers in his many publications.

2. Klass and Costello (2003) offer a tremendously important contribution in their family-friendly volume which, among many other things, walks parents through the sometimes complex and emotionally loaded process of assessment.

3. One of Greenspan's (1992) powerful contributions to our understanding of children with complex neurodevelopmental profiles is his hopeful approach to developing individualized profiles and his conviction that when we understand a child's vulnerabilities with specificity—and intervene based on that understanding—we may see remarkable progress.

4. See endnote 1 for the important work on which these stages are based.

5. See endnotes 7 and 8, Chapter 2.

6. Greenspan has written about this challenge in many ways over the years. See *Infancy and Early Childhood* (1992, pp. 479–486) for one example, in which he discusses how we help a child build on her use of symbolic representation and support her ability to make logical connections between one idea and another.

7. In addition to the usefulness of Klass and Costello's (2003) explorations of possibilities for and issues related to testing and assessment, see the parent-directed volume of Braaten and Felopulos (2004). For an overview of neuropsychology as it applies to school and learning issues—including a focus on applications of assessment for intervention—see Hale and Fiorello (2004).

8. See the compassionate elucidation of this process in Klass and Costello's (2003, pp. 32–63) chapter "Specialists, Labels, and Alphabet Soup: Arriving at a Diagnosis."

Chapter 14

1. See Osofsky (2004) and Weinreb and Groves (2007) for documentation and elaboration of such responses to trauma.

2. For an excellent overview of the connection between brain function and trauma, see National Scientific Council on the Developing Child (2005).

3. The literature on helping caregivers and teachers help children cope with the aftermath of trauma is growing. See Zero to Three's superb publication for caregivers, *Hope and Healing* (Fitzgerald Rice and Groves, 2005) and the Massachusetts Advocates for Children's *Helping Traumatized Children Learn* (Cole et al., 2005). For an overview of consultative issues vis-à-vis traumatized children, see "Intervention for Young Children Affected by Trauma" in Donahue, Falk, and Gersony Provet (2000, pp. 189–242). For cogent explorations of the issues facing such children, see Groves (2002). For aspects of intervention, including therapeutic approaches that can help traumatized youngsters, see Gil (1991), Lieberman and Van Horn (2004), and Osofsky (2004). For a brilliant exploration of how preschools can support these children, see Koplow (1996).

4. For explorations of the issues facing children who have lost a parent, see Lieberman et al. (2003) and Worden (1996). For general information on the process of talking with children about death, see Grollman's (1968) classic *Explaining Death to Children*. For information on clinical intervention with bereaved youngsters, see Boyd Webb (2002). For parent-friendly explanations of talking with children about loss, see Grollman (1991) and Trozzi and Massimini (1999). Finally, for an invaluable resource for clinicians (and parents) to have on hand that speaks to a variety of circumstances surrounding loss, see Schaefer, Lyons, and Peretz's (2002) *How Do We Tell the Children: A Step-by-Step Guide for Helping Children Cope When Someone Dies.*

5. For a general overview about helping children cope with divorce and separation, see Taylor (2001). For easily accessed online guidelines for parents, see the American Academy of Child and Adolescent Psychiatry's "Facts for Families: Children and Divorce" (at www.aacap.org) and Family Communications' "Helping Children with Divorce" (see "Resources for Families" at www.fci.org). For an exploration of issues involved for children caught between battling parents, see Garrity and Baris (1997).

6. The following statistics come from the Kaiser Family Foundation's comprehensive *The Media Family: Electronic Media in the Lives of Infants, Toddlers, Preschoolers, and their Parents* (Rideout, Hamel, and the Kaiser Family Foundation, 2006). This publication does an impressive job of examining the ways in which media exposure is now embedded in the lives of many young children, and some of the potential impact of that exposure.

7. For more information on computer game dependence, see Keepers (1990), Fisher (1994), Griffiths and Hunt (1998), and Tejeiro Salguero and Bersabe Moran (2002).

8. For cogent explorations of children and media exposure, see Levin (1998) and Singer and Singer (2002). For parent-friendly material on toy choices and media exposure, see TRUCE's (Teachers Resisting Unhealthy Children's Entertainment) "Toy Action Guide," "TV and Your Child," and "Media Violence and Children: Action Guide." (See www.truceteachers.org)

9. Amy Bamforth of the Somerville Community Partnerships for Children has been an inspiration to many New England area practitioners in her commitment to developing written resources—often in multiple languages—for the parents and teachers of young children. In addition to the bibliography project mentioned here, she has partnered with other gifted early childhood professionals in producing *Planting the Seeds for Success in Life: Supporting Children's Resilience, Your Child's Emotional Health: A Guide for the Parents and Caregivers of Young Children,* and *Helping All Children Succeed: A Family Companion to the Massachusetts Department of Education Guidelines for Preschool Learning Experiences.* All are available through the Somerville Community Partnerships for Children, Somerville, MA.

References

Aber, J. L., Pederson, S., Brown, J. L., Jones, S. M., & Gershoff, E. T. (2003). *Changing children's trajectories of development*. New York: National Center for Children in Poverty.

Ainsworth, M. (1973). The development of infant-mother attachment. In B. Caldwell & H. Riccuiti (Eds.), *Review of child development research, Vol. 3* (pp. 1–94). Chicago: University of Chicago Press.

Aponte, H. (1994). *Bread and spirit: Therapy and the new poor*. New York: W. W. Norton.

Ayres, J. A. (1979). *Sensory integration and child*. Los Angeles: Western Psychological Services.

Barkley, R. A. (1997a). Behavioral inhibition, sustained attention, and executive functions: Constructing a unifying theory of ADHD. *Psychological Bulletin, 121*, 65–94.

———. (1997b). *Defiant children: A clinician's manual for assessment and parent training* (2nd ed.). New York: Guilford Press.

———. (1998). *Attention-deficit hyperactivity disorder: A handbook for diagnosis and treatment* (2nd ed.). New York: Guilford Press.

———. (2000). *Taking charge of ADHD: The complete, authoritative guide for parents*. New York: Guilford Press.

———. (2005). *ADHD and the nature of self-control*. New York: Guilford Press.

Barkley, R. A., & Benton, C. (1998). *Your defiant child: Eight steps to better behavior*. New York: Guilford Press.

Barnett, D. W., Bell, S. H., & Carey, K. T. (1998). *Designing preschool interventions: A practitioner's guide*. New York: Guilford Press.

Bates, J. E., & MacFadyen-Ketchum, S. (2000). Temperament and parent-child relations as interacting factors in children's behavioral adjustment. In V.J. Molfese & D. L. Molfese (Eds.), *Temperament and personality development across the life span* (pp. 141–176). Mahwah, NJ: Lawrence Erlbaum Associates, Publishers.

Bean, B. J., Biss, C. A., & Hepburn, K. S. (2007). Vermont's Children's Upstream Project: Statewide early childhood mental health services and supports. In D. F. Perry, R. F. Kaufman, & J. Knitzer (Eds.), *Social and emotional health in early childhood: Building bridges between services and systems* (pp. 169–188). Baltimore: Paul H. Brookes Publishing Co.

Berk, L. (2001). *Awakening children's minds: How parents and teachers can make a difference*. New York: Oxford University Press.

———. (2005). *Child development*. Boston: Allyn & Bacon.

Bettelheim, B. (1987). The importance of play. *Atlantic Monthly, 259* (3), 35–46.

Bilmes, J. (2004). *Beyond behavior management: The six life skills children need to thrive in today's world*. St. Paul, MN: Redleaf Press.

Bishop, D. V. M. (1997). *Uncommon understanding: Development and disorders of language comprehension in children*. East Sussex, UK: Psychology Press.

Black, B. (1996). Social anxiety and selective mutism. In L. J. Dickstein, M. B. Riba, & J. M. Oldham (Eds.), *American Psychiatric Press review of psychiatry* (pp. 469–496). Washington: American Psychiatric Press.

Blair, K. C., Umbreit, J., & Bos, C. S. (1999). Using functional assessment and children's preferences to improve the behavior of young children with behavioral disorders. *Behavioral Disorders, 24*, 151–166.

Boehm, A., & Weinberg, R. A. (1996). *The classroom observer: Developing observation skills in early childhood settings* (3rd ed.). New York: Teachers College Press.

Bonniwell Haslett, B., & Samter, W. (1997). *Children communicating: The first five years.* Mahwah, NJ: Lawrence Erlbaum Associates, Publishers.

Bowlby, J. S. (1969). *Attachment and loss: Vol. 1, Attachment.* New York: Basic Books.

———. (1973). *Attachment and loss: Vol. 2, Separation.* New York: Basic Books.

Boyce, W. T. (1996). The dilemma of developmental and behavioral diagnosis. In A. M. Rudolph, J. I. E. Hoffman, & C. D. Rudolph (Eds.), *Rudolph's pediatrics* (pp. 94–95). Stamford, CT: Appleton & Lange.

Boyd Webb, N. (Ed.). (2007). *Play therapy with children in crisis: Individual, group, and family treatment* (3rd ed.). New York: Guilford Press.

——— (Ed.). (2002). *Helping bereaved children: A handbook for practitioners* (2nd ed.). New York: Guilford Press.

Braaten, E., & Felopulos, G. (2004). *Straight talk about psychological testing for kids.* New York: Guilford Press.

Bradley, S. (2000). *Affect regulation and the development of psychopathology.* New York: Guilford Press.

Brassard, M. R., & Boehm, A. E. (2007). *Preschool assessment and principles: Principles and practices.* New York: Guilford Press.

Brazelton, T. B. (1983). *Infants and mothers: Differences in development.* New York: Dell Publishers.

Brazelton, T. B., & Sparrow, J. D. (2001). *Touchpoints Three to Six: Your child's emotional and behavioral development.* Cambridge, MA: Perseus Books.

Brennan, E., Bradley, J., Allen, M. D., Perry, D., & Tsega, A. (2005). *The evidence base for mental health consultation in early childhood settings: Research synthesis and review.* Paper presented at an invitational meeting sponsored by the Georgetown University National Technical Assistance Center for Children's Mental Health, Tampa, FL.

Bretherton, I., Fritz, J., Zahn-Waxler, C., & Ridgeway, D. (1986). Learning to talk about emotions: A functionalist perspective. *Child Development, 55*, 529–548.

Brody, J., & McGarry, K. (2005). Using social stories to ease children's transitions. *Young Children, 60* (5), 38–42.

Bromfield, R. (1992). *Playing for real: A child therapist explores the world of play therapy and the inner worlds of children.* New York: Plume.

Brooks, R. (2001). *The self-esteem teacher.* Loveland, OH: Treehaus Communications.

Brooks, R., & Goldstein, S. (2001). *Raising resilient children.* Chicago: Contemporary Books.

Brown, R. (1958). *Words and things.* New York: The Free Press of Glencoe.

Brown, R. T., Arnstein Carpenter, L., & Simerly, E. (2005). *Mental health medications for children: A primer.* New York: Guilford Press.

Buckley, B. (2003). *Children's communication skills: From birth to give years.* London: Routledge.

Burke, R. V., Kuhn, B. R., & Peterson, J. L. (2004). Brief report: A "storybook" ending to children's bedtime problems—The use of a rewarding social story to reduce bedtime resistance and frequent nighttime waking. *Journal of Pediatric Psychology, 29* (5), 389–396.

Bushman, B., & Anderson, C. A. (2001). Media violence and the American public. *American Psychologist, 56* (6/7), 477–489.

Byrnes, J. P. (2001). *Minds, brains, and learning: Understanding the psychological and educational relevance of neuroscientific research.* New York: Guilford Press.

Calkins, S., & Johnson, M. C. (1998). Toddler regulation of distress to frustrating events: Temperamental and maternal correlates. *Infant Behavior and Development, 21,* 379–395.

Cambell, S. (2002). *Behavior problems in preschool children.* New York: Guilford Press.

Caselman, T. (2005). *Stop and think: Impulse control for children.* Chapin, SC: YouthLight, Inc.

Cassidy, J., & Shaver, P. R. (1999). *Handbook of attachment: Theory, research, and clinical applications.* New York: Guilford Press.

Chambless, D. L., & Gracely, E. J. (1989). Fear of fear and the anxiety disorders. *Cognitive Therapy and Research, 13* (1), 9–20.

Chance, P. (2003). *Learning and behavior* (5th ed.). Pacific Grove, CA: Thomson-Brooks/Cole Publishing.

Chang, H. (1993). *Affirming children's roots: Cultural and linguistic diversity in early care and education.* San Francisco: California Tomorrow.

Chansky, T. (2000). *Freeing your child from obsessive-compulsive disorder.* New York: Three Rivers Press.

Chen, X., Hastings, P. D., Rubin, K. H., Chen, H., Cen, G., & Stewart, S. L. (1998). Child-rearing attitudes and behavioral inhibition in Chinese and Canadian toddlers: A cross-cultural study. *Developmental Psychology, 34* (4), 677–686.

Chess, S., & Thomas, A. (1996). *Temperament: Theory and practice.* New York: Brunner/Mazel.

Chomsky, N. (1965). *Aspects of a theory of syntax.* Cambridge, MA: MIT Press.

Christakis, D. A., Zimmerman, F. J., DiGiuseppe, D. L., & McCarty, C. A. (2004). Early television exposure and subsequent attentional problems in children. *Pediatrics, 113* (4), 708–713.

Clark, L. (1996). *SOS, help for parents: A practical guide for handling everyday behavior problems.* Bowling Green, KY: Parents Press.

Cohen, N. J., Davine, M., & Meloche-Kelly, M. (1989). The prevalence of unsuspected language disorders in a child psychiatric population. *Journal of the American Academy of Child and Adolescent Psychiatry, 28,* 107–111.

Cole, S., Greenwald O'Brien, J., Geron Gadd, M., Ristuccia, J., Luray Wallace, D., & Gregory, M. (2005). *Helping traumatized children learn: A report and policy agenda.* Boston: Massachusetts Advocates for Children.

Costa, G. (2006). Mental health principles, practices, strategies, and dynamics pertinent to early intervention practitioners. In G. Foley & J. D. Hochman (Eds.), *Mental health in early intervention: Achieving unity in principles and practice* (pp. 113–138). Baltimore: Paul H. Brookes Publishing Co.

Curtis, D., & Carter, M. (2003). *Designs for living and learning: Transforming early childhood environments.* St. Paul, MN: Redleaf Press.

DeGangi, G. A., Craft, P., & Castellan, J. (1991). Treatment of sensory, emotional, and attentional problems in regulatory disordered infants. *Infants and Young Children, 3,* 9–19.

DeGangi, G. A., DiPietro, J. A., Greenspan, S. I., & Porges, S. W. (1991). Psychophysiological characteristics of the regulatory disordered infant. *Infant Behavior and Development, 14,* 37–50.

de Villiers, P., & de Villiers, J. (1979). *Early Language.* Cambridge, MA: Harvard University Press.

DiLalla, L. F., Kagan, J., & Reznick, J. S. (1994). Genetic etiology of behavioral inhibition among two year olds. *Infant Behavior and Development, 17,* 401–408.

Dilg, M. (2003). *Thriving in the multicultural classroom: Principles and practices for effective teaching.* New York: Teachers College Press.

Diller, L. H. (2006). *The last normal child: Essays on the intersection of kids, culture, and psychiatric drugs.* Westport, CT: Praeger Publishers.

Donahue, P., Falk, B., & Gersony Provet, A. (2000). *Mental health consultation in early childhood.* Baltimore: Paul H. Brookes Publishing Co.

Duhl, F., Duhl, B., & Kantor, D. (1973). Learning, space, and action in family therapy: A primer of sculpture. In D. Block (Ed.), *Techniques of family psychotherapy.* New York: Grune & Stratton.

Dummit, E. S., Klein, R. G., Tancer, N. K., Asche, B. A., & Martin, J. (1996). Fluoxetine treatment of children with selective mutism: An open trial. *Journal of the American Academy of Child and Adolescent Psychiatry, 35* (5), 615–621.

Eisenberg, N. (2002). Emotion-related regulation and its relation to quality of social functioning. In W. Hartrup & R. Weinburg (Eds.), *Minnesota Symposium on Child Psychology, Vol. 32* (pp. 133–171). Mahwah, NJ: Lawrence Erlbaum Associates, Publishers.

Fabes, R. A., Eisenberg, N., Jones, S., Smith, M., Guthrie, I., Poulin, R., et al. (1999). Regulation, emotionality, and preschoolers' socially competent peer interactions. *Child Development, 55,* 432–442.

Faculty of Tufts University's Eliot-Pearson Department of Child Development. (2003). *Proactive parenting: Guiding your child from two to six.* New York: Berkley Books.

Fisher, S. (1994). Identifying video game addiction in children and adolescents. *Addictive Behaviors, 19* (5), 545–553.

Fitzgerald Rice, K., & Groves, B. M. (2005). *Hope and healing: A caregiver's guide to helping young children affected by trauma.* Washington DC: Zero to Three Press.

Forehand, R., & Long, N. (1996). *Parenting the strong-willed child.* Chicago: contemporary Books.

Fox, L., & Harper Lantini, R. (2006). Teaching children a vocabulary for emotions. *Young Children* (November). Retrieved July, 2007 from http://www.journal.naeyc.org

Fraiberg, S. (Ed.). (1980). *Clinical studies in infant mental health.* New York: Basic Books.

Freeman, J., Epston, D., & Lobovits, D. (1997). *Playful approaches to serious problems: Narrative therapy with children and their families.* New York: W. W. Norton.

Garmezy, N., & Rutter, T. (1983). *Stress, coping, and development in children.* New York: McGraw-Hill.

Garrity, C., & Baris, M. (1997). *Caught in the middle: Protecting the children of high conflict divorce.* San Francisco: Jossey-Bass.

Genesee, F., Paradis, J., & Crago, M. B. (2004). *Dual language development and disorders: A handbook in bilingualism and second language learning.* Baltimore: Paul H. Brookes Publishing Co.

Gentile, D. A., Walsh, D. A., Ellison, P. R., Fox, M., & Cameron, J. (2004). *Media violence as a risk factor for children: A longitudinal study.* Paper presented at the American Psychological Association 16th Annual Convention, Chicago.

Gil, E. (1991). *The healing power of play: Working with abused children.* New York: Guilford Press.

Gilliam, W. S. (2005). *Prekindergarteners left behind: Expulsion rates in state prekindergarten systems.* Unpublished manuscript, Yale University Child Study Center.

Gilliam W. S., & de Mesquita, P. B. (2000). The relationship between language and cognitive development and emotional-behavioral problems in financially-disadvantaged preschoolers: A longitudinal investigation. *Early Child Development and Care, 162,* 9–24.

Gimbel, G. A., & Holland, M. L. (2003). *Emotional and behavioral problems of young children: Effective interventions in the preschool and kindergarten years.* New York: Guilford Press.

Gladding, S. (2006). *Family therapy: History, theory, and practice* (2nd ed.). Englewood Cliffs, NJ: Prentice Hall.

Goldenberg, I., & Goldenberg, H. (1996). *Family therapy: An overview* (4th ed.). Pacific Groves, CA: Brooks/Cole.

Goldstein, S., Hagar, K., & Brooks, R. (2002). *Seven steps to help your child worry less.* Plantation, FL: Specialty Press, Inc.

Golwyn, D. H., & Sevlie, C. P. (1999). Phenelzine treatment of selective mutism in four prepubertal children. *Journal of Child and Adolescent Psychopharmacology, 9* (2), 109–113.

Gopnick, A., & Meltzoff, A. (1988). The development of categorization in the second year and its relationship to other cognitive and linguistic developments. *Child Development, 58,* 1523–1531.

Gray, C. (1994). *The new social story book.* Arlinton, TX: Future Horizons.

Gray, C., & White, A. L. (2003). *My social stories book.* London: Jessica Kingsley Publishers.

Greene, R. W. (1998). *The explosive child: A new approach for understanding and parenting easily frustrated, "chronically inflexible" children.* New York: Harper Collins Publishers.

Greene, R. W., & Ablon, S. (2006). *Treating explosive kids: The collaborative, problem-solving approach.* New York: Guilford Press.

Greenhill, L., & Blumer, J. (2003). Developing strategies for psychopharmacological studies in preschool children. *Journal of the American Academy of Child and Adolescent Psychiatry, 42* (4), 406–414.

Greenspan, S. I. (1992). *Infancy and early childhood: The practice of clinical assessment and intervention with emotional and developmental challenges.* Madison, CT: International Universities Press.

Greenspan, S., with Salmon, J. (1995). *The challenging child: Understanding, raising, and enjoying the five "difficult" types of children.* Reading, MA: Addison-Wesley Publishing Co.

Greenspan, S. I., & Thorndike Greenspan, N. (1985). *First feelings: Milestones in the emotional development of your baby and child.* New York: Penguin Books.

Greenspan, S., & Wieder, S. (1998). *The child with special needs: Encouraging intellectual and emotional growth.* Reading, MA: Perseus Books.

———. (2006). *Engaging autism: Using the floortime approach to help children relate, communicate, and think.* Cambridge, MA: DaCapo Press.

Griffiths, M. D., & Hunt, N. (1998). Dependence on computer games by adolescents. *Psychological Reports, 82* (2), 475–480.

Grollman, E. A. (1968). *Explaining death to children.* Boston: Beacon Press.

———. (1991). *Talking about death: A dialogue between parent and child.* Boston: Beacon Press.

Grossman, K. E., & Grossman, K. (2005). *Attachment from infancy to adulthood: The major longitudinal studies.* New York: Guilford Press.

Groves, B. (2002). *Children who see too much: Lessons from the child witness to violence project.* Boston: Beacon Press.

Hale, J. B., & Fiorello, C. A. (2004). *School neuropsychology: A practitioner's handbook.* New York: Guilford Press.

Haley, J. (1977). *Problem-solving therapy.* San Francisco: Jossey-Bass.

Happé, F. (1994). *Autism: An introduction to psychological theory.* Cambridge, MA: Harvard University Press.

Hepburn, K. (2004). *Building culturally and linguistically competent services to support young children, their families, and school readiness.* Baltimore: Annie E. Casey Foundation.

Hettema, J. M., Neale, M. C., & Kendler, K. S. (2001). A review and meta-analysis of the genetic epidemiology of anxiety disorders. *American Journal of Psychiatry, 158,* 1568–1578.

Hoffman, E. (2004). *Magic capes, amazing powers.* St. Paul, MN: Redleaf Press.

Hoffman, L. (1981). *Foundations of family therapy: A conceptual framework for systems change.* New York: Basic Books.

Isbell, R., & Exelby, B. (2001). *Early learning environments that work.* Beltsville, MD: Gryphon House.

Johnston, K., & Brinamen, C. (2006). *Mental health consultation in child care: Transforming relationships among directors, staff, and families.* Washington DC: Zero to Three Press.

Kagan, J. (1997). Temperament and reactions to unfamiliarity. *Child Development, 68,* 139–143.

Kagan, J., & Snidman, N. (2004). *The long shadow of temperament.* Cambridge, MA: Harvard University Press.

Kaiser, B., & Rasminsky, J. S. (2003). *Challenging behavior in young children: Understanding, preventing, and responding effectively.* Boston: Allyn & Bacon.

Kaplan, B. J., McNichol, J., Conte, R. A., & Moghadam, H. K. (1987). Sleep disturbance in preschool-aged hyperactive and nonhyperactive children. *Pediatrics, 80,* 839–844.

Katch, J. (2001). *Under dead man's skin: Discovering the meaning of children's violent play.* Boston: Beacon Press.

Kaufmann, R., & Wischman, A. L. (1999). Communities supporting the mental health of young children and their families. In R. N. Roberts & P. R. Magrab (Eds.), *Where Children Live: Solutions for serving young children and their families* (pp. 177–210). Stamford, CT: Ablex Publishing Corporations.

Keepers, G. A. (1990). Pathological preoccupation with video games. *Journal of the American Academy of Child and Adolescent Psychiatry, 29,* 49–50.

Kindlon, D. (2001). *Too much of a good thing: Raising children of character in an indulgent age.* New York: Hyperion.

Klass, P., & Costello, E. (2003). *Quirky kids: Understanding and helping your child who doesn't fit in.* New York: Ballantine Books.

Knapp, J. V., & Womack, K. (2003). *Reading the family dance: Family systems theory and literary study.* Newark, DE: University of Delaware Press.

Koplow, L. (Ed.). (1996). *Unsmiling faces: How preschools can heal.* New York: Teachers College Press.

Krupa-Kwiatkowski, M. (1998). "You shouldn't have brought me here!": Interaction strategies in the silent period of an inner-directed second language learner. *Research on Language and Social Interaction, 31* (2), 133–175.

Kumpulainen, K. (2002). Phenomenology and treatment of selective mutism. *CNS Drugs, 16* (3), 175–180.

Kutcher, S., Reiter, S., & Gardner, D. (1995). Pharmacotherapy: Approaches and applications. In J. S. March (Ed.), *Anxiety disorders in children and adolescents.* New York: Guilford Press.

Landy, S. (2002). *Pathways to competence: Encouraging healthy social and emotional development in young children.* Baltimore: Paul H. Brookes Publishing Co.

Larson, N., Henthorne, M., & Plum, B. (1994). *Transition magician: Strategies for guiding young children in early childhood settings.* St. Paul, MN: Redleaf Press.

Lawrence, E. C. (2006). Guidelines for a Family Assessment Protocol. In L. Combrinck-Grahm (Ed.), *Children in family contexts: Perspectives on treatment* (2nd ed., 51–70). New York: Guilford Press.

Leung, E. K. (1990). Early risks: Transition from culturally/linguistically diverse homes to formal schooling. *Journal of Educational Issues of Language Minority Students, 7,* 35–51.

Levin, D. (1998). *Remote control childhood? Combating the hazards of a media culture.* Washington DC: NAEYC.

Levine, M. (1995). The disabling of labeling: A phenomenological approach to understanding and helping children who have learning disorders. In A. Thomas (Ed.), *Plain talk about kids* (pp. 1–14). Cambridge, MA: Educators Publishing Service.

———. (2001). *Educational care: A system for understanding and helping children with learning problems at home and in school* (2nd ed.). Cambridge, MA: Educators Publishing Service.

———. (2002). *A mind at a time.* New York: Simon & Schuster.

Lieberman, A., Compton, N., Horn, P. V., & Gosh Ippen, C. (2003). *Losing a parent to death in the early years: Guidelines for the treatment of traumatic bereavement in infancy and early childhood.* Washington DC: Zero to Three Press.

Lieberman, A., & Pawl, H. J. (1993). Infant-parent psychotherapy. In C. H. Zeannah (Ed.), *Handbook of infant mental health* (pp. 427–442). New York: Guilford Press.

Lieberman, A., & Van Horn, P. (2004). Assessment and treatment of young children exposed to traumatic events. In J. Osofsky (Ed.), *Young children and trauma: Intervention and treatment* (pp. 111–138). New York: Guilford Press.

Linares, L. O., Heeren, T., Bronfman, E., Zuckerman, B., Augustyn, M., & Tronick, E. (2001). A meditational model for the impact of exposure to community violence on early childhood behavior problems. *Child Development, 72* (2), 639–652.

Loeber, R., & Hay, D. (1997). Key issues in the development of aggression and violence from childhood to early adulthood. *Annual Review of Psychology, 48,* 371–410.

Lynch, E. W., & Hanson, M. J. (2004). *Developing cross-cultural competence: A guide for working with children and their families.* Baltimore: Paul. H. Brookes Publishing Co.

Main, M., & Solomon, J. (1986). Discovery of an insecure-disorganized/disoriented attachment pattern during the Ainsworth Strange Situation. In M. T. Greenberg, D. Cicchetti, & E. M. Cummings (Eds.), *Attachment in the preschool years: Theory, research, and intervention* (pp. 121–160). Norwood, NJ: Ablex Publishing Corporations.

Malenfant, N. (2006). *Routines and transitions: A guide for early childhood professionals.* St. Paul, MN: Redleaf Press.

March, J. (Ed.). (1995). *Anxiety disorders in children and adolescents.* New York: Guilford Press.

March, J., & Mulle, K. (1998). *OCD in children and adolescents: A cognitive behavioral treatment manual.* New York: Guilford Press.

Masten, A., & Coatsworth, J. D. (1998). The development of competence in favorable and unfavorable environments: Lessons from research on successful children. *American Psychologist, 53,* 205–220.

McGoldrick, M., Giordano, J., & Garcia-Preto, N. (2005). *Ethnicity and family therapy.* New York: Guilford Press.

Merrell, K. W. (2001). *Helping students overcome depression and anxiety: A practical guide.* New York: Guilford Press.

Minuchin, P., Colapinto, J., & Minuchin, S. (2007). *Working with families of the poor* (2nd ed.). New York: Guilford Press.

Minuchin, S., Nichols, M., & Lee, W. (2007). *Assessing families and couples: From symptom to system.* Boston: Allyn & Bacon.

Monteiro Musten, L., Firestone, P., Pisterman, S., & Mercer, J. (1997). Effects of methylphenidate on preschool children with ADHD: Cognitive and behavioral functions. *Journal of the American Academy of Child and Adolescent Psychiatry, 36,* 1407–1415.

Moore, C., & Dunham, P. J. (Eds.). (1995). *Joint attention: Its origins and role in development.* Mahwah, NJ: Lawrence Erlbaum Associates, Publishers.

Morris, T. L., & March, J. (Eds.). (2004). *Anxiety disorders in children and adolescents* (2nd ed.). New York: Guilford Press.

National Scientific Council on the Developing Child. (2004). *Young children develop in an environment of relationships.* Working paper #1.

National Scientific Council on the Developing Child. (2005). *Excessive stress disrupts the architecture of the developing brain.* Working paper #3.

Nelson, K. (1996). *Language in cognitive development: The emergence of the mediated mind.* New York: Cambridge University Press.

———. (2007). *Young minds in social worlds: Experience, meaning, and memory.* Cambridge, MA: Harvard University Press.

Nichols, M. P., & Schwartz, R. C. (Eds.). (2004). *Family therapy: Concepts and methods* (4th ed.). Boston, MA: Allyn & Bacon.

Olson, D. H., & Gorall, D. M. (2003). Circumplex model of marital and family systems. In F. Walsh (Ed.), *Normal family processes: Growing diversity and complexity* (3rd ed., pp. 514–548). New York: Guilford Press.

O'Neill, R. E., Horner, R. H., Albin, R. W., Sprague, J. R., Storey, K., & Newton, J. S. (1997). *Functional assessment and program development for problem behavior: A practical handbook.* Pacific Grove, CA: Brooks/Cole Publishing Co.

Osofsky, J. (Ed.). (2004). *Young children and trauma: Intervention and treatment.* New York: Guilford Press.

Paley, V. G. (1981). *Wally's stories: Conversations in the kindergarten.* Cambridge, MA: Harvard University Press.

———. (1983). *Molly is three: Growing up in school.* Chicago: University of Chicago Press.

———. (2004). *A child's work: The importance of fantasy play.* Chicago: University of Chicago Press.

Papp, P. (1976). Family choreography. In P. Guerin (Ed.), *Family therapy: Theory and practice* (pp. 465–477). New York: Gardner Press.

Parlakian, R. (2002). *Reflective supervision in practice: Stories from the field.* Washington DC: Zero to Three Press.

Pawl, J. H., & Milburn, L. A. (2006). Family and relationship-centered principles and practices. In G. M. Foley & J. D. Hochman (Eds.), *Mental health in early intervention: Achieving unity in principles and practice* (pp. 191–226). Baltimore: Paul H. Brookes Publishing Co.

Pearson, P. D., & Gallagher, M. C. (1983). The instruction of reading comprehension. *Contemporary Educational Psychology, 8,* 317–334.

Perry, D. F., Kaufman, R. K., & Knitzer, J. (Eds.). (2007). *Social and emotional health in early childhood: Building bridges between services and systems.* Baltimore: Paul H. Brookes Publishing Co.

Perry D. F., Woodbridge, M., & Rosman, E. (2007). Evaluating outcomes in systems delivering early childhood mental health services. In D. F. Perry, R. F. Kaufmann, & J. Knitzer (Eds.), *Social and emotional health in early childhood: Building bridges between services and systems* (pp. 121–146). Baltimore: Paul H. Brookes Publishing Co.

Phelan, T. (2003). *One-Two-Three Magic: Effective discipline for children two to twelve* (3rd ed.). Glen Ellyn, IL: ParentMagic, Inc.

Pumariega, A. J., & Winters, N. C. (Eds). (2003). *The handbook of child and adolescent systems of care: The new community psychiatry.* San Francisco: Jossey-Bass.

Rapoport, J. (1991). *The boy who couldn't stop washing: The experience and treatment of obsessive-compulsive disorder.* New York: Penguin Books.Rhodes, R., Ochoa, S. H., & Ortiz, S. O. (2005). *Assessing culturally and linguistically diverse students: A practical guide.* New York: Guilford Press.

Rideout, V., Hamel, E., & the Kaiser Family Foundation. (2006). *The media family: Electronic media in the lives of infants, toddlers, preschoolers, and their parents.* Menlo Park, CA: Henry J. Kaiser Family Foundation.

Robinson, J. L., Kagan, J., Reznick, J. S., & Corley, R. (1992). The heritability of inhibited and uninhibited behavior: A twin study. *Developmental Psychology, 28,* 1030–1037.

Roumaine, S. (1999). Bilingual language development. In M. Barrett (Ed.), *The development of language.* East Sussex, UK: Psychology Press.

Routh, D. K. (1978). Hyperactivity. In P. Magrab (Ed.), *Psychological management of pediatric problems* (pp. 3–48). Baltimore: University Park Press.

Rowena, F. (Ed.). (2004). *Culturally competent practice with immigrant and refugee children and families.* New York: Guilford Press.

Roznowski, F. (1999). Building community through literacy resource bags. *Field Notes: Harvard Graduate School of Education, 2* (5), 5.

Rutter, M., & the English and Romanian Adoptees Study Team. (1998). Developmental catch-up and deficit following adoption after severe early global privation. *Journal of Child Psychology and Psychiatry, 40,* 19–55.

Saville-Troike, M. (1988). Private speech: Evidence for second language learning strategies during the 'silent' period. *Journal of Child Language, 15,* 567–590.

Scarlett, W. G. (1998). *Trouble in the classroom: Managing the behavior problems of young children.* San Francisco: Jossey-Bass.

Schaefer, D., Lyons, C., & Peretz, D. (2002). *How do we tell the children: A step-by-step guide for helping children cope when someone dies.* New York: Newmarket Press.

Schneider, W., Schumann-Hengsteler, R. S., & Sodian, B. (2005). *Young children's cognitive development: Interrelationships among executive functioning, working memory, verbal ability, and theory of mind.* Mahwah, NJ: Lawrence Erlbaum Associates, Publishers.

Sears, W., & Thompson, L. (1998). *The ADD book: New understandings, new approaches to parenting your child.* Boston: Little Brown & Company.

Shahmoon-Shanak. (2006). Reflective supervision for an integrated model. In G. M. Foley & J. D. Hochman (Eds.), *Mental heath in early intervention: Achieving unity in principles and practice* (pp. 343–382). Baltimore: Paul H. Brooks Publishing Co.

Shonkoff, J., & Phillips, D. (Eds.). (2000). *From Neurons to neighborhoods: The science of early childhood development.* Washington DC: National Academies Press.

Shore, A. (2001a). The effects of a secure attachment relationship on right brain development, affect regulation, and infant mental health. *Infant Mental Health Journal, 22* (1–2), 7–66.

———. (2001b). The effects of early relational trauma on right brain development, affect regulation, and infant mental health. *Infant Mental Health Journal, 22* (1–2), 201–269.

Siegel, D. J. (1999). *The developing mind: How relationships and the brain interact to shape who we are.* New York: Guilford Press.

Siegel, D., & Hartzell, M. (2003). *Parenting from the inside out.* New York: Putnam.

Sigman, M., & Capps, L. (1997). *Children with autism: A developmental perspective.* Cambridge, MA: Harvard University Press.

Singer, D., & Singer, J. (Eds.). (2002). *Handbook of children and the media.* Thousand Oaks, CA: Sage Publications.

Stock Kranovitz, C. (1998). *The out-of-synch child: Recognizing and coping with sensory integration dysfunction.* New York: Perigree.

Sturm, C. (1997). Creating parent-teacher dialogue: Intercultural communications in child care. *Young Children, 52* (5), 34–38.

Szatmari, P. (2004). *A mind apart: Understanding children with autism and Asperger's disorder.* New York: Guilford Press.

Tabors, P. (1997). *One child, two languages: A guide for preschool educators of children learning English as a second language.* Baltimore: Paul H. Brookes Publishing Co.

Taylor, E. (2001). *Helping children cope with divorce.* San Francisco: Jossey-Bass.

Tejeiro Salguero, R. A., & Bersabe Moran, R. M. (2002). Measuring problem video game playing in adolescents. *Addiction, 97* (12), 1601–1606.

Thomas, A., Chess, S., & Birch, H. G. (1968). *Temperament and behavior disorders in children.* New York: New York University Press.

Thompson, S. (1997). *The source for nonverbal learning disorders.* East Moline, IL: LinguiSystems, Inc.

Trevarthen, C. (1980). The foundations of intersubjectivity: Development of interpersonal and cooperative understanding in infants. In D. Olsen (Ed.), *The social foundations of language and thought: Essays in honor of Jerome Bruner* (pp. 316–342). New York: W. W. Norton.

———. (1993). The functions of emotions in early infant communication and development. In J. Nadel & L. Camaioni (Eds.), *New perspectives in early communication development* (pp. 43–81). London: Routledge.

Tronick, E. Z. (1989). Emotions and emotional communication in infants. *American Psychologist, 44* (2), 112–119.

Tronick, E. Z., & Weinberg, M. (1997). Depressed mothers and infants: The failure to form dyadic states of consciousness. In M. L. Murray & P. Cooper (Eds.),

Postpartum depression and child development (pp. 54–81). New York: Guilford Press.

Trozzi, M., & Massimini, K. (1999). *Talking with children about loss: Words, strategies, and wisdom to help children cope with death, divorce, and other difficult times.* New York: Berkley Books.

Turecki, S. (2000). *The difficult child.* New York: Bantam Books.

van der Kolk, B., & Streck-Fischer, A. (2000). Down will come baby, cradle and all: Diagnostic implications of chronic trauma on child development. *Australian and New Zealand Journal of Child Psychiatry, 34,* 903–918.

Vygotsky, L. S. (1978). *Mind in society: The development of higher psychological processes.* Cambridge: MA: Harvard University Press.

Wachtel, E. (1994). *Treating troubled children and their families.* New York: Guilford Press.

Walsh, F. (1998). *Strengthening family resilience.* New York: Guilford Press.

Watson, T. S., & Steege, M. W. (2003). *Conducting school-based functional behavioral assessments: A practitioner's guide.* New York: Guilford Press.

Watzlawick, P., Weakland, J., & Fisch, R. (1974). *Change: The principles of problem formation and problem resolution.* New York: W. W. Norton.

Webster-Stratton, C. & Hammond, M. (1999). Marital conflict management skills, parenting style, and early-onset conduct problems: Processes and pathways. *Journal of Child Psychology and Psychiatry, 40,* 917–927.

Weinreb, M., & Groves, B. M. (2007). Child exposure to violence: Case of Amanda, age 4. In N. Boyd Webb (Ed.), *Play therapy with children in crisis: Individual, group, and family treatment* (pp. 73–90). New York: Guilford Press.

Werner, E. E. (2000). Protective factors and individual resilience. In J. P. Shonkoff & S. J. Meisels (Eds.), *Handbook of early childhood intervention* (pp. 115–134). Cambridge, UK: Cambridge University Press.

Whitaker, C., & Bumberry, W. M. (1987). *Dancing with the family: A symbolic approach.* New York: Brunner-Routledge.

Wilens, T. E. (2004). *Straight talk about psychiatric medications for kids.* New York: Guilford Press.

Williams, M. S., & Shellenberger, S. (1996). *How does your engine run: A leader's guide to the alert program.* Albuquerque: TherapyWorks, Inc.

Willis, D. J. (2003). The drugging of young children: Why is psychology mute? *The Clinical Psychologist, 56* (3), 1–3.

Wing, L., Gould, J., Yeates, S. R., & Brierley, L. M. (1977). Symbolic play in severely mentally retarded and autistic children. *Journal of Child Psychology and Psychiatry, 18,* 167–178.

Winsler, A., de Léon, J. R., Wallace, B. A., Carlton, M. P., & Willson-Quayle, A. (2003). Private speech in preschool children: Developmental stability and change, across-task consistency, and relations with classroom behavior. *Journal of Child Language, 30,* 583–608.

Worden, J. W. (1996). *Children and grief: When a parent dies.* New York: Guilford Press.

Zelazo, P. D., Qu, L., & Mueller, U. (2005). Hot and cool aspects of executive function: Relations in early development. In W. Schneider, R. Schumann-Hengsteler, & B. Sodian (Eds.), *Young children's cognitive development: Interrelationships among executive functioning, working memory, verbal ability, and theory of mind* (pp. 71–93). Mahwah, NJ: Lawrence Erlbaum Associates, Publishers.

Index